The Lighthouses of Massachusetts

Dear Kristina –

I hope these are lighthouses you get to visit someday!

Love
Julie

The Lighthouses of Massachusetts

Jeremy D'Entremont

Commonwealth Editions
Beverly, Massachusetts

ISBN-13: 978-1-933212-33-3
ISBN-10: 1-933212-33-0

Library of Congress Cataloging-in-Publication Data
D'Entremont, Jeremy.
  The Lighthouses of Massachusetts / Jeremy D'Entremont.
    p. cm.
  Includes bibliographical references and index.
  ISBN 978-1-933212-33-3 (alk. paper)
  1. Lighthouses—Massachusetts—History. I. Title.
  VK1024.M35D46 2007
  387.1'5509744—dc22

                                  2007003652

Cover and interior design by Stephen Bridges
Layout by Anne Lenihan Rolland

Printed in the United States of America

Published by Commonwealth Editions,
an imprint of Memoirs Unlimited, Inc.,
266 Cabot Street, Beverly, Massachusetts 01915
www.commonwealtheditions.com

Lighthouse Treasury Series:
The Lighthouses of Connecticut
The Lighthouses of Rhode Island

The large photo on the cover is Plymouth Light. The small photos are, top to bottom, Boston Light, Sankaty Head Light, Eastern Point Light, Graves Light, Monomoy Point Light, Brant Point Light, and Nobska Point Light.

Contents

Preface   ix

1   Borden Flats Light   1

2   Dumpling Rock Light   5

3   Clark's Point Light   11

4   Butler Flats Light   15

5   Palmer's Island Light   21

6   Ned's Point Light   29

7   Bird Island Light   33

8   Cleveland Ledge Light   41

9   Wing's Neck Light   45

10   Cuttyhunk Light   51

11   Tarpaulin Cove Light   59

12   Nobska Point Light   63

13   Gay Head Light   71

14   West Chop Light   79

15   East Chop Light   87

16   Edgartown Light   91

17   Cape Poge Light   97

18   Brant Point Light   105

19   Great Point Light   113

20   Sankaty Head Light   125

21 Point Gammon Light   135

22 Bishop and Clerks Light   139

23 Hyannis Harbor Light   143

24 Bass River Light   149

25 Stage Harbor Light   155

26 Monomoy Point Light   159

27 Chatham Light   169

28 The Three Sisters of Nauset
      and Nauset Light   177

29 Highland Light   187

30 Race Point Light   201

31 Wood End Light   209

32 Long Point Light   213

33 Mayo's Beach Light   219

34 Billingsgate Light   223

35 Sandy Neck Light   229

36 Duxbury Pier Light   237

37 Plymouth Light   245

38 Scituate Light   255

39 Minot's Ledge Light   265

40 Long Island Head Light   285

41 Spectacle Island Range Lights/
      Broad Sound Range Lights   291

42 Deer Island Light   295

43 Lovell's Island Range Lights   301

44 Narrows Light   307

45 Boston Light 311

46 Graves Light 331

47 Egg Rock Light 339

48 Marblehead Light 351

49 Derby Wharf Light 359

50 Fort Pickering Light 363

51 Hospital Point Light 367

52 Baker's Island Light 371

53 Ten Pound Island Light 383

54 Eastern Point Light 387

55 Thacher Island Twin Lights 395

56 Straitsmouth Island Light 409

57 Annisquam Light 415

58 Ipswich Range Lights 421

59 Plum Island Light 429

60 Newburyport Harbor Range Lights 435

61 Miscellaneous Lights and Lightships 437

Selected Bibliography 448

Index 455

Preface

Before I made the New Hampshire seacoast my adopted home, I lived for nearly four decades on the coast of Massachusetts. As I worked on this book, it was great fun becoming reacquainted with locations that are like old friends, and in many cases I learned new and surprising things as I deepened my studies. My research on many of these lighthouses goes back more than 20 years, making it a challenge to list all the people and organizations that deserve my thanks. I'll do my best; I apologize to anyone I've omitted.

The staffs of the National Archives in Washington, D.C., and their Northeast Region branch in Waltham, Massachusetts, have always been helpful and professional. The same is true of the Library of Congress in Washington, the Massachusetts Historical Society, the Boston Public Library, and the Phillips Library of the Peabody Essex Museum in Salem.

It's always a pleasure dealing with the men and women of the United States Coast Guard; I particularly want to thank Chief Warrant Officer Dave Waldrip and his successor, Chief Warrant Officer Pete Boardman, of the First Coast Guard District Aids to Navigation office in Boston. Dr. Bob Browning and Scott T. Price of the U.S. Coast Guard Historian's Office were very helpful when I visited their facility. The personnel of Civil Engineering Unit Providence, particularly architect Marsha Levy, have been generous with their time over a number of years.

Jennifer Perunko, Maritime Historian and Preservation Specialist of the Maritime Heritage Program, National Park Service, helped me obtain copies of the nomination forms for the National Register of Historic Places for a number of lighthouses.

Tim Harrison, Kathleen Finnegan, and Dee Leveille of Foghorn Publishing (publishers of *Lighthouse Digest* magazine) have always been generous with research materials and photos.

The Somerset Public Library and the Fall River Public Library provided information on Borden Flats Light, and the friendly people of the Borden Light Marina got me out to photograph the lighthouse. Arthur

P. Motta Jr. of the New Bedford Office of Tourism and Marketing has been a vital source of information on the past and present of his city's lighthouses. Helen Paradis kindly shared information on Keeper Arthur Small of New Bedford's Palmer's Island.

Volunteer keeper Clayton Hagy shared his time and expertise during a visit to Ned's Point Light several years ago, and the present volunteer keeper, Bert Theriault, has been every bit as helpful. Thanks also to the Mattapoisett Historical Society for their assistance.

Charles Bradley, Marion's former harbormaster and founder of the Bird Island Lighthouse Preservation Society, got me to Bird Island and provided helpful information. The Sippican Historical Society was vital to my research on Bird Island Light. Pat Evenson of Wareham provided copies of useful articles from her own collection on Bird Island and also arranged a memorable boat ride with her friend Ingrid Morse.

Christina Stevens of the Wings Neck Lighthouse Trust arranged for me to visit that lighthouse for the first time since the late 1980s, when I met the famous "Lady of the Lighthouse," the late Irene Flanagan. I enjoyed corresponding with Bruce Howard, grandson of Keeper George Howard. The Bourne Historical Society also helped with research.

The Cuttyhunk Historical Society helped with my chapters on Cuttyhunk and Tarpaulin Cove lights. Ray Terpeny provided information on his great-grandfather, Cuttyhunk's Keeper Eugene Terpeny. John D. Ross provided information on his ancestor, Nobska Point Light's Keeper Frederick Ray. Also helpful with research on Nobska Point Light were Sandy Abt of the Coast Guard Auxiliary and the Falmouth Historical Society.

The Martha's Vineyard Historical Society has been vital to my research of the island's lighthouses for many years. Rob Hammett opened East Chop Lighthouse for a tour and shared his research. Cindy Jacobs helped with information on the Children's Lighthouse Memorial at Edgartown Lighthouse.

The Nantucket Historical Association, the Nantucket Whaling Museum, and the Nantucket Lifesaving Museum are important repositories of that island's heritage. Robert Felch of the 'Sconset Trust very kindly opened Sankaty Head Light for a tour and helped with my research.

Mary Sicchio of the Nickerson Room at the Wilkens Library at Cape Cod Community College was a great help, and the library was a source of much valuable material. The Sturgis Library in Barnstable,

Hyannis Public Library, Wellfleet Public Library, Provincetown Public Library, and the Falmouth Public Library were also vital to my research on lighthouses on Cape Cod. Special recognition goes to the friendly staff of the Chatham Historical Society and Atwood House Museum.

I have fond feelings for the Lighthouse inn in West Dennis, the former Bass River Lighthouse. Particularly, I extend my sincere gratitude to Mary Stone and Nelson Cook of the inn for their generous assistance.

Thanks to Lee Hall and Rulon Wilcox, who were responsible for my first visit to Point Gammon Lighthouse in the spring of 2006. My trip to Monomoy would have been impossible without the generosity of Janice Lincoln. Thanks also to Mike Brady of the Monomoy National Wildlife Refuge.

The fine people of the Nauset Light Preservation Society, including Shirley Sabin and Bud Griffin, have been a boon to my work for years. Thanks also to the Truro Historical Society for their help with Highland Light, particularly Gordon Russell, Bob Firminger, Francene Webster, and Susan Kurtzman.

Jim Walker of the Cape Cod Chapter of the American Lighthouse Foundation has provided personal tours of Race Point Light Station on several occasions and has aided my research. Ken Morton, manager of the Sandy Neck Lighthouse property in Barnstable, provided a wonderful tour and also helped with historical photos and articles.

Dolly Bicknell of Project Gurnet and Bug Lights, in addition to being a great friend (and daughter of my hero, Edward Rowe Snow), shared her research on that lighthouse and Duxbury Pier Light. The Plymouth Public Library also provided some important materials. Paul Christian has been very generous in sharing his happy memories and photos of the Plymouth Light Station. Richard Boonisar also shared his impressive historical collection on the Gurnet section of Plymouth.

David Ball of the Scituate Historical Society shared his expertise and provided a tour of Scituate Lighthouse. The Cohasset Historical Society helped with my research on Minot's Ledge Light, and Gil Nadeau provided information on his father, Pierre Nadeau, an assistant keeper at Minot's. The Mystic Seaport Museum graciously allowed me to quote a segment of an interview with Molly Tornberg Orr, daughter of Keeper Per Frederick Tornberg.

The Lynn Historical Society and the Nahant Historical Society were very helpful with research on Egg Rock Light. Bill Conly, the Abbott Public Library, and the Marblehead Museum and Historical Society provided information on Marblehead Light. The Beverly Historical Society and Beverly Public Library helped with Hospital Point Light.

The Salem Public Library and the Salem Maritime National Historic Site provided material on the lighthouses in their area. Nelson Dionne kindly copied many useful articles for me from back issues of the *Salem Evening News*. Charlie Arnold, manager of Winter Island Marine Park in Salem, lent his assistance, as did former manager Gary Moore.

My research on the lighthouses of Cape Ann was greatly aided by the Cape Ann Historical Society. I've had a long, pleasant involvement with the Thacher Island Association, and I particularly thank Paul St. Germain, Dottie Carroll, and George Carroll for all their help and support over the years.

The Ipswich Public Library and the Newburyport Public Library were excellent sources of articles and historical materials on the light-houses of the northern Massachusetts coast. Special thanks go to my old friends with the Friends of Plum Island Light, particularly Barbara Kezer, Jim Frey, and Roslin Esposito.

Doug Bingham has always generously shared his considerable knowledge of our nation's lightships.

My "Flying Santa" accomplice and friend Brian Tague is a constant source of support. Bob Trapani, executive director of the American Lighthouse Foundation, is always there to help or simply to listen as a friend. Others whose friendship and knowledge have helped make this book possible include John Forbes, Skip Empey, Elinor De Wire, Michel Forand, Russ Rowlett, Suzanne Gall Marsh, Bill Edwards, Bob and Sandra Shanklin, Jim Claflin, Ross Tracy, and Candace Clifford. Thanks also to my local circle of lighthouse friends, the volunteers of the Friends of Portsmouth Harbor Lighthouse.

My friend, keeper's daughter Seamond Ponsart Roberts, has been a font of information, support, and good humor. Her real-life light-house experiences are included in several chapters. The late Harold Jennings, son of Keeper Charles Jennings (Boston, Monomoy, and Lovell's Island) shared a wealth of information and anecdotes through his writing and personal tours of Lovell's Island. Many other keepers and family members are mentioned in the pages of this book, and they all have my heartfelt gratitude.

Commonwealth Editions has provided me an opportunity for which I'll always be grateful, and without exception, everyone involved with the publication of these books has been professional and gracious.

My wife, Charlotte Raczkowski, is constant in her support. My older brothers, Jim and John, have long inspired me with their own writing.

More than 20 years ago, my mother suggested I produce a video project on historian and "Flying Santa" Edward Rowe Snow. That offhand suggestion led to a deepening of my interest in maritime history and to my enjoyable career as a lighthouse historian. This book is dedicated to her memory.

CHAPTER 1

Borden Flats Light in September 2006. *Photo by the author.*

Borden Flats Light

1881

The city of Fall River, situated where the Taunton River flows into Mount Hope Bay, was famed as the "Textile Capital of the World" in the nineteenth century.

The city's location also allowed easy travel by water to Providence, Newport, and beyond. Beginning in 1847, the Fall River Line of steamships provided a link to Boston and New York City. For many years, Borden Flats Lighthouse welcomed these magnificent vessels.

Fall River is famous as the home of Lizzie Borden, who was acquitted of the 1892 murders of her father and stepmother. The wealthy Borden family, for whom Borden Flats was named, had been prominent in the area since the seventeenth century.

For a number of years before the lighthouse was built to warn of a dangerous reef at the mouth of the Taunton River, an unlighted day beacon marked the spot. The 1872 annual report of the Lighthouse Board described a "stone beacon, with iron column and day-mark." On June 16, 1880, a sum of $25,000 was appropriated for a lighthouse on Borden Flats, and construction soon commenced.

A cylindrical cast-iron caisson was sunk in place on the reef and then filled with concrete. The components of the superstructure were delivered in July 1881. The cast-iron tower, which doubled as living quarters for a keeper, was erected on the caisson, and the light went into service on October 1, 1881, with a fourth-order Fresnel lens producing a fixed red light 47 feet above mean high water. A fog bell, with automatic striking machinery, was installed on the side of the tower.

There were five stories above the basement, including the lantern; two levels were used as living quarters. Rainwater was collected in gutters and deposited into a cistern in the structure's basement, providing the keeper's water supply.

Herman Georgie (or Georgy, by some accounts) was keeper from 1885 to 1898. The *Boston Globe* reported in September 1897 that Georgie was found acutely ill with appendicitis at the lighthouse. His wife had been sounding the fog bell and waving to passing boats for some time before people onshore realized something was wrong, and the keeper was quickly rushed to a hospital. "For two days," said the *Globe*, "he suffered intense agony at the lighthouse, attended only by his wife."

The year 1900 saw a change to a fifth-order lens exhibiting a fixed white light, and during the following year it was changed to a flashing light because the fixed light was hard to distinguish from the lights of the city.

Joseph Meyer was keeper on October 8, 1907, when a severe storm hit the area. In the station's log, now at the National Archives in Washington, D.C., Meyer wrote: "Violent SW gale. Occasional heavy squalls. 11 a.m. —A barge of about 800 tons of coal sank in the harbor—two men drowned, and a sloop of 10 tons was wrecked on the beach." In the log Meyer frequently described the area around the lighthouse as frozen or surrounded by chunks of ice in winter. His entry for February 15, 1908: "Started fog bell 6:30 a.m. Bell broke 11 a.m.—struck by hand until 1 p.m."

In early 1912, the area around the lighthouse was completely frozen over. The *Boston Globe* reported that Meyer was able to get ashore on February 1 for the first time since January 4.

Getting back to the lighthouse proved just as difficult. "The tug which brought him ashore was obliged to leave the harbor before he was ready to return," reported the newspaper, "and the keeper set out at midnight for the lighthouse, but got caught in the drift ice and was more than two hours getting back to shore. In consequence of his absence the beacon failed to shine for the first time in seven years."

Borden Flats Light in the early 1900s. *From the collection of the author.*

John H. Paul became keeper in July 1912 and stayed until 1927. Many of his log entries describe endless scraping and painting of the lighthouse. In the middle of the afternoon on August 3, 1912, Keeper Paul was involved in a dramatic rescue. Two Fall River men were passing near the lighthouse in a rowboat. As the men attempted to change places, the boat overturned.

Paul saw the accident and immediately launched his boat. One of the men, James Parker, was unable to swim and was lost in the waves. The other man, Matthew Loftus, clung to the overturned boat and was swiftly rescued by Paul. The keeper later received a bronze Carnegie lifesaving medal.

Joseph Covo was keeper from 1927 to 1943. His daughter, Elaine, later summed up life at Borden Flats: "Everything was brass. You polished brass from morning to night with government polish."

The lighthouse was battered in the hurricane of September 21, 1938, as were most lighthouses on New England's south-facing coast. The storm left the tower with a pronounced tilt, which it still has. A new, much-wider cylindrical caisson was subsequently added around the old one to provide more protection.

During a cold snap around 1948, a Coast Guard keeper named Archie DeMille was stranded at the lighthouse as the area froze over. DeMille eventually managed to walk across the ice for several miles to his home in Swansea, Massachusetts.

Truman Sawyer, now of Houston, Texas, served at Borden Flats Light as a young Coast Guardsman from November 1955 to December 1956. The light still ran on kerosene, as did a refrigerator and stove. The fog-bell mechanism was still wound by hand. Although he now looks back on the experience fondly, Sawyer says that at the time, "It was like punishment."

The lighthouse was converted to electric operation in 1957, but the old kerosene lamp was kept on hand as a backup.

The light was automated in the spring of 1963, and the last Coast Guard crew of four was reassigned. For a while a civilian "lamplighter" was employed by the Coast Guard to turn on the fog bell as needed from shore, with the flick of a switch.

In 1977 a modern optic replaced the old Fresnel lens. The station's fog bell stayed in service for a full century, but it was replaced by an automatic horn and subsequently removed from the lighthouse in 1983. The light was converted to solar power in 1989.

Today the tower is about a half mile from the Braga Bridge, built in 1965. The lighthouse remains an active aid to navigation, with a white flash every 2.5 seconds.

In September 2006, it was announced that the lighthouse would be available for transfer to a suitable applicant under the provisions of the Lighthouse Preservation Act of 2000.

Borden Flats Light can be seen from the Borden Light Marina, a half mile south of Battleship Cove (home to the battleship *Massachusetts*) on the Fall River waterfront. See www.bordenlight.com for directions. The excellent Fall River Marine Museum is nearby, with exhibits on the *Titanic* and the old Fall River Line's steamships.

ock Light, (Buzzard's Bay) Mass.

Dumpling Rock Light, New Bedf

Two views of Dumpling Rock Light on early-1900s postcards.
From the collection of the author.

Dumpling Rock Light

1828, 1890–1942

The town of Dartmouth, on the south coast of Massachusetts at the west side of the entrance to Buzzards Bay, grew as a center for shipbuilding and whaling in the early nineteenth century. A lighthouse was needed to help guide local shipping traffic, and Dumpling Rock, a few hundred yards offshore from Round Hill Point, was an ideal location.

A light on Dumpling Rock would also help mariners heading for New Bedford Harbor, and it would serve to warn mariners of the dangerous ledges off Round Hill Point. On May 23, 1828, a sum of $4,000 was appropriated for the lighthouse.

The initial structure on Dumpling Rock consisted of a two-story stone dwelling with a lantern on its roof. It was first lighted on October 19, 1828, and Levi Smith was the first keeper, at a yearly salary of $400. The lantern held a system of 10 lamps and 14-inch reflectors, exhibiting a fixed white light 43 feet above the sea, visible for 10 nautical miles.

For some years in the station's early history, the keeper at Dumpling Rock Light operated a signaling system. When a ship was approaching New Bedford Harbor, the keeper would drop a signal arm on a post. The merchants of New Bedford, seeing the signal, would vie with each other to sell their goods to the incoming mariners.

Life at Dumpling Rock was difficult for the early keepers. The seas often encroached on the light station during storms, until the government finally built a stone wall, six feet high, around the dwelling.

Lt. Edward W. Carpender of the U.S. Navy visited this station, among many others, in 1838. He called the light a useful one, but "larger than is necessary." He recommended a reduction in the number of lamps. Carpender also found the work of the keeper lacking: "I visited this light in the afternoon, and found the keeper absent on the main, without having paid the least attention to the lamps since he extinguished them in the morning. The reflectors appeared not to have been burnished for some time, and the lantern was covered with smoke."

Carpender displayed some sympathy toward Keeper Smith in another part of his report: "Located as this light is, on a small barren rock, with fewer advantages to the keeper than, perhaps, any other light in the district, it would seem proper that I should notice the fact of the salary being smaller by $50 than that of many others."

A civil engineer, I. W. P. Lewis, inspected the station in 1842 for a report he would make to Congress the following year. The dwelling was "laid up in bad lime mortar," he reported, which had led to cracks in the walls. The windows were leaky, and the cistern filled with seawater in stormy weather. Keeper Smith, in a statement provided to Lewis, called the lantern "a very bad one." It shook in the wind and leaked profusely.

A fourth-order Fresnel lens replaced the old lamps and reflectors in 1857. A new lantern was installed in 1863. Beginning in 1867, the station had an assistant keeper to help with the added duties of maintaining a fog bell and striking machinery.

Charles Hinckley, formerly an assistant at Bishop and Clerks Light, was principal keeper from 1884 to 1892. In 1888, during Hinckley's term, the Lighthouse Board announced that the dwelling was in such bad condition that it would have been a "waste of money to give it further repair." Instead, a new wood-frame dwelling, 26 by 34 feet, was built on the old foundation in 1890.

A square wooden tower was attached to the house, with a lantern containing a fourth-order lens. A new protective bulkhead, 90 feet long and made of hard pine timber, was bolted to the rock and reinforced by stones salvaged from the old dwelling.

The 1893 light list provides further description of the station: "A black lantern on a white frame tower which rises 48 feet above high water mark, attached to NE corner of a white frame dwelling—it is lit by a fixed white light visible for a distance of 12 nautical miles. The bell tower is about 100 feet south of light. The fog signal bell is struck by machinery alternating a single and double blow with intervals of 30 seconds."

It was often foggy in the vicinity, and it was decided that a more powerful fog signal was needed. A Daboll trumpet, operated by a steam engine, was put into service on October 12, 1897.

Octave Ponsart, later at Cuttyhunk and West Chop lights, became keeper in 1937, after working as an assistant at Great Point Light on Nantucket. Ponsart's daughter Seamond Ponsart Roberts was born in 1940, while her parents lived on Dumpling Rock. Roberts has written a good deal about her family's lighthouse years. Despite the rugged conditions, she says her parents enjoyed life at Dumpling Rock. She recalls stories about one of the area's best-known residents: "Colonel Edward Howland Robinson Green was a railroad tycoon who had an experimental airport at Round Hill. Atomic scientists were often there at Colonel Green's estate, and these scientists would sometimes go out to Dumpling Rock to visit the keepers and eat lobster." One of those visiting scientists was the renowned Wernher von Braun.

Day-to-day life could be an adventure on Dumpling Rock. Once, Seamond's mother, Emma Ponsart, was hanging clothes on a line when she heard her husband yell, "Run!" She got out of the way just as a rogue wave swept the laundry into the ocean. There were more serious dangers, too, such as the pack ice that would pile up against the station, endangering the buildings. One winter the ice carried away the outhouse.

The worst hurricane in recorded New England history slammed into the south-facing coast on September 21, 1938. Roberts tells the story of the storm's devastating impact on Dumpling Rock:

> On that gray Wednesday, September 21, 1938, my parents, my sister Bette and my cousin were scheduled to leave the Rock for a long-awaited vacation. It was to be their first vacation since the Depression. Assistant Keeper Henry Fontenot's wife, May, helped Mom to pack and supplied gentle chatter as they were about to row ashore. They had the suitcases in the dory, ready to go, when the wind suddenly rose and the water got really rough. The storm came on quickly. "Just like that!" they would later say with a snap of the fingers.
>
> Dad was not about to launch the dory in that kind of weather. He headed Mom, my sister Bette, and cousin Connie back to the house. Dad and Henry tried to secure the dory, but their efforts were fruitless and the boat was swept seaward. They headed for the oil house and the light tower to secure what they could. The task of securing anything soon became impossible. Dad and Henry headed for the keeper's house as waves began to wash the rocks, flooding the first floor.
>
> My father hung onto a doorknob on the front door as he hollered to my mother, sister, and cousin to get upstairs and go to the assistant keeper's rooms on the lee side of the building. The dog, Rexena, was swimming in the living room. Henry pointed seaward, and all he and Dad could see was foggy foam and mountainous combers heading directly for their rocky island.
>
> From what they could see, the waves were getting progressively larger. Dad said that even the first ones coming in looked like they would engulf the tower. At that point, they were both sure they would not survive.

Charles Hinckley was keeper at Dumpling Rock Light 1884–92.
Courtesy of William L. Crocker.

Octave Ponsart, keeper 1937–42, with his daughter Seamond circa 1942. *Courtesy of Seamond Ponsart Roberts.*

Henry said, "Octave, I think we're going to lose the light." Dad nodded and they headed upstairs to be with the women and children. There was nowhere else to go. My father had been on lightships, and he said he had never seen such a "quick sea" develop. In quick succession many waves hit, breaking completely over the house and lighthouse.

The keepers had been doing carpentry in one of the bedrooms and had nails and boards ready. They nailed boards over the windows and braced the floors with the biggest spikes they had in the toolbox. The window glass was quickly broken and the whole house was wet inside. Outside, boards were being torn from their nails and the screeching noise was terrible.

Pieces of the roof tore off. The house shuddered with each wave, and the side facing the sea caved in and was leaning. Henry and May talked of lashing themselves to a mattress to try to make it to Round Hill. Dad argued they would never last.

May Fontenot was crying. She told my mother, "I think we are all going to die, but at least I know we have been such good friends. I'm so glad you're here with me." My mother cried too, because May was such a sweet person. Mom would tell me this story later and she'd always cry, saying, "That May, she was one of the best friends I ever had." And she'd add, "We really thought we were going to die. In a few minutes, even."

My mother, sister, and cousin were in shock, huddled on the bed, wrapped in sheets. My cousin had a massive nosebleed, apparently from fear, and Dad tried to help her. Then there was a noise "like a freight train or what an earthquake must sound like," as Mom described it. Then came a tremendous long-lasting blast of water and a huge pounding shock with a splintering of wood. Those on the bed were hurled to the floor.

Henry and Dad knew something even more drastic had happened. The water on the first floor was now almost up to the ceiling. They

*opened the bedroom door and peered around the whirling water to
see a bit of sky through the side of the living room and a massive
obstruction where just before the ceiling and walls had been.*

*A huge piece of rock had been torn free by the hurricane waves,
lifted up, and hurled through the side of the first-floor living room.
Now it sat there, actually anchoring the house and lighthouse to
Dumpling Rock.*

*The rock had opened up a channel through the house, easing the
flow of water entering and exiting the building now without too
much of an obstruction. Henry and Dad turned back to report this,
and May cried and cried.*

*Blow after blow came after that and yet the rock in the living room
held firm. Mom said later when she sang the hymn,* Rock of Ages,
Cleft for Me, *it had a new and much more personal meaning.*

*The six remained upstairs through the dreadful night. When morn-
ing came and the waters had receded, they ventured downstairs.*

*Nothing was left. Nothing except Rexena, who had spent the storm
in the linen closet, going to the top shelf as the water rose. This was
proven by the dog's footprints that had been left on each shelf.*

*The waters that swirled around Dumpling Rock were filled with
debris, telephone poles, and pieces of homes and trees. There was
seaweed on top of the light tower. The keeper's quarters were in
shambles. There were no clothes or furnishings or anything else left
except a few canned goods still in a closet. A pile of canned goods
was found a few weeks later, wedged between the rocks below the
tide line, as well as one silver spoon inherited from a Cornell grandmother. On shore, Dad's new car, which had been parked at the boat
launch at Round Hill, was gone, probably washed into Buzzards Bay.*

Roberts "learned to walk," she says, "on the very rocks that were
nearly a death trap for my parents and my sister in the 1938 hurricane."
The family had another harrowing experience in 1942, when a mysterious group of men—possibly Italian spies—arrived at the station and
threatened to take the fuel. Keeper Ponsart radioed for help, and the
men were soon chased away by a Coast Guard boat from New Bedford.

Ponsart and Assistant Keeper Fontenot completed some
makeshift repairs and did what they could to keep the station livable,
but the Coast Guard decided not to renovate the lighthouse after the
hurricane. The keepers left in 1942.

The lighthouse was removed and a skeleton tower was erected
in its place, exhibiting a flashing green light. The light remains in
operation today.

CHAPTER 3

Clark's Point Light in June 2001. *Photo by the author.*

Clark's Point Light

1797, 1799, 1804, 1869

Clark's Point is the southernmost extension of the city of New Bedford, in Buzzards Bay on the west side of the entrance to the Acushnet River and New Bedford Harbor. British troops landed in Clark's Cove, just west of the point, on September 5, 1778, and burned much of New Bedford before being stopped by American troops from Wareham. The area's fledgling whaling industry eventually rebounded and flourished, making New Bedford one of the richest cities in the world.

Clark's Point was an ideal location for a lighthouse to help mariners heading to New Bedford. Local merchants erected the first wooden lighthouse on the point in 1797. Daniel Ricketson described the building of the lighthouse in his 1858 book, *The History of New Bedford*: "A wooden lighthouse was built at Clark's Point, at the raising of which, to induce the people to assist, and for the sake of a general jollification at so important an event, a hundred gallon try-pot of chowder, with other entertainment, was prepared. Much to the credit of the sobriety of our predecessors, no one became intoxicated on this occasion."

Little is known of the structure, which burned down about a year later. The lighthouse was promptly rebuilt, financed by local merchants and mariners. The *Columbian Courier* of October 16, 1799, reported that the lighthouse had been completed and lighted for the first time on October 12. Another fire, apparently caused by lightning, destroyed the tower on August 5, 1803. It took until the following March for Congress to appropriate $2,500 for yet another rebuilding.

An octagonal rubblestone tower, 38 feet tall, was completed in 1804. The lighthouse underwent extensive renovations in 1818, including an increase of four feet in height and the installation of a new octagonal iron lantern.

U.S. Navy Lt. Edward W. Carpender inspected the lighthouse in 1838. He noted that a dwelling was not provided for the keeper, who lived in his own house. Carpender believed the lighthouse would have been of greater service to navigation if it had been erected about 150 yards farther to the south, on the southwestern point of Egg Island Shoal. He also felt that the 10 oil lamps in the lighthouse could be judiciously reduced to six.

After a light was established atop Fort Taber in 1869, the earlier lighthouse tower remained standing for some years, minus its lantern. *From the collection of the author.*

Edward W. Howland became keeper in early 1835, replacing his father, Capt. Cornelius Howland, who had recently died at 77. The elder Howland was born in Dartmouth, Massachusetts, and was master of a vessel by the age of 18. He was taken prisoner during the Revolution and survived 15 months of captivity in Edinburgh Castle.

After more adventures, Captain Howland settled down on a farm at Clark's Point, and eventually he received the lighthouse-keeping appointment.

The book *New Bedford's Story for New Bedford's Children,* by Emma Gartland, tells an interesting but undated story. It seems the master of a vessel that delivered supplies to the lighthouse once smuggled a slave woman and her two children, a boy and a girl, to the lighthouse. The family remained in New Bedford, and the boy—identified as "Charlie"—grew to be a popular hack (carriage) driver in the city for many years.

In 1851 a new cast-iron deck was added, and new lamps and reflectors were installed. The tower still had its 1818 lantern—the last remaining "old-style lantern" in the district, according to the Lighthouse Board—a dozen years later, but the lantern and lighting apparatus were replaced in 1865.

In 1857 a new fort began to take shape next to the lighthouse. The fort became known as Fort Taber in honor of the city's mayor in the early 1860s, Isaac C. Taber.

The high walls of the fort eventually blocked the view of the light. In 1869, a rectangular wooden tower, 11 by 20½ feet and 8 feet high, was erected on the northerly tower of the fort. A cushioning system was devised to protect the new light from any concussions resulting from the firing of the fort's cannons. The lantern from the old stone tower was relocated to the new structure, and the new light went into service on June 15, 1869. In its new position, the light was 68 feet above the sea. The old stone tower remained standing until it was demolished in 1906.

In 1898 the establishment of Butler Flats Light offshore rendered Clark's Point Light obsolete. The light on the fort was discontinued in April 1898. Capt. Amos C. Baker Jr., keeper of the light at Clark's Point since 1879, became the first keeper at Butler Flats Light.

The deteriorating fort and lighthouse were restored in the early 1970s, only to fall victim to extensive vandalism and theft. The lighthouse gradually became a shabby ruin.

In July 1997, the city of New Bedford unveiled an ambitious plan to create a new public park around the fort. City officials also decided to fully restore and relight the historic lighthouse on the fort. Restoration was carried out during the winter months of 2000–2001, funded in part by a grant from the utility company Nstar. A gala relighting ceremony was held on the evening of Friday, June 15, 2001—the 132nd anniversary of the lighthouse's first illumination. Approximately 3,000 people attended the event. The program featured a seaside pops concert by the New Bedford Symphony Orchestra, a special postal cancellation, and remarks from city, state, and federal representatives.

For New Bedford, this was the third lighthouse restoration in three years, following the successful relightings of the Butler Flats and Palmer Island lights.

The light was switched on by New Bedford's director of tourism and marketing, Arthur Motta, at 9:00 p.m., followed by cannons blasting, fireworks, and the playing of the *1812 Overture*.

🔦 **Fort Taber Park and Clark's Point Lighthouse are easily reached by following Route 18 in New Bedford to a traffic light at its southern end. Turn left at the light and continue for two miles to the park entrance. The interior of the fort and lighthouse are not now open to the public, but good photo opportunities are available from the grounds.**

CHAPTER 4

Butler Flats Light in September 2006. *Photo by the author.*

Butler Flats Light

1898

Its days as a whaling center were long past, but New Bedford was still an important port in the late nineteenth century. It was the third-largest manufacturing city in Massachusetts; about 500,000 tons of shipping entered the port in 1890 alone. In 1887 ferries to Martha's Vineyard, Nantucket, and other nearby points carried 75,000 passengers in and out of the city. The 1891 annual report of the Lighthouse Board made a case for a new lighthouse:

> *The entrance near buoy no. 9, on the point of Butler Flats, is narrow, obscure, and difficult to find in snowstorms, fogs, and dark nights. If a light with a fog signal was placed on that point, it would mark both the entrance and turning point, would guide vessels to an anchorage in the lower harbor, and, with the light on Palmer Island, would guide them clear of North Ledge, Henrietta and Hurricane Rocks, in Buzzards Bay, and be of great service to the navigation of this important port.*

Butler Flats Light, built at a cost of $32,800, rendered the old Clark's Point Light, at the southernmost tip of New Bedford, obsolete. F. Hopkinson Smith, who was also known as an artist and writer, designed the new lighthouse. Smith's place in lighthouse history is secure largely because of his planning of Race Rock Light in Fisher's Island Sound. He also built the foundation of the Statue of Liberty.

Built in shallow water with no solid rock for a foundation, Butler Flats Light was a challenge to construct. A cast-iron cylinder, 35 feet in diameter, was put into place after 5 feet of mud was dredged. The cylinder was filled with stone and concrete, and then the brick super-structure was built on top. The lantern originally held a fifth-order kerosene-fueled Fresnel lens, displaying a white flash every five seconds, 53 feet above mean high water. It was first lighted on April 30, 1898. The tower was painted red at first, but its color was changed to white in 1899.

From its first lighting until 1942, when the Coast Guard took over, Butler Flats Light had only two keepers: Amos C. Baker Jr. and his son, Charles A. Baker, who initially served as assistant keeper under his

An early view of Butler Flats Light. *From the collection of Edward Rowe Snow, courtesy of Dorothy Snow Bicknell.*

father. Amos C. Baker Jr. had been in charge at Clark's Point Light since 1879, and his father was keeper there before him. In total, the Bakers kept the two lights for about 80 years.

Amos C. Baker Jr., a native of Dartmouth, Massachusetts, had first gone to sea as a 12-year-old cabin boy on the whaling ship *Messenger,* of which his father was captain. In 1862, as third mate on the bark *Stafford,* Baker had his leg broken in two places by a whale and spent 80 days on his back. By 1874 he was the captain of the bark *A. R. Tucker.* He became keeper at Clark's Point after his second voyage as captain, a trip that lasted 29 months.

After arriving at Butler Flats Light in April 1898, Keeper Baker wrote: "At 7 a.m. took charge of Butler Flats Lighthouse with Charles A. Baker as Assistant Keeper. The lighthouse is new but found it very wet and leaky and very dirty and everything topsy-turvy."

The Bakers soon had the station in good order. A newspaper article described life at the new lighthouse:

> Passing the lighthouse in going down the bay, it seems hardly possible that there is room for housekeeping within its walls, but a visit to the lighthouse will convince the most skeptical. The few who have been privileged to visit Captain Baker when on duty have returned to their own homes more than surprised at the show of comfort and ease found.
>
> The main entrance to the structure . . . leads directly into the kitchen, which is 16 feet in diameter. This room opens directly into the engine room, which can be reached without going outside. In the room are the usual utensils found in a kitchen—stove, sinks, closets, sideboard and locker—for this department is used as a dining room. The drudgery of housekeeping is all on this floor. It is seven feet in the clear, and so well provided with windows that even in the warmest weather it is comparatively cool. Everything is as handy as a pocket in a shirt, and when Mrs. Baker joins her husband next week, for the summer months, she will find everything in readiness for her.

Below the kitchen was a basement that contained cisterns (water was collected off the roof of the main gallery) and storage space, as well as a workroom for the keeper. One floor up from the kitchen was the parlor, called the "coziest room in the lighthouse" in the newspaper article. Above that were the sleeping quarters for the keeper and the assistant keeper. The next level was the watchroom and kerosene storage, topped by the cast-iron lantern. A weight was suspended from the lantern all the way down to the cellar. A single winding of a clockwork mechanism each evening raised the weight and set the revolving lens in motion.

Amos C. Baker Jr. was widowed twice during his years at Butler Flats, but his loneliness was eased by the fact that his son was the assistant keeper. He also had occasional visits from his daughter, Amy. Some of the logs of Captain Baker are in the possession of the Old Dartmouth Historical Society. The entry for Christmas in 1907 reads: "A pleasant Christmas Day. . . . Squally in the evening, but we had some music from the phonograph so we had sunshine inside."

A fog bell was sounded by an automatic striking mechanism when needed, producing a double blow every 15 seconds. Amy Baker enjoyed saluting passing vessels with the bell. The renowned Capt. Joshua Slocum gave Amy a copy of a booklet about his sloop *Spray* with the inscription, "To the little girl who rang the bell each time I passed the light." Amy Baker later wrote of the fog bell: "To one not used to it, it would seem almost unbearable when going for any length of time, but I have often been told in the morning that it had been running during the night, when I knew nothing of it, sleeping soundly all the while. Vessels are saluted by this bell."

The Baker family found Butler Flats Light a pleasant place to live in summer, but winters were a different story. Amy Baker wrote: "In the winter ice shakes the light a good deal at times, and it is scarcely pleasant to have the chair in which you sit shake and realize what might happen if the ice proved stronger than the iron plates of the caisson."

In 1905, 200 tons of riprap stones (large blocks of granite) were placed around the base of the lighthouse to help protect it against damage from ice.

When Amos C. Baker Jr. died in 1911, his obituary stated: "For 13 years he lived in Butler Flats Lighthouse. Visitors occasionally came alongside, and Captain Baker's cheery, 'Come aboard!' always made them glad to obey and see the old seaman's comfortable house." Visitors' signatures in the register included that of President Grover Cleveland.

Charles A. Baker, who replaced his father as keeper, was alone at Butler Flats Light during the great hurricane of September 21, 1938, which battered the south-facing New England coast. Someone later told Baker that since he could see from shore that the light was on, he knew Baker was all right. Baker responded, "What a foolish remark. As long as I could crawl, I would get the light going."

Hugh Murray, a volunteer, works on the lighthouse's optic on the day of its one-hundredth birthday celebration, April 30, 1998. *Photo by the author.*

Charles A. Baker retired in 1941. For a brief period Octave Ponsart, the principal keeper at Dumpling Rock Light until 1942, visited the lighthouse every morning and evening to tend the light while he lived with his family on Merrimack Street in New Bedford. Soon Coast Guard crews took over the operation of the lighthouse.

Among the Coast Guard keepers was Leland S. Rose, who was in charge from 1943 to 1946. During that period, he also looked after the automated lights at Palmer's Island and Dumpling Rock. Rose later recalled that there were five crewmen assigned to the lighthouse; three were on duty at a time and two onshore. Rose said he was "always busy doing something" at the lighthouse.

The City of New Bedford honored Rose by presenting him with a citation at a luncheon on May 2, 2003. Before he died in November 2003 at the age of 90, Rose was among the last living employees of the old Lighthouse Service. He entered the service as a lightship sailor in 1938 and joined the Coast Guard two years later.

In 1975 a new automatic light and fog signal were placed on New Bedford's hurricane barrier, which had been built to protect the harbor after the hurricane of 1938. The Coast Guard deemed Butler Flats Light unnecessary, and it was leased to the City of New Bedford in 1978. Private citizens took responsibility for the maintenance of the light.

In 1978 the lighthouse became one of the first in the nation to use solar power. A New Bedford surgeon, John B. O'Toole III, rowed out to the lighthouse often to replace the batteries and clean the solar panels. He claimed to have a secret method for keeping birds off the panels.

He told the *Boston Globe*, "Everybody in New Bedford loves the lighthouse." A plaque dedicated to Dr. O'Toole, who died in 1991, is now on the shore near the lighthouse.

An underwater electrical cable was run out to the lighthouse in 1992. In 1993 the lighthouse was fitted with a new optic, and it was made more secure by the addition of an exterior lighting system. The tower was also made more difficult to enter in an effort to curb vandalism.

In September 1997, inmates from the Bristol County House of Correction went to work at the lighthouse. The project was a joint venture of Bristol County Sheriff Thomas Hodgson and New Bedford Mayor Rosemary S. Tierney. The inmates rewired the electrical system and did work on the tower's walls, ceilings, floors, and stairway.

On April 30, 1998, more than 600 people attended a celebration of Butler Flats Light's one-hundredth birthday. A new, brighter optic had been installed by Hugh Murray, a retired New Bedford wire inspector who in recent years has led the preservation efforts, along with Peter Duff, a retired plumber, and Manuel Mendonca, a retired firefighter. Anne Blum Brengle, director of the Old Dartmouth Historical Society, read excerpts from the writings of Amy Baker. "Just as the Old Light successfully withstood the storms," she read, "let us hope that Butler Flats may be a guide to sailors for many a long year."

Also at the 1998 celebration, Edward P. Talbot, chief of staff of the Bristol County Sheriff's Office, spoke about the practice of having inmates from the Bristol County House of Correction do maintenance at the lighthouse. "The most impressive statement of all," said Talbot, "came from an individual who has been in and out of our facilities for the past 10 years. He was assigned to this project last summer, and he told us he was very pleased to work out here because it was fun. But most important, he had a five-year-old son who could never be proud of an awful lot of things he had done in his life. But he could always stand along the beach and point to the lighthouse and say, 'I had something to do with keeping that place alive.'"

A good view of Butler Flats Light can be obtained from the New Bedford–Martha's Vineyard ferry. Call (866) 453-6800 or visit www.mvexpressferry.com for more information. The ferry from New Bedford to Cuttyhunk also passes the lighthouse; see www.cuttyhunk.com or call (508) 992-1432.

The lighthouse can be seen offshore along East Rodney French Boulevard in New Bedford, especially near the intersection with Ricketson Street.

CHAPTER 5

Palmer's Island Light in September 2006. *Photo by the author.*

Palmer's Island Light

1849

Six-acre Palmer's Island, in the Acushnet River on the west side of the entrance to New Bedford's harbor, has been the scene of great heroism and tragedy. The island is named for one of the earliest settlers of Dartmouth, William Palmer. Like Boston Harbor's Deer Island, Palmer's Island was used as an internment camp for Indians during King Philip's War in 1675–76.

New Bedford was the whaling capital of the nation in the midnineteenth century, with a fleet of 239 ships. About half of the country's supply of whale oil came through the city. A June 27, 1843, letter from a branch pilot, Benjamin Akin, made a case for a lighthouse on Palmer's Island: "I have always found it extremely difficult in the night, even with a fair wind, to bring a ship past Palmer's Island and the fort, when the passage is narrow and the channel crooked; and therefore, [I] state it as my opinion, that a light-house is much needed there upon Palmer's Island."

In his 1843 report, the engineer I. W. P. Lewis wrote: "This island lies directly within the entrance to New Bedford Harbor. A single lamp beacon placed upon it would add materially to the facilities required on entering this important harbor."

A lighthouse was built on the northern point of the island for $1,951 by Charles M. Pierce, a mason. The 24-foot, conical tower was built of rubblestone, with wooden windows and floors. Three flights of wooden stairs and a short iron stairway led to the "birdcage-style" lantern. A walkway connected the lighthouse to the higher part of the island; the walkway was covered for a time beginning in 1902. A boathouse was added in 1869, and an oil house was built in 1905.

The light, 34 feet above mean high water, was put into service on August 30, 1849, by the first keeper, William Sherman. Like many of the nation's lighthouses at that time, the lamps were fueled by New Bedford whale oil.

An 1850 report described the station: "Tower of the light-house built of stone, and tight; dwelling is of wood and somewhat leaky; lantern is a good one, and the whole taken together is a fair piece of work. . . . Found the apparatus clean; but the dome of the lantern, which was painted white, was just as black as could be. . . . Dwelling is too small and needs a porch."

In 1857 a fifth-order Fresnel lens and a single oil lamp replaced the earlier system of multiple lamps and reflectors. A new lantern was installed in 1863.

Keeper Sherman left to become the toll collector on the Fairhaven Bridge in 1853. Charles D. Tuell, who remained keeper until 1861, replaced him.

George Cowie served as keeper from 1872 to 1891. He complained that the well water was brackish and that the smoke from New Bedford factories blew across the island, contaminating the cistern with soot. It's unclear if anything was done to remedy the situation.

From 1888 to 1891, a red light on the nearby Fairhaven Bridge served as a range light with Palmer's Island Light; mariners would align the two lights to navigate safely past Butler Flats before the lighthouse was established there. Later, a light on the Wamsutta Mill also served for a time as a range light with Palmer's Island Light.

The early part of the twentieth century saw a number of changes. A new fog bell and striking machinery were installed in 1900 in a pyramidal wooden tower. Later, the fog-bell machinery was removed from this tower and placed in a structure that was attached to the lighthouse. New stairs were also installed in the lighthouse in 1900. In the following year, 75 tons of riprap stones were placed on the beach to afford some protection in storms.

Arthur Small, a native of Brockton, Massachusetts, came to Palmer's Island with his wife, Mabel, in 1922, after five years at Boston Harbor's Narrows ("Bug") Light. Small witnessed the end of New Bedford's whaling era, when the last square-rigger, the *Wanderer*, left the harbor on August 25, 1924. Known widely as Captain Small, he was

Palmer's Island Light Station in the early 1900s. *From the collection of Edward Rowe Snow, courtesy of Dorothy Snow Bicknell.*

Keeper Arthur Small. *Courtesy of Jeremy Burnham.*

a well-traveled seaman who had first gone to sea on a Maine fishing schooner at the age of 14.

According to Edward Rowe Snow in his book *Famous Lighthouses of New England,* Small practically had to rebuild the keeper's house at Palmer's Island in 1932, because it was listing badly. Small jacked up the entire house and put in new sills, a chimney, and a fireplace.

Arthur Small was a gifted artist of sailing ships and harbor scenes, praised for his attention to detail. Mary Jean Blasdale's book *Artists of New Bedford* informs us that Small started painting on scraps of sail as a hobby during his years at sea, and he later took classes to sharpen his skills.

Small was a member of the Mariners' Club, which met for conversation and chowder at the Peirce and Kilburn Shipyard in Fairhaven, just across the Acushnet River from New Bedford. A number of Small's paintings were displayed in the area where the club met, and he also painted a large compass rose on the floor.

Edward Rowe Snow quoted Arthur Small's comments on the importance of his work to the commerce of New Bedford Harbor:

> *It is a popular idea that there is very little to do except for striking a match once a day to light the lamp. Few of these landlubbers realize that if a fog comes in during the middle of the night, the keeper must be ready to turn on the fog signal at once, for if the fog bell is silent for a moment, even then a great vessel may be feeling her way up into the harbor, depending on the ringing of the fog signal bell for her safety.*

> *The channel in New Bedford Harbor is so narrow that if a large vessel went down, all shipping in or out of the harbor would be at a standstill. The coal for the electric light company would not reach the pier, and the cotton steamers likewise would find it impossible to dock. In a short time all the city would be seriously crippled. That is what makes me angry when I hear of the easy job of a lighthouse keeper, as described by some fair-weather sailor or inland resident.*

In another interview, Keeper Small downplayed the so-called heroism of keepers: "Whenever they say anything about a lighthouse keeper, they always act as if he were some kind of hero. We're not heroes. Here I am on this island, perfectly safe, working and painting pictures, while you wander around in New Bedford, crossing streets with automobiles and trolley cars whizzing by, just missing you by a few feet. Why, you people take more chances in a week than I do in ten years."

On September 20, 1938, Mabel Small took part in one of her regular activities, a sewing circle in Fairhaven. One of the other women there saw Mrs. Small looking anxiously out at the water. The woman asked what was wrong, and Mabel Small replied that the seas were rough and she feared that Arthur would not be able to row over from Palmer's Island to pick her up. But her husband was waiting at the landing at the usual time, and Mabel shouted, "See you girls next week!" as she headed home to Palmer's Island.

The very next day, a ferocious hurricane took the area by surprise. During the afternoon of the storm, 53-year-old Arthur Small attempted to walk the 350 feet from the house to the lighthouse on Palmer's Island. He left his wife at the oil house, which he considered to be relatively safe, as it was on the island's highest point.

As he struggled to reach the tower, Keeper Small was struck by a large wave and was swept underwater. He managed to swim back to safety. He looked back and saw his wife attempting to launch a row-

Arthur and Mabel Small with some of their cats on Palmer's Island. *From the collection of the author.*

boat to come to his aid. As Mabel Small tried to launch the boat, a tremendous wave destroyed the boathouse, and Arthur Small lost sight of his wife.

Keeper Small later said: "I was hurt and she knew it. Seeing the wave hit the boathouse was about the last thing I remember. I must have been hit by a big piece of timber and knocked unconscious. I came to some hours later, but all I remember was that I was in the middle of some wreckage standing on it. There was a window under me. Then I must have lost my senses for good, for I remember nothing more."

Somehow Arthur Small kept the light burning through the night. The morning after the hurricane, two friends of the Smalls rowed to the island. They took the keeper to St. Luke's Hospital in New Bedford under police escort. They had first contacted the Lighthouse Service for permission, as no keeper was to leave his post until relieved "if he is able to walk." Small was later transferred to the Chelsea Marine Hospital.

Mabel Small had not survived. Her body was later found and identified in Fairhaven. Many of Keeper Small's paintings were lost in the hurricane, along with his large library of several hundred books. His wife had their savings of about $7,500 in her possession when she drowned, and this was also lost.

The *Boston Traveler* reported: "Mrs. Small, wife and mother, perished in a moment of high bravery attempting to go the aid of her man. Arthur Small went through a living death during those black hours of Wednesday night while held captive in the lighthouse tower. High bravery was his in not challenging hopeless odds that the storm had set up."

Three days after the storm, Commissioner Harold D. King of the Bureau of Lighthouses called Arthur Small's performance during the storm "one of the most outstanding cases of loyalty and devotion that has come to the attention of this office."

Small asked for no compensation for his paintings, but in his official report he assigned a value of $75 to his library and $100 to his records and notes on sailing ships, "the result of thirty years' work and used for reference in painting the history of sailing ships, a spare-time hobby." After an extended leave that included time in Panama, Small became keeper at Hospital Point Light in Beverly, Massachusetts, in 1939.

When Arthur Small died in 1958, the Coast Guard honored him with a burial at Arlington National Cemetery. A plaque honoring Arthur and Mabel Small can be seen today on the Fairhaven side of the harbor at Fort Phoenix.

Detail from one of Arthur Small's paintings at the Fairhaven Shipyard. *Reproduced with the consent of Max Isaksen.*

After the hurricane, Franklin Ponte, formerly an assistant at Boston Light, went to Palmer's Island as a temporary keeper. Ponte's nephew Joseph Ponte served as an assistant. All that was left was the lighthouse and the oil house, and Joseph Ponte later recalled that he and his uncle lived for almost a month in the lighthouse tower before the Coast Guard sent a garage that was converted into living quarters. The light was automated in 1941; Martin Maloney was the last keeper.

With the construction of a massive hurricane wall in New Bedford Harbor in 1963, the lighthouse was deemed superfluous. Palmer's Island, adjacent to the new wall, became more accessible to lighthouse seekers and vandals alike. The island passed through various owners, including radio station WBSM. In 1966 the tower was burned by arsonists; the interior was gutted and the lantern practically destroyed.

In 1978 ownership of Palmer's Island passed from Norlantic Diesel to the city of New Bedford, and a local resident, Dr. John B. O'Toole III, mounted a preservation effort. New Bedford youngsters picked up 20 tons of trash and debris from the island, which they converted into $300 for the lighthouse fund. A new fiberglass lantern was constructed to replace the badly burned one, and a 500-pound steel door was installed. The New Bedford Fire Department contributed a new iron spiral staircase.

After another restoration in 1989, the lighthouse soon fell victim to more vandalism. It remained dark through most of the 1990s.

In 1999, it was decided that restoring and relighting Palmer's Island Lighthouse would be one of the city's Millennium projects. The badly damaged lantern was removed on July 20, 1999, and taken to the city's wastewater division. Jose Pereira, a welder, rebuilt the lantern, preserving the original metal frame. The four-foot-high, seven-foot-diameter lantern was reinstalled on August 25. The tower was repainted by a crew provided by the Bristol County Sheriff Department's Pre-Release Program, under the direction of Peter Duff, a volunteer.

A new solar-powered beacon was installed, with a 250-millimeter clear acrylic lens. The light—originally fixed white, later fixed red and then fixed green—now has a white light with a characteristic of two seconds on, six seconds off. The new lighting apparatus was paid for with donated funds.

A large crowd gathered on New Bedford's State Pier on the pleasant evening of August 30, 1999, to witness the relighting of Palmer's Island Light, 150 years—almost to the minute—after its first lighting in 1849.

In a dramatic tribute to the city's past as the whaling capital of the nation, three crews from the Whaling City Rowing Club took part in the relighting ceremony. Mayor Frederick M. Kalisz Jr. handed out lighted oil lanterns to the crews on board the whaleboats *Herman Melville, Flying Fish,* and *Skylark.* The three boats made their way to the island. As the crowd watched quietly, Mayor Kalisz waved another lantern in the air and the lighthouse soon began to flash.

Palmer Island Light is pictured on New Bedford's city seal, which was developed in the mid-1800s, along with a whaling ship. The city's motto—*Lucem Diffundo,* meaning "I Spread the Light"—has a double meaning, referring to the city's famed whale oil business as well as the city's many Quaker residents, who referred to themselves as the "Children of Light."

At this writing, in the fall of 2006, the lighthouse is again in need of repairs and painting. The base is underwater at high tide, which is accelerating the wear and tear on the masonry.

Palmer's Island is accessible by foot at low tide only from New Bedford's hurricane wall. The lighthouse can be seen from the New Bedford Whaling Museum and other spots onshore. The ferry to Cuttyhunk Island passes the island; call (508) 992-1432 or see www.cuttyhunk.com. A daily harbor tour offered in season also provides a view; see www.whalingcityexpeditions.com or call (508) 984-4979.

CHAPTER 6

Ned's Point Light in September 2006. *Photo by the author.*

Ned's Point Light

1838

Mattapoisett—a few miles east of New Bedford in southeastern Massachusetts—was a village of the town of Rochester until 1857, when it was incorporated as a separate town. With a commodious harbor on Buzzards Bay, Mattapoisett developed as a center for ship-building, whaling, and coastal trade.

With the support of the Massachusetts congressman (and former president) John Quincy Adams playing a vital role, Congress appropriated $5,000 on March 3, 1837, for a lighthouse at Ned's Point, at the north side of the entrance to Mattapoisett's harbor. The point's name comes from Edwin "Ned" Dexter, who once owned a farm there. A landowner at the point, Barnabas Hiller, sold four acres to the government for the light station for $240.

Leonard Hammond, a prominent local shipbuilder and business-man widely known as "Uncle Leonard," was the contractor chosen to build the new lighthouse and keeper's house. Edward Rowe Snow tells an amusing story in his book *Famous Lighthouses of New England*. Hammond, who also ran a saltworks and a tavern, apparently was unable to complete construction in the specified time. He had to take drastic action when an inspector arrived, expecting to see a finished lighthouse.

Hammond convinced the inspector to spend some time at his tavern before heading to Ned's Point. Meanwhile, some of Hammond's work crew scurried around to make it appear that the job had been finished. Where a finished floor should have been, they placed loose planking over barrels. Hammond and the inspector soon arrived. The unsuspecting man stepped on the end of one of the loose boards and disappeared into the foundation of the tower, angry but unhurt.

The conical lighthouse—built of stone from a nearby beach—originally had a "birdcage-style" lantern, holding a system of 11 lamps and parabolic reflectors showing a fixed white light 41 feet above the sea. A small stone dwelling was built close to the lighthouse. An unusual architectural touch in the tower is the cantilevered granite stairway, with 32 steps embedded in the inner wall without the use of mortar.

Lt. Edward W. Carpender inspected the station just a few months after it went into service in March 1838. Carpender felt that the light was far more powerful than it needed to be, and he recommended suppressing seven of the lamps. (Records indicate that for some years in the 1840s, only eight lamps were used.) Carpender also found the construction of the tower and house lacking.

> *The unskillfulness of the work extended to the lantern, the dome of which likewise leaked, rendering it prudent for the keeper to remain by the lamps during the rain, lest the light should become extinguished. I removed the surface of the mortar or cement, in several places, and found the stone to be laid in what appeared to be very little more than mere sand.*

Most of the early keepers stayed at the station for only a few years, until the former stage driver Larnet Hall Jr.'s split stint of 20 total years (1848–53 and 1859–74). An inspection in 1850 called the station "a first-rate concern." A report in the following year told a different story; it found the lighthouse to be badly built and leaky, with a poor lighting system. The lantern was only 5 feet 8 inches high—"too low . . . for the convenience of the keeper with his hat on."

The original birdcage-style lantern was replaced by an octagonal lantern at some point before 1888, probably at the same time that a fifth-order Fresnel lens was installed in 1857. The present lantern was installed in 1896.

Ned's Point Light with its original "birdcage-style" lantern. *U.S. Coast Guard photo.*

The 1868–69 period saw many repairs and improvements to the dwelling. A new wood-frame house, built on the original foundation in 1888, replaced the stone house. A new covered walkway was built between the house and tower in 1892. A brick oil house was added in 1907.

After 17 years as keeper of nearby Bird Island Light, Zimri Tobias "Toby" Robinson, a Civil War veteran, became keeper in 1912. Keeper Robinson died in 1914 and was followed by Russell B. Eastman, who would be the light's final keeper. The keeper's house was removed in 1923, when the light was converted to automatic operation. The house was loaded onto the scow *Eva* and floated across Buzzards Bay to Wing's Neck Light Station in Bourne. According to legend, Eastman cooked his breakfast inside the house on the way across the bay.

The Coast Guard decommissioned the lighthouse in 1952. According to Edward Rowe Snow, a bureaucratic error led to the lighthouse being inadvertently offered for sale "to the lowest bidder." James Stowell of Mattapoisett—determined not to be underbid—promptly offered one cent, but the sale was canceled.

In 1958 the site, except the lighthouse itself, was sold to the town of Mattapoisett. The town developed a beautiful and popular park at Ned's Point. The light became active again, with a new modern lens, in 1961.

In 1993 the local Coast Guard Auxiliary flotilla adopted the lighthouse. Auxiliary members renovated the lighthouse in 1995–96. Also in 1995, the Coast Guard installed a new 250-millimeter optic. The light's characteristic since 1961 has been isophase six seconds—a white light on for three seconds, alternating with three seconds of darkness.

The lighthouse stands in Veterans Park at the end of Ned's Point Road in Mattapoisett, and there is a large free parking area. In recent years, the lighthouse has been open during July and August, on Thursdays from 10 a.m. to noon. E-mail Bert Theriault at nedspointlight@comcast.net for more information.

CHAPTER 7

Bird Island Light in September 2005. *Photo by the author.*

Bird Island Light

1819

Stark little Bird Island—less than two acres—is just a few hundred yards off Butler's Point near the entrance to Marion's Sippican Harbor, on the west side of Buzzards Bay. The name "Sippican," the local Indians' word for "long river" or "land of many waters," according to different sources, once applied to a much-wider area.

Bird Island was an ideal place to establish a lighthouse that would serve to guide mariners to Sippican Harbor and points north. Congress appropriated $11,500 on March 3, 1819, for three separate aids to navigation, including a lighthouse on Bird Island.

Henry A. S. Dearborn, customs collector for the port of Boston and the local lighthouse superintendent, contracted Bela Pratt of Weymouth, Massachusetts, to build the tower and other buildings at a cost of $4,040. A conical rubblestone tower was constructed, 25 feet tall, with an 18-foot diameter at the base and a 10-foot diameter at the top. A 12-foot-tall iron lantern surmounted the tower. The accompanying stone dwelling was 20 by 34 feet, and a covered walkway connected the house and tower. William S. Moore, a veteran of the War of 1812, was appointed as the first keeper, and the light went into operation on September 1, 1819.

A severe storm struck the area at the end of December 1819, devastating the new light station. Keeper Moore, who lost his boat and a large supply of wood, described the damage in a letter to Dearborn: "A very violent gale . . . has swept away every thing moveable from the island; and among other things my boat. . . . I was under the necessity of removing with my family into the light house, as the seas breaking against the dwelling house threatened to fill the low part. . . . In the course of being at sea, I have experienced much severe weather, particularly the tornadoes of Africa, and other tropical climates, and they hardly exceed the violence of this gale for a short time."

Letters from Moore to Dearborn indicate that the keeper conducted experiments with the heating of whale oil to keep it from freezing in the winter months. He also worked on the development of "air boxes" to be stored on boats to help prevent sinking.

In a letter dated February 25, 1821, Moore explained that after he had served in the War of 1812, he was accused of owing money to the

U.S. Army. He denied the charge, although he admitted to careless accounting. Moore told Dearborn that he wanted to remain at Bird Island so he could pursue his various experiments. He explained, "As the keeping of a lighthouse is calculated to afford me more leisure than almost any other employment, I shall give it up with great regret."

Persistent local legend claims that Moore was a pirate who was banished to Bird Island as punishment. Some versions of the story claim—preposterously—that he was left without a boat, supplies being delivered periodically. Since his boat is mentioned frequently in correspondence, that is clearly untrue. In any case, properly functioning lighthouses were vital to maritime commerce, and the authorities strove to hire responsible and reliable men, not accused pirates.

Some accounts claim that Moore murdered his wife—described as a "Boston society girl"—at the light station. A rifle was purportedly found in a secret hiding place, along with a bag of tobacco, when the original keeper's house was torn down in 1889. The gun was believed by some to be the murder weapon. Others have claimed that Moore prevented his ailing wife from seeking medical attention on the mainland and that she died as a result.

Although she is supposedly buried on the island, there is no sign of the grave of Moore's wife today. With the gun was found a note signed by Moore, which eventually came into the possession of Marion's longtime town historian, H. Edmund Tripp. It reads: "This bag contains tobacco, found among the clothes of my wife after her decease. It was furnished by certain individuals in and about Sippican. May the curses of the High Heaven rest upon the heads of those who destroyed the peace of my family and the health and happiness of a wife whom I Dearly Loved."

Another far-fetched part of the lore surrounding William Moore is that he disappeared, never to be seen again, shortly after his wife's death was discovered. In reality, records clearly show that Moore was assigned to the new Billingsgate Lighthouse near Wellfleet in 1822. It isn't clear if he was able to continue his experiments there.

The truth about Keeper Moore will probably never be completely separated from the fantastic legends concerning his life. But his wife did die on the island, and there are those who say it has been haunted or cursed ever since. According to a newspaper article in the *Standard Times,* legend has it that the "ghost of a hunched-over old woman, rapping at the door during the night" frightened some later keepers.

John Clark was keeper from 1834 to 1849 and again from 1853 to 1861. (John Delano was keeper from 1849 to 1853.) In 1837 Clark reported that the tower and lantern deck were leaky and that the stairs were "considerably decayed." He warned that the seas were washing away the shoreline and could potentially split the island in two if not checked. He also complained of a bad whale-oil supply that was "as thick as porage." Bird Island Light was one of the few lighthouses of the early 1800s to have a revolving optic. Lt. Edward W. Carpender, in his important 1838 survey, questioned the necessity of a revolving light. He pointed out that there was no chance of this light's being mistaken for another, since it was "aloof from all other lights." He recommended that it be changed from a flashing white light to a fixed red light and that the number of lamps be reduced from 10 to 6. This would, said Carpender, save taxpayers $143.50 yearly. Carpender also noted that the harbor was frozen for long periods in winter, but the light was kept in service year-round nevertheless. Carpender's recommendations went unheeded.

The engineer I. W. P. Lewis visited Bird Island during his survey of 1842, and Clark provided him with this gloomy statement:

I was appointed keeper of this light in 1834, upon a salary of $400. . . . The tower is in a bad state, very leaky, and wood work all more or less rotted. The lantern contains ten lamps; the reflectors on one side are very old, and much worn; the lantern is crowded exceedingly, and leaks badly at all the angles; the glass is continually broken by the rust; the lantern sweats very much, and makes ice upon the glass in winter half an inch thick. The whole light-house is in a bad state, and I think was not built in a faithful and workmanlike manner.

The dwelling-house is tolerably comfortable, but requires shingling; the chimneys smoke; the east and south sides of the island are washing away fast. Last winter the stone wall on three sides was knocked away by the sea. I have been at work this summer rebuilding the wall on a more substantial scale. The superintendent allowed me forty dollars for the work. My boat-house has become so rotten in the framing that I expect it will blow down, if not repaired. The boat ways are so placed as to receive the whole rake of the sea from the northeast. This exposes the boat to considerable danger, and repeatedly damages the ways. My oil is good. There is a well here, but no water. I am therefore obliged to boat my water from the main land, over two miles distant, and carry all our clothing on shore to be washed. I have no rain-water cistern.

Lewis corroborated Clark's observations, writing that the "construction of the house and tower evinces a great want of fidelity on the part of the contractor, and renders complete and thorough repairs necessary."

A report by the local lighthouse superintendent in early 1843 was far less critical, describing the station as "in good order, and well kept." The report did recommend more protection from the sea and an improved boat landing. An authorization of $1,000 in 1843 paid for a new 600-foot stone seawall, a 25-foot extension to the wharf, the construction of a cistern for the water supply, the reshingling of the dwelling roof, and the painting of the buildings. More repairs were carried out during the 1840s, including the reglazing of the lantern in 1849. New clockwork machinery for the revolving lens was installed in 1850.

In 1856, a fourth-order Fresnel lens replaced the old lamps and reflectors. The 1863 annual report of the Lighthouse Board noted that a new lantern had been installed on the tower.

In November 1866, during Marshall V. Simmons's stint as keeper (1861–69), a severe storm swept the island, flooding the cellar and the well, damaging the seawall, and carrying away part of the enclosure fence. Repairs were swiftly completed.

Simmons was still the keeper on September 8, 1869, when a storm of "unprecedented severity" caused widespread destruction in New England. The seas covered Bird Island completely during the height of the storm, demolishing 280 feet of the seawall. The waves also destroyed a barn and carried away other outbuildings and fences. The official report stated that the station was reduced "from a condition of perfect order to a perfect wreck."

William A. Simmons, formerly an assistant, became principal keeper a week after the 1869 storm. In February 1872, a newspaper reported that Simmons had seen more than 300 seals on the ice near Bird Island at one time. "He shot one and obtained from it two gallons of oil," according to the article.

Periodic repairs kept the station inhabitable, but the keeper's dwelling was reported to be dilapidated in 1888. A new wood-frame house, 28 by 31 feet, was built on the old foundation.

The station had an assistant keeper for a few years in the 1860s and 1870s. Charles A. Clark filled that role for a brief period before he became the principal keeper in 1872, and he would remain in charge until 1891.

Peter Murray followed Charles Clark as keeper. In 1980 Murray's daughter, 91-year-old Frances Murray Rathbeg, recalled the family's life on the island, which she called a "sad place." The harsh winters, said Rathbeg, were especially difficult.

During one winter, Keeper Murray's 11-month-old son, Gerald, became ill with pneumonia. "We had no way to get off the island," Rathbeg recalled. "The baby coughed and screamed." With no other way to signal for help, the desperate keeper extinguished the light to attract attention. Help eventually arrived, but too late; the baby had died. The Murrays buried their child on the mainland and never returned to Bird Island.

Zimri Tobias "Uncle Toby" Robinson became keeper in May 1895, and he would remain for 17 years. The families on Bird Island kept animals to augment their food supply. According to his brother's grandson, Keeper Robinson transported a cow to the island by attaching a rope to the animal and tying it to his skiff. He then rowed to the island with the cow swimming behind him.

Robinson and his wife, Angie, also kept a flock of chickens and a substantial garden. Angie Robinson always had a chicken dinner ready for visiting lighthouse inspectors.

During a tremendous storm on the night of September 30, 1907, Keeper Robinson spotted a motor vessel in distress with two men aboard. Robinson went out in his boat and rescued the men, but they were not able to return to safety until the next morning, after hours of drifting in the gale.

On another occasion during Robinson's tenure, the entire island was almost completely underwater for about an hour during an extreme high tide, and seawater poured into the cellar of the house. At the opposite extreme, it was reported that during one unusually low tide it was possible to walk from the island all the way to Kittansett Point in Marion.

Bird Island Light Station, circa early 1900s. *From the collection of the author.*

The lantern and deck were again replaced in 1899, and a fifth-order lens replaced the earlier fourth-order lens. In 1902 a wooden bell tower was added to the station, with a 1,000-pound bell and striking machinery.

Elliot C. Hadley, previously the first keeper of Graves Light in Boston Harbor, was in charge of Bird Island Light from late 1912 until early 1917, when H. H. Davis took over. Maurice A. Babcock was the next keeper, staying from 1919 to 1926. Babcock's next stop was Boston Light.

George T. Gustavus, a Wisconsin native, father of 10 children, and a 16-year veteran of lighthouse keeping, was the next and—as it turned out—the last keeper.

Gustavus and his family left Bird Island Light when it was taken out of service on June 15, 1933. The building of the Cape Cod Canal had led to more traffic in Buzzards Bay, but lighted buoys close to the main shipping channels eliminated the need for Bird Island Light.

The hurricane of September 21, 1938, caused widespread destruction all along the south coast of New England, and Marion was hit hard. High tide in the evening of the hurricane was 14 feet above normal. The great storm swept away every building on Bird Island except the lighthouse tower.

In March 1940, the government sold the island at auction to George Harmon of Bar Harbor, Maine, for $654. Just a month later, Augustus Fiske of Providence, Rhode Island, purchased the island. It appears that little was done with the property over the ensuing 25 years.

In early 1965, the Marion Conservation Commission announced that donations were being accepted toward the purchase of the island. The town bought the island from Fiske's heirs in May 1966 for $2,500.

By 1973, $12,500 had been raised for the restoration of the lighthouse and to erect a fence, designed to protect the island's nesting tern colony. The lighthouse was relighted on July 9, 1976, as part of Marion's celebration of the nation's bicentennial, but the tower subsequently fell into further disrepair and the light was again extinguished.

By the 1990s, stones and mortar were loose and green moss covered much of the tower. Broken panes of glass allowed starlings to nest in the roof of the lantern. The white paint had faded so that the dark tower blended with the coastline behind it.

A new effort was mounted in 1994, when Charles J. Bradley, a local shellfish officer, formed the Bird Island Preservation Society. By the fall of 1996, the society had raised more than $70,000 through direct mailings, an open house on the island, and a donation from the town. They also secured another $30,000 in federal funds.

International Chimney Corporation of Buffalo, New York, was hired to do the restoration work. The company had gained fame in lighthouse circles after their successful moves of Block Island Southeast Light in Rhode Island and Highland and Nauset lights in Massachusetts.

The International Chimney crew arrived on the island in October 1996 and began with the sandblasting and repointing of the exterior. After completing much of the project that fall, the workers returned the following spring to finish the job.

In June 1997, the Marion Board of Selectmen asked Charles Bradley if his group had the funds for a new optic to be installed in the tower. Bradley replied that they didn't, so the selectmen decided to provide $3,000 for a new solar-powered flashing 300-millimeter lens and its installation. At 9:00 p.m. on July 4, 1997, with 3,000 people gathered on the shore, Bird Island Light was relighted as a private aid to navigation. "It's a gift from heaven," said Bradley.

Bradley was Marion's harbormaster from 1999 to 2005, and he has been the de facto keeper of the lighthouse. Despite the legends that swirl around the island, Bradley says he's never experienced a ghost there himself. But some people, he says, have found the lighthouse "eerie." For one thing, it's home to countless spiders. A young man once entered the lantern room to find it full of spiders. "He was airborne," Bradley told the *Standard Times*, "back to the boat before I could even say, 'Ernie, where'd you go?'"

Custody of Bird Island was transferred to the Marion Marine Department in 1998. The nesting population of roseate terns—an endangered species—on the island is around 1,500 pairs. It's the largest breeding colony of the species in North America. In fact, it represents about half the known breeding population on the continent. Ram Island in nearby Mattapoisett is also an important nesting site.

The presence of these rare terns on Bird Island means that the island receives much attention from researchers. It also means that the island is officially off-limits to the public during much of the spring and summer.

🔆 **Bird Island Light can be seen distantly from shore in Marion, but it's best viewed by private boat. For more information, or to help with the ongoing preservation of the lighthouse, write to Bird Island Light Preservation Society, 2 Spring Street, Marion, MA 02738, call (508) 748-0550, or visit www.by-the-sea.com/birdislandlight/.**

CHAPTER 8

Cleveland Ledge Light in September 2005. *Photo by the author.*

Cleveland Ledge Light

(Cleveland East Ledge Light)
1943

Cleveland Ledge, west of Bourne in Buzzards Bay and eight miles from the entrance to the Cape Cod Canal, is named for President Grover Cleveland, who frequently visited the area to fish in the days when his summer White House was at the Gray Gables mansion in Bourne. The unique tower built here was the last commissioned lighthouse in New England.

According to the *Coast Guard Bulletin* of August 1940, the decision to build a lighthouse at Cleveland Ledge was part of a plan to convert the aids to navigation in Buzzards Bay from their original purpose of serving local navigation to the new purpose of guiding major shipping traffic through the Cape Cod Canal, which opened in 1914. The lighthouse is about 1.8 miles from the nearest point of land, and it marks the eastern side of the southern approach to the canal.

The contract for the construction of the lighthouse was awarded to the J. F. Fitzgerald Company of Boston in the amount of $198,851. On October 7, 1940, the caisson that would serve as the lighthouse's foundation was towed to the ledge from New London, Connecticut, where it had been constructed. It took 19 hours to tow the caisson into position. Commercial tugs were aided by the Coast Guard cable ship *Pequot.*

The 52-foot-high caisson was sunk in 21 feet of water and then filled with stone and concrete. Below the main deck were an engine room, fuel tanks, and four water tanks with a capacity of 4,800 gallons. On top of the caisson, a two-story building was constructed to house resident keepers, and this was surmounted by a 50-foot, reinforced-concrete light tower. The sleek architecture of the structure is classified as Art Moderne, a trendy style of the 1930s and 1940s. A number of similarly styled lighthouses were constructed elsewhere, including Alaska, but this is the only Art Moderne lighthouse ever built in New England.

The partially built lighthouse was transferred to the government in September 1941 because of the threat of war, and, after the onset of World War II, construction was delayed because of the shortage of many materials. The new lighthouse was completed and commissioned on June 1, 1943. It was put through a grueling test a little over a year later.

Construction of Cleveland Ledge Lighthouse. *U.S. Coast Guard photo.*

On September 14, 1944, a hurricane battered the area. When the storm hit, a crew of nine men (and a dog) under the command of Lt. Olie P. Swenson were in the lighthouse. A newspaper reported a few days later: "Every member of the crew will frankly admit today that he was surprised and, to put it mildly, gratified that the hitherto untried cement and steel structure withstood the storm. All had misgivings about their immediate futures at one time or another throughout that night, and during those hectic, fearful hours during which they alternately hoped and prayed that the next wave wouldn't be the one to bowl them all into the sea."

During the height of the storm, at about 12:30 a.m., a crash brought the entire crew running to an engine room in the lighthouse's base. A skylight had partially dislodged, and seawater was flooding the engine room. The men grabbed buckets and began bailing frantically. The water rose to within two inches of the tops of batteries that provided power for the light, but a barricade made of planks and mattresses stopped the water level from rising any higher.

Later, when the seas had subsided slightly, two of the men, with lifelines around their waists, made it to the broken skylight and managed to plug the break with oil drums, mattresses, and planking. A damaged boat, hanging on davits nearly 40 feet above the sea, indicated how high the waves had reached during the storm. The telephone and radio were dead, but the light had continued to flash through the hurricane.

Four men were assigned to the lighthouse at the time of a newspaper article in December 1967. Each of the men had two weeks at the station followed by a week off. When asked how the crew felt about spending their holidays at the lighthouse, the officer in charge, Boatswain's Mate First Class Ronald E. Glass of Birmingham, Alabama, said: "Of course, the men would rather be home, but you always look forward to going there when you are off. Everyone here understands our mission. We earn our liberty and eventually we get it." That holiday season, two of the men got time off around Christmas while the other two were off at New Year's.

At the time of the 1967 article, the interior of the lighthouse was described as "spit and polish spotless" and as "warm as toast" thanks to a large oil furnace. The living facilities included a galley, a lounge with a small television, sleeping quarters, and a lavatory. A 44-foot patrol boat from the Woods Hole Coast Guard station visited weekly with supplies, which were hauled up to the deck at the lighthouse in a sling.

In late January 1977, the resident crew had some excitement when a barge carrying 3.3 million gallons of home heating oil ran aground near the lighthouse while under tow on the way to Portland, Maine. Some of the oil leaked out, but a major catastrophe was averted.

The lighthouse originally had a fourth-order Fresnel lens. In 1978, the lens was replaced and the light was automated, after the laying of an underwater cable to supply power. The Coast Guard crew was reassigned in September 1978, and the lighthouse was sealed off. Coast Guard personnel later spent three weeks in 1990 renovating the lighthouse.

When he was a boy in the 1960s, James M. Howe of North Falmouth frequently visited the Coast Guard keepers at Cleveland Ledge, along with his two brothers. The men befriended the local boys, who gave them a hand by delivering newspapers and helping with painting and repairs. In 2005, with his good memories as an inspiration, Howe founded a preservation organization and was granted a license to care for the lighthouse.

Howe died in December 2005, but others say they will carry on caring for the lighthouse he loved. Within the next few years, the lighthouse will most likely be transferred to a new owner under the provisions of the National Historic Lighthouse Preservation Act of 2000.

☀ **Cleveland Ledge Light remains an active aid to navigation, with a modern 190-millimeter optic displaying a white flash every 10 seconds and an automated fog horn sounding every 15 seconds. It can be seen distantly from shore (from Old Silver Beach in North Falmouth, for example) but is much better viewed by boat.**

CHAPTER 9

Wing's Neck Light in September 2005. *Photo by the author.*

Wing's Neck Light

1849, 1890

Pocasset, on Buzzards Bay just north of North Falmouth, became a part of the newly incorporated town of Bourne in 1884. The Wing's Neck peninsula in Pocasset (said to be a Wampanoag Indian word for "where the stream widens") extends about two miles westward into the bay, north of Pocasset Harbor.

Congress first appropriated $5,000 for a lighthouse at the tip of Wing's Neck in 1837, but the project was delayed after some debate about whether the light was really needed.

There was plentiful iron ore in the area's swampy terrain, and several foundries—including the Pocasset Iron Company—were established by the mid-1800s. These businesses and related manufacturing companies added volume to the local shipping traffic, as many vessels traveled to and from Sandwich and Wareham, to the northwest. Maritime traffic in the vicinity increased, leading Congress to appropriate $3,500 for a lighthouse in August 1848. Almost 10 acres of land were acquired for the station from George and Nancy Ellis in the following March for $250.

The contractor John Vina erected a stone dwelling, topped by a hexagonal wooden tower and lantern, for $3,251. The fixed white light, established in August 1849, was 38 feet above the ground and 50 feet above mean high water, and it could be seen for 14 nautical miles.

The first keeper, Edward D. Lawrence, was removed in 1854 for belonging to the wrong political party (the Whigs) and was replaced by Samuel Barlow. Lawrence returned as keeper in 1865 and remained until 1887, serving a total of 28 years at the station. John Maxim, another keeper in the 1850s, was killed during the Civil War, in the Battle of Gettysburg.

The Lighthouse Board reported in 1857 that a fourth-order Fresnel lens had replaced the earlier system of multiple lamps and reflectors. In 1928, the lens was replaced and the light was changed from fixed to flashing. The light was converted to electricity in 1934.

It was noted in 1863 that repairs to the building had been completed, including the installation of a new lantern. Despite these improvements, the building was in poor condition by 1878, as is reflected in the annual report that year: "The lantern is on top of the dwelling, the roof has been crushed."

A fire did further damage to the building later that year, but repairs sufficed until 1888, when funds were finally appropriated to rebuild the station. The new dwelling, completed in 1890 on the original foundation, was a wood-frame structure, 28 by 31 feet. A hexagonal wooden lighthouse tower was erected next to the dwelling, with the light 44 feet above the water; the two structures were connected by an enclosed walkway in 1899. A pyramidal wooden bell tower and a 1,000-pound fog bell were added to the station in 1902.

Albert Gifford served as keeper at Wing's Neck for 21 years, beginning in 1887. His wife, Carry H. Gifford, served as his assistant. Edward D. Nickerson, the local undertaker, described what happened the night Albert Gifford died at the lighthouse in October 1908:

> One mean and foggy night he died in his house. I hitched up my old nag and drove down there. Mrs. Gifford was alone [and] as I worked on his body, she carried on through that beastly, cold, foggy, night, tending the light and clocking the fog bell. After finishing my work I stayed the night there. I could not leave her way out there alone with her husband lying dead in the parlor. The light streaming out into the foggy night and the weird clang-clang-clang of that great bell every 1/2-minute. I never forgot that night or the woman all alone there sticking to her husband's responsible job.

Carry Gifford kept the station operating for two weeks before being relieved by Wallace Eldredge, the son of a Nantucket whaler. Eldredge had previously been stationed at Nantucket's Sankaty Head Light and Cape Poge Light on Chappaquiddick Island.

A 1916 article described the lighthouse during the stay of Eldredge and his wife, Louise: "The keeper's wife is fully as popular as her husband—and one of those women who never tire. The polished floors and walls and the immaculate ceilings assure the visitor that the man of the house should share with his better half in the credit for this model of tidiness."

After the opening of the Cape Cod Canal in 1914, with its western entrance just a few miles northeast of Wing's Neck, local maritime traffic greatly increased. Personnel at the light station had to watch for any vessel approaching the canal from the south, and they would telephone ahead so that a tugboat and pilot could meet the vessel for its passage through the canal. For a time, Louise Eldredge served as the official day dispatcher for the canal. She also had the duty of flying storm signal flags at the station as needed.

The assistant keeper under Eldredge for some years was his wife's brother, Benjamin Whitford Joy, another Nantucket native, who had

The first (1849) Wing's Neck Lighthouse. *From the collection of the author.*

been the captain of clipper ships sailing out of New York for San Francisco and China.

President Harding once passed near the station in the presidential yacht *Mayflower*. Because of bad weather, the yacht anchored near Wing's Neck. In the morning, Keeper Eldredge gave the president a 21-"gun" salute using the station's fog bell. He then cranked up his Model T automobile and drove his family to the Cape Cod Canal office, where they got a view of the president at closer range.

Eldredge earned five Efficiency Gold Stars for excellent service during his years at Wing's Neck. He retired at the age of 65, after 33 years of lightkeeping, in 1921. Eldredge bragged that he had never "tasted a drop of a doctor's medicine" in all that time, although an accident once necessitated the amputation of part of his right thumb. On the Eldredges' retirement, their Wing's Neck neighbors presented them with a solid silver tray inscribed, "To Captain and Mrs. Wallace A. Eldredge, 1908–1921, with best wishes from their friends on Wing's Neck."

George Addison Howard, formerly at several other Massachusetts light stations, became keeper in 1921. In 1909 Howard had become the youngest principal keeper in the nation at Duxbury Pier Light at the age of 23. His brother, William James Howard, previously at Boston Light and a navy veteran, became his assistant in 1926. The Howard brothers—sons of the captain of the Cross Rip Lightship in Vineyard Sound—gained widespread fame as lifesavers. Both brothers were commended in 1930 for saving a man whose small sloop had capsized near the lighthouse in high winds. According to a newspaper account,

Wing's Neck Light Station in the early 1900s. *From the collection of the author.*

the struggle to row their rowboat back to shore against the wind left the brothers exhausted.

In another instance, on July 14, 1931, a small boat overturned with a man and four young boys on board. William Howard went out in the station's boat and rescued all five. In 1932 alone, the Howard brothers were credited with eight lives saved. An article written that year described George Howard sitting in his typical spot near the edge of the bluff, staring at the sea with a pair of powerful binoculars at his side. He described another of his brother's rescues one night that summer:

> Bill heard the men shout across the water after the four, two girls and two young men, had tipped over. It was pretty rough, you can believe. They were trying out a brand new racing boat and I suppose turning in the sea they had hit a broad-backed comber and just flopped over like a duck. But the boat remained upside down.
>
> One of the girls could swim. She said she couldn't, but when she got into the water she found, she told us, she could—because she had to. They get like that. Pluck! Just pluck! Well, I was away, ashore on an errand connected with the light. Bill heard them shouting. He got his son, Gilbert.

One of the young women and one of the young men reached shore on their own. William Howard launched his small boat. Aiming for the shouts he heard coming from the darkness, he located the drifting young man, who was hanging on to a rubber cushion. It was too rough to pull the man into the boat, so Howard pulled his arms into the stern and rowed ashore with the nearly drowned man holding on. It isn't clear from the article what happened to the fourth passenger of the racing boat.

Just nine days later, William Howard saved the lives of a man and four boys—aged 12 to 15—whose boat was swamped about a mile offshore.

"I wish they wouldn't go off here fishing or cruising in such small craft," said William Howard in 1932. "If it comes up a quick blow, there's sure to be trouble." By the end of William's career, it was estimated that he had saved 37 people.

In 1923 the keeper's house at Ned's Point Light in Mattapoisett—on the opposite side of Buzzards Bay—was floated to Wing's Neck to become an assistant keeper's house at Wing's Neck Light Station. (The house is now privately owned.)

With the establishment of Cleveland Ledge Light in 1943 as a guide to the canal, Wing's Neck Light was considered expendable. The station was discontinued in 1945 and went up for sale in 1947. Frank Flanagan of Boston bought it for $13,738. Years later, his wife, Irene Kelly Flanagan, loved to tell visitors about how surprised she was when Frank came home one day and asked, "How'd you like to live in a lighthouse?"

The Flanagans were a musical family, and Wing's Neck Light became a center of musical activity in the area. According to an article in *Yankee* magazine, Frank believed that singing made for a happier world. "Keep the world singing," he often said.

The Flanagans' daughter, Beth, was a concert pianist. Barbershop quartet concerts frequently took place on the lawn, and the von Trapp family singers of *Sound of Music* fame spent some time at the lighthouse. Known to many as "the lady in the lighthouse," Irene Flanagan died in 1999 at the age of 96.

The area around the lighthouse remains a monitoring station for the Cape Cod Canal; it contains radar and a closed-circuit television system.

☀ **Wing's Neck Light is on private property, and the grounds are not accessible to the public. A fairly good view is available from a gate about 100 yards from the lighthouse, reached by leaving Route 28 in Pocasset and following Barlow's Landing Road for 2.2 miles and turning right onto Wing's Neck Road, which leads to the end of the peninsula.**

The lighthouse was renovated in 2003 and is now available for vacation rentals, with sleeping accommodations for eight people. For more information, call the Wing's Neck Lighthouse Trust at (508) 460-0506 or see www.wingsnecklighthouse.com.

CHAPTER 10

Top: The 1860 Cuttyhunk Lighthouse. *Bottom:* The 1891 Cuttyhunk Lighthouse. *Both U.S. Coast Guard photos.*

Cuttyhunk Light

1823, 1860, 1891–1947

Cuttyhunk Island—about two miles long by a mile wide—is at the southwestern end of the Elizabeth Islands, a chain that extends for about 16 miles from the village of Woods Hole in Falmouth on Cape Cod. The 16 islands, which mark the boundary between Vineyard Sound and Buzzards Bay, constitute the town of Gosnold.

The island's name comes from the Algonquin Indian word "Poocutohhunkunnoh," which is generally translated as "point of departure" or "land's end."

The English explorer Bartholomew Gosnold established a short-lived settlement on the island in 1602. Gosnold used the island as a base to explore the area, including Martha's Vineyard.

Coastal shipping traffic in the area was heavy by the early 1800s. In 1830 a total of 12,603 vessels were observed passing Cuttyhunk. The island's southwestern tip was an obvious location for a lighthouse to help guide traffic into Buzzards Bay and eastward into Vineyard Sound.

After Congress appropriated $3,000 for a lighthouse on May 7, 1822, the government paid two local men $300 for "three acres and 139 rods" of suitable land for the station. The plans called for a conical stone tower, 25 feet tall, 18 feet in diameter at the bottom and 10 feet at the top. The tower was to be surmounted by an octagonal iron lantern. A separate, one-floor dwelling was called for, 20 by 34 feet and built of stone.

The buildings were finished and the light went into service on May 1, 1823, with a system of nine lamps and reflectors showing a fixed white light, 48 feet above the water. The first keeper, a man named Sayre, ran into controversy in late 1825. Capt. Cornelius Howland of the brig *Wm. Thacher* complained that he had been near Cuttyhunk for four hours one night and never saw the light from the lighthouse. A scathing report soon appeared in the *New Bedford Mercury:* "We have heard it stated from respectable authority, that the objects for which the Light House was erected on Cutterhunk, have been but partially realized; or in other words, that great neglect on the part of the keeper, in not having it properly lighted, frequently renders the navigation in its vicinity more hazardous that it would have been had no Light House ever been erected there."

Keeper Sayre responded in the January 20, 1826, edition of the *Mercury*: "As it respects the Light-house under my care, I can affirm that it has never been out since May 1st, 1823, until put out at a proper time in the morning."

Sayre explained that the tower had a severe dampness problem and that heavy steam continually clouded the lantern glass. In addition, insufficient ventilation in the lantern kept the lamps from burning brightly except during times of high wind. Finally, he said, spray from the ocean often covered the lantern and blocked the light. There were light winds on the night of Captain Howland's report. Sayre saw the brig and took it to be at least nine miles away, not between four and eight miles, as Captain Howland had claimed.

It isn't clear how—or if—this dispute was ever settled. A footnote: Cornelius Howland became a lighthouse keeper himself a few years later, at Clark's Point Light in New Bedford.

When Lt. Edward Carpender inspected the station in 1838, there were 10 lamps with 13-inch reflectors in use. The reflectors, said Carpender, had not been well cleaned, and the frame of the lantern was badly corroded. He recommended a new lantern and a more com-pact arrangement of the lamps. Carpender also mentioned that the stone tower had twice been encased in brick, which lends credence to Sayre's assertion that it was poorly built and prone to dampness.

I. W. P. Lewis's examination, reported to Congress in 1843, force-fully confirmed that the lighthouse was not well built. Lewis described the tower as leaky from roof to base, and he said the "whole establish-ment [is] conducted in the worst manner." His criticism didn't end there:

> The light, which should be one among the best, is not only the poor-est one among all in the vicinity, but is hidden away under a side hill, by which location it is of little or no use to navigation. A reef extends from the southwest end of Cuttahunk about two miles, and is one of the most dangerous in the sound; lying directly at and across the entrance to Buzzard's Bay. Vessels approaching from the eastward cannot see Cuttahunk light until they are close aboard this reef, called the Sow and Pigs, over which the tide sets with fearful rapidity. If a light were erected on the extremity of this reef, it would be of immense value, not only to the coasting trade through Vineyard and Long Island sounds, but as the key to Buzzard's Bay, by which all the dan-gers of the west shore might be avoided.

In an attempt to remedy this situation, a light vessel was assigned to a spot near the Sow and Pigs Reef—2.3 miles from the Cuttyhunk Lighthouse—in 1847.

A Fresnel lens replaced Cuttyhunk Light's old lamps and reflectors in 1857. In 1860 the dilapidated old tower was torn down. A second story was added to the keeper's dwelling, and a lantern was erected on the roof.

S. Austin Smith was keeper from the end of January 1864 until 1881. About two weeks after he took over, on February 9, 1864, he noted in the station's log that he was taking care of his sick family. Four days later, the entry was even more plaintive: "Employed washing, cooking, cleaning the light. This is lonesome. We are all sick." Two weeks later, Smith and his wife were finally feeling much better.

William Atchison followed Smith with a nine-year stint. The next keeper was Alfred G. Eisener, a Maine native. According to a newspaper account, the old dwelling when Eisener moved in was "very damp, and somewhat dilapidated." Funds were soon appropriated for the rebuilding of the dwelling and for a new 45-foot stone lighthouse.

The first floor of the new one-and-a-half-story, wood-frame keeper's house contained a living room, dining room, kitchen, and pantry, and three bedrooms were located upstairs. A fifth-order Fresnel lens was installed in the new tower, presumably relocated away from the old structure. The new light went into service in 1891.

Eisener was involved in a dramatic rescue on March 11, 1892. A tremendous storm was bearing down on the area, and the keeper noticed debris coming ashore. With a telescope, he spotted a disabled ship offshore. Four men could be seen hanging on to wreckage on the deck. Eisener roused two neighbors, and soon a party of five—the keeper, his wife, their daughter, and two men who lived nearby— launched a lifeboat supplied by the Massachusetts Humane Society.

After a grueling half hour they reached the wreck, which was a British ship called the *Rob and Harry*. A line was secured to the ship's bowsprit and two of the ship's crewmen were able to drop themselves into the lifeboat. A large wave severed the connection between the two vessels, and the lifeboat was driven back to shore with two men still aboard the *Rob and Harry*.

By this time, the captain and some of the crew from the island's life-saving station arrived on the scene. The lifeboat was repaired, and Keeper Eisener and some of the lifesavers rowed back to the wrecked ship. They got the last two crewmen aboard, but one of them had already died.

Eisener moved on to Plymouth Light in 1894. A succession of keepers came and went over the next few decades. Eugene Terpeny stayed for the longest stretch (1894–1909). Before the family arrived, word got around among the island's young men that the Terpeny family included two daughters. Their hopes were high, but it was reported that a large sigh could be heard when it was learned that the daughters were little girls.

Terpeny's daughter Alice Terpeny Petty recalled her early life at the lighthouse many years later. She said that her father—between visits of the government supply boat—went to the village on the island to buy supplies and would bring them back in a wheelbarrow. As many as 10 or 12 people would come to the house for Sunday dinners, and the Terpenys' island neighbors would often visit to play whist, to sew, or to dance. The visitors would bring lanterns to light the way on their return trip.

Keeper Terpeny died at the age of 60 in 1909, three months after a lingering illness forced him to step down as keeper. His obituary appeared in the publication *Along the Coast:* "Mr. Terpeny was well known and liked by every visitor to Cuttyhunk, while among the islanders he was a friend to everyone." Alice remembered the family's years at Cuttyhunk as happy and said they were heartbroken to leave.

George Gustavus, a native of Wisconsin, was keeper from 1919 to 1926. Gustavus and his wife, Mabel, raised 10 children during their lighthouse years.

Octave Ponsart, a New Bedford native and the son of Belgian immigrants, became keeper in 1943 and moved into the keeper's house with his wife, Emma, and their daughters, Bette and Seamond. Seamond fondly recalls the family's years at the Cuttyhunk Light Station. After hearing stories of the area's early English explorers, she loved to "play Gosnold."

Keeper Octave Ponsart (right), his wife, Emma (center), and her daughter Bette (left). *Courtesy of Seamond Ponsart Roberts.*

Mom and Dad would ask me if I had a busy day, and I'd say Rex [her dog] and I sure did and that Gosnold had to hurry up and get back to England. And when I told them that, they knew for sure what I had been up to. Dad made me a little play sword (with a blunt end on it, as Mom insisted) and a hat out of newspaper that to me looked more like what a sailor would use, but Dad assured me that Gosnold could have worn one of those. And if Dad told me something solemn like that, I really figured it was the gospel truth.

Cuttyhunk Island was just a wonderful place for children. It was magic for sure. And it still is, I am glad to report.

But the best magic was that my Daddy was a lighthouse keeper. He was just the best man and most patient father anyone could ever have, and he had this neat occupation that provided me with a lighthouse tower to play in and help care for. Besides playing Gosnold on the rocks, I would be the damsel in the tower or Rapunzel letting down her long hair in the fairy tale, even though my hair was brown and short. In my imagination I could do anything, and having a tower was a great accessory for my daydreams of fairy tales and dragons.

The island for me was an endless playground. I had the pond to play in with my little boats and floating toys. I had my chickens, which were my dear friends and providers of eggs and chicken dinners. I loved gathering eggs and this was my morning chore. I also had a little garden and I always seemed to eat more baby carrots than I grew. I'd pull them up too soon to see how they were growing, then wash them off at the pump and eat them right there.

Seamond remembers her father being continually busy with his duties as keeper.

My father had so many duties connected with the little lighthouse on Cuttyhunk. He whitewashed and cleaned the tower, the house and the barn. He would polish the brass daily, and there was a lot of brass. He would clean the lens, make sure the lamps (the main one and the spare one) were ready in the tower, and lots of other mundane stuff that went along with being a lighthouse keeper.

Everything had to be shipshape, and if any damage was done it had to be noted and explained. The dwelling that was provided for us was part of my father's salary. He got a "report card" on the inspections, and if he got any less than an overall "very good," which was like getting a B on a report card, his annual salary could be reduced. So he was very busy all the time.

The crewmen from two local lightships—Vineyard Sound and the Hen and Chickens—often stopped at the Cuttyhunk Light Station on their way to or from their stations, and sometimes they spent the night on bunks provided by the Ponsarts. Seamond thought of the young men as uncles. "When my lightship 'uncles' visited we'd have a big dinner, more than likely seafood. Then we'd sit on the porch and Dad would play his mandolin or harmonica and sing. Sometimes the men

Left: Seamond, daughter of Keeper Octave Ponsart, with Skipper, one of her dogs, at Cuttyhunk. *Right:* During her birthday party in 1944 at Cuttyhunk Light Station, navy planes surprised Seamond Ponsart and her family by dropping bombs on the station. The bombs were supposed to be dropped for target practice on Noman's Land, a deserted island some distance away. Here Seamond poses with one of the bombs on the pier at the West End Pond. *Both photos courtesy of Seamond Ponsart Roberts.*

would tell stories. And my mother, a Cuttyhunker herself, would chip in with stories of local people or fishing stories she knew oh so well."

A hurricane on September 14, 1944, hit Cuttyhunk directly, changing the shape of the island. Ponsart weathered the storm and managed to keep the light going through the night, with the help of little Seamond, who ran up and down the stairs fetching supplies and coffee. Her sister, Bette, who had married a Coast Guardsman, was pregnant and went into labor on the same night (false labor, as it turned out). As the wind reached its highest point, at about 2:00 a.m., there was a crash in the keeper's house—a chimney had crashed through the roof. It landed on Seamond's bed, where she would have been sleeping if she hadn't been with her father.

During a visit to Cuttyhunk Island in July 2001, Seamond Ponsart Roberts placed a wreath in the water in memory of her parents, Octave and Emma Ponsart. *Photo by the author.*

Every night, the Ponsarts could see the lights of the Vineyard Sound lightship offshore. During the night of the hurricane, Seamond and her father checked periodically to see if the lightship could still be seen. The last time they saw it was around the time the chimney had fallen into the house. Seamond recalls:

When the big blow came, it was so strong that the whole tower was shaking and we were holding on to the lens stand. Dad was not so sure that the tower was not going to blow down! I was really, really scared. I had never felt the tower shake like that. Since then I've been in earthquakes, and that's what it felt like.

Dad said to me, "Seamond, do you see the lightship?" And I did for a few seconds. Then, as we looked where the lights had been just seconds before, they were gone. When the next clear patch of sight came, no lights. We both knew.

My father said, "The iron men in the iron ship, gone to the bottom." I knew he was thinking of days past when he too was a lightship man, and the peril they faced out there. And we were both crying because I knew all my uncles were gone. He told me to go tell Mom and Bette. And I did, making a dangerous trip down the stairs as the tower was still shaking badly.

Bette and Mom were so upset. Mother went up with Dad in the tower while I stayed with Bette. We all knew it was the worst for these men, our dear, dear friends. Daylight was coming. I went to the living room and did something strange, yet comforting for me. I went over and hugged each of their pillows and then fell asleep on one of the lightship crewmen's bunks.

The Ponsarts were still at Cuttyhunk Light in December 1945 when the "Flying Santa," in the person of the historian-storyteller Edward Rowe Snow, dropped packages for the family from a plane. One package contained a doll for little Seamond. Unfortunately, the doll was broken on the rocks, despite heavy packing. Seamond was heartbroken. The following Christmas, the Ponsarts were at West Chop Light on Martha's Vineyard. Edward Rowe Snow chartered a helicopter, flew to the island, and hand-delivered a new doll to Seamond.

The station had been badly damaged by the hurricane in 1944, and the Coast Guard felt that erosion would soon cause the tower to fall into the ocean. In 1947 a modern skeleton tower with an automatic light was erected nearby, and the lighthouse was demolished. All that remains today is the skeleton tower and the station's oil house.

The skeleton tower continues to exhibit a white flashing light, visible for 12 miles, from 63 feet above the water.

You can visit Cuttyhunk by taking the ferry *Alert II* from New Bedford. The island may no longer be worth visiting as a lighthouse destination, but it's still a fascinating place. See www.cuttyhunk.com, or call (508) 992-1432 for information on the ferry.

CHAPTER 11

Tarpaulin Cove Light in September 2005. *Photo by the author.*

Tarpaulin Cove Light

1817, 1891

Naushon Island, about seven miles long and 5,000 acres in area, is the largest of the Elizabeth Islands, a chain of 16 islands that extend about 16 miles westward into Buzzards Bay from Falmouth on Cape Cod. Naushon Island's name comes from the local Indians' name for the entire chain, "Nashanow," thought to mean "midway islands," referring to the islands' position separating Vineyard Sound and Buzzards Bay.

Tarpaulin Cove, on the east shore of the island, was for many years a bustling little place where the local farmers did business with the crews of incoming vessels. Seamen traveling through Vineyard Sound often stopped for a meal or a night's stay at a tavern run for many years in by Zaccheus Lumbert.

Lumbert established an early navigational light in 1759, for the "public good of Whalemen & Coasters." Except for the whale oil the people of Nantucket gave him, Lumbert paid for the upkeep of the light himself. When he petitioned the colonial governor for some financial relief in 1762, Lumbert was awarded a sum of six pounds. Lumbert and his successors maintained the light for nearly six decades.

In spite of the light, shipwrecks in the vicinity were not uncommon. The first government appropriation for a proper lighthouse at Tarpaulin Cove was made in 1807, but no action was taken for another decade—apparently largely because a local landowner and tavern keeper, James Bowdoin, feared that the lighthouse keeper could start a competing tavern business and possibly harbor disreputable types who might steal from Bowdoin's large flock of sheep. Progress couldn't be made until after Bowdoin's death, when the federal government paid $216 for suitable property for the establishment of a lighthouse on the west side of Tarpaulin Cove in 1817.

A rubblestone tower—described as 38 feet tall in some sources, but reported as 25 feet tall in Lt. Edward W. Carpender's 1838 inspection—was built for a little over $6,000. It went into service in October 1817, exhibiting a fixed white light 71 feet above the water. John Hayden became the first keeper.

The lantern held a system of 10 lamps and reflectors when Lieutenant Carpender inspected the station in 1838. Carpender

Tarpaulin Cove Light Station before 1888. *U.S. Coast Guard photo.*

stated the opinion that a "single series of six lamps, compactly arranged" would serve local navigation sufficiently.

Hayden had been living at the station for a quarter century when he provided a statement for I. W. P. Lewis's 1843 report that painted a dire picture:

> *The tower is leaky from top to bottom, so that I have to cut the ice off the staircase in winter. All the staircase and window frames are more or less rotten—the landing of the stairs dangerous to tread upon. The lantern sweats so as to make quantities of ice on the glass and floor. The tower is not high enough to clear the land to the westward, so that the light in that direction is of no use to vessels near the shore. The dwelling-house leaks badly about the windows, the frames of which are rotten; cellar stairs rotten, and ridge boards of the roof old and rotten. . . . There is a boat-house and landing; the landing is a kind of trestle bridge made of rough poles, and is nearly knocked to pieces in the surf. . . .*
>
> *I have a well, thirty-six feet deep, without a drop of water in it; also a cistern, the pump of which always freezes up in winter, for want of covering.*
>
> *I consider the establishment was not faithfully built in the first instance. The plastering is more or less fallen off in the chambers and sides of the other rooms; chimneys are all smoky, and the house cold and uncomfortable.*

An 1850 inspection praised Hayden and indicated that repairs had improved life at the station somewhat. "Light-house is in good order.

Some repairs to the work (wood) to the dwelling have been made since I supplied last year, such as a new outside cellar door; and lighting apparatus is in good order and clean; and, in fact, so is the whole establishment. Keeper is a hard-working, likely man, and has brought up a large family."

A fifth-order Fresnel lens from L. Sautter and Company of Paris was installed in 1856. In April 1870, the characteristic was changed from a fixed white light to fixed white punctuated by brighter flashes every 30 seconds, in an effort to make it easier to differentiate the station from other fixed lights in the vicinity,

Richard Norton, keeper from 1871 to 1882, had been the captain of a square-rigger in the Civil War. Captain Norton lost all his possessions when a Confederate raider sank the ship, and he was appointed keeper at Tarpaulin Cove as compensation.

In 1888 the old stone house was replaced, and in 1891 a new, 38-foot brick lighthouse tower was built, with an iron lantern and a fourth-order Fresnel lens. A 1,200-pound fog bell in a tower with striking machinery was installed. The bell tower was destroyed in the great hurricane of September 1938.

On November 13, 1904, the two-masted schooner *Earcularious* ran aground on jagged rocks less than a mile west of the lighthouse during a northeast gale, and four crewmen were lost. Frank S. Carson, keeper from 1886 to 1910, witnessed the wreck of the schooner just before sunset, but there was nothing that could be done to help the crew as darkness fell over the stormy sea.

Frank Allen Davis was keeper through most of the 1920s. On one occasion, a schooner, the *Tanzy Bitters,* caught fire nearby. Davis rescued two badly burned men and brought them into the kitchen of the keeper's house. His wife did her best to treat the men while Davis went to Martha's Vineyard to get a doctor. The men died, but the doctor said he couldn't have done more for them than Mrs. Davis had. While her husband was away, Mrs. Davis also tended the light.

After the light was automated in 1941, the house and other buildings fell into disrepair and were torn down in 1962. A 300-millimeter modern optic is now in use, and the light continues as an active aid to navigation, with a white flash every six seconds visible for 9 nautical miles, 78 feet above mean high water.

Naushon Island is owned by the Forbes family and is off-limits to the public. No regular public cruises pass near the lighthouse, which makes viewing difficult. The Cuttyhunk Historical Society now manages the lighthouse. For more information, write to them at P.O. Box 165, Cuttyhunk, MA 02713, or call (508) 971-0932 (summer only).

CHAPTER 12

Nobska Point Light in September 2005. *Photo by the author.*

Nobska Point Light

(Nobsque Point Light)
1829, 1876

Falmouth, at the southwestern corner of Cape Cod, was named for Falmouth, England, home port of the explorer Bartholomew Gosnold, who gave Cape Cod its name in 1602. The part of Falmouth known as Woods Hole was purchased from the local Quissett Indians, a tribe of the Wampanoags, by Jonathan Hatch in 1679. Woods Hole was used primarily for farming in the early days.

Today, the village is famous as the home of the Woods Hole Oceanographic Institute, one of the leading centers for oceanographic research in the country. Woods Hole also has a sizable tourist industry, largely because it's the point of departure for today's large car-carrying ferries to popular Martha's Vineyard. There have been ferries of one kind or another traveling this route since about 1700. Nobska Point, at the southeastern tip of Woods Hole, was mostly unused by the settlers until the establishment of a smallpox inoculation hospital there in 1797.

Woods Hole, with its deep harbor, developed a substantial whaling fleet in the early years of the nineteenth century. Besides the local maritime traffic, Nobska Point was passed by a stream of vessels crossing through Vineyard Sound, bordered by Falmouth and the Elizabeth Islands to the north and Martha's Vineyard to the south. In 1829, the year the lighthouse was established, it was reported that more than 10,000 vessels passed through the area.

Prominent Nobska Point was an ideal place for a lighthouse. Congress appropriated $3,000 for that purpose on May 23, 1828, and the federal government purchased four acres for the light station from William and Hannah Lawrence, Andrew Davis, and Elizabeth Lawrence, at a cost of $160.

The first Nobska Point Light, built in 1828 for $2,249, was a typical Cape Cod–style structure with an octagonal lantern on top of the keeper's house. There were three rooms on the first floor of the dwelling and two small rooms upstairs. Like some similar lighthouses, this one had problems with leaks, as the lantern created too much stress on the roof. The lantern held a lighting system of 10 lamps and 14-inch reflectors, displaying a fixed white light 78 feet above the sea.

The first (1829) Nobska Point Lighthouse. *U.S. Coast Guard photo.*

Because the lighthouse was on the mainland, the keeper was not provided with a boat. Lt. Edward W. Carpender surveyed the station in 1838 and recommended that an exception be made, saying: "Should the regulation be waived in favor of any one, I hope it will be extended to this individual, who once had it in his power, with the government boat, no longer serviceable, to rescue some persons from drowning."

Carpender also expressed the opinion that four of the 10 lamps should be suppressed, as the light, "though useful, requires to be seen only for a short distance." In his 1843 report, the engineer I. W. P. Lewis stated his opinion: "One lamp of a proper form is alone required for this place, instead of the 10 now used."

Peter Daggett, a veteran of the War of 1812, was keeper in the 1840s. Some of Daggett's papers are in the possession of the Falmouth Historical Society. It appears he was generally a man of few words, although he did complain to the local superintendent several times about the poor quality of the oil he received for the light. In May 1847, he reported that he had whitewashed the lighthouse. "All that is wanting at this time," Daggett wrote, "is a new pump to the cistern and a new sail for the boat and three sheat iorn [*sic*] pipes for the chimneys."

Daggett was removed from the position in the summer of 1849, "for no other reason," according to a contemporary newspaper, "than because he is a democrat." The newspaper praised Daggett's service: "No light in the world was better kept. Honesty, fidelity and capacity in the keeper were evident to all." Lightkeeping positions were political appointments in those days, and there was no stopping the wheels of politics. William Davis became the next keeper.

Through much of the nineteenth century, the keepers had to count the vessels that passed the light. On one day alone in 1864, Keeper Frederick Ray counted 188 vessels—including 175 schooners—passing the point.

After numerous repairs to the original building, the Lighthouse Board announced in 1875 that the station was "in a dilapidated condition, and should be rebuilt." The same year's annual report announced that a fog bell and striking machinery had been put into operation.

In 1876 the lighthouse was rebuilt as a 40-foot, cast-iron tower lined with brick. The fifth-order Fresnel lens had a focal plane height of 87 feet. The individual sections of the lighthouse were cast in Chelsea, Massachusetts, and transported to Woods Hole in four sections. The new tower was painted a dark reddish brown. This tower is one of a handful of lighthouses (Edgartown Light on Martha's Vineyard and Cape Neddick Light and Lubec Channel Light in Maine are some others) to have miniature lighthouses as ornamentation at the top of each balustrade on its gallery.

The lens was upgraded to fourth order in 1888, and a red sector was added to warn mariners of the dangerous L'Hommedieu and Hedge Fence shoals. New striking machinery for the fog bell was installed in the same year. Four years later, a 100-foot stone wall was added to protect the fog bell tower, which was closer to the water than the lighthouse. Further protection was added in 1900, and a new building was added to house the striking machinery.

A covered walkway between the lighthouse and dwelling was added in 1899, and a brick oil house was built in 1901. A second dwelling for an assistant keeper and his family was added in 1907. The two houses were joined many years later.

The fog-bell tower at Nobska Point in the late 1800s. *From the collection of Edward Rowe Snow, courtesy of Dorothy Snow Bicknell.*

Oliver A. Nickerson had the longest stay of any keeper in the station's history, from 1874 to 1911. A 1908 article described the duties of the keeper's daughter, Florence Nickerson. For the previous seven years, she had been the official "observer" at Nobska, keeping track of all the vessels passing by in daylight hours. "She is shrewd and kindly," said the article, "one of

Nobska Point Light Station in the early 1900s. *From the collection of the author.*

those Yankee girls who fear nothing and take life cheerfully." Besides her observational duties, Florence kept house at the station and tended a flock of chickens.

In 1910, a new brick fog signal building was erected, and there were plans to install a fog whistle operated by compressed air. The plan ran into stern opposition from local residents, who feared the new signal would disturb their sleep. The signal did soon go into operation; it was reported in 1911 that it was powered by two gasoline engines. It doesn't appear that any concessions were made regarding its volume. The keepers started the signal when visibility dropped below five miles.

George I. Cameron of Southport, Maine—formerly at Graves Light and Baker's Island Light Station, near Salem, Massachusetts—was briefly assistant keeper under Nickerson, and he became the next keeper in 1911. Cameron's assistant early in his stay was George Gustavus, who would go on to a long career at several light stations. Gustavus returned to Woods Hole late in his career and was the principal keeper from 1939 to 1941.

Cameron was in charge in early August 1911 when the Boston-bound steamer *Bunker Hill,* with more than 300 passengers on board, ran aground close to the light station on a clear night, in calm seas. "If the pilot or captain, whoever was in charge of the steamer, was trying to hit Nobska Lighthouse," wrote one passenger, "he was a very poor shot, as he didn't come within 100 feet of it, and if he was trying to avoid hitting it he was equally a poor shot, as he had plenty of water in the broad Vineyard sound to escape striking the beacon, the rays of which must nearly have blinded him as he was running his vessel toward it." The steamer was backed off the rocks and made it to Vineyard Haven, where all the passengers were safely unloaded.

Keeper Nickerson's son, Herman, remained at the lighthouse as a boarder while Cameron was keeper. A newspaper item in October 1911 indicates that Cameron's wife had taken their six children and run away to parts unknown with Herman Nickerson.

John M. Scharff had a 30-year stay as keeper (1925–55). Early one morning in May 1930, the 15,000-ton steel freighter *Kearny,* with about 25 men on board, ran into the rocks near the lighthouse in a light fog. Keeper Scharff quickly phoned the Woods Hole Coast Guard station and aid was hurried to the vessel. There were no injuries.

On August 26, 1935, Keeper Scharff and Assistant Keeper Waldo Leighton rescued a man who had fallen overboard from his sailboat during a squall.

The Coast Guard took over the management of lighthouses in 1939, but civilian keepers remained at Nobska Point Light until November 1973. Osborne Hallett was in charge from 1955 to 1968, and Joseph Hindley was his assistant.

The historian and "Flying Santa" Edward Rowe Snow once dropped a holiday package for the Halletts from a plane. This was one of the rare occasions when Snow experimented with the use of parachutes on the Santa packages. The parachute was caught on the station's flagpole, and it took a ladder crew from the Woods Hole Fire Department to disentangle it.

Hindley took over as keeper in 1968. When he retired in 1973, Hindley was believed to be the last civilian lighthouse keeper in New England. His career in the Lighthouse Service dated back to 1927, when he was an assistant at Whale Rock Light in Rhode Island.

At the time of their retirement and move to a home in East Falmouth, the keeper's wife, Charlotte Hindley, said that the couple's years at lighthouses were "very uneventful," and she observed, "People always try to romanticize it." She said that after so many years of learning to talk between foghorn blasts, it would be hard to sleep without the sound.

The Coast Guard's officer in charge at the time of a 1983 article was 25-year-old Gary Williams of Groton, Massachusetts, who lived in the larger of the two keepers' houses with his wife, Donna, and their 14-month-old son, Christopher. "You couldn't ask for a better spot on the Cape," said Williams. "The beach gets busy in the summer, but it always seems quiet here, and although we're only three-quarters of a mile from town, it seems like it's far away. We've got front row seats for the Falmouth Road Race, which goes right by our front door."

The light was automated and the Coast Guard keepers were removed in 1985. The last officer in charge was Charles Tebo, who lived at the lighthouse with his wife, Gina, and their two young children.

After automation, the station became the home for the commander of U.S. Coast Guard Group Woods Hole, which was renamed in 2006 as Coast Guard Sector Southeastern New England. The group serves the mainland and islands from Plymouth, Massachusetts, to the Rhode Island–Connecticut border. While Capt. Frederick M. Hamilton and his wife, Bonnie, were living at the station in 1988, they suggested to the Falmouth Historical Commission that a plaque be placed on the lighthouse, telling about its history. The plaque was installed late that year, and it's still in place.

For three years ending in July 2001, Captain Russell Webster lived at the station. His wife, Elizabeth B. Webster, recalled good times and bad in an article in the *Boston Globe*.

> *Every room but one offers gorgeous ocean views, and from these windows we have seen it all: blood-red sunsets, soaring red-tail hawks, a double rainbow following a December snowstorm, and the latest, best, and worst in bridal fashion and etiquette.*
>
> *One year ago, on the evening of my daughter Noelle's 6th birthday, she screeched in delight at seeing a huge wild turkey from our family room window. The turkey circled the house all day then was never seen again. Maybe it was scared away by the life-size Barbie doll that we put in the lighthouse cupola that night in preparation for my daughter's Barbie treasure hunt birthday party the next day. That night, we heard drivers slowing their cars to gawk at the apparent damsel in distress in the lighthouse.*

With tens of thousands of tourists visiting the lighthouse yearly, life frequently took on a circus atmosphere for the Websters. It wasn't rare for people to come to their door well into the evening, expecting a lighthouse tour. One photographer demanded to be let into the house, claiming, "This is federal property, and I'm a taxpayer, so I'm entitled to come in." The Websters witnessed many weddings held on the grounds, including seven ceremonies on a single banner day in June. Once, the Websters arrived home to find more than 40 cars parked on their lawn and a state trooper who told them they couldn't enter their own house. The wedding couple had invited more than 200 people and put up a huge tent. After that, weddings were limited to 50 people.

December 29, 1967: Osborne E. Hallett, Joseph G. Hindley Jr., and Harry A. Wilbur are awarded Gallatin Certificates by Capt. Frederick J. Hancox, commanding officer of Coast Guard Group Woods Hole. The men were the last three civilian lighthouse keepers in New England. (Wilbur was keeper at Warwick Light, Rhode Island.) *Courtesy of Anne Ames.*

In spite of the inconveniences, the Websters were sad to leave. "We undoubtedly will be on the lighthouse catwalk at sunset," wrote Elizabeth, "teary-eyed, as our views from Nobska come to an end."

The lighthouse has been "adopted" by the members of the Coast Guard Auxiliary Flotilla 11-02, and there are public open houses in season. For some years starting in 1996, the volunteer "keeper" was Payson A. Jones of North Falmouth, a veteran of more than 40 years in the Coast Guard Auxiliary. Jones loved greeting visitors in his old-fashioned keeper's uniform. He told visiting children, "We don't do two things at Nobska. We don't go out on the catwalk at the top of the light and we don't touch the 100-year-old Fresnel lens that's valued at $250,000."

The lighthouse is easily reached by following Route 28 into Falmouth. Take a right onto Woods Hole Road and follow the signs for the Woods Hole Ferry Terminal. Take a left onto Church Street and follow it to the lighthouse.

There's a small parking area nearby, and the grounds are open to the public until dusk every day. There are frequent public open houses at the lighthouse from spring through fall. Tours are conducted by U.S. Coast Guard Auxiliary Flotilla 11-02. Admission is free. A schedule of the open houses is posted at www.lighthouse.cc/nobska/.

CHAPTER 13

Gay Head Light in August 2006. *Photo by the author.*

Gay Head Light

(Aquinnah Light)
1799, 1856

The handsome Gay Head Lighthouse stands in one of the most picturesque locations in New England, atop the 130-foot, multicolored-clay
cliffs at the western end of Martha's Vineyard. Wampanoag Indians
have lived at this location for at least 10,000 years, and native people
still make up most of the small population of the town of Aquinnah,
which roughly means "end of the island." The town's name was changed
from Gay Head in 1998 to better reflect the heritage of its residents.

The Englishman Bartholomew Gosnold, the first European to
explore the area, called the headland Dover Cliff in 1602, after the
famous formation on the English Channel. The Gay Head name was
in common usage by the 1660s.

Massachusetts State Senator Peleg Coffin of Nantucket requested
a lighthouse at Gay Head in 1796 because of the heavy maritime traffic
passing through Vineyard Sound. The passage between the Gay Head
cliffs and the Elizabeth Islands was treacherous because of the long
underwater obstruction called Devil's Bridge that extends out from
Gay Head.

Congress appropriated $5,750 for the lighthouse on July 16, 1798.
A 47-foot (57 feet to the top of the lantern) octagonal wooden lighthouse was erected on a stone base, along with a wood-frame keeper's
house, barn, and oil vault. The light went into service on November 18,
1799. The initial keeper, Ebenezer Skiff, was the first white man to live
in the town of Gay Head.

Skiff found the conditions harsh and requested a pay raise in a
letter to Albert Gallatin, secretary of the Treasury, in October 1805.

> Clay and Oker of different colours from which this place derived
> its name ascend in a Sheet of wind from the high Cliffs and catch on
> the light House Glass, which often requires cleaning on the outside—
> tedious service in cold weather, and additional to what is necessary
> in any other part of Massachusetts.
>
> The Spring of water in the edge of the Clift is not sufficient. I have
> carted almost the whole of the water used in my family during the
> last Summer and until this Month commenced, from nearly one
> mile distant.

For Skiff's troubles, President Thomas Jefferson authorized a raise from $200 to $250 yearly. Ten years later, Skiff described more of his hardships in a plea for another raise.

> When I hire an Indian to work I usually give him a dollar per day when the days are long and seventy five cents a day when the days are short and give him three meals: Now supposing the meals worth twenty-five cents each they amount to seventy-five cents which is seven cents more than the wages for my service both day and night (while I board myself) only sixty-eight cents, computing my Salary (as it now is) at two hundred and fifty dollars a year and the year to consist of three hundred and sixty-five days.

Skiff got another raise of $50 yearly—authorized by President James Madison—and he remained at the lighthouse for a total of 29 years. In 1828, his son, Ellis Skiff, became keeper at $350 per year, a higher salary than most keepers received at the time.

In October 1812, Gay Head Light became one of the earliest American lighthouses to use the system of oil lamps and parabolic reflectors devised by Winslow Lewis of Boston. These devices replaced the earlier spider-lamp system, which consisted of a shallow pan containing oil and several wicks. The new apparatus consisted of 10 oil lamps, each backed by a 14-inch reflector. The entire apparatus revolved, thus producing a flashing light.

In 1838, a New Bedford blacksmith rebuilt the lantern and deck, and the tower was lowered by three feet. Earlier the tower had been cut down by 14 feet to lessen the problem of the light's being obscured by fog. The engineer I. W. P. Lewis visited the station during his landmark survey in the fall of 1842. He described the tower as "decayed in several places" and said the keeper's house was "shaken like a reed" by storms. Both the tower and house required rebuilding, said Lewis. Included in his report was a statement ascribed to Ellis Skiff:

> Both buildings [the tower and house] are defective, through age and bad construction originally. From the want of any foundations, they have been repeatedly thrown by the frost, so as to require numerous repairs to make them tenable. . . . The ground on the north side of the tower has settled by a slide of the cliff, so that I was obliged to pry it up and raise the underpinning. Since then it has settled again on the south side, so as to throw the tower out of perpendicular. The lantern leaks and sweats very much. There is no way of getting air into it, except through the scuttle in the floor; and ice and frost make thick upon the glass in winter, obscuring the light. The revolving appa-

ratus stopped last July on account of the pulley being so bad. . . . The old clock stopped frequently, and in cold weather would not go, so that I was obliged to let the light stand still, and appear as a fixed light. The reflectors are all worn out. The chambers of my house are not lathed, plastered, or ceiled; and the house is not only cold and uncomfortable, but, from its elevated situation, likely to be blown down, as it shakes fearfully with every gale of wind.

Leavitt Thaxter, the collector of customs in Edgartown and the local lighthouse superintendent, believed that I. W. P. Lewis was too harsh in his criticisms, and he claimed that Skiff had been misquoted. In a letter to Thaxter, Skiff stated, "In regard to some of the statements in Mr. Lewis's report having my signature, I can only say, if they were all on the paper I signed, I knew it not, and they are different than I supposed them to be, and from what I told him. It will at least learn me a lesson for the future, not to sign a paper for any man until I understand its contents." Skiff may have been misrepresented, but it's also possible that he feared losing his job once the survey was made public and was seeking to cover his tracks. Lewis's survey was ultimately a major factor in the reorganization of the nation's lighthouse service, with the formation of a new Lighthouse Board in 1852.

The tower had to be moved back about 75 feet from the edge of the eroding bluff in 1844. John Mayhew, a contractor from Edgartown, completed this task. Ellis Skiff remained keeper until he was removed for political reasons in 1845.

An 1852 report on lighthouses in the United States ranked Gay Head Light as the ninth most important seacoast light, the highest rank of any light north of New York. In October of the following year, Joseph T. Pease, the customs collector at Edgartown, wrote to the newly formed Lighthouse Board requesting the immediate rebuilding of the lighthouse. "The tower is too low," he wrote. "In my opinion, a first-class lens light should be erected there as soon as is practicable."

Congress appropriated $30,000 on August 3, 1854, and by the following summer Caleb King was contracted to build the new tower and dwelling. A first-order Fresnel lens was obtained from the Henry-Lepaute company of Paris. A new 51-foot conical brick lighthouse was built to hold the enormous lens, which contained 1,008 prisms. The new light went into service on December 1, 1856. A clockwork mechanism had to be wound every four hours to keep the lens revolving and producing a flash every 10 seconds. Gen. David Hunter wrote in *Harper's:* "Of all the heavenly phenomena that I have had the good fortune to witness— borealis lights, mock suns or meteoric showers—I have never seen anything that, in mystic splendor, equaled the trick of the magic lantern of Gay Head."

The magnificent new lens heightened Gay Head Light's fame as a tourist attraction. Excursion boats brought parties of the curious from other parts of Martha's Vineyard and from New Bedford and other locations on the mainland. The local Wampanoag Indians transported the tourists in oxcarts from the dock to the lighthouse.

Samuel Flanders, a native of Chilmark on Martha's Vineyard, was keeper from 1845 to 1849 and again from 1853 to 1861. An 1860 article in *Harper's* sang the praises of Flanders:

> *A natural and moral philosopher according to the teaching of St. Paul and Professor Agassiz, he lectures with equal clearness on antediluvian ichthyology and the ethics of scripture. In short, no one can long sojourn with Squire Flanders without being touched by his obliging and amiable character and impressed with his substantial worth and honesty. It is a matter of conscience with him to keep his lamp always trimmed and his light set upon a hill. Long may it shine, a luminous example to federal office holders, a beacon of safety to the homeward-bound mariner!*

In spite of the powerful light, shipwrecks in the vicinity occurred with regularity. The worst of them was in the early morning of January 19, 1884, when the 275-foot passenger steamer *City of Columbus* hit Devil's Bridge en route from Boston to Savannah with about 130 passengers and crew. The captain stopped the engine and had the ship put into reverse, but it was too late. The steamer rapidly filled with water and sank, and within a short time about 100 persons drowned.

Horatio N. Pease of Edgartown, a veteran of 14 years as keeper at Gay Head and six years as assistant keeper before that, was in charge at the time of the *City of Columbus* disaster. His assistant, Frederick Poole, spotted a light from the stranded ship at 5:00 a.m. Pease extinguished the light as Poole frantically aroused their neighbors. A Humane Society lifeboat was kept at the light station, and soon a volunteer crew of Gay Head Indians plunged the boat into the icy seas to assist the survivors, who were clinging to the ship's frozen rigging.

After multiple trips, a number of people were saved by the brave actions of the volunteer lifesavers and by the crew of the revenue cutter *Dexter,* which soon arrived on the scene. Some of the Wampanoag rescuers received medals from the Massachusetts Humane Society, which have been proudly passed from generation to generation. A certificate and cash award were given to Keeper Pease.

Pease remained keeper until 1890, when William Atchison, previously keeper at Cuttyhunk Light, replaced him. Atchison, a Civil War veteran who was born in Ireland, had to resign after several months because of a mysterious illness. His replacement, Edward Lowe, died at the age of 44, after only a year at the station. A few years later, four children of Keeper Crosby L. Crocker died within 15 months. A fifth child of Keeper Crocker died ten years later at the age of 15.

It was belatedly decided that the causes of all these illnesses were the extreme dampness of the keeper's house and the accompanying mold and mildew. (Some thought the culprit might be the drinking water, which was hauled from a spring a good distance from the station.) The 1856 brick house was torn down and replaced by a wooden house in 1902. The new gambrel-roofed house was built on a much higher foundation so it would remain dry.

In spite of his family tragedies, Crocker remained keeper until 1920. Charles Vanderhoop, a native Gay Head Indian, was an assistant to Crocker. He advanced to the position of principal keeper when Crocker retired, and he soon became one of the light's most popular keepers. Vanderhoop was born in 1882, the son of a teacher at the Gay Head School. He continued his education in Boston and Providence and attended classes at Harvard University. Vanderhoop first joined the U.S. Life-Saving Service, then the Lighthouse Service; he was stationed at Nantucket's Sankaty Head Light before being assigned to Gay Head.

It was estimated that Vanderhoop and his assistant, Max Attaquin, took approximately one-third of a million visitors to the top of the lighthouse before Vanderhoop's retirement in 1933. The wives of Vanderhoop and Attaquin each had two children during their years at the station. Vanderhoop was very active in the community, serving as sheriff, Republican town chairman, and a member of other civic organizations. He was also an amateur scientist and once found a giant petrified shark's tooth in the cliff at Gay Head.

Frank Grieder was keeper from 1937 to 1948. The light was dimmed as a defense measure in 1941, and the assistant keeper's house was occupied by Coast Guardsmen who patrolled the local beaches.

The light was returned to its full brilliance in 1946. The station had long had multiple keepers, but it was made a single-keeper light during the war and retained that status when the war ended. The keeper's son, Bill Grieder, remembers keeping busy:

> *I went up to help whitewash or paint the tower, and mow the lawn of course. Lug the kerosene up in the tower. Polish the lens. It had to*

be cleaned and dusted all the time. We had a dust cover over that. In the wintertime we used to put glycerin on the outside of the [lantern] glass, so if you got rain it wouldn't ice up.

When Frank Grieder was keeper at Nantucket's Great Point Light in the 1930s, his assistant was Octave Ponsart. Ponsart became the keeper at West Chop Light on Martha's Vineyard in 1946, and his daughter Seamond Ponsart Roberts recalls visits to the Grieders at Gay Head.

Dad and Mr. Grieder would go into the tower and look at and polish the magnificent Gay Head lens. Dad said that even when the wind was blowing there, it was like a church inside the tower because the lens was so gorgeous. They would be in there for hours cleaning the glass, polishing the brass and "talking lighthouse stuff," while we visited with Mrs. Grieder inside the house and had our own social hour.

A Coast Guard family—Arthur and Rita Bettencourt and their five children—moved into the keeper's house after the Grieders left in 1948.

The light had been converted to kerosene operation in 1885. The year 1952 saw the end of the kerosene era, as a high-intensity electric beacon replaced the Fresnel lens. The lens can be seen today in a structure resembling a short tower and lantern on the grounds of

Gay Head Light Station in the late 1800s. *From the collection of Edward Rowe Snow, courtesy of Dorothy Snow Bicknell.*

Charles Vanderhoop was a popular keeper at Gay Head; he retired in 1933. *U.S. Coast Guard photo.*

the Martha's Vineyard Historical Society Museum in Edgartown. Seamond Ponsart Roberts remembers collections of pennies from island schoolchildren to help pay for the lens display. When the display was dedicated in 1952, the former keeper Charles Vanderhoop lighted the lens for the assembled crowd.

Joseph Hindley succeeded Arthur Bettencourt and would be the last keeper at Gay Head, leaving when the light was fully automated in 1956. The dwelling was razed after automation.

The Vineyard Environmental Research Institute (VERI) leased the lighthouse from the Coast Guard in 1985, and some repairs were completed in 1989. The Coast Guard installed a new DCB 224 aerobeacon during the same year. The license was transferred to the Martha's Vineyard Historical Society in 1994. Much work has been done on the tower and grounds in recent years.

Craig Dripps, chairman of the Martha's Vineyard Historical Society's Lighthouse Committee, says that the lighthouse is in need of some work. Rust has caused the gallery surrounding the lantern to lift, which has allowed rainwater to get inside. "This moisture not only leaves dampness on the inner walls," according to Dripps, "but also, more seriously, freezes and expands during colder months, adversely affecting the integrity of the structure." The society is working to raise sufficient funds for a full restoration.

The Martha's Vineyard Historical Society held a celebration marking the lighthouse's 150th birthday in August 2006. The light continues as an active aid to navigation, exhibiting an alternating red and white flash every 15 seconds, 170 feet above the water.

☀ The best views of the lighthouse and cliffs are from a scenic lookout near the small strip of shops and restaurants at Gay Head. The cliffs are closed to the public because of erosion concerns, but the lighthouse is opened by the Martha's Vineyard Historical Society on Friday, Saturday, and Sunday evenings from one hour before sunset to a half hour after sunset, from the summer solstice to the fall equinox.

For information on open houses at Gay Head Light, write to the Martha's Vineyard Historical Society, P.O. Box 1310, Edgartown, MA 02539, call (508) 645-2211, or visit www.marthasvineyardhistory.org.

CHAPTER 14

West Chop Light in August 2006. *Photo by the author.*

West Chop Light

(Holmes Hole Light)
1817, 1846, 1891

The spacious harbor of Vineyard Haven in the town of Tisbury on Martha's Vineyard—protected by two areas of land known as East Chop and West Chop—was bustling with maritime traffic in the nineteenth century. West Chop, which overlooks the dividing point between Vineyard Sound to the west and Nantucket Sound to the east, was mainly a sheep pasture for many years. It grew into an exclusive summer resort by the late 1800s, and the little colony at West Chop eventually had its own ferry service from the mainland.

The harbor and the village around it were long called Holmes Hole—named for a settler from Plymouth, according to some sources, or stemming from an Indian word meaning "old house or dwelling," according to others. The lighthouse is often referred to as "Holmes [or Holmes's] Hole Light" in old records.

The people of Holmes Hole were disappointed that the harbor at Edgartown—at the eastern end of the island—got a lighthouse (at Cape Poge) in 1801, even though Holmes Hole's harbor was busier. When another lighthouse was commissioned in 1817 at Tarpaulin Cove on Naushon Island, about a dozen miles to the west, the Holmes Holers were incredulous. The residents petitioned their congressman, John Reed, with success.

To aid vessels heading in and out of the harbor as well as coastal traffic passing through Vineyard Sound, Congress appropriated $5,000 on March 3, 1817. Four acres of land for the station were purchased from Abijah and Mary Luce of Boston for $225. The contractor, Duncan McBean, built the lighthouse and keeper's house for $4,850.

The first lighthouse at West Chop, a 25-foot rubblestone tower, was swiftly erected along with a stone dwelling, 20 by 34 feet. A fixed white light was exhibited from about 60 feet above the water. The light went into service on October 5, 1817.

James Shaw West, a Tisbury native, became the first keeper at $350 per year. He and his wife, Charlotte, had 11 children, including two who died in early childhood.

Lt. Edward W. Carpender, in his 1838 survey, called the light "exceedingly useful." Everything was in excellent order, "justifying the high reputation" the light enjoyed along the coast. Carpender believed, however, that the 10 lamps and accompanying 14-inch reflectors could easily be reduced to six. He also recommended raising the tower by a few feet so that it could be seen from the passage between the west side of the island and dangerous Middleground Shoal. The station was continually plagued by erosion, and Carpender felt the light could be advantageously moved about 300 yards to the south.

I. W. P. Lewis recognized the importance of West Chop Light in his survey of 1843: "This light being placed at the Chops of the Vineyard sound, is exceedingly useful for all coasters bound east or west. It also affords an excellent mark for clearing various shoals, and indicates the position of Holmes's Hole anchorage. It should be maintained in the highest state of efficiency. The present keeper deserves praise for the great neatness of the establishment." Lewis found much to criticize in the construction of the station's buildings. The tower, he wrote, was "laid in bad lime mortar; base resting on the gravel, one foot below the surface; walls cracked and leaky; roof soapstone, loose and leaky; wood work rotten; whole structure out of repair." James West was still the keeper, and he held nothing back in his assessment of the dwelling and tower in a statement for Lewis's report:

> Both buildings are leaky, in consequence of the mortar with which they were built being bad. The wood work of both buildings is rotten; in consequence of the leaks in the walls. . . . The house is damp and cold. The inside of the house is coated with ice in the winter. The lantern sweats badly at all times, and so much so in winter as to cover the glass with ice and frost. I have removed large quantities of ice from the lantern, having to cut it off the deck with an axe. . . . The bluff on which the tower stands has washed away to within 37 feet of the base, and I consider the buildings unsafe in their present position. I have known 30 feet of the bluff to wash away in one storm. . . . I am not allowed a boat, which prevents me from rendering assistance to the many vessels that get ashore in this neighborhood.

The station was finally rebuilt in 1846. A round stone tower and a stone Cape-style keeper's house were constructed about 1,000 feet southeast of the old location. The old stone house was later relocated to Music Street in West Tisbury, where it became the home of Keeper West's son, Gustavus. The 1846 tower was later enclosed in shingled wooden sheathing, in an octagonal form. This was apparently done to cut down on leaks—an 1850 inspection referred to the tower as "somewhat leaky."

The 1846 tower (with its original "birdcage-style" lantern) and keeper's house. *U.S. Coast Guard photo.*

James West was still keeper when the new tower was completed. He resigned in 1847 and was succeeded by Charles West (not one of his sons).

Winslow Lewis installed a new system of lamps and reflectors in 1848. A fourth-order Fresnel lens later replaced this apparatus. For a time, beginning in 1857, there was an additional light shown from a lantern on the roof of the keeper's house; the Lighthouse Board explained that this light replaced a system of three range lights that served as a guide into the harbor.

According to Edward Rowe Snow, a schooner laden with bricks ran aground near the lighthouse in 1877. Tons of bricks were thrown overboard so the vessel could float, and the bricks could be seen for many decades at low tide.

Charles West remained keeper until 1868, when his son—also named Charles—succeeded him. The younger West remained at the station until 1909, ending a remarkable 62-year father-son dynasty.

A steam-driven fog signal housed in a new building was added in 1882, and the same year a one-and-a-half-story wood-frame assistant keeper's house was built. The first assistant keeper was George Dolby, who later became the principal keeper (1909–19). In 1888, the stone dwelling built in 1846 was removed and a second wood-frame house was erected.

By the early 1890s, West Chop had become a summer resort and the proliferation of large houses in the area began to obscure the light.

A 17-foot mast with the light on top was added to the tower for a brief period. In 1891 a 45-foot, cylindrical brick tower, painted red, replaced the old tower. The new tower was painted white in 1899.

Octave Ponsart, formerly at Dumpling Rock and Cuttyhunk lights, became keeper in 1946. As part of his duties, Ponsart also had to check periodically on the automated lights at Edgartown, East Chop, and Cape Poge.

Because Sam Fuller, the assistant keeper, and his wife were already settled in the principal keeper's house next to the tower, the Ponsarts moved into what was supposed to be the assistant keeper's house. Octave Ponsard's daughter Seamond was thrilled at the modern conveniences at West Chop after years of primitive conditions at Cuttyhunk.

> *First and foremost, this place had town electricity! No more oil lamps to read by! Next—and most amazing to us—a real flushing toilet! No more hazardous trips to an outhouse! It had running water. It was a beautiful two-story, three-bedroom home. It had a "real" telephone, not a crank one with limited use like at Cuttyhunk, and one with which you could speak to an operator who could potentially hook you up with not only local calls, but even long distance.*
>
> *And then it really dawned on us that we had just stepped into civilization. There outside the gate was a road where you drove your car, and within minutes you were at real stores. No more rowing ashore,*

A circa 1890s view of the light station, with the fog signal building in the foreground. *From the collection of Edward Rowe Snow, courtesy of Dorothy Snow Bicknell.*

*no more carrying groceries on Dad's back or sledding in the food, no
more waiting for mailboat deliveries for our stuff. Oh, we had definitely stumbled into heaven and we felt so, so blessed.*

*I spent my first minutes there running up and down the stairs push-
ing the light switch buttons. There was one at the bottom and one at
the top that turned on and off the same hallway light. I couldn't figure
out how this could work. Then I spent plenty of time flushing the toilet.
Like a hick from the sticks! Other marvels awaited me as I turned on
faucets and looked all over the cellar.*

The Ponsarts—including Seamond, who was only six years old
when the family moved to West Chop—enjoyed fishing from the lighthouse property and from boats. Once, Seamond went fishing with a
group that included the actor James Cagney, who helped her haul in
her first bluefish. A few days later, Cagney showed up at the light
station and received a private tour from Seamond.

Keeper Ponsart's wife, Emma, was a regular contributor to a
newspaper called the *Maine Coast Fisherman,* which ran a column of
reports from light stations. Here are some excerpts from her letters:

November 1954

*Hurricane Carol took all the docks down at West Chop. . . . I was
out to look at the surf during it and it came way up over our bank.
We had no electricity for three days. Many yachts were driven on the
land. Then, Hurricane Edna came along. What a mess I had to clean
up around the place! It took our skiff into two yards down from us.
Up to Menemsha Creek, it was a sight to see the fishing boats, yachts
and fish buildings all wrecked. By now, the lighter has come and
hoisted the smaller boats out. My husband went to East Chop Light
to put on the kerosene lamp during the two storms and to Edgartown
too. It was too fierce to take the little ferry across to Chappaquiddick
and so he could not get to Cape Pogue. Luckily, the batteries out
there held out and the light stayed on. Our friends, the Nortons in
Edgartown, phoned us to say they could see Cape Pogue Light still
burning, which was a great relief to my husband as he worried it
would be out and no way to relight it during the hurricanes. Here at
the lighthouses, we were lucky that most of the heavy damage was at
the other end of the island.*

*My garden was ripped to pieces in the storm. It broke our bird-
houses too. I have been raking leaves and tree limbs ever since the
two storms. I don't feel so good. I got a cold since there was no heat
in the place during the storms. Our government house is a good one
though to have stood all it took.*

July 1955

The inspectors were out to Gay Head Light Station yesterday and the Coast Guard Station, but didn't come out to our light this time.

We have planted our tomato plants and all kinds of flower seeds. We have many different kinds of birds in our birdhouses. We put stale bread out every day to feed them and the seagulls.

I have caught one flounder and one tautog so far this week. I expect to go fishing every evening on our beach and see if we can do better than that.

The summer people have started to come big time on the isle and up to Menemsha Creek there are a lot of fishermen tied up to the wharf. We expect the government carpenters here to shingle the roof and put in all new windows due to the hurricanes.

We have two tame wild rabbits in our yard and a flock of quail. The wild rabbits are thick up-island and quite a few deer too. My dog, Rexy, like to chase the rabbits and Rexy goes and digs moles out of the banks by the shore.

February 1957

CHRISTMAS AT WEST CHOP

Edward Rowe Snow, the Flying Santa Claus, came to the airport in his shining red airplane and brought Seamond a package, also one to us, and one to Mr. and Mrs. Fuller, the assistant keepers. Books were given out to the keepers who were not present. The Coast Guard received two packages from Santa also. There was quite a blow on and so it was necessary for him to leave almost immediately for the next stop, Block Island. Joseph Chase Allen, noted author and correspondent to The Vineyard Gazette, was on hand to greet Santa and discuss with him his new book, The Vengeful Sea, printed by Dodd, Mead and Company, which came out just this fall.

Well, tomorrow we'll begin to deck the halls and the tree too. I wanted to deck the tower with a big star, but my husband said that we are just supposed to guide the ships, not wreck them! However, I managed to get him to put lights in the living room and even that was a struggle because all he wants to do now is make sailor mats. Once a sailor, always a sailor. Anybody that served on the lightship from the years 1919–1929, drop my husband a line because he'd like to hear from some old shipmates.

The tradition of the Flying Santa's flights to lighthouse keepers and their families, carried on by Bill Wincapaw and Edward Rowe Snow for more than 50 years, is still going strong. A nonprofit organization, the Friends of Flying Santa, flies to lighthouses and Coast

Guard stations each December and distributes gifts to the children of Coast Guard families. In December 2003, the Friends of Flying Santa invited Seamond Ponsart Roberts to fly along as an "elf" on part of their Massachusetts route. One of the stops was West Chop Light, where she had lived for more than a decade as a girl. She later wrote about the experience:

> The children of the Coast Guard from Station Menemsha were there to greet us and we had a great toy giveaway sitting on the very back porch where I had played many years. There were a few minutes to spare and so I was allowed to go into our old house. The house is ever so beautified now, as it is a guesthouse and certainly not the regulation- type quarters we lived in, but still home. To see the real old home I lived in, I went into the cellar. Ah yes, there it was the same. Now, for a quick scramble up the tower. Once atop, I was really home. There was the beautiful lens, and the view was every bit as wonderful as it used to be.

Keeper Ponsart retired in 1956, and Coast Guard keepers eventually staffed the station. According to an article in the *Vineyard Gazette*, it wasn't unusual for Fred P. Gallop, the officer in charge in 1969, and his assistant, Edward Trenn, to make as many as 25 trips to the top of the lighthouse with tourists on a summer day. After Gallop was transferred in 1971, Chief Boatswain's Mate Edward T. Williams was in charge of both Gay Head and West Chop lights, and rotating personnel kept watch at West Chop.

In 1976 West Chop Light became the last Martha's Vineyard lighthouse to be automated. Later, for some years, the Vineyard Environmental Research Institute used the houses at the station for its offices.

The house closest to the lighthouse now serves as living quarters for the officer in charge of Coast Guard Station Menemsha. The other house is a vacation home for people in all branches of the military.

West Chop Light continues to exhibit its white flash, visible for 15 miles, as an active aid to navigation. The fourth-order Fresnel lens remains in place. There's a red sector to warn mariners away from two dangerous shoals.

The grounds are closed to the public, but the lighthouse can be seen from West Chop Road and is also easily viewed from the ferries to and from Vineyard Haven.

CHAPTER 15

East Chop Light in August 2006. *Photo by the author.*

East Chop Light

1878

The word *chop* (or *chap*) was long used in England to describe land at the entrance to a channel, river, bay, or harbor. The name was adopted in the seventeenth century for the two prominent points marking the east and west sides of the entrance to the harbor of Holmes Hole (now known as Vineyard Haven) in the town of Tisbury, on the north side of Martha's Vineyard.

There had been a lighthouse at West Chop, across the entrance to the harbor since 1817. A local mariner, Capt. Silas Daggett, lobbied for a lighthouse at East Chop, but the authorities apparently believed a single light was adequate for the harbor. In 1869 Daggett took it upon himself to erect a lighthouse at East Chop.

Daggett's lighthouse burned down in 1871 and was rebuilt as a light on top of a house. The Lighthouse Board announced in 1872 that three 21-inch reflectors for the light had been loaned to Daggett. The following year's annual report revealed plans for a proper lighthouse: "A light has been maintained for several years at this point by the sub-scription of the owners of steamships and by other private individuals. As there is no doubt of the utility of the light, it is recommended that an appropriation for erecting a fourth-order light be made."

The plea was repeated the following year, and on March 3, 1875, Congress appropriated $5,000 for the lighthouse. The old structure, described as "little better than a shanty," was removed. Daggett returned to his life at sea, coming back to Tisbury late in life to serve as the town's first water commissioner in 1905.

A conical cast-iron lighthouse tower, 40 feet tall, was erected in 1878, along with a one-and-a-half-story keeper's house. The tower, made of several cast-iron segments bolted together and lined with brick, is very similar to several towers constructed in New England in the 1870s and 1880s, including Edgartown Light on Martha's Vineyard.

The fourth-order Fresnel lens, with its focal plane 79 feet above mean high water, originally showed a fixed light; it was changed to flashing red in 1898 and to flashing green in 1934. An oil house was added to the station in 1897.

The lighthouse was painted white at first, but sometime in the 1880s it was changed to a reddish-brown color that earned it the nickname "the Chocolate Lighthouse." It has been white again since 1988.

George Walter Purdy was keeper from 1902 to 1934, after stints at Sankaty Head and Gay Head lights. Purdy was a former lobsterman who had lost an arm in an accident in the engine room of the lighthouse tender *Azalea*. Purdy's daughter, Alice, had been born just a few months before the family moved from Sankaty Head on Nantucket to East Chop. The keeper and his wife, Mary Jane, had their fourth child—a son named Luther—during their stay on Martha's Vineyard.

Alice Purdy Ray was later interviewed by Linsey Lee of the Martha's Vineyard Historical Society. She fondly recalled the station at East Chop.

> *The house there, they don't build them like that anymore. . . . In the wintertime it was beautiful. You would never know whether it was raining, blowing, sleet. . . . It was just as nice and warm as could be. In the summertime it was cool.*
>
> *There was another building they called a tool shed, and there was a barn across the street. You see, Dad decided he had to have a cow. So he asked the town if he could put a cow across the street. There*

Capt. Silas Daggett's privately owned lighthouse at East Chop. *Courtesy of the Martha's Vineyard Historical Society.*

wasn't anybody there. It was just open field. They said, "Go ahead,"
so he went out and bought himself a cow.
    And we used to have a vegetable garden. You should have seen the
garden my family used to have in there. Oh, those rambling roses.

Years later, Alice was watching a Coast Guardsman scraping paint from the tower. She told the man, "I know a one-armed man used to scrape that all by himself." The man asked, "How long did it take him?" Alice answered, "Two days," to the man's amazement.

In 1934, when the light was being converted to automatic operation, the Purdy family was offered the chance to stay in the house for $100 a month rent. They refused the offer, so the keeper's house and oil house were removed. According to Alice, the crew had trouble demolishing the house because it turned out that brick walls were hidden under the wooden exterior. Alice said later, "I could never understand why the government pulled it down. Why didn't they sell it to somebody? It was pretty nice up there."

Octave Ponsart, keeper at West Chop Light from 1946 to 1956, had the extra duty of looking after the East Chop, Edgartown, and Cape Poge lights. Ponsart, often with the help of his daughter Seamond, visited the station every few days to keep the lens polished, the grounds clean, and the grass mowed.

In 1957 the Coast Guard sold the land surrounding the lighthouse to the town of Oak Bluffs for use as a park. The original Fresnel lens was replaced by a modern optic in 1984. The following year, the Vineyard Environmental Research Institute (VERI) became responsible for the maintenance of the lighthouse under a license agreement with the Coast Guard.

The tower absorbed a great deal of heat on hot days, and the rising heat and humidity caused water to drip from the lantern. The situation was improved when the exterior was painted white in 1988.

In 1994 the license was transferred to the Dukes County Historical Society (now the Martha's Vineyard Historical Society), along with the licenses for the Gay Head and Edgartown Lights.

Only the lighthouse tower remains on the site today, exhibiting a three-second green flash every six seconds. The grounds around the lighthouse are beautifully maintained. Tours are offered on Sundays from mid-June to mid-September, from one and a half hours before sunset to a half hour after. For details, write to the Martha's Vineyard Historical Society, P.O. Box 1310, Edgartown, MA 02539, call (508) 627-4441, or visit www.marthasvineyardhistory.org.

CHAPTER 16

Edgartown Light in August 2006. *Photo by the author.*

Edgartown Harbor Light

1828, 1939

The first white settlement on Martha's Vineyard was established at the eastern end of the island in 1642, and the early settler Thomas Mayhew called the spot Great Harbor. Nobody seems to know for sure where the town's eventual name, Edgartown, came from, but it may be a corruption of Egerton, a parish in England. The town's spacious harbor is bounded by Chappaquiddick Island to the south and east.

Martha's Vineyard, like Nantucket, developed a booming whaling industry in the late 1700s and early 1800s. Between them, Nantucket and Martha's Vineyard owned one-quarter of America's whaling fleet just before the American Revolution. By the early nineteenth century, more than a hundred Edgartown men were captains of whaling ships. The magnificent houses built for these captains on North Water Street remain among the most beautiful in New England.

The whaling industry was thriving in 1828 when Congress appropriated $5,500 and the federal government purchased a plot of land from Seth Vincent for $80 for the purpose of building a lighthouse at the entrance to Edgartown Harbor. A two-story dwelling was constructed, with three rooms on the first floor and two on the second. A lantern on the roof contained a system of lamps and reflectors showing a fixed white light visible for 14 nautical miles. A local man named Bowker, working for the contractor Winslow Lewis, erected the building.

The lighthouse sat offshore on pilings, meaning the keeper originally had to row a short distance to reach the mainland. In 1830 a wooden causeway was built to the lighthouse at a cost of $2,500. The causeway became known locally as the "Bridge of Sighs," because men about to leave on whaling voyages would frequently walk there with their wives or girlfriends.

The first keeper, Jeremiah Pease, was also an accountant and surveyor. In 1830 a Nantucket newspaper charged that the lighthouse was a "rendezvous for all kinds of dissipating." A young man—a future Harvard student named Charles Thomas—was boarding with Pease at the time and may have had something to do with the allegations.

Pease's reputation was salvaged, and he kept the light for two separate stretches of 13 and 6 years. Pease, a Democrat, was removed from his job twice for political reasons by the Whigs. The political winds played a large role in the appointment of keepers before the formation of the Lighthouse Board in 1852.

In 1838 Lt. Edward W. Carpender wrote after visiting the station, "It cannot be long before Government will have to reconstruct this breakwater and light-house, as the worms have made great havoc with them, and the sea threatens them, particularly the latter, with total destruction." Carpender also recommended suppressing six of the ten lamps. He felt that four lamps, properly aligned, were sufficient for a local harbor light.

Sylvanus Crocker was keeper between Pease's two stints, at $350 per year. Crocker had been employed in the original construction of the lighthouse as a carpenter, but that didn't keep him from being severely critical in a statement for I. W. P. Lewis's 1843 report:

> *The whole structure was badly done. The light-house originally stood on a wooden pier; three years ago it was necessary to replace this with one of stone, the old pier being entirely decayed and rotten. The frame of the house was light and weak, and the building always leaky. The lantern stands upon the roof of the house, and is shaken by the force of storms, causing other leaks in the roof. . . . The causeway has been knocked to pieces five or six times, and has been an expensive concern to keep in sufficient order to cross it with safety. It is my opinion, the whole establishment was very badly built in the first place.*

Lewis described more faults in his report to Congress:

> *This house stands at the extremity of a trestle bridge, fifteen hundred feet long, which has been magnified into a breakwater. The house was erected on piles, but these giving way, and letting the chimneys overboard, it became necessary to build a stone pier for its support. This pier was built three years since, is a square block of rough-split stone, filled in with ballast, has settled thirteen inches out of level on the east side . . . but answers a better purpose than the original plan of piling. . . . The frame of the house is decayed in several places, plastering cracked and fallen off in large patches, roofs and sides of house leaky, and lantern rickety.*

In 1847 a new stone breakwater was built for $4,700. An 1850 inspection revealed that Crocker—who had returned for his second stretch as keeper in 1849—was not living on the premises. "The dwelling is unoccupied by the keeper, he living in his own, not a great

The first Edgartown Lighthouse. *U.S. Coast Guard photo.*

distance from the light-house. Lantern is very rusty; sashes are large and the lantern glass small."

A fourth-order Fresnel lens replaced the old lamps and reflectors in 1856. The dwelling and walkway were repaired many times through the years. A storage building, 9 by 28 feet, was added to the station in 1885, and an oil house was built in 1896. At some point, a fog bell and striking machinery were also installed.

Probably because of the building's defects and its vulnerable location, the keepers generally stayed for only a few years. Henry L. Thomas —after a dozen years as keeper at Cape Poge Light on nearby Chappaquiddick Island—was in charge from 1931 to 1938, and conditions at the lighthouse had improved somewhat by the time a 1934 newspaper article described his family's life: "Their lighthouse home has practically all the conveniences that go to make the modern home comfortable, except for electricity. As the lighthouse is located a quarter of a mile out from shore it has never been wired for electricity, although they have a radio, running water, and a modern heating plant."

In the summer of 1938, the government announced plans to replace the old lighthouse with a utilitarian steel skeleton tower. Capt. George E. Eaton, superintendent of the district's lighthouses, called the 1828 lighthouse a "rat-infested box" with no scenic or historical value. Many local residents disagreed, and they circulated a petition on the island to keep the structure intact.

Even so, Commissioner Harold D. King of the Bureau of Lighthouses announced in August that plans would proceed to replace the lighthouse. He explained his rationale in a letter to Martha's Vineyard officials: "Its continued maintenance by the Service would necessarily in accordance with the trend of the time, involve expenditure for modernization and improvements, which under the circumstances are not felt to be warranted."

The great hurricane of September 21, 1938, did great damage to the lighthouse. The Coast Guard took over the management of the nation's aids to navigation in 1939, and they quickly demolished the dilapidated structure.

As it turned out, the news wasn't all bad for Edgartown residents. The Coast Guard came up with an alternative plan to the installation of a skeleton tower in Edgartown—the relocation of an 1873 45-foot cast-iron tower from Crane's Beach in Ipswich, Massachusetts. The tower was disassembled and brought by barge to Edgartown. The "new" lighthouse was soon in service, with an automatic flashing red light every six seconds.

After its relocation to Edgartown, the iron tower was not given a typical spiral staircase or a brick lining. Instead of stairs, there's simply a ladder to the top. Seamond Ponsart Roberts, whose father, Octave Ponsart, was keeper at West Chop Light and had to keep an eye on Edgartown Light for some years, recalls the climb being a bit treacherous.

> Dad rigged up a pulley system so that he would not have to carry heavy stuff to the top. Before he did that, a climb up there was downright dangerous. Sam Fuller [assistant keeper at West Chop] was a big man, probably close to 300 pounds, and he just told Dad he was flat not going up that damn ladder to the top of the Edgartown Lighthouse. I can't say I blame him. While I would climb it myself, I was always in horror at the thought of falling all the way down that ladder. I slipped a few rungs one time and thought my little life was going to be snuffed out instantly.

The Coast Guard refurbished the lighthouse in 1985. They sandblasted and repainted the tower and repaired damage done by vandals, some of it from gunshots.

The lighthouse was leased to the Vineyard Environmental Research Institute (VERI) in 1985. A new plastic lens was installed in 1990, and the light was converted to solar power. In 1994 the license was transferred to the Dukes County Historical Society, now the Martha's Vineyard Historical Society.

Rick Harrington, whose son, Ricky, had died in a car accident just three weeks after his sixteenth birthday in 1996, approached the Martha's Vineyard Historical Society with the idea of turning the lighthouse into a children's memorial. A fund-raising effort to restore the lighthouse and establish a memorial was spearheaded by the historical society's executive director, Matthew Stackpole, and a board member, Craig Dripps.

The large base surrounding the lighthouse had fallen into disrepair. It was rebuilt and enlarged for the memorial, which was designed by the architect Geoffrey White, with an additional 3,500 granite cobblestones. Most of the stones are designed to hold a child's name. The stones are surrounded by a polished granite border and are divided into quadrants by granite spokes meant to evoke the light emanating from the lighthouse's lantern above.

A plaque on the ocean side of the base commemorates the memorial's creation and includes the concluding lines from a poem by from Tomas Napoleon called *A Remembrance of an Unforgotten Vineyard Summer:*

> *Let the celebration of all our children and their endless youth,*
> *When the world was to them still without problem,*
> *Always be that Unforgotten Vineyard Summer—an everlasting day.*

Napoleon, a friend of the Harrington family, had written the poem in memory of Ricky Harrington and read it at his memorial service. "I wrote that poem as a celebration of life," he said. Matthew Stackpole adds, "In some ways there's nothing you can do to mitigate that kind of loss. But there's a feeling that the place is magical and brings some peace. It's a great gift."

The Children's Memorial at the Edgartown Lighthouse presently contains the names of more than 300 children from all over, not just Martha's Vineyard. Cindy Jacobs, who maintains a Web site about the memorial, says, "For those of you who have visited the memorial or have children who are part of it, I hope the site can help maintain that connection. For those of you that cannot visit the Memorial, I hope the Web site can bring you a sense of its quiet wonder and simple grace. Martha's Vineyard is a place of great beauty and of kindness."

Over the decades sand gradually filled in the area between the lighthouse and the mainland, so that today Edgartown Light is on a beach. The Harbor View Hotel overlooks the picturesque site, and wedding parties frequently walk down to the lighthouse for photographs.

The Martha's Vineyard Historical Society is raising funds for the maintenance of the three lighthouses under its care. To learn more, go to www.marthasvineyardhistory.org. For more information on the lighthouses or memorial, you can also write to Martha's Vineyard Historical Society, P.O. Box 1310, Edgartown, MA 02539, or call (508) 627-4441.

For information or to donate to the Martha's Vineyard Children's Lighthouse Memorial, write to Children's Lighthouse Memorial, c/o Martha's Vineyard Historical Society, P.O. Box 1310, Edgartown, MA 02539, or visit www.childrenslighthousememorial.org.

CHAPTER 17

Cape Poge Light in 1999. *Photo by the author.*

Cape Poge Light

(Cape Pogue Light)
1801, 1844, 1893

Cape Poge (sometimes spelled "Pogue") is a lonely, windswept point at
the northeast tip of Chappaquiddick, an island of about five square
miles just east of Martha's Vineyard. The two islands are connected
at their southern ends by a narrow barrier beach, but most people
get to Chappaquiddick by taking the tiny "On Time" ferry from
Edgartown.

With Edgartown's whaling business flourishing at the dawn of the
nineteenth century, Congress recognized the need for a navigational
light at Cape Poge to help direct traffic to the town's harbor. An appropriation of $2,000 was made on January 30, 1801, and by early March,
four acres of land had been purchased for a light station from four
local men at a cost of $36.

Duncan McBean, a contractor from Hingham, Massachusetts, completed a 35-foot, octagonal wooden lighthouse tower in November 1801.
A small, two-room keeper's house, 12 by 15 feet, was also built. A primitive "spider lamp" in the small lantern (less than 6 feet tall and 5 feet in
diameter) exhibited a fixed white light 55 feet above sea level. Winslow
Lewis installed a new system of multiple oil lamps and parabolic reflectors in 1812, and a more spacious lantern was installed in 1817.

President Thomas Jefferson appointed Matthew Mayhew—of
the prominent Edgartown Mayhews—the first keeper, at $200 a year.
Mayhew and his wife, Magdalen Burroughs Mayhew, had eight
children, several of them born during their years at Cape Poge. It was
a difficult and isolated place for a family to live. At first, Mayhew was
not provided a boat, but he requested one and was allowed to buy one
in late 1802—provided it cost no more than $70.

During the War of 1812, the light was extinguished for a few
months and the lighting apparatus was hidden in the cellar of a
Chappaquiddick house four miles away. After the war, life for the
Mayhews became marginally more comfortable with an addition to
the dwelling, completed in 1816. Even with the addition, there were
still only three rooms in the house.

In 1825 Mayhew reported that two acres of land—half the station's original size—had been lost to erosion. He wrote: "If we are not

in danger of falling immediately down the clift, it is very unpleasant, particular to females to be thus situated in storms when the Sea is beating with such violance as for the spray to fly against and over the House and no other dwelling House within 5 miles for a refuge." Four more acres of land were purchased, and Mayhew's brother was paid $250 to move the dwelling to safer ground.

Mayhew died at 68 in December 1834. His successor, 63-year-old Lott Norton of Edgartown, couldn't reach the station for two weeks because of ice. There's no record of whether the light was kept in operation during the interim, but Mayhew's widow may have filled in. In early January, before a new keeper arrived, a schooner was wrecked at Cape Poge. Several passengers froze to death, including one who died after reaching the lighthouse. It is not known if the light was operating at the time of the wreck.

In October 1836, the local lighthouse superintendent, John Presbury Norton, wrote to Stephen Pleasanton, fifth auditor of the Treasury, who was in charge of the nation's lighthouses, about the erosion problem. The lighthouse tower at that point was only 40 feet from the cliff. Norton suggested the construction of a stone wall under the cliff, at a cost of $120. Pleasanton agreed to the suggestion and the wall was built, but it afforded little protection.

When Lt. Edward W. Carpender inspected the station in 1838, the tower was being moved "a few yards" farther back from the edge of the eroding bluff. Carpender recognized the importance of the light as a local harbor guide and also "to the trade entering the 'shoals' from the southward, and to vessels crossing them in all directions." But he recommended reducing the number of lamps to six, and he noted that the tower had "suffered from the action of the wind."

Lott Norton was still keeper when the engineer I. W. P. Lewis visited in 1842. Lewis agreed with Carpender that the light was "essentially important to the navigation of Vineyard sound, as well as of local value to all vessels entering Edgartown." But he was very critical of the buildings' construction in his 1843 report.

> An octagonal frame building, rotten from base to roof, and requires to be rebuilt at once; has been moved from its original position several hundred feet on account of the inroads of the sea. The keeper states that, four years since, a breakwater, (so called,) consisting of pilings, planks, and ballast, was constructed, to protect the point from further decay; but the whole was demolished the following winter, and its remains (the ballast) are now visible under water about seventy-five feet outside of the present beach.

Lewis wrote that the dwelling was leaky and "unfit to repair," and the lighthouse's lantern was "very much corroded, leaky, and racked by storms." He concluded, "The entire establishment requires rebuilding." Keeper Norton had been supplied with a boat, but, he complained, "she is old and rotten." Norton, in a statement for Lewis, added: "I am very much troubled to find sleeping room for my family. The house being so old, and never repaired much, is now in a decaying state. . . . There is not a single closet in the house, nor any convenience."

Winslow Lewis completed a new tower, with new lighting equipment, in 1844 at a cost of $1,600. Lott Norton died just a few months after the new tower was completed and was succeeded as keeper by Aaron Norton (no relation). A fourth-order Fresnel lens replaced the lamps and reflectors installed by Lewis in 1857, and a new lantern was installed on the tower at the same time.

In August 1856, while Daniel Smith was keeper, a 13-year-old girl was playing in a small boat on the beach at Cape Poge when the tide carried the boat into the ocean. Joshua Smith, the 11-year-old son of the keeper, saw the girl and fetched help. The boy and others went out in a boat and rescued the girl, whose boat was filling with water and would have sunk. Her father subsequently published a note of thanks to his daughter's rescuers in the *Vineyard Gazette*.

In a severe storm in January 1866, the schooner *Christiana* went aground on a shoal near Cape Poge. Several people died as they clung

A nineteenth-century view showing the 1844 lighthouse. *U.S. Coast Guard photo.*

Cape Poge Light Station around 1900. *From the collection of Edward Rowe Snow, courtesy of Dorothy Snow Bicknell.*

to the frozen rigging. One man, the first mate, Charles F. Tallman, managed to survive four days before help could arrive. He lost parts of his hands and feet from frostbite but later operated a newsstand in Oak Bluffs.

The ocean continued to tear away the land at Cape Poge. The 1878 annual report of the Lighthouse Board reported that the keeper's house would probably "fall into the sea within two years." A new, larger dwelling was built, farther from the shore, in 1880. The bigger house was needed largely because the station had had an assistant keeper since 1867. The station's first assistant keeper was Jethro Worth, son of Keeper Edward Worth.

The father and son keepers lived at Cape Poge together until 1882, when the assistant position was abolished. Edward Worth retired that day, and Jethro became the next principal keeper. The following year, Jethro Worth became keeper of Edgartown Light and George H. Fisher came to Cape Poge. He remained in charge until 1898.

A wooden tower, 40 feet inland from the previous one, was built in 1893. The lantern from the previous tower was transferred to the new one, and a week later the 1844 tower was destroyed. The rebuilding came just in time; stones from the earlier foundation were falling down the eroding bank by 1896. The Lighthouse Board called the 1893 tower a "temporary" structure, but it has survived to this day. The wooden, shingled tower is 35 feet tall, and its light is 65 feet above mean high water.

Because of complaints that the fixed white light at Cape Poge could easily be confused with the light from the Cross Rip Lightship, the characteristic at Cape Poge was changed to flashing white and red in the summer of 1898.

George E. Dolby followed George Fisher as keeper in 1898, and Dolby's four-year stay was punctuated by tragedy and hardship. A brutal November storm on November 26–27, 1898—a storm that would be remembered as the Portland Gale—destroyed the station's boathouse and knocked down fences. During the following July, a three-year-old son of the keeper died after an illness of a few days.

The keeper's wife, Mabel Jane Dolby, blamed the poor conditions at Cape Poge for her son's death, and she wrote to the lighthouse authorities requesting a transfer to a less isolated station. There was no immediate transfer, so Mabel and her two surviving children spent the winter in Edgartown. When Dolby was relocated to the Cliff Beacons on Nantucket, Mabel Jane and the children remained in Edgartown. George and Mabel Jane Dolby were finally reunited when Dolby was appointed keeper at West Chop Light in 1909.

Cape Poge again was assigned an assistant keeper beginning in 1900, apparently in part because the new flashing characteristic required the winding of a clockwork mechanism every five or six hours. In 1911 the apparatus that turned the lens malfunctioned, and Keeper J. E. Barrus and his assistant had to turn the lens by hand for four nights until new bearings finally arrived.

A 1934 article reported that Keeper Marcus Pieffer made trips to Edgartown twice weekly for supplies. He had to travel the length of Chappaquiddick Island to get to the ferry that took him to Edgartown. During the winter, he used a motorboat to make the trip by water. On rare occasions, the harbor between Edgartown and Cape Poge was frozen over in winter, which made travel for the keepers especially difficult. The *Vineyard Gazette*'s editor Henry Beetle Hough recorded walking over the ice to Cape Poge during a stretch of severe cold in 1933.

The light was automated in 1943, and the last keeper, Joseph Dubois, was removed. A Coast Guard patrol lived at the station during World War II. In 1954 the keeper's house was sold to a Chappaquiddick resident. It was subsequently torn down for the lumber.

For some years, the keeper at West Chop Light kept an eye on the automated lights at Cape Poge, Edgartown, and East Chop. Octave Ponsart was keeper at West Chop from 1946 to 1956. His daughter,

Seamond Ponsart Roberts, recalls visits to Cape Poge, especially on one particular day.

We got over to the ferry and onto the island just fine. We got to the lighthouse and Dad did his cleaning and fixing and it was about 4 p.m. It was time to go. Everyone was having a good time until we came over the little hill and came to the part of the trip where the water would sometimes go through. It had turned high tide and a storm was whipping up and there had to be a good six feet of water there in front of us. Even with our "bomb truck," there was no way we could go through this because at this point Chappaquiddick Island had just divided itself. We were on the end with the lighthouse and the other end had the road to the ferry, with a whole bunch of the Atlantic Ocean between the two parts.

Dad just turned the truck around and we headed back to the lighthouse. And then it started to rain. You have to remember the house had not been occupied for years. It was boarded up tight and Dad opened the door. He had gotten the kerosene lamp, the one you used in emergencies, from the tower. I remember clearly that the door was not even locked. It just turned and opened.

Meanwhile, the weather turned into a northeaster with all the wind and cold rain you could imagine. About two seconds into the house, the rats realized someone had opened up their den. A few came running past us.

We found an old stack of newspapers and books in one of the living rooms, and once we got the cook stove lit with some of these papers and some old wood, the kitchen warmed for the first time in years. We spent the night cuddled up in the corner of the cupboards near the stove with Mom screaming every time a rat went by.

The storm went on all night, and I must tell you it probably was the longest night of my life. Mom woke up from one of her catnaps during this time and she told my father, "Octave, a lady just came and said, 'Why are you in my kitchen?' and touched me." My mother had turned just as white as the ghost she thought had touched her. She was convinced. I know I was convinced, and none of us slept for the next few hours.

The 1893 tower has been moved four times, the first time in 1907. It was moved 95 feet inland in 1922. In 1960 the tower was moved back another 150 feet. In 1987 it had to be relocated about 500 feet from the eroding shoreline. On that occasion, a U.S. Army helicopter moved the lighthouse, and the lantern was moved separately.

The new location was on land owned by the Trustees of Reservations, a nonprofit organization dedicated to the preservation of properties of exceptional scenic, historic, and ecological value in Massachusetts. The lighthouse now stands in the 516-acre Cape Poge Wildlife Refuge.

Some refurbishing of the tower was done in the new location and a modern optic was installed. The tower was repainted a few years later, and the workers found that the windows had been broken and birds had taken up residence inside the lighthouse.

The Coast Guard still owns the lighthouse and maintains the light and related equipment, but the Trustees have cared for the tower since 1994. In October 1997, the 2,300-pound lantern was removed by helicopter. It was taken to Falmouth and then trucked to New Bedford, where it was sandblasted and repainted, and broken panes of glass were replaced. The Coast Guard and the Trustees of Reservations cohosted a 200th birthday celebration for the lighthouse in May 2001.

Despite its remoteness, thousands of people visit Cape Poge Light each year. The lighthouse can be reached via a three-and-a-half-mile hike from Chappaquiddick's Dike Bridge or with the use of a four-wheel drive vehicle, for which you must obtain a permit.

The lighthouse can also be visited on an excellent 90-minute tour offered in season (end of May to Columbus Day weekend in October) by the Trustees of Reservations. Reservations are required; call (508) 627-3599 or see www.thetrustees.org for details.

CHAPTER 18

Brant Point Light in August 2006.
Photo by the author.

Brant Point Light

1746, 1758, 1774, 1783, 1786, 1788, 1825, 1856, 1901

This is America's second-oldest light station, after Boston Light (1716), and an astounding total of nine different lighthouse structures have stood here over the years, not including a bonfire on a hogshead, or barrel, that was said to be in use as early as 1700. The present tower on Nantucket Island may rank among the shortest lighthouses in New England, but in combination with its picturesque surroundings it makes up in charm what it lacks in stature.

Nantucket's whaling industry was born in the early eighteenth century and was booming by the 1740s. At its peak as the whaling capital of the world, the island had a population of 10,000—in Massachusetts, only Boston and Salem were larger. At a town meeting in January 1746, the merchants and mariners of Sherburne—as the town was then called—voted that the town should erect a lighthouse at Brant Point, on the west side of the entrance to the island's harbor. The sum of £200 was appropriated, and a wooden lighthouse was soon in operation. The maintenance of the lighthouse was paid for by the town and by ship owners and merchants.

No detailed description survives of the wooden 1746 lighthouse, which burned down in 1757—probably the result of an oil fire. At a town meeting on July 26 of the following year, the citizens voted to build a new lighthouse and assigned a committee of three local men to "carry on the affair till the Light House be Completed." A small conical wooden tower on piles was completed shortly thereafter.

Early in the morning of March 9, 1774, a strong storm—almost definitely a tornado—laid the lighthouse flat. A newspaper reported:

> *About Eight o'Clock this Morning we had the most violent Gust of Wind, that perhaps was ever known here, it lasted but about a Minute, it seemed to come in a narrow Vein, and in its Progress blew down our Light-House, and totally destroyed it, besides several Barns, Shops, &c. Had it lasted fifteen Minutes I really believe it would not have left more than one Half the Buildings standing in the Course that it passed. I do not hear of any Persons receiving much Hurt, or much Damage done, except the Loss of the Light-House, which in every Respect is considerable.*

Just two weeks later, it was voted that the lighthouse should be rebuilt "as High as the former one that blew down lately at the Town's Expense." The third lighthouse was financed by a tax on shipping coming into the harbor. All vessels of 15 tons or more were charged six shillings at the time of their first coming or going each year.

Brant Point played a role in the American Revolution in September 1781, when a band of about a hundred Loyalist privateers entered the harbor. American forces from Cape Cod arrived and set up cannons at Brant Point. They fired on the Loyalist vessels and forced them from the harbor. The lighthouse escaped the skirmish unscathed.

The bad-luck beacon—which had been extinguished for a period during the war—was again destroyed by fire on September 17, 1783. A new light was erected, no more than a lantern hoisted up between two spars. The dim light was likened to a lightning bug, thus the nickname "Bug Light." The structure burned down in 1786.

The fifth lighthouse—a simple wooden framework structure—lasted only two years before it was destroyed by a storm. The next lighthouse—a small wooden tower with a cramped wooden lantern—was built by the Commonwealth of Massachusetts in 1788 and ceded to the federal government in 1795, the same year the town changed its name from Sherburne to Nantucket.

A brief newspaper story reported that the lighthouse was blown down on October 26, 1800, but it was apparently repaired and not rebuilt. Information on the lighthouse during this period is sketchy, but we know that the light was extinguished for a time during the War of 1812.

Nantucket's whaling industry continued to expand and a more efficient lighthouse was in order. In April 1824, some of the merchants and mariners of Nantucket petitioned the federal Lighthouse Establishment to build a new lighthouse. Congress appropriated $1,600 on March 3, 1825, and a new wood-frame dwelling was erected with a lighthouse tower attached to its eastern end, showing a fixed white light 38 feet above mean high water.

Lt. Edward W. Carpender of the navy inspected the station in 1838 and his report didn't reflect well on Keeper David Coffin, who had replaced his ailing father as keeper in 1831. "I found the lantern smoked, tube-glasses the same, lamps not trimmed, and reflectors really looking as if weeks or months had elapsed since they had been cleaned, they were so black and spotted."

There were eight oil lamps with 12 ½-inch reflectors in use when Carpender visited, and he expressed the belief that two lamps, "differently attended" were all that was needed. Carpender also described a

A late-nineteenth-century view showing the 1856 lighthouse. *From the collection of Edward Rowe Snow, courtesy of Dorothy Snow Bicknell.*

range light that had been erected nearby, known as the Nantucket Beacon. Mariners would align the Beacon with Brant Point Light as they came into the harbor.

The Nantucket Beacon was a small building, 11 feet high, with two lamps exhibiting a light through a window. There was also another pair of range lights under construction nearby. Seeing that an additional keeper's dwelling was being erected near the new range lights, Carpender suggested that the keeper of Brant Point Light could easily attend to them. Instead, the new range lights were assigned their own keeper, and the first in the position was Peleg Easton.

When the engineer I. W. P. Lewis inspected the Brant Point station in 1842, Coffin had been keeper for 11 years. Coffin provided a description for Lewis's 1843 report: "Two years ago the house and tower required repair, the foundations having settled away; these repairs were made, and the only foundations now supporting the whole tower and dwelling house are cedar posts, stuck in the sand, about eight feet deep. These posts are not tenoned into the sills or other timber of the frame; nor is there any security whatever, in case of a very high tide, to prevent the whole concern from floating away or being destroyed."

Coffin went on to describe the tower as leaky, the lantern as "nearly rusted to pieces," and the lighting apparatus as "defective in the extreme." He also complained that he was not provided a boat and thus had no means of saving his family "should a storm destroy the

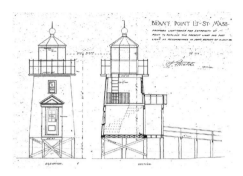

Part of the plans for the 1901 lighthouse. *Courtesy of U.S. Coast Guard.*

house." The cellar, where oil was stored, was often flooded. Lewis concurred with the keeper's assessment, asserting that "the whole structure might be swept away" in a high flood tide.

An 1850 inspection report, when James Allen was keeper, described the lighthouse as "an old one, and what I call a poor concern." In November 1853, Maj. C. A. Ogden of the Army Corps of Engineers recommended the erection of a new tower at Brant Point, as the 1825 structure was "so completely rotted as to require reconstruction with the least possible delay." At about the same time, Eben W. Allen, collector for the port of Nantucket, wrote to Thornton A. Jenkins, secretary of the new Lighthouse Board, asking for a more "permanent and commodious structure at Brant Point."

On August 3, 1854, Congress finally appropriated $15,000 for a new lighthouse. This time a 47-foot brick tower (the bottom part was granite) and an attached one-and-a-half-story brick dwelling were built, about 135 feet south of the earlier lighthouses. A fourth-order Fresnel lens was installed, showing a fixed red light. A boathouse was built at the water's edge at the same time. The 1856 lighthouse still stands, without its lantern, as part of U.S. Coast Guard Station Brant Point.

W. H. Swain was keeper at the time of an 1867 article in the *New York Times,* by a correspondent who spent some time living at the lighthouse.

> There is a magnificent sea view from the top through thick plate windows; the keeper told us that insects annoyed him considerably by striking against the panes, but that morning the panes were polished as bright as those of any drawing room in New York. . . . The keeper has also been a sailor, as indeed have most of the men on the island. Every few steps one "runs afoul" of an old salt with weather-beaten face and uncertain gait, who sings out in a cheery voice, as if from the deck of a whaler. Every morning we are awakened by three stamps at the foot of the stairway and a stentorian cry, "All hands ahoy!" And then we rise, laughing, and go down to breakfast with the Captain.

The Captain is a jovial fellow of 55 years or thereabouts, who has made nine voyages as mate and master of a whaler, and who has at last settled down for a green old age. A lazy life here on land, it seems to me. To watch the boat come into the harbor every afternoon, to go to the Post-office for occasional letters, to read the Boston Advertiser *every evening with, perhaps, a game at euchre with a neighboring sailor; to turn in (as he phrases it) at 9 o'clock and "turn out" at 5 in the morning, these make up the sum of daily living, and it is scarcely less monotonous than the life at sea.*

With a decline in the whaling industry, Nantucket's population had fallen from 10,000 to 4,000 by 1870. Meanwhile, tourism blossomed into a major business. In the late 1880s, as Nantucket developed as a summer resort, a battle was waged between the federal government and developers who built houses and a hotel that encroached on the land reserved for the light station.

The Lighthouse Board's annual report of 1889 described a "protracted and laborious investigation" that had been completed in 1887, followed by the building of a fence around the property. But that didn't stop the neighbors, who trespassed and "molested the fence, and menaced the engineer of the district with prosecution." The 1890 annual report stated that the matter was in the hands of the U.S. attorney. The situation was presumably resolved for good when the government sold off five lots of land bordering the light station, encompassing 5.9 acres, in 1901.

A new lantern and deck were installed on the lighthouse in 1895, but it remained in service for just a few more years. Because of shifts in

Early 1900s postcard showing the steamer *Gay Head* rounding Brant Point. *From the collection of the author.*

Keeper Gerald M. Reed (left) and Assistant Keeper Frank W. Craig in August 1932. *From the collection of Edward Rowe Snow, courtesy of Dorothy Snow Bicknell.*

the channel, the 1856 lighthouse had to be discontinued in 1900. It was replaced for a short time by a fixed red light on a pole.

In 1901 the present lighthouse was built 596 feet east of the 1856 tower. The 1895 lantern from the earlier tower was relocated to the new one and fitted with a fifth-order Fresnel lens. The new light went into service on January 31, 1901.

The diminutive wooden tower is 26 feet tall and was built on wooden pilings, and the entrance door was reached via an elevated wooden walkway. Large blocks of stone were later placed around the base to protect the structure. A pyramidal wooden fog-bell tower was erected nearby, with a 1,000-pound bell. (A fog bell from the station is now on display at Coast Guard Station Brant Point.) An oil house was added to the station in 1904.

John Chapman, keeper beginning in 1898, was the first man in charge of the new light. When Chapman died in 1907, his wife briefly assumed his lightkeeping duties. Everett Joy became keeper later that year.

Beginning in 1908, Joy had the additional duty of caring for a new pair of range lights nearby, a pair of wooden skeleton towers standing 500 feet apart. In December 1910, he was given the increased responsibility of tending two more lights at the ends of two jetties about a mile away. He had to reach the jetties by boat, and since there were no good landing places, the job was often treacherous. A previous attendant of the jetty light had once been stranded for six hours when his boat was smashed. An article in the *Boston Globe* on December 26, 1910, was highly sympathetic to Joy:

> *As the keeper is one of the most popular men in the service on this part of the coast, his fellow citizens of Nantucket have faith to believe that his case will receive prompt official attention when the facts are laid out before the proper authorities.*

*As for talking about it for publication, keeper Joy does not enter-
tain the proposition for a moment.*

*"I'm too busy looking out for these five lights to talk," he said today.
"Besides," he added with a quiet smile, "it's against the regulations to
give information to newspapers."*

*Then the keeper went on rubbing lamp chimneys. From the
appearance of the station, he must spend most of his time polishing
things. What he doesn't find to polish his housekeeper, Mrs. Flagg,
polishes in her own department. Her fame as a polisher, and housekeeper and cook is second only to that of the keeper as a lightkeeper
of multiple duties and unconquerable good humor.*

As it turned out, Keeper Joy was only human and his good humor
was conquerable after all. After numerous unheeded requests for an
assistant to help with the jetty lights, Joy resigned as keeper in August
1911. He told the *Globe* that he planned to take a good long vacation
and then resume his former occupation as a house painter.

Richard Dixon had a 16-year stay as keeper, and Gerald M. Reed,
formerly at the Plymouth Light Station, followed him. There was eventually an assistant keeper mercifully assigned to the station to help
with the extra duties. A small assistant keeper's house was also added.

The white light at Brant Point was changed to red in 1933 to avoid
confusion with nearby house lights. The light was automated in 1965.
The occulting red light—with an eclipse every four seconds—remains
an active aid to navigation.

In the fall of 2000, the Coast Guard hired the Campbell
Construction Group to carry out an overhaul of the 1901 lighthouse.
The six-week project entailed removing the lead paint from the lantern
and replacing all the lantern glass, reshingling the tower, repainting
the entire structure, and replacing the interior stuccowork.

This pretty little lighthouse is seen by thousands each year as they
enter and leave Nantucket on ferries, and the long tradition of arriving
at Nantucket by "coming 'round Brant Point" appears destined to continue well into the future.

**For information on getting to Nantucket, check www.nantucketchamber.
org or call the Nantucket Island Chamber of Commerce at (508) 228-1700.
Brant Point is within walking distance of the ferry terminal, and there are
also guided tours that include the lighthouse. The Coast Guard station at
Brant Point is not open to the public, but the 1856 lighthouse can be easily
viewed from the road leading to the currently active lighthouse.**

CHAPTER 19

Great Point Light in September 2000. *Photo by the author.*

Great Point Light

1784, 1818, 1986

The gap between Great Point on Nantucket and Monomoy Island—the dividing line between the Atlantic Ocean and Nantucket Sound—was one of the busiest sections of the Atlantic Coast for many years. Menacing currents and dangerous shoals in the area made navigation a challenge.

With Nantucket's whaling industry going strong, local merchants and mariners first clamored in 1770 for a lighthouse at Great Point (known then as Sandy Point) at the terminus of a seven-and-a-half-mile stretch of white sand and rolling dunes. The initial push for a lighthouse stalled because of the American Revolution, but the effort was revived after the war.

On February 5, 1784, the General Court of Massachusetts passed a resolution for the construction of a lighthouse, and a wooden tower was promptly built. A newspaper notice on September 24, 1784, announced, "The public are hereby informed, That the Light-House on the North-East Sandy Point at Nantucket, is completed, and the Lamps will be lighted in a few days." The light was put into service during the month of October.

Capt. Paul Pinkham, a former whaleman and pilot, was the first keeper, at a salary of $166.66 yearly, soon raised to $250. During the year the light was established, Pinkham surveyed the shoals around Nantucket, and his work was later published as the era's best chart of the area.

For the first few years there was no keeper's house at Great Point, so the keeper had to walk more than seven miles or get to the station on horseback. Pinkham sometimes traveled by boat to Brant Point in Nantucket Harbor to get food and supplies.

Pinkham wrote a letter in 1795 pleading for another raise, calling the $250 salary "scanty support for a family" in such an isolated location. He was given another raise and also an assistant, who was provided the use of a bedroom and half the kitchen in the newly built wood-frame keeper's house.

In June 1795, a recently opened bank on Nantucket was robbed of $20,000 in coins by three men who had stolen Pinkham's small boat. The men used the boat to transport the stolen loot to their sloop.

Pinkham issued a description of his missing boat and offered incentive for its return: "Whoever will Deteck the thief and return the property shall be handsomely Rewarded by Paul Pinkham, Keeper of the Lighthouse at Nantucket."

Pinkham died in late 1799 and was succeeded by George Swain. In October 1804, the schooner *Republican* ran ashore near the lighthouse. The captain, his wife, and the crew all managed to swim to shore. In his book *Storms and Shipwrecks of New England,* Edward Rowe Snow wrote, "So grateful was the master of the ship to Keeper George Swain for his hospitality and friendliness that he sold the schooner just as it lay on the shore to the keeper for the bargain price of $50. Swain later broke up the schooner for salvage."

The first keeper's house was destroyed by fire in 1812. Again, until 1825, the keepers had to commute the great distance from their own homes to the station. And in the meantime, in November 1816, while Jonathan Coffin was keeper, the *Nantucket Gazetteer* reported: "The Light House on Nantucket Great Point was consumed by Fire; a small temporary Light is already erected in its place, but a larger and more permanent one will be completed in a few days, under the direction of Daniel Coffin, Esq. Collector of the Customs of this port."

Some believed the fire was deliberately set, but nothing was proved. The temporary light, consisting of a lantern hoisted on a triangle to a height of 36 feet above mean high water, served until a new 60-foot, conical rubblestone tower was erected in 1818, at a cost of about $7,400.

In 1829, after Obed Bunker became keeper, a petition was circulated among Nantucket's citizens to have Bunker removed for purported intemperance. It eventually became evident that the effort was started by a local man who wanted the keeper position for himself, and Bunker kept his job for a few more years.

Lt. Edward W. Carpender's report of 1838 provides an excellent description of the lighting apparatus:

> *Seven miles from Nantucket harbor, on the northern extremity of the island, stands the great light of Nantucket. This light is 70 feet above the level of the sea, in a stone tower 60 feet high. It consists of 14 lamps, 3 with fifteen, and 11 with sixteen-inch reflectors, arranged in the usual way, in two circles parallel to each other and to the horizon. The keeper has removed 7 lamps from the chandelier, and placed them on a shelf against the window, on the familiar principle of doing the same when we would throw a light into the yard. I confess the lamps against the window seemed to show with more power than those back upon the chandelier near the centre of the lantern.*

By placing the lamps against the window, the keeper also solved the common problem of frost forming on the glass in winter. The normally conservative Carpender recommended that all of the lamps be kept in operation, recognizing Great Point as "an exterior and important light."

I. W. P. Lewis visited for his report of 1843, and he was uncharacteristically complimentary of the tower's construction. The rubble masonry, he wrote, was "laid in good lime mortar," with "strong foundations." The dwelling was in good condition, except for a leaky kitchen. Lewis saved his harshest criticisms for the lantern, which was "very leaky," and the lighting apparatus, which he said was "worn out, and kept in the most filthy manner." Lewis stressed the location's importance:

> This light is one of the highest importance to our coasting trade, placed as it is at the entrance to a great thoroughfare, celebrated among seamen for the intricacy and danger of its navigation. No establishment on our coast requires a more efficient light, and not one, save Monomoy, on the opposite side of the same channel, is in so bad condition in respect to the illuminating apparatus and effects produced by it; nor is there any thing by which a stranger can distinguish one from the other, both being fixed lights, both located on flat sand beaches, and both environed with shoals and currents of the most dangerous and deceptive character.

Lewis's report was in sharp contrast with an inspection report by the local lighthouse superintendent in the same year, which was brief: "This light-house is well kept, and in good order, excepting a small part of the roof of the dwelling-house, which needs some slight repairs. Estimated expense, $5."

Things hadn't improved much by the time of an inspection in July 1850, when Oliver C. Gardner was keeper. The roof still needed shingling, and the gutters were rotten. A new cistern had been built, but it remained useless because there was nothing to lead the water into it.

In 1857 a third-order Fresnel lens replaced the old system of lamps and reflectors. The same year, the tower was lined with brick and housing was added for an assistant keeper. Great Point had been a single-family station until this time, except for a period during which the first keeper, Paul Pinkham, had an assistant.

George Folger Coggeshall was principal keeper beginning in 1861. There were several wrecks near Great Point during his stay, including that of the bark *Elwine Frederick* in a gale on April 20, 1863. The bark was a complete loss, but the crew escaped to a nearby schooner.

Some wrecks occurred because Great Point Light was easily confused with the fixed white light of the Cross Rip Lightship. One of the wrecks blamed on this confusion occurred on October 12, 1865, when a schooner hit a bar off Great Point during a severe storm. The captain was able to get his wife, three children, and the boat's crew to shore in a longboat. Keeper Coggeshall met them with a carriage and got them to the warmth of the keeper's house.

There were at least 43 wrecks in the vicinity of Great Point between 1863 and 1890. The problem was finally solved when a red sector was added to Great Point Light in 1889, which helped to keep mariners from straying from the proper channel.

The Nantucket Historical Association has preserved an 1862 letter written by Keeper Coggeshall's 21-year-old daughter, Elizabeth. The letter, addressed to Elizabeth's cousin Henry R. Gardner, is proof that life at Great Point wasn't ideal for a young adult. "I was very much disappointed when I opened your letter not to find your picture. I think if you knew what a comfort it is to look at my friends, when I am out to the Point, and get entirely tired of seeing the faces of my family, you would send it. . . . I think when father is removed from the point, I shall have served an apprenticeship at lightkeeping as long as I care to."

Elizabeth also commented on the Civil War: "I am disgusted with this war for I can't see that we gain one inch of ground." Coggeshall was still keeper in August 1867, when a writer described a visit to Great Point in the *New York Times*.

Great Point Light Station in the late 1800s. *From the collection of Edward Rowe Snow, courtesy of Dorothy Snow Bicknell.*

Great Point Lighthouse is nine miles from the town; the road is the worst possible for man or beast. But it is a pleasant sail thither. The keeper's salary is only $450 per annum, out of which he has to keep a horse. . . . I expressed my belief that the solitude would be favorable for study. "Oh, you'd like it for a month, perhaps. But think of passing twenty-eight days without a newspaper or letter! My son has walked five miles many a day in the hope of getting a paper from some one. When we expected our daughter home the letter naming the day was thirty-six days getting to us. Yet we had visitors, and were glad to see them." He spoke in the past tense, because he had sent in his resignation; he had served six years.

W. S. Allen had been assistant keeper since 1857, and he became the next principal keeper after Coggeshall's resignation, remaining until 1886. In 1889, while Charles F. Swain was principal keeper, the old keeper's house was demolished and a new duplex dwelling was built on the same spot.

In May 1898, during the Spanish-American War, there was widespread fear that Spain was sending warships to attack the East Coast. On May 16, a newspaper reported the startling word that the keeper of Great Point Light had sighted a "war vessel with two masts and one funnel, and quite low in the water." The vessel, according to the report, "kept up a cannonading about an hour," breaking several panes of glass at the Coskata Lifesaving Station. This and other similar reports on the coast had the U.S. military preparing to retaliate, but nothing more ever materialized of the threat.

Assistant Keeper Marcus E. Howes had a night he'd never forget in early April 1902. During his watch, Howes left the lighthouse watchroom momentarily to get a drink of water. Seconds after he left, he heard a loud crash and saw that the light was out. Howes ran up the stairs to the lantern and found that two large canvasback ducks (rare in New England) had flown right through the thick lantern glass, extinguished the light, and smashed fatally into the opposite panes. This type of occurrence was not unheard of on the New England coast, but the extreme violence of this incident was unusual.

Judah Berry, a Cape Cod native and a veteran sea captain and lightship sailor from a prominent seafaring family, became principal keeper in the summer of 1903. Just a few months later, shortly after a blizzard in January 1904, the captain of the lighthouse tender *Azalea* noticed the flag flying at half-staff at Great Point. Concerned that something might be amiss, the captain took the tender past ice floes to the light station.

He discovered that Berry had died, apparently of heart disease, as he sat in his armchair watching the lighthouse through a window. His wife and daughter, after keeping a lonely vigil through the night, accompanied Berry's body aboard the *Azalea,* leaving the assistant keeper in charge. Berry, who was 70 years old, was buried in his home-town of Harwich. Alfred A. Howard became the next principal keeper.

Theodore L. Chase was keeper on September 23, 1931, when the fishing schooner *Elizabeth Foley* caught fire two miles from the light. Chase and Assistant Keeper Otis E. Walsh rescued the entire crew from a sinking dory.

William L. Anderson was principal keeper from 1932 to 1935. Anderson equipped his automobile with special balloon tires to make the trip to town easier. In 1933 he used this vehicle to take 350 visitors to the lighthouse.

Frank Grieder, a Maine native, succeeded Anderson as principal keeper. His son, Bill, lives today in the Madaket section of Nantucket. In an interview in 2001, he recalled many details of life at Great Point.

> We came to Great Point. My mother came by steamer. My Dad and I came down on the lighthouse tender. All the furniture was brought to Great Point—they brought all the furniture and landed it on the beach. And then it had to be taken up to the lighthouse.
>
> By the same token, all the coal and oil had to come in. The oil was put in a storage building just a short way from the lighthouse. The coal was brought up to the house. It was that really big, heavy coal. I used to have to go down in the cellar and stack it up against the back side so we could get our winter supply of coal in.
>
> A lot of things about Great Point were a little different from the norm. We had a cistern down in the cellar and we used to collect rainwater. There were gutters and they used to come down on the drainpipes and into the basement. They had these—like funnels, with a narrow end on it—so when it rained you pulled them out of the cistern pipes so you'd wash the roof off for 15 or 20 minutes or a half hour, because a lot of bird stuff got on it. Once it washed off, you took these funnel-shaped things and turned them so the water would fill up the cistern.
>
> I used to have to clean the cistern every year—get down inside it, scrub it down. Occasionally you'd find some bones—some mice fell in. Of course you didn't advertise that to too many people.
>
> The [district] superintendent of the Lighthouse Service used to come to the lighthouses on his tour of inspection. And he used to ask for a glass of "God's water." That's what he called it. And if he'd known what was in it, I don't know if he would've wanted it.

Assistant Keeper John Taylor (left) and Keeper Frank Grieder. *Courtesy of Bill Grieder.*

Of course, when he came down for his inspection, the lighthouse people knew he was coming, probably before he did, because he'd be at the other stations and word would get around. We had a telephone, but you had to go through the Coast Guard station to get an outside line.

They [keepers] spent a lot of time on maintenance work. There were very few lighthouses that I ever saw that weren't kept up. They took pride in their lighthouses. You wanted to get a high rating.

If you wanted a new paintbrush, a new saucer, a new fork— anything pertaining to the lighthouse— "Show me the old one, I'll give you a new one." They ran a tight ship. They just didn't have that kind of money.

There were times during northeasters—gales—we'd have ducks flying into the windows and they'd break the plate glass, and that had to be replaced. The light blinded them and they just ran into it.

There was a big pond there at Great Point. That's where I learned to go fishing and sailing and all kinds of stuff. I used to do a lot of hunting. I did a lot of things out there. I had a golf course up in the sand dunes. I used tomato cans. I did a lot of beachcombing. I'd swim with sand sharks, eels, all that kind of stuff. And there was a huge nesting area for terns. Thousands and thousands of terns.

We had a truck, a Ford truck, and the Coast Guard had a truck. And that's about the only vehicles that were around. We had big balloon tires, called sand tires. You could go to Wauwinet in the track you left a week before, and it was still there except where the tide came in and washed it out. You could just get in the ruts, pull the throttle out, take your hands off the wheel, and she'd track right to Wauwinet.

The Flying Santa [Bill Wincapaw or Edward Rowe Snow] dropped presents at Great Point at Christmas. I didn't know what it was at first. I thought somebody was dropping bombs.

There might have been three cars out there in the summer. That was it. After I got out of the service I got out there—I hadn't been there in a long time—and I counted 75 jeeps in one weekend. I said, "This place has changed!"

Octave Ponsart served as assistant keeper in the mid-1930s. His daughter Seamond Ponsart Roberts recalls that her father described the periodic inspections as rigorous in those days. At the end of the inspections, the keepers were given efficiency ratings. A rating below "good" could mean a reduction in pay. A tower that hadn't been white-washed for too long could result in a poor rating.

Dad said that at Great Point one time the tower needed a white-wash job. Mr. Grieder came running to Dad saying, "Quick, help me get the staging over to the tower and open up those whitewash cans. The tender is laying off the station." They just got it over there and the brushes ready and all when the inspectors arrived. They were saved!

Archford ("Ted") Vernon Haskins, previously an assistant at Boston Light, succeeded Grieder as principal keeper at Great Point in August 1937. Haskins moved to the station with his wife, Betty, and their seven children. His daughter Beverly Haskins described life at the station in a letter to Edward Rowe Snow in the 1940s. Beverly lived in town during the school year, but she always looked forward to summers at the light station.

As a few weeks passed we had names for almost every place on the Point. A few of the names were Arizona, Rose Bowl, Mountain, Little Pond, The Point, Betty Bush Corner. Each name had its own meaning so that when we left the house to go anyplace to play our parents would know where we were.

We had such pets as dogs, turtles, rabbits, seals, birds, field mice, goldfish, and pheasants. We always had some sort of animal around . . . . Every spring we would catch small deer mice and feed them with a medicine dropper until they would be real tame and then sit on our shoulders and eat out of our hand.

In the summer when July came it was berry picking time at Great Point. Gooseberries, raspberries, huckleberries and blueberries were plentiful and we often took our lunch and spent the whole day picking berries. Mom would put them up and how good they were when the snow began to fly and we had a blueberry or huckleberry pie. When we went swimming we always dug clams and quahogs before we enjoyed our swim.

Many days and usually after the day was done we would go out in the yard and play games such as baseball, tag, hide and seek, and on our nice lawn we played croquet and had our own small golf course. We used to practice target shooting with Dad's 22 rifle under his guidance, and we all enjoyed that.

I will always remember my seven years at Great Point as some of the happiest hours I have spent. I always feel a little lonesome to know they are over, and I hope some day I can go out to Great Point again.

Beverly's sister, Jeanette Haskins Killen, later wrote to Edward Rowe Snow about her years at Great Point.

I always loved storms and still do. The storms there were beautiful. The wind swept along the dunes and at the top of the house, but never came low in our little valley. I used to love to walk in the brisk wind along the beach and feel the sting of the sand.

It is strange how I feel about God, too. Living as I have has influenced my belief. We have never had a chance to attend church regularly, but when I look at all the beautiful things of nature I feel my religion lies there. I feel that such a service as the lighthouse has something to do with God. When men are lost at sea most of them pray for light and when the light is seen it might be a beacon guiding these men back to shore and life. When I light the light (which I do sometimes), I feel as if I am believing and helping God.

It is hard to put into words about the things that leave you spellbound such as the first flight of birds north, the first fish found in the lagoon, the first robin on the lawn, but they all go to make up a life you can look back on as being lived to the fullest.

Coast Guard crews ran the station after the Haskins family left in 1944. Nicholas Norton, a Martha's Vineyard native who was the officer in charge when Edward Rowe Snow visited in March 1945, had been awarded a lifesaving medal for his part in the rescue of "thirteen men, one woman, and a cat" from the vessel *Marcus L. Urann,* around 1915 near Edgartown.

The light was automated in the 1950s, and the Coast Guard crew was removed. In October 1966, the abandoned keeper's house was razed by a suspicious fire, which left the old stone lighthouse tower standing by itself at Great Point.

The lighthouse originally was built well inland, but erosion gradually brought the ocean perilously close. A study in 1979 showed that 50 feet of land had been lost in the previous four years. The Coast Guard rejected Nantucket Islanders' pleas to move the lighthouse inland, saying the tower was in no immediate danger.

A study in 1982 recommended moving the tower 1,000 feet to the west, at an estimated cost of $450,000—a figure the Coast Guard said was beyond their means. Some islanders talked of building an artificial reef around Great Point to protect the lighthouse. Unfortunately, they never had the chance.

A severe three-day storm punished Nantucket in late March 1984. On the morning of March 30, word spread that the lighthouse had fallen. The storm had broken through the barrier beach, temporarily turning the point into an island.

For the next few months, locals and sightseers took away chunks of the lighthouse by the armload and the carload. The lantern roof was salvaged and is now incorporated into a display featuring the lighthouse's old third-order lens at the Nantucket Lifesaving Museum.

In 1982 the Coast Guard had replaced Deer Island Lighthouse in Boston Harbor with a 33-foot fiberglass tower. The white structure was often difficult to see, so it was replaced by a brown tower in September 1984. The Coast Guard announced plans to move the white tower to Great Point. Before they could get around to the move, a new plan was unveiled.

With the help of Massachusetts Senator Edward M. Kennedy, $2 million in federal funds was appropriated for the building of a new Great Point Lighthouse in October 1984. A 45-foot-tall temporary wooden structure was placed at Great Point, and plans proceeded for the building of a new tower.

It was determined that the new lighthouse would have the same dimensions as its predecessor—70 feet tall to the very top, 45 feet in diameter at the base. The replica was constructed about 150 feet inland from the old site by Hydro-Dredge, a New Bedford construction company, with some help from Rosado and Sons of Boston. Work began in the fall of 1985 and progressed through the summer of the following year.

The foundation for the new reinforced concrete tower was sunk 35 feet below the ground. A rubble veneer was added to the outer surface, made partly of stone recycled from the old structure. The tower was designed to withstand 130-mile-per-hour winds and 15-foot breaking waves, and to be completely vandal-proof. A two-inch-thick steel door guards the entrance. An aluminum spiral stairway was created that is very similar to the nineteenth-century iron stairway. To power the automatic light, eight 35-watt solar panels were installed in a false window near the top of the tower. The Coast Guard installed a 190-millimeter optic, which has been replaced in recent years by a rotating VRB-25 that shows a white flash every five seconds.

The final cost of the replica tower was over a million dollars—more than 200 times the cost of the tower in 1818. The surplus funds from the $2 million appropriation went toward the rehabilitation of Cape Poge Light and Monomoy Point Light.

On September 6, 1986, Senator Kennedy and other dignitaries visited the Nantucket Elementary School as part of the celebration for the new lighthouse. A relighting ceremony was scheduled for that evening, but thick fog caused it to be postponed for a day. With more than 200 people on hand, including Jeanette Haskins Killen, 95-year-old Elsie Grieder, and other keepers' relatives and descendants, Senator Kennedy smashed a bottle of champagne against the tower and announced, "Great Point is alive and well again." Senator Kennedy and Rear Adm. Robert L. Johanson of the Coast Guard raised a Coast Guard flag, signaling Electrician's Mate Second Class Bob Hughes to turn the light on.

☼ Great Point is now part of Coskata-Coatue Wildlife Refuge, managed by the Trustees of Reservations. Much of the area is off-limits at times because it is a nesting site for the endangered piping plover. There is an access fee to the reservation, and a four-wheel drive vehicle is needed to drive over the more than seven miles of soft sand.

From May to October the Trustees of Reservations present a daily natural history tour at Coskata-Coatue Wildlife Refuge. A naturalist guide leads participants on an over-sand vehicle tour through the salt marsh to learn about the geology, ecology, and history of the refuge. Participants also get to climb the Great Point Lighthouse. Reservations are required. Call (508) 228-6799 or see www.thetrustees.org for more information.

Great Point Light's third-order Fresnel lens is on display at the Nantucket Lifesaving Museum at 158 Polpis Road. Visit the museum's Web site at www.nantucketlifesavingmuseum.com or call (508) 228-1885 for more information.

CHAPTER 20

Sankaty Head Light in August 2006. *Photo by the author.*

Sankaty Head Light

1850

Nantucket, the world's leading whaling port for about a century, had lighthouses at Brant Point and Great Point by 1784. Meanwhile, the island's east and south coasts remained devoid of lighthouses well into the nineteenth century, in spite of the high volume of shipping traffic passing the island and the presence of dangerous shoals.

The English explorer Bartholomew Gosnold may have sighted Sankaty Head—at what is now the village of Siasconset on the island's southeast coast—during his 1602 voyage, and in 1605 the English captain George Weymouth recorded it as a "whitish sandy cliffe." Approximately 2,000 people of the Wampanoag tribe inhabited the island at that time. The name "Sankaty"—sometimes spelled "Sankoty" or "Sancoty"—is said to come from a Wampanoag word for a highland or "cool hill." Local tradition informs us that the bluffs, nearly 100 feet high, were used as a lookout for whales by some of the early European settlers, who went after whales close to shore before advancing to longer expeditions.

A writer in the *Boston Post* in 1838, referring to himself simply as "A Sailor," made a strong case for a lighthouse on the bluffs at Sankaty Head, the most southeasterly headland on the coast of New England.

> *There is a passage inside South Shoal, near Sankaty Head, deep enough for the largest ships to pass—sounding five fathoms. Now, the difficulty to us is that we have no directions to govern us in going through this passage, except some vague ones in* Blunt's Coast Pilot. *None of these directions would answer for the* night time. *What the mariner wants is the outside passage surveyed and a lighthouse placed on Sankaty Head, Nantucket Island. It would help coming up the coast and going down, and, for those utilizing the inside route, a saving of 24 hours would be made. Having the lighthouse would mark a place of refuge for any ship running into a strong westerly, which might anchor under the lee of the high shore at Sankaty.*

In his influential 1843 report to Congress, the civil engineer I. W. P. Lewis echoed the plea of "A Sailor."

There is a . . . fatal spot upon the coast of Massachusetts, where many a brave heart and many a gallant ship lie buried in one common grave. The shoals of Nantucket are known and dreaded by every navigator on the Atlantic seaboard; and, among the great number of "missing vessels" recorded at the insurance offices, there are doubtless many that have been swallowed up in these treacherous quicksands. . . . An accurate and detailed, hydrographical survey of all these shoals . . . is of vital importance. . . . A more important measure, however, is the erection of a first class light-house upon the highlands near Siasconsett, and it is really very remarkable that this most striking omission in the lighting of our sea coast has not before been observed. By establishing a powerful light on the southeastern elbow of Nantucket Island, all the vessels that now feel their dubious way around the South shoal . . . could coast the south shore of the island, and pass between Sancoty Head and Bass rip in a deep safe channel. . . . The establishment of a light-house at Siasconsett would be more generally useful to the commerce of the United States than any other position on the seaboard.

After a survey in 1847 included the discovery of previously uncharted shoals, the superintendent of the Coast Survey recommended a lighthouse. Congress complied with an appropriation of $12,000 on August 14, 1848. Ten acres of land for the station were purchased from George Myrick for $250.

Sankaty Head Light Station in the late 1800s. *From the collection of the author.*

Overseeing construction was Benjamin F. Isherwood, who was later chief engineer for the U.S. Navy during the Civil War. Early in the summer of 1849, schooners brought building materials into Nantucket Harbor. From there the materials were carted to the bluff in Siasconset.

The contractor Cabet King built the 53-foot conical tower and accompanying dwelling for $10,333. The tower was constructed of brick, with a five-foot-deep foundation below the earth. The top six feet of the tower were constructed of granite, and atop the tower a nine-foot-tall cast-iron lantern was installed. A one-and-a-half-story brick dwelling was built adjacent to the lighthouse, which from its earliest days has been white with a broad red central band.

Additional Congressional appropriations of $6,000 in 1848 and $2,000 in 1850 were needed for the purchase and installation of a second-order Fresnel lens from the firm of Henry-Lepaute in Paris. Benjamin Isherwood traveled to France to purchase the lens, and he oversaw its installation himself. Sankaty Head Light became the first Massachusetts lighthouse with a Fresnel lens, and the first lighthouse in the United States with a Fresnel lens as part of its original equipment.

Heavy weights attached to a clockwork mechanism descended into the tower to rotate the lens, which exhibited a fixed white light with more brilliant flashes at set intervals. The light went into service on February 1, 1850. Three days later, the *Nantucket Inquirer* reported, "The flashes of light are very brilliant and must be visible at a distance of twenty-five miles." There were other claims that the light could be seen at the unlikely distance of 40 miles.

The newly formed U.S. Lighthouse Board included an extensive description of the light station in a report in January 1852. The lens and the light's first keeper, Alexander D. Bunker, received high praise.

> *This lens is acknowledged universally, so far as could be ascertained, to be, if not the best light in point of brilliancy and power, greatly superior to all others (except, perhaps, those on the Highlands of Navesink, New Jersey) on the entire coast of the United States.*
>
> *The present principal light-keeper in charge of this establishment is a most respectable and intelligent retired sea captain, who commanded a merchant ship for twenty-five years, and who knows the importance of his trust, and evinces a most praiseworthy interest in the performance of all his duties.*
>
> *He is assisted by two persons, who, for want of quarters at the light-house, are compelled to reside at some distance from it, to the detriment of the service.*

The present keeper took charge of the light on the night it was first lighted without previous knowledge or instruction as to its management, but encountered no other difficulty . . . than that arising from the use of bad oil, which he has frequently had.

The two assistants and the keeper take a regular watch during the night, relieving each other every four hours.

The 1853 annual report of the Lighthouse Board again referred to the shortage of housing at the station. The assistant at the time had to travel seven miles each day to do his job. "This, in the winter season," stated the report, "is not only an arduous task to perform, but is attended with great inconvenience to the keeper, as the daily absence of the assistant from the station is necessarily considerable." The housing crunch was solved with the addition of an assistant keeper's house in 1855.

Bunker was keeper until 1854, when he was put in charge of the newly established Nantucket South Shoals Lightship, more than 23 miles south of the island. Bunker was succeeded by his former assistant, Samuel G. Swain, who stayed until 1861.

As Nantucket evolved from whaling capital to vacation resort, the lighthouse became a popular attraction; many people climbed to its lantern to enjoy the view and the magnificent lens. An accommodation was made to the styles of the period, according to the *Nantucket Mirror* of October 25, 1856: "The narrow aperture on the platform under the lantern at Sankaty lighthouse has been widened to allow ladies with hoop skirts to pass through to see the reflectors."

In his 1875 book *Nooks and Corners of the New England Coast,* the popular historian Samuel Adams Drake provided a vivid snapshot of the village of Siasconset and its lighthouse.

The village is an odd collection of one-story cottages, so alike that the first erected might have served as a pattern for all the others. . . . On many houses were the names of wrecks that had the seeming grave-stones overlooking the sands that had entombed the ships that wore them. In one front yard was the carved figure of a woman that had been filliped by the foam of many a sea. Fresh from the loftier buildings and broader streets of the town, this seemed like one of those miniature villages that children delight in.

We returned by the foreland of Sankaty Head, on which a light-house stands. From an eminence here the sea is visible on both sides of the island. When built, this light was unsurpassed in brilliancy by any on the coast, and was considered equal to the magnificent beacon of the Morro. Fishermen called it the blazing star. Its flashes are very full, vivid, and striking, and its position is one of great

importance, as warning the mariner to steer wide of the great
Southern Shoal. Seven miles at sea the white flash takes a
reddish hue.

George Franklin Folger, who became principal keeper in 1873 after a few years as assistant keeper, had worked in the construction of whaling ships as a young man. He served in the Civil War and was wounded in the second day of the battle at Gettysburg. The *Boston Globe* interviewed Folger in 1910, well after his retirement. "I am Folger, Starbuck, Coffin, Ray, and you can't beat that in Nantucket stock. My middle name is Franklin, and I am descended from Peter Folger, Benjamin Franklin's grandfather. You know Franklin's mother was born on Nantucket. I believe he got a great deal of his ability from her."

Folger became the custodian of the Nantucket Athenaeum in his later years. He was said to have an unusually retentive memory, recalling island events dating to his boyhood. He vividly remembered the great Nantucket fire of 1846, which took place when he was 13. The fire destroyed more than 250 buildings—about a third of the town—and did $1 million in damage, contributing heavily to Nantucket's decline as a whaling capital. Folger also remembered a man named Abram Quarry, who died in 1854 and was said to be the island's last Indian.

Extensive repairs were completed in 1868–69, including the installation of new panes of glass in the lantern. In spite of the strong glass—almost half an inch thick—a news item from January 1876 informs us that a black duck smashed into one of the panes and broke it, killing itself instantly.

The 1884 annual report of the Lighthouse Board announced that new iron stairs had been put in the tower. In 1886 telegraph and telephone lines reached the lighthouse, and a 50-foot pole was added for the display of weather signals. As described in the Lighthouse Board's annual report of 1888, the "unsightly and dilapidated dwellings" at the station were torn down and replaced by a double wood-frame dwelling. The new house was completed in early 1888 at a cost of $6,700.

Later in 1888, the top part of the tower, the deck, and the lantern were replaced, leaving the tower 70 feet tall. While this work was in progress, the light was exhibited for a few months from a fourth-order lens on a temporary skeleton tower. Some leftover components of the old houses and lantern were sold at public auction.

Calvin Hamblin, assistant keeper from 1880 to 1882, succeeded Folger as principal keeper in 1882 and stayed until 1891. A 1950 article tells an amusing story of a tiff between Hamblin and an assistant,

Early 1900s postcard of Sankaty Head Light Station. *From the collection of the author.*

Benjamin Brown. As the story goes, Brown was about to go to town without permission. Hamblin told him, "Ben—if you go to town I shall have to log you as leaving the station without giving notice—that you are refusing duty!" The angry but outwardly calm Brown replied, "But, Calvin, I am giving notice—I'm not refusing duty—you can put me down in the log as resigning—here and now!"

A small brick oil house was added to the station for the storage of kerosene in 1892. In the same year, after a brief stint by Ethan Allen, Joseph Remsen became the principal keeper. Remsen remained for 27 years. Remsen, a veteran of the U.S. Life-Saving Service, had been keeper at Nantucket's Brant Point Light and was briefly in charge of the Nantucket South Shoals Lightship.

On a stormy day in January 1892, soon after he became keeper, Remsen spotted a three-masted schooner in trouble on shoals 15 miles to the east. He telephoned the lifesaving station a few miles away at Coskata. A crew of lifesavers made their way to the vessel, but when night arrived and the men hadn't returned, townspeople believed they had perished.

The next morning, the lifesaving crew and the men they had saved from the schooner arrived safely on the beach at Siasconset. They had struggled against the seas for 26 long hours before their return.

An 1898 newspaper article described Remsen's courteous and informative tours of the lighthouse. "As we reached the foot of the tower," wrote the reporter, "we met another party who were waiting to make the ascent to the top, and I noticed the keeper re-entered the tower with them, and started to retrace his steps up the long, winding stairs without the least sign of resentment on his bronzed and weather-beaten face."

Before 1898, the light station was reachable by land via a rough road across private property. The property owner told the government he would no longer allow access unless the road was improved. After a congressional appropriation of $300, an improved road was established to the station.

Like much of the New England coast, Nantucket was battered by a tremendous storm on November 26–27, 1898. The storm, nicknamed the Portland Gale after a steamship that sank with about 200 lives, brought winds of 90 miles per hour to Nantucket. At Sankaty Head, Remsen reported that a chimney on the house was blown down, the walls were badly cracked, and all the fences were "blown down and scattered to the winds."

Seven different assistant keepers served under Remsen, including Charles Vanderhoop, a Gay Head Wampanoag Indian who later became the very popular principal keeper of Gay Head Light on Martha's Vineyard. Before he returned to his home at Gay Head, Vanderhoop succeeded Remsen as principal keeper at Sankaty Head and served from April 1919 to May 1920 in that capacity.

Eugene N. Larsen, a native of Norway who went to sea at 16 and came to America as a young man in 1901, was principal keeper for

Keeper Eugene Larsen posed for this ad for the Granger Tobacco Company. *From the collection of the author.*

about 24 years beginning in 1920. Larsen had been an assistant keeper for six years, and he had previously served at the Massachusetts light stations at Minot's Ledge, Thacher Island, and Graves Ledge. He and his wife, Edvardine, arrived on Nantucket with two children and had five more daughters during their years at the light-house. His grandson Renny Stackpole later remembered being taken into the light-house on his birthday by "Papa" Larsen and being placed inside the giant revolving lens.

Several times during his career at Sankaty Head, Larsen won the coveted Lighthouse Pennant, which was awarded for keeping a clean and orderly station. Larsen also achieved some degree of national fame when his photo was used in a magazine advertisement for the Granger Tobacco Company.

An incandescent oil-vapor lamp was installed in 1912, replacing the old wick lamp. The light was converted to electric operation in 1933, and the characteristic was changed to a white flash every 15 seconds. A modern motor replaced the old clockwork mechanism that turned the lens, and the position of assistant keeper was abolished. In August 1933, the Lighthouse Service claimed that the newly electrified light could be seen as far as the Nantucket Shoals Lightship, 41 miles away, although the normal range was only 19 miles.

Coast Guard personnel from the cutter *Penobscot Bay,* homeported in Bayonne, New Jersey, painted the Sankaty tower in September 2000. *Photo by the author.*

After a century of service, the Fresnel lens was removed in 1950 and was replaced by modern rotating aerobeacons. The old lens can now be seen at the Nantucket Whaling Museum. The person in charge of the installation of the lens at the museum was Renny Stackpole, who many years earlier was given an intimate look at the lens on his birthday.

After Larsen's retirement, Archford Haskins, previously at Boston Light and Nantucket's Great Point Light, succeeded him as keeper in 1944. In its last years before automation, the station was staffed by a succession of Coast Guard crews. In 1953 the double keeper's house was razed and replaced by nondescript ranch-style housing. The light was automated in 1965, but Coast Guard personnel continued to occupy the house until 1992.

The Coast Guard removed the lantern in 1969, leaving the rotating aerobeacons "naked" and exposed to the elements. Residents and visitors to Nantucket complained until a new aluminum lantern, somewhat similar in appearance to the old one, was installed.

The house and other buildings have been removed from the rapidly eroding bluff. In 1990 the Army Corps of Engineers estimated that the lighthouse itself would be in danger of falling over the bluff within 10 years. At that time, a move of the tower was estimated at $840,000.

In 1991 concerned islanders formed a nonprofit organization called Save Our Sankaty to raise funds toward the tower's move. Legislation was passed in 1994 to transfer ownership of the lighthouse to the Nantucket Historical Association. The association ultimately decided against taking ownership, and the 'Sconset Trust, a nonprofit conservation and preservation organization, became the lead group in the preservation effort.

Erosion control measures that use arrays of pipes and pumps under the sand have been somewhat successful in recent years, delaying the inevitable move or extinction of the lighthouse. A blizzard in early 2005 exacerbated the situation, however, leaving the tower 80 feet from the bluff's edge. It's estimated that once the distance is down to 60 feet, it will be too late to save the tower.

In the fall of 2005, the 'Sconset Trust announced that it was working with the Nantucket Historical Association to gain ownership of the lighthouse, with a goal of relocating it to safer ground. At this writing, it's hoped the move will take place in 2007.

The light remains an active aid to navigation, with a white flash every 7.5 seconds, 158 feet above mean high water. Sankaty Head, in the village of Siasconset, can easily be reached from the ferry terminal on Nantucket by car or bicycle, and the lighthouse is also included in some guided tours of the island. The tower is not open to the public, but the grounds are open every day.

The Nantucket Whaling Museum, home to the old Fresnel lens from Sankaty Head Light, is open most of the year. For more information, visit www.nha.org or call (508) 228-1894.

For more information about the preservation of Sankaty Head Light, write to the 'Sconset Trust, P.O. Box 821, Siasconset, MA 02564, call (508) 228-9917, or visit www.sconsettrust.org.

CHAPTER 21

Point Gammon Light in April 2006. *Photo by the author.*

Point Gammon Light

1816

Great Island, encompassing some 550 acres and attached to Cape Cod at West Yarmouth by a narrow isthmus, was home to generations of Native Americans before Europeans arrived. Point Gammon is at the southern tip of Great Island, east of the entrance to Lewis Bay and Hyannis Harbor, and slightly more than two miles north of the dangerous ledges known as Bishop and Clerks. The point's name comes from an old term used in the game of backgammon. Mariners trying to pass between the point and the offshore ledges were deceived, or "gammoned," which often resulted in disaster.

As Hyannis grew in importance as a port for maritime trade, it was obvious that a navigational aid was needed to help mariners negotiate the area. The residents of Barnstable, Yarmouth, and Dennis petitioned Congress, and funds were appropriated in 1816.

The specifications for the tower and dwelling at Point Gammon were identical to those issued at the same time for a light station at Race Point, in Provincetown. The conical tower was to be built of stone, with a diameter at the base of 16 feet. The walls were to be 20 feet high, and the tower was to be topped by an octagonal iron lantern. The one-and-a-half-story dwelling was to be 16 by 30 feet, with a 10-by-12-foot porch.

Construction was swiftly completed and the light went into service on November 21, 1816, with seven lamps and reflectors exhibiting a fixed white light. The first keeper was a local resident, Samuel Adams Peak, who died in June 1824 at the age of 41. His son, John A. Peak, who was only 18 years old at the time he took the position at a salary of $350 yearly, succeeded him.

When Lt. Edward W. Carpender inspected the station in 1838, there were 10 lamps and 13½-inch reflectors in use, arranged in two tiers, six on the lower tier and four above. Carpender recommended the suppression of the upper four lamps and a more compact arrangement of the other six.

Carpender noted that the dwelling was connected to the tower via the kitchen, and he reported that the premises were in good order after some recent repairs. The tower had been raised in height by six feet shortly before his visit.

The engineer I. W. P. Lewis visited four years later. In his 1843 report, Lewis noted that there were still 10 lamps in use. He found fault with many aspects of the station.

> *Tower of rubble masonry, to which has been added a superstructure of brick, making the entire height 25 feet; masonry rough-cast outside, but in bad condition; roof soapstone, and leaky; walls leaky; wood work rotten; whole structure out of repair.*
>
> *Dwelling-house of rubble stone, rough-cast outside with gravel and cement; roof shingled; whole structure leaky . . .*

Included in Lewis's report was a statement from Keeper John Peak. The keeper added that the lantern was rickety and shook so much in storms that the glass sometimes broke and the lamps rattled. In addition to the numerous problems with the buildings, Peak noted that he was provided a boat but no boathouse and added, "The curb of the well is so rotten that we have difficulty in obtaining water."

John Peak and his wife, Martha, raised nine children at Point Gammon, including two sons who became lighthouse keepers. In his 1946 book, *A Pilgrim Returns to Cape Cod*, the historian Edward Rowe Snow wrote about Imogene Peak, one of John Peak's children: "School for her meant a walk of six miles each way. One of nine Peak children at the light, she said later that the walk of twelve miles daily with other children of the family was beautiful in spring, summer, and fall, but lonely in the winter."

Some repairs were carried out, but problems remained at the time of an 1850 inspection. The lantern was still leaky, and the woodwork in the tower was still described as rotten. But the dwelling was "in good order" and "nice and clean," and the inspector complimented Peak as a good keeper.

Peak counted 4,969 schooners, 1,455 sloops, 216 brigs, and four steamboats passing his station in 1855. As the traffic increased, the lighthouse was considered inadequate to warn vessels away from the offshore ledges. A lightship was briefly stationed close to Bishop and Clerks, but the vessel had problems with the heavy ice in the vicinity. In 1858 a new lighthouse was built at the Bishop and Clerks ledges, and John Peak became its first keeper.

The lighthouse at Point Gammon was discontinued and, along with the keeper's house, fell into disrepair in the next few years. There was talk of demolishing the lighthouse, but the property was instead sold into private ownership.

Charles Barney Cory, a wealthy ornithologist from Boston, purchased the island in 1882 and established it as a game preserve, with elk, deer,

A view of the tower and keeper's house, circa 1880s. *Courtesy of Nancy Finco.*

antelopes, pheasants, and other animals. Nongame birds were protected, and the island thus became one of the nation's earliest bird sanctuaries.

The lighthouse's iron lantern was removed at some point after the light was discontinued. Cory added a taller structure to the top, designed to facilitate the use of the tower as a viewing platform. The old stone dwelling was used as a museum for the butterfly collection amassed by Cory and his wife, Harriet.

In 1902 Cory and some associates built the luxurious 45-room Great Island Club on the island, which included an 18-hole golf course. (Cory was an avid golfer and winner of a hundred prizes, including the championship of Massachusetts.) Cory later lost his fortune in the stock market and sold his Great Island property. The club became the Aberdeen Hall Hotel; it burned down in 1924.

Malcolm G. Chace, a banker from Rhode Island who had visited Great Island as a boy, purchased the property in 1914. The old lighthouse dwelling was dismantled in the 1930s and then rebuilt at Uncle Ben's Cove on the bay side of the island, where it remains a private residence. The lighthouse's observatory-lantern installed by Cory has been rebuilt in relatively recent years.

Most of Great Island has remained in the ownership of the Chace family, but they have surrendered development rights for 266 acres through an agreement with the Trustees of Reservations, which ensures it will remain in its natural state.

Great Island, including the lighthouse, is off-limits to the public. The lighthouse can be viewed distantly from the Hyannis-Nantucket ferry, or from excursion boats and fishing charters leaving Hyannis.

You can take a scenic sail on Capt. Marcus Sherman's catboat *Eventide* from Hyannis from spring to fall. Views of Point Gammon Light might be distant, depending on the wind and sea conditions. Call (508) 775-0222 or visit www.catboat.com for more information.

CHAPTER 22

Nineteenth-century view of Bishop and Clerks Light.
U.S. Coast Guard photo.

Bishop and Clerks Light

1858–1952

Point Gammon and the offshore ledges known as Bishop (largest of the ledges) and Clerks (smaller rocks) were, for many years, scourges to mariners traveling near Hyannis along the south coast of Cape Cod—one writer dubbed them the "Scylla and Charybdis" of Nantucket Sound.

A day beacon marked the spot for some years, before the Lighthouse Board announced in 1855 that a lightship had been built at the navy yard in Boston to be placed at Bishop and Clerks. It wasn't long before the lightship was deemed insufficient. On August 18, 1856, Congress appropriated $20,000 for a lighthouse at the location.

The massive granite blocks were cut onshore and ferried to the site, where they were pieced together on a cylindrical base. The Lighthouse Board announced that the stonework had almost been completed in 1857, but the 65-foot tower wasn't finished until the following year. The light went into operation on October 1, 1858, and the lightship (the LV 4) was removed.

Point Gammon Light was extinguished when the new lighthouse went into service. The lighthouse received a fourth-order Fresnel lens, which exhibited a white flash every 30 seconds from a point 56 feet above the water. (A red sector, warning of Cross Rip and Tuckernuck shoals, was added in 1889.) The lighthouse also had an automatic fog bell, operated by a clockwork mechanism. The striking machinery and associated weights were housed in a wooden addition to the side of the lighthouse.

A principal keeper and two assistants (usually only two men would be on duty at the lighthouse at the same time) lived inside the tower, which had a kitchen and two bedrooms. The first principal keeper was John Peak of Hyannis. His father, Samuel Adams Peak, had been keeper of the Point Gammon Light from the time it was built in 1816 until his death in 1824. John took over and remained keeper at Point Gammon until the new tower was completed at Bishop and Clerks.

Payroll records indicate that W. W. Baker took over as principal keeper in 1859. At least 35 men served at the lighthouse in its 65 years as a staffed station.

Captain Charles H. Hinckley, a native of Barnstable, was an assistant keeper from 1881 to 1884. He left for a few years at Dumpling Rock Light, but he returned as principal keeper at Bishop and Clerks in 1892. His wife, Dorinda (Bearse), sometimes visited the lighthouse to stay with her husband. Hinckley remained at the lighthouse until 1919, when he was 70. Hinckley, who was 4 feet 9 inches (or 4 feet 6 inches in his stocking feet, according to one account), has been called the shortest lighthouse keeper in the world.

Hinckley, whose father was a prominent Cape Cod doctor, had gone to sea at the age of 16 as a cabin boy on an East Indies–bound ship. He said the first and most important thing he learned about seafaring life was "to move when spoken to, to jump quickly to one side and avoid the real attack that was sure to come." He "knocked about" in a variety of vessels for 15 years before becoming a lighthouse keeper.

The *Boston Herald* interviewed Hinckley in 1907, and Betty Bugbee Cusack included much of the interview in a 1995 article for *Lighthouse Digest* magazine. Here's an excerpt:

> It requires lots of philosophy to be a light-keeper on an outside station. At Bishop and Clerks, for example, the keeper has twenty days on and ten days off. The past two years has been the best that has ever been known. Only twice during the winter periods, have conditions been such that we could not get ashore. In the year 1903, for 48 days the sound was full of ice and at times it was piled around the light to the height of twenty feet.
>
> The government tender *Azalea* comes once a month with a fresh supply of rations, and twice a year the oil boat comes with six months' supply of oil.

In 1909 the magazine *Along the Coast* quoted Keeper Hinckley: "There ain't a great deal of me so far as height goes but I am all right from my feet up. I've laid many a man bigger than me on his back if I do say it myself."

Betty Bugbee Cusack, in her book *Collector's Luck: A Thousand Years at Lewis Bay, Cape Cod*, remembered her friend Mrs. Cook of Hyannis, who often visited the lighthouse as a girl. Mrs. Cook was the niece of Keeper Hinckley. Mrs. Cook said she could "just smell the cornbread and those boiling lobsters now, thinking about those trips."

Cusack also wrote that Hinckley was a familiar sight in Hyannis after his lighthouse-keeping days (he retired in 1919): "He was always busy, either digging and selling a few clams, doing an odd job here and there, or tending somebody's furnace . . . doing it all with a cheerful

Keeper Charles Hinckley with Walter Carney of Hyannisport, a local ferry captain. Hinckley referred to himself and Carney as the "long and short of the service." *From the collection of the author.*

optimism." Father of four and a lighthouse keeper for 38 years, Charles Hinckley died in 1932.

One of the last assistant keepers was Luther Chapman, described in the book *Once upon a River,* by Ted Frothingham, as a great story-teller who had a habit of "beginning and ending all his sentences with cuss words."

The lighthouse was converted to automatic acetylene gas operation in 1923 and discontinued in 1928. It remained as a day beacon, but it suffered from the sea's battering as well as vandalism. A storm in 1935 did considerable damage.

By 1952 the tower tilted to one side and was missing many blocks. The Coast Guard decided to raze the structure. Hired to carry out the demolition was the McKie Lighter Company and U. O. MacDonald of Boston, a blasting expert. Preparations took a week. Dynamite was placed strategically in drilled holes in such a way to direct the blast upward, so the debris wouldn't scatter over too large an area. It was hoped that some of the materials could be salvaged.

As hundreds of people in pleasure craft watched on September 11, 1952, the tugboat *Irene and Mary* flew a red flag of warning. When the proper time came—12:57 p.m.—the tug blew six blasts on its whistle. The *Boston Globe* described the aftermath of the blast that came 10 seconds later: "A cloud of smoke partly hid the old tower, which stood swaying for a moment and then toppled to one side like a pile of child's blocks. . . . The historic Bishop and Clerks Lighthouse was no more."

For many years, a 30-foot, white pyramidal day beacon marked the spot where the lighthouse once stood. There's now a small white-and red-lighted tower. In addition, several buoys warn mariners away from the dangerous shoals that were guarded by the lighthouse for nearly a century.

CHAPTER 23

Top: Hyannis Harbor Light in the late 1800s. *From the collection of Edward Rowe Snow, courtesy of Dorothy Snow Bicknell.*
Bottom: Hyannis Harbor Light in April 2006. *Photo by the author.*

Hyannis Harbor Light

(South Hyannis Light)
1849

Tucked away on a residential side street, Hyannis Harbor Light is seen
by only a small number of the tourists who come to Hyannis to shop,
to catch the ferries to Nantucket and Martha's Vineyard, or to get a
glimpse of the Kennedy family's Hyannisport compound. The privately
owned lighthouse and keeper's house have been altered so much
through the decades that only an informed visitor would be likely to
recognize what was an important nineteenth-century light station.

Hyannis (a corruption of the name of a Cummaquid Indian
sachem) is one of seven villages of the Cape Cod town of Barnstable.
The village grew into a busy fishing and trade port in the 1800s, and
today it's the largest community on Cape Cod. By 1840 more than 200
shipmasters were living in Hyannis and Hyannisport. Point Gammon
Light had been established at the southern approach to the harbor in
1816, but it became increasingly apparent that a navigational light was
needed to guide shipping into the inner harbor.

A local man, Daniel Snow Hallett, took it upon himself to provide
a light in the early 1840s, a few years before the government decided to
erect one. The light established by Hallett was shown from a one-room
shack that was known locally as "The Bug." A whale-oil lantern hung in
a window, backed by a reflector that was discarded from nearby Point
Gammon Light. The light was financed in part by money Hallett made
by selling printed directions for sailing into Hyannis Harbor.

"The Bug" was maintained by Hallett, who was assisted in his
lightkeeping duties by his son, Daniel Bunker Hallett, who would grow
up to be a banker in Boston. He recalled years later: "As a boy of ten or
twelve, I often used to walk from Pickens Cove, where my father lived,
down across the fields two miles to the harbor light, after school, to
light the lamp and remain all night alone, with only my dog Pilot as
company, then return home in the morning in time to get breakfast
and go to school."

In 1848 Congress authorized the building of a more substantial
lighthouse at South Hyannis for $2,000. The Treasury Department
reported: "With much difficulty a small piece of land was purchased, a
small tower erected and fitted up with lamps and reflectors, for the sum

Hyannis Harbor Light with its original "birdcage-style" lantern. *U.S. Coast Guard photo.*

appropriated. A man has been employed to attend it, who has a house of his own in the neighborhood, at the rate of fifteen dollars per month."

A 19-foot (to the base of the lantern), conical brick tower was built, and the light went into service on May 7, 1849. A system of five oil lamps and parabolic reflectors produced a fixed white light, 43 feet above the water, with a red sector that warned mariners away from dangerous Southwest Shoal. Two years later, an additional $800 was appropriated for a wooden keeper's dwelling, attached to the lighthouse by a covered walkway. A barn, a summer kitchen, and an oil house were added in later years. A fifth-order Fresnel lens replaced the original lighting apparatus in 1856, and a new cast-iron lantern was installed in 1863.

Daniel Snow Hallett was appropriately appointed keeper, but he was replaced two years later for political reasons. His brother, Capt. Almoran Hallett, served as keeper for eight years starting in 1853. James Bearse was in charge between the Hallett brothers. An 1850 inspection praised Bearse, reporting, "Everything is nice and clean about the premises, and the apparatus is in good order."

Franklin Baker was the keeper for a decade beginning in 1861. He was followed by "Pilot John" Lothrop of Hyannis, who was appointed keeper after a long career as a "branch pilot," helping to guide vessels from Maine to Virginia. In 1874, during Lothrop's tenure, one of the vessels landing in Hyannis brought President Ulysses S. Grant, who had been visiting Nantucket. The keeper and his wife, Hannah, celebrated their fiftieth wedding anniversary at the light station in 1876.

Lothrop was assisted by his son, Alonzo Freeman Lothrop, who became keeper after his father's death in 1878. The figures Alonzo

Lothrop kept for 1882 underscore the importance of the lighthouse. The statistics show 6,000 tons of coal discharged in the harbor, along with 1,250,000 feet of lumber and 4,000 barrels of fish. A total of 1,400 schooners and 100 steamers arrived in Hyannis that year. These numbers rose even higher during the last part of the nineteenth century.

Alonzo Lothrop remained at the station until 1899, when he resigned because of ill health, ending nearly three decades of the Lothrop family at the station. The *Barnstable Patriot* reported that the keeper had "made many friends especially among the many summer people visiting the light, for he was always pleasant and agreeable."

John A. Peak Jr., a former captain of lighthouse tenders and part of a family dynasty of local lighthouse keepers, took over at Hyannis Harbor Light after Alonzo Lothrop's resignation and remained until his own poor health forced him to retire in 1915.

While John Peak and his wife, Grace, lived at the lighthouse, local children would visit for sailing lessons. Captain Peak also let some of the children help with lighthouse chores, such as polishing the brass parts of the tower. Peak's great-niece Marilyn Peak Rogers later recalled the extravagant morning meals served by the keeper. "Folks were amazed at the breakfasts they had at Uncle John's—fried potatoes, pie, beef—whatever was left from the night before."

Peak is said to have hung a mirror in his bedroom so he could monitor the light from his bed, probably saving many trips to the top of the tower in the dead of night. "Why should I get up to look when I can see it in the mirror?" he asked.

Alonzo Lothrop was keeper 1878–99.
Courtesy of Ruth E. Alt.

In 1885 a front range light was added on the Old Colony Railroad Wharf, about 1,000 feet from the lighthouse. It was a simple lamp hoisted to the top of a 20-foot wooden tower. The new front range light and the lighthouse would be aligned by mariners, one above the other, as a guide into Hyannis Harbor.

John Peak's great-nephew Howard recalled years later that he would walk to the wharf with the keeper. "Every night he raised the lantern," Howard remembered, "filled it with oil, and pulled it down every morning." A member of the

Peak family reported that railroad cars would often be left in a position that blocked the range light, and Keeper Peak would have to argue with railroad personnel until they would move the cars.

A 1922 inspection showed a kerosene-fueled lamp and a fifth-order Fresnel lens in use. The report stated that access to the station was via a road from town. The keeper had no boat, and there was no landing place for a boat other than a small beach.

Waldo Leighton, formerly at Race Point Light in Provincetown, became keeper in 1915 after Peak resigned because of illness. One of Leighton's three sons, Harvard, later described the station as "a wonderful location, a nice place to live, a picturesque site overlooking the whole bay. . . . Our home was a charming two-story dwelling with a full cellar and an outhouse. It had no electricity or running water."

Keeper Leighton made extra money by working as caretaker for several properties belonging to local summer residents, including the Kennedy family's property in Hyannisport. He also worked as a carpenter and a clammer. "Most anytime in season," Harvard said in 1985, "we could also scoop up a bushel of scallops in front of our house. These delicious morsels produced both food and money from sales to a market. We could not have survived without them."

Waldo Leighton was the last keeper of the lighthouse, and he moved to Nobska Point Light in Woods Hole when Hyannis Harbor Light was discontinued on June 30, 1929. The closing of the light station came about because the primary ship-landing site in the area was moved to Lewis Bay.

The lantern was removed from the lighthouse, leaving it with a headless look. The light on the wharf continued for some years as an automatic acetylene gas beacon. Today only a trace of the old wharf can be seen on Keyes Beach.

A. W. Fuller bought the lighthouse at auction for over $7,000 and subsequently sold it to Annie V. Stevenson. The property has reportedly changed hands seven times since then.

Janice Hyland and Alan Granby, former elementary school teachers with PhDs who deal in eighteenth- and nineteenth-century marine antiques, bought the property in 1985. They found that much of the wood in the house was rotten. In fact, when they first bought the house, Hyland fell right through the floor twice. She had the house boarded up and wouldn't discuss it for a year, but work on the property eventually resumed, thanks to Granby's prodding.

Granby and Hyland oversaw a three-year renovation that began with the virtual gutting of the interior of the keeper's house and a large 1938 addition. After Hyland pulled out the kitchen cabinets, took

This wooden tower served as the Hyannis Front Range Light for a time. *U.S. Coast Guard photo.*

down the curtains, ripped up carpeting, and pulled down a plaster ceiling in the living room, the debris filled 12 dump trucks.

All the floors, floor joists, sills, inside walls, and ceilings had to be replaced, as did the electrical and heating systems. The kitchen was remodeled with a marble bar, mahogany cabinets, and Portuguese ceramic tile on the counters. There was plenty of display space created for the couple's maritime antiques and art.

A post-and-beam addition, 30 by 32 feet, was erected on the ocean side of the house; it serves as a library—with an extensive maritime research collection—and living room. A garage on the property was in rough shape, so it was torn down and replaced with a guesthouse.

Thirty coats of paint were sandblasted off the lighthouse tower to expose the original red brick, and the exterior was then repainted. On the day before Halloween in 1986, a new top was installed on the tower. The oversized lantern is not traditional, but it provides a great view at sunset. Alan Granby says he especially enjoys "the panoramic view of Nantucket Sound and the particular excitement of the year-round boating activity in the area."

A high fence makes it difficult to get a good view of the lighthouse from the nearby road, but if you park at Keyes Beach in Hyannis and walk east for a few minutes, you'll get a good view from the beach.

Another way to get a view is to take a ride on Capt. Marcus Sherman's catboat *Eventide,* which offers scenic sails from spring to fall. Call (508) 775-0222 or visit www.catboat.com. If you sail with Captain Sherman, be sure to tell him of your interest in the lighthouse and he'll take you closer.

For more information on Hyland Granby Antiques, you can visit their Web site at www.hylandgranby.com.

CHAPTER 24

Top: Bass River Lighthouse in the late 1800s. *Courtesy of the Lighthouse Inn.* *Bottom:* The former Bass River Lighthouse, now the Lighthouse Inn, in 2001. *Photo by the author.*

Bass River Light

(Lighthouse Inn, West Dennis Light)
1855

The town of Dennis is bounded by Cape Cod Bay on the north and Nantucket Sound to the south. West Dennis—one of Dennis's five villages—is in the southwestern part of the town, separated from South Yarmouth by the Bass River. The Dennis side of the river once had saltworks and facilities for building small vessels, and many West Dennis residents were involved in fishing and coastal trade.

For some years before a lighthouse was built near the mouth of the Bass River in 1855, a West Dennis resident, Warren Crowell, aided local navigation by keeping a lantern burning in the attic window of his house at Wrinkle Point. Local ship captains each donated 25 cents monthly so that Crowell could buy the oil he needed to keep the lantern lit.

As traffic in the area increased, so did the demand for a lighthouse. A small beacon on a breakwater at the mouth of the river was proposed. The *Yarmouth Register* of January 24, 1850, reported: "A petition is in circulation . . . asking Congress to substitute a Light House for the Beacon which has been ordered to be built on the breakwater at the mouth of the Bass River. There is much more need of such a guide and safeguard to the navigation through the Sound than of many similar ones on the coast. Certainly a light house it should be, rather than a beacon."

Congress appropriated $4,000 for a lighthouse on September 28, 1850. An officer of the Revenue Marine was sent to examine the site, and he promptly declared the lighthouse unnecessary. But in their annual report of 1852, the newly formed Lighthouse Board disagreed: "It is apparent, however, to this board, from the information received from various reliable sources—among which may be included that of the officer of the coast survey who was charged with examining this locality with reference to another object—that a small light is required at or near the Bass river breakwater."

Congress reappropriated the $4,000 for the lighthouse on March 3, 1853, and a site near the breakwater was soon selected. The land for the light station was purchased from George W. Richardson in March 1854.

Oxen hauled building materials across the local marshes, and when the lighthouse was finished Warren Crowell appropriately became its first keeper. The light went into service on April 30, 1855, with a fifth-order Fresnel lens displaying a fixed white light. The lighthouse consisted of a two-story, wood-frame dwelling with the lantern mounted on the roof.

In 1972 Marion Crowell Ryder painted a vivid picture of the lighthouse's early years in *Cape Cod Remembrances:*

> *The house stood tall and solid and foursquare, quite a distance back from the edge of the water. In those days the beach presented a busy scene. . . . It was lined with fishing dories, moored or drawn up on the sand, and great piles of long, slender weir poles were stacked here and there. . . . Atop the sand dunes straggled an uneven line of small, weather-beaten fish shanties where their owners could store their gear and warm themselves about battered little stoves in inclement weather. When we went to the beach as children we never tired of wandering along the shore, watching the fishermen mending their nets, setting out for their weirs, or bringing in a shining catch. . . . The lighthouse itself always dominated the beach with its purpose and significance.*

Warren Crowell served as keeper until 1863. He was wounded and taken prisoner in Virginia during the Civil War, and he eventually returned as keeper in the early 1870s. Crowell arranged for his wife and nine children to live in a house on Fisk Street in West Dennis during his war service. This might have been a welcome change for the children after being crowded into the small bedrooms of the lighthouse.

Captain James Chase became keeper when Crowell left for the war. His granddaughter Carrie May Sheridan later remembered seeing ships anchored offshore while friends and families waited on the West Dennis Beach for the passengers' arrival. "Horse-drawn wagons drove into the shallow water's edge to take them ashore," she recalled.

Another keeper during the 1860s was Zelotes Wixon of Dennis. Wixon complained that when he arrived at the lighthouse expecting to be trained, James Chase was not cooperative. "[He] refused me all access to the light until the first day of August though I several times requested permission to look at it and examine the same in order to fit me for my position and the proper discharge of my duties," wrote Wixon. He also reported that the outgoing keeper was apparently adulterating the oil used in the lighthouse.

Everything apparently worked out eventually, as a couple of months later an inspector stated, "Mr. Wixon is now performing his

The Lighthouse Inn, circa 1940s. *Courtesy of the Lighthouse Inn.*

duty with entire faithfulness and ability and has been ever since his misfortune in August last."

On August 1, 1880, the lighthouse was discontinued and the property was sold at auction after the lighting of Stage Harbor Light a few miles to the east, in Chatham. A newspaper reported that Keeper Crowell returned "to his former residence where he is having a barn built."

Six months later, complaints caused the government to buy the lighthouse back and relight it on July 1, 1881. Capt. Samuel Adams Peak of Hyannis became keeper, remaining until his death in 1906. Captain Peak had gone to sea as a boy and served as master of two barks before becoming a lighthouse keeper. His father and grandfather had also served as lightkeepers in the Hyannis area.

After Peak's death, Russell Eastman became the station's final keeper. Marion Crowell Ryder later described Eastman as "taciturn and unceasingly busy keeping the lighthouse and its out-buildings in spotless condition."

The government deemed the lighthouse unnecessary after the advent of the Cape Cod Canal. Thanks to the efforts of Congressman Thomas C. Thacher, a new automatic light was established on the Bass River west jetty at the entrance to the river. The lighthouse was extinguished on June 15, 1914, and its Fresnel lens was removed. Keeper Eastman was transferred to Ned's Point Light in Mattapoisett, Massachusetts.

Inside the Lighthouse Inn. *Photo by the author.*

The property was soon sold at auction. Harry K. Noyes—of the Noyes Buick Company in Boston—used it as a summer residence for a while. Noyes expanded the main house and added several new buildings.

After Noyes's death, the property was unoccupied for about five years, until 1938, when it was bought by State Senator Everett Stone and his wife, Gladys, for $22,000. The Stones began to have overnight guests at the lighthouse, and their hospitality became so popular that they soon opened it to the public as the Lighthouse Inn. In 1939 a night's stay for two—including three meals—cost five dollars.

Everett and Gladys Stone's son, Bob, became the first head of the food service for the inn. Bob Stone hired three waitresses from Wheaton College. One of them was Mary Packard of Brockton, Massachusetts. Bob and Mary married in 1942.

Mary Stone recalls that during World War II, American planes bombed the rocks near the inn for practice. The guests would gather on the beach and cheer the show.

A 1944 hurricane destroyed the dining room and the station's old oil house, but the Stones continued to expand. Two more hurricanes battered the property in 1954, and Hurricane Bob in 1991 sent seawater cascading through the windows of a downstairs lounge and out through the doors on the opposite side. The inn lost power for six days as a result of the storm, but Mary Stone told the *Cape Cod Times.* "That was nothing. You should have seen '44."

Bob Stone died in October 2004 at the age of 86, but Mary and other family members remain involved with the inn's operation. There's a summer staff of about 90. Bob and Mary's son Greg Stone is president, and his wife, Patricia, is the general manager. Nelson Cook, who worked as a waiter at the inn in 1957, returned years later as director of marketing.

For years Greg Stone found it difficult to return to the inn when coming back from Nantucket or Martha's Vineyard. The area's small

Mary Stone at the Lighthouse Inn in 2001. *Photo by the author.*

navigation lights blended with other lights on the shore. He convinced the Coast Guard that a relighted Bass River Lighthouse would provide a needed service to local boaters.

In 1989 the Stone family had their lighthouse relighted as a seasonal aid to navigation, with a 300-millimeter optic providing a white light that flashes every six seconds. The relighting took place on August 7, 1989, which was National Lighthouse Day, the celebration of the 200th anniversary of the national Lighthouse Service. The light, officially designated the West Dennis Light, now operates each summer.

The old 1855 lantern atop the inn got a much-needed overhaul in March 2002. Marty Nally and Clem Fraize of the Campbell Construction Group of Beverly, Massachusetts, did the job, which included the installation of six new panes of heat-resistant glass.

For many years the Lighthouse Inn has been a beacon to mariners and travelers, and it now also serves as a beacon for education. There is a program that enables local third-grade schoolchildren to tour the inn and lighthouse as part of a curriculum on maritime history. The program was originally designed with the help of the Cape Cod Discovery Museum.

The Lighthouse Inn features 700 feet of private beach, 61 rooms and cottages (with working fireplaces), tennis courts, a heated pool, miniature golf, a playground, a cocktail lounge, and a waterfront dining room offering a five-course dinner every evening. The inn also has a special children's program in the summer, with a children's director who plans and supervises activities for the children of guests. If you stay at the inn, you might also be able to arrange a tour of the lighthouse and lantern.

For more information, write to the Lighthouse Inn, P.O. Box 128, 1 Lighthouse Inn Rd., West Dennis, MA 02670, call (508) 398-2244, or visit www.lighthouseinn.com.

CHAPTER 25

Top: Stage Harbor Light in the early-1900s. *From the collection of the author. Bottom:* Stage Harbor Light in September 2006. *Photo by the author.*

Stage Harbor Light

(Harding's Beach Light)
1880

The area now known as Stage Harbor in Chatham was visited by the French explorer Samuel de Champlain in 1606, but skirmishes with the Monomoyick Indians convinced him not to remain there. English settlers arrived about a half century later, and Stage Harbor (named for racks used for drying fish) developed into a busy fishing port.

In 1878 the Lighthouse Board recommended the establishment of a lighthouse on Harding's Beach (named for Joseph Harding, a farmer who had once owned the land), on the northeast side of the channel known as Chatham Roads, saying that the light "would serve as a guide into old Stage Harbor, and would be of great value to vessels seeking refuge there and during bad weather." Congress appropriated $10,000 for the lighthouse on March 3, 1879.

A 48-foot cast-iron tower and a wood-frame keeper's house were finished at a cost of $9,862.74, and the light went into service on July 15, 1880. The lighthouse was fitted with a fifth-order Fresnel lens that exhibited a fixed white light visible for 12 nautical miles. A well was added in 1902, and an oil house and another small outbuilding were constructed in 1905.

Enoch Eldredge, the first keeper, was paid $560 per year. Eldredge died in 1884 and was succeeded by George W. Folger, who remained until 1900. Alfred Howard, who became keeper in 1906 and stayed for a decade, was commended several times for going to the aid of boaters in trouble.

In 1912 Howard received praise for towing four people to safety after their boat had run out of fuel. Later that same year, he guided the yacht *Arcturus* to safe anchorage, as the captain was unfamiliar with the vicinity.

Just a few months later, on March 30, 1913, Howard saved the life of Walter C. Harding of the Monomoy Life-Saving Station. Harding's boat had capsized in a strong wind. "Had it not been for the prompt assistance of A. A. Howard, Keeper of Hardings Beach Light," wrote Harding, "it would have ended seriously. . . . I was taken from the bottom of my dory and carried to the lighthouse where I was furnished with dry clothing and made as comfortable as possible."

In December 1914, Capt. Ephraim Smith of Chatham wrote to the lighthouse authorities in Boston, describing Howard's latest act of heroism:

> *I deem it my duty to report to you the valuable assistance rendered me by Alfred A. Howard, Keeper, Stage Harbor Light Station, in saving my horse from drowning; also supplying my man with rubber boots and dry stockings, etc. On the 18th inst. p.m. I sent my man after seaweed on Harding's Beach, who is quite elderly and his sight not very good. In driving the horse across the marshland, the horse got mired and went down in mud and water. My man couldn't do anything to save the horse, so he ran for Mr. Howard, the light keeper, at the station; who responded to the call readily and through some very hard work got the wagon and harness clear and then got the horse out of the quicksand and mud and water to hard land all right. And as he would not take money for his very kind service, I take these means to write you for your kind consideration towards commending him for his prompt and efficient aid towards saving my pet and valuable property.*

Howard's pay was raised in the following year from $560 yearly to $600. He was again commended in October 1915 for rendering assistance to the passengers of a disabled pleasure boat.

Keeper Mills Gunderson came to Stage Harbor Light from Boston Light in 1916. In 1919 Keeper Gunderson committed suicide, hanging himself in a shed for reasons unknown. His son, Stanley, took over as keeper and stayed at the light until it was decommissioned in 1933.

Alfred Howard was keeper 1906–16. *From the collection of Edward Rowe Snow; courtesy of Dorothy Snow Bicknell.*

According to Admont G. Clark's book *Lighthouses of Cape Cod, Martha's Vineyard and Nantucket,* the floor under the covered walkway between the house and tower became a hiding place for liquor for a time during Prohibition. An inspector on a surprise visit noticed the loose floorboards. Much to the keeper's relief, he merely told him to nail them down more securely.

Stanley Gunderson rescued the passengers of a disabled yacht in 1929. Lighthouse Commissioner George Putnam praised the keeper for his "timely assistance." Gunderson was also perennially commended for the excellent condition of the station.

In 1933 an automated light on a skeleton tower replaced Stage Harbor Light. Gunderson complained to the *Boston Post:* "To save money they put in something that is far more expensive and less reliable and call that economy and put another employee on the unemployment list. Rather a poor way to reduce unemployment and surely no help toward better times."

Gunderson stayed briefly in the Lighthouse Service, moving to Great Point on Nantucket as an assistant keeper for a year, after which he resigned.

The government removed the lantern and capped the tower, and the lighthouse and three surrounding acres were sold at auction to an army officer. In early 1936, the property was again for sale. Henry Sears Hoyt told *Yankee* magazine about his first visit to inspect the property:

> *One day in January with the thermometer about five degrees above zero and a fifty-mile northwester blowing (that day Nantucket Lightship broke loose from her moorings), my brother and I drove to Chatham in an ancient Buick open car. Locating a guide to our prospective property, we drove to a point from which, through spray and wind haze, we could see, far out, a desolate looking group of buildings dominated by a faded white tower. . . .*
>
> *A more desolate spot would be hard to imagine. Doors had broken down, rocks were all over the floor where they had been thrown through the lower windows. Since then we have never found a stone worth throwing, and have calculated the vandals must have carried their ammunition out from the mainland. A howling gale, whistling around angry sea, but nevertheless a grand place.*

Hoyt later learned that the lighthouse property was a portion of an original grant of 4,000 acres made by the local Indians to his ancestor William Nickerson, founder of Chatham. Hoyt commented, "Old great-great, etc., grandfather got all of Chatham for less than his descendants paid for a small portion, showing a weakening of New England trading ability."

The Hoyt family still owns the property, and they've opened it to the public occasionally as part of Cape Cod Maritime Week in May. There has never been electricity at the station, and no plumbing except a single pump. The nearby skeleton tower continues as an active aid to navigation, exhibiting a white flash.

The lighthouse can be viewed across the water from the town landing at the end of Sears Road, or it can be reached after a one-mile hike on Harding's Beach; keep in mind that the house and tower are private property.

CHAPTER 26

Top: Monomoy Point Light in the early 1900s. *From the collection of Edward Rowe Snow, courtesy of Dorothy Snow Bicknell.* Bottom: Monomoy Point Light in September 2006. *Photo by the author.*

Monomoy Point Light

1823, 1849

Monomoy was once a peninsula some eight miles or so in length and barely a quarter mile in width, extending southward from Chatham at the elbow of Cape Cod's flexed arm. For a thousand years or more before the arrival of Europeans, native peoples used this windswept stretch of sand as a summer base for shellfishing and hunting. The name comes from "Munumuhkemoo," an Algonquian word roughly meaning "mighty rush of water."

Monomoy was first separated from the mainland around 1800, but it was later rejoined. It was separated again by winter storms in 1958. Today the former peninsula is divided into two islands, North Monomoy and South Monomoy. The ever-shifting contours of South Monomoy have left acres of sand between the lighthouse and the shore, so that some liken it to a "minaret in the Sahara."

The grassy inland part of Monomoy was suitable for pasturing livestock, and Chatham farmers took advantage of this for many decades. A tavern opened in 1711 at Wreck Cove on the west shore, designed to serve the mariners who came there seeking shelter.

In the early nineteenth century, a small fishing community evolved around a harbor (now reduced to a shallow pond called Powder Hole) on the west side of the point. Whitewash Village, as it was called, reached its apex around 1850. Monomoy fishermen caught cod and mackerel in nearby waters, and they also had easy access to plentiful lobsters. A destructive storm helped bring an end to Whitewash Village in the 1860s.

Monomoy is at the dividing line between Nantucket Sound to the west and the deeper, colder Atlantic Ocean to the east. Where the sound and ocean meet—east and south of Monomoy—dangerous "rips" occur as rapid ocean waves pass over shallow shoals and bars. Early French visitors knew Monomoy as Cape Malabar—"Cape of Evil Bars." Despite the menacing conditions, the passage between the southern end of Monomoy and Great Point, the northern extremity of Nantucket, was one of the Atlantic coast's busiest stretches for many years.

According to an 1864 article in *Harper's*, Monomoy's first aid to navigation took a primitive form. "'Eighty years ago,' said a Monomoy

Pointer, 'we had no light-house here. But in a shanty up there on Sim's Knoll . . . there lived an old couple who used to answer the purpose pretty well. One or the other would come out on the risin' above the water whenever any vessel was passing by into the Sound, and would pint [sic] out the course and the marks. Channel ran pretty close inshore for schooners, and so on, and so mostways 'twant hard to hear.' "

Lightships were stationed in the vicinity over the years, at Pollock Rip (1849–1969), Stonehorse Shoal (1852–1963), Handkerchief Shoal (1858–1951), and Great Round Shoal (1890–1932). Congress appropriated $3,000 for Monomoy's first lighthouse—the fifth on Cape Cod—on March 3, 1823. Five landowners sold a four-acre parcel to the government for the establishment of the light station at the southern tip of Monomoy, also known as Sandy Point.

Like many early lighthouses on Cape Cod, the first Monomoy Point Light consisted of a wooden tower and iron lantern situated on the roof of a brick dwelling; it was built by the contractor James B. Gill. The fixed white light was established on November 1, 1823.

When Lt. Edward W. Carpender visited for his 1838 survey, the lantern held eight lamps with 13-inch reflectors. Carpender wrote:

> *This memorable light stands on Sandy point, eight miles from Chatham, a long, low beach that reaches off right into the very heart of the whole coasting navigation, and requires to be lighted, perhaps, more conspicuously than any other part or point in the district. This light, on the keeper's dwelling, elevated only 25 feet above the level of the sea, has but a single series of lamps, while almost every other light in the district (most of them more elevated and interior to this) has a double. I acquainted myself with the operation of this light, and found it perfectly satisfactory and good. I myself saw this light from Nantucket, 15 feet above the level of the sea, a distance of 13 miles. . . .*
>
> *This point of land has received an accession of several hundred yards from the sea, making it probable that, in the course of a few years, when the land shall have formed a little higher, it will be advisable to remove this light farther to the southward.*

Carpender, who recommended fewer lamps at most other locations, proposed a second series of lamps at Monomoy. But there were still only eight lamps when I. W. P. Lewis visited in 1842. Lewis described the reflectors as out of position and at "unequal distances apart." Lewis, like Carpender, stressed the need for a sufficient light:

This is one of the most important locations on the coast of the United States. Thousands of vessels pass here annually, amid the numerous and very dangerous shoals that obstruct the navigation. The light originally stood within sixty yards of the beach; now it is five hundred yards distant therefrom, owing to the alteration of the sands; and vessels frequently get ashore directly abreast of the light, which is one of the worst on the coast of Massachusetts, saving and excepting its next neighbor, Nantucket [Great Point] light, which is equally bad.

Solomon Doane, who became keeper in 1841 at a yearly salary of $400, complained to Lewis that the roof leaked where it joined the tower, and he reported, "the lantern has been so much racked by storms that it shakes so as to break the glass continually." He continued:

The lantern leaks very badly in all wet weather, and is entirely out of repair. . . . The coasters complain of the feebleness of this light. . . . The reflectors are worn out. The well of water has been spoiled by the drain, &c, breaking into it. I am allowed a boat, but there is no boat-house. . . . The kitchen chimney leaks and smokes, and the oven has fallen to pieces, and is useless. Owing to the loss of my well, I am dependent upon my neighbors for water, as there is no rain-water cistern on the premises.

An inspection report by the local lighthouse superintendent in 1842 was less critical than Lewis's, but it noted:

The effect of high winds is to blow the sand from the house, and thereby undermine it. The keeper, at his own expense, has carted away many loads of sea weed, and put them around the buildings, to protect them, which has had a good effect. More sea weed is yearly required.

The keeper's boat is very old, and good for nothing. It seems absolutely necessary that he should have a new one. I respectfully ask for authority to furnish him with one. Cost of boat, $90.

There's much disagreement among various sources concerning the year the present lighthouse tower was built. Some claim 1855 as the date, and others the 1870s, but it's clear that the extant tower was built in 1849. A contract in the National Archives indicates Cyrus Alger built the new tower that year, and Pelham Bonney built a two-story, wood-frame dwelling. A short covered passageway connected the house and tower.

The 40-foot cast-iron tower erected in 1849 was one of the first cast-iron lighthouses in the United States; towers at Boston's Long Island Head (1844) and Vermont's Juniper Island (1846) were among the earlier ones. Among surviving American towers of this type, only those at Juniper Island in Lake Champlain and at Biloxi, Mississippi (1848), are older.

An inspection report in 1850 was critical of the new lighthouse:

This is a new establishment altogether—an iron light-house, a wooden dwelling, and a new fashionable apparatus. The workmanship to the light-house, I presume, is good, but it is neither large enough, nor high enough, nor stiff enough; for I can take hold with one hand of any part of the lantern and shake it to such a degree as to break the tube glasses on the lamps.

The ventilator to the dome is such as to admit rain and snow into the lantern freely, and is troublesome to the keeper, and in strong winds it might prevent the smoke from passing through it. As I have already said, the dwelling is of wood, and a poor concern; it is tight.

The Lighthouse Board recommended the installation of a second-order Fresnel lens in 1850, pointing out that the lighthouse was the primary guide for vessels in the vicinity. Instead, a fourth-order Fresnel lens replaced the old system of multiple lamps and reflectors in 1855. Two of the reflectors were salvaged and converted into washbasins by a local resident, and they eventually were donated to the Chatham Historical Society.

The Lighthouse Board's annual report for 1857 mentioned that the tower had been lined with brick, and the annual report for 1869 announced that the illuminating apparatus and fixtures had been overhauled and a new globe ventilator for the lantern dome had been made. Presumably, these improvements ended the problems described in the 1850 report.

In 1871, and in each of the following three years, the Lighthouse Board recommended that the light be upgraded to second order. The board noted that one of the light's original purposes, to guide mariners to Chatham's Stage Harbor, had been rendered moot since that harbor had filled with sand. "But," the board stated, "inasmuch as nearly all vessels (both steamers and sailing) plying between New York and the eastern ports pass this point . . . it is considered a matter of the greatest importance that this light should be replaced by one of sufficient power to guide vessels safely through this intricate passage."

Despite this plea, the light was never upgraded. The tower was, however, painted red in 1882 in an effort to improve its visibility in the daytime. In 1892 iron trusses were added to the tower to prevent vibration.

For years, the Massachusetts Humane Society maintained four little huts, called houses of refuge, along Monomoy's outer coast. In 1873, soon after the formation of the U.S. Life-Saving Service, a lifesaving station was built on Monomoy, about two miles north of the lighthouse. A second station was added in 1902, about three-quarters of a mile from the lighthouse. Six or seven surfmen and a captain lived at the stations, patrolling the beaches for wrecks each night. Often the lighthouse keepers were the first to spot wrecks and would notify the lifesaving crews. In 1902 one of the worst tragedies in Life-Saving Service history occurred when seven men from the Monomoy Station died attempting to save the crew of a schooner-barge on Shovelful Shoal.

Asa L. Jones, a native of the Cape Cod town of Harwich, was keeper from 1875 to 1886. Jones, who was born in 1840, had been wounded in the Civil War. His young son, Maro B. Jones, kept a diary that provides a glimpse of life at the light station in the 1884–86 period. Here are some excerpts, beginning when Maro was eight or nine years old.

March 25, 1884: Good weather. Papa killed a black duck.

March 31, 1884: Good weather. Papa bound a book. Seven geese came to the pond. Papa tried to shoot them.

April 6, 1884: Good weather. Papa got three shelldrakes. I scared them for Papa to shoot.

May 3, 1884: Papa went to Harwich. A lonesome day. I sent a letter to Harper's Young People.

May 16, 1884: Very pleasant day. Papa painted his lantern.

May 29, 1884: Windy. I went with Uncle Willie to haul his nets. I went to the Station. Mama and Papa were worried about me.

June 17, 1884: Awful hot. Papa caught a rabbit.

June 22, 1884: Very good weather. THE INSPECTOR WAS HERE.

August 8, 1884: Mama and I went blackberrying.

August 10, 1884: Papa caught 81 bluefish.

June 19, 1886: The surveyors went home. Papa carried them to Chatham. The ass't inspector came and wrote "Station in good order."

June 28, 1886: Papa went to Harwich and he carried the first load of things from here so the people knew we were to move off. The weir men have got a live sturgeon tied and he is tame.

July 4, 1886: Not much of a Fourth of July for me. I never saw as much as an explosion with gunpowder. It is funny that today has been the most lonesome day of the summer. In the PM the drinkers of Harwich Center came after some quahogs for bait to catch black bass.

July 26, 1886: Mr. Ben Mallowes has got a sort of turtle and it looks like a sea cow. No one knows what it is, not even old whalers and Papa is going to write a man to come and get it.

July 30, 1886: Eddie Marshall came up and said the monster was dead. Thank the lord we came off for good. The wind was south west and Mama was seasick. In the bay were the largest waves I ever saw.

After retiring as keeper, Asa Jones ran an undertaking business in Harwich.

For many years, the chief means of travel between Monomoy Point and Chatham was by boat. In later years, one resourceful keeper converted his Model T Ford into an early dune buggy, making the trip by land to Chatham much faster.

James P. Smith, a native of Copenhagen and a former assistant keeper at Boston Light, became keeper in 1899. His wife died early in his stay at Monomoy, but Keeper Smith had three daughters—aged 24, 17, and 13 at the time of a 1904 article—who assisted him in his duties. (A fourth daughter was married and lived in Provincetown.) The oldest daughter, Annie, acted as housekeeper and tended the light when her father was away.

In February 1902, Keeper Smith and his daughters found the body of a Nova Scotia fisherman from the wrecked vessel *Elsie M. Smith*. The man's clothes had filled with sand, and Emma Smith said that he must

The three daughters of Keeper James P. Smith, circa 1904. *From the collection of the author.*

have weighed 300 pounds. It took Keeper Smith and his daughters Annie and Emma to pull the body from the surf.

A reporter once asked the Smith sisters if life at the lighthouse was lonely. Annie replied, "Oh, no! We don't have time to be lonesome. There is always something to do, with the housekeeping and the light." The place was immaculate, according to the reporter, who commented, "Even the stove shines like a new dollar."

In 1987, 95-year-old James Wilson recalled his days as a Life-Saving Service surfman at Monomoy when Smith was still the lightkeeper. "The lighthouse keeper had a farm, chickens, pigeons, and three daughters," Wilson recalled. "One day, ol' Capt. Smith went up there to put the light out in the morning and didn't come down. It was too much for him. He died coming down the stairs."

Charles Jennings, a native of Provincetown, became keeper in 1909 at a salary of $660 yearly. His son, Harold Jennings, wrote in his book, *A Lighthouse Family*, that his parents had a cow, chickens, and a horse at the light station. In those days, it was possible to take a horse-drawn buggy across the mud flats to Chatham, but there were areas where it was necessary to get out and lead the horse so it wouldn't become mired. This led to a problem on one occasion, according to Harold.

This particular day, Dad was leading the horse and the reins slipped from his hands. When he reached down for the reigns, a ring my mother had given him slipped off his finger. He searched in vain but could not find it. Every time he crossed the flats for the next three years he would look for it. Mom would say, "Charles, you know you can't find that ring, especially with the tide coming in and out across these flats." In the meantime, in May 1916, Dad applied for and was accepted as keeper of the Boston Light. The day before he was to leave the Monomoy station, he told Mom that he was going to go and find the ring. She told him he was wasting his time. Believe it or not, he went to the area where he had lost the ring a few years earlier and there it was!

With the opening of the Cape Cod Canal in 1914, traffic past Monomoy decreased. One of the two lights at Chatham was moved to Eastham in 1923, and the power of the remaining light was increased. With these changes, Monomoy Point Light was considered expendable. The light was discontinued in 1923 and the property passed into private hands. The first owner was George Dunbar of Chatham, who paid $500.

The property was eventually sold to George Smith Bearse, a Chatham automobile dealer whose great-grandfather David Bearse

This early dune buggy was used for travel between Monomoy Point Light Station and Chatham. *From the collection of Edward Rowe Snow, courtesy of Dorothy Snow Bicknell.*

had been an early keeper of the light. When he came to visit the property, Bearse was startled to find that navy planes had been using it for machine-gunning target practice. One bullet had come through a wall of the keeper's house and knocked out a rung on a rocking chair; another had lodged itself in a four-by-four beam.

The last private owners sold the buildings to the Massachusetts Audubon Society in 1964. The property came under the management of the U.S. Fish and Wildlife Service (USFWS) in the 1970s. North Monomoy, South Monomoy, and a portion of Morris Island, which is attached to the mainland at Chatham, now constitute the 2,750-acre Monomoy National Wildlife Refuge, established in 1944.

In 1988 the USFWS hired K & K Painting of Baltimore to carry out a major overhaul of the lighthouse and keeper's house. The Lighthouse Preservation Society had helped initiate the project when it was learned that the USFWS was considering demolishing the lighthouse dwelling. The work was funded mostly by money left over from the rebuilding of Great Point Light on Nantucket, which was funneled to Monomoy with the help of Massachusetts Senator Edward M. Kennedy.

K & K replaced glass and repainted the tower, re-sided the keeper's house, rebuilt a deck, installed new windows and doors, built a new stairway to the basement, and revamped the closets—all for $148,200. The K & K crew spent most nights sleeping in the keeper's house, which made it possible for them to put in 16-hour workdays. The company's owner, Engelo Kaliakoudas, claimed that before the renovation, "The bricks inside were holding the tower up. One storm would have taken it down."

Also in 1988, the USFWS announced a partnership with the Cape Cod Museum of Natural History of Brewster. Peter Trull, the museum's education coordinator, explained the appeal of the lighthouse to the *Cape Codder* newspaper: "You could have climbed Mount Everest or been to Antarctica, but if you haven't lain up on the lighthouse deck at Monomoy and seen the stars in total darkness, well, that's something to experience."

For a number of years, museum staff took birdwatchers and lighthouse buffs on trips to the property, and some of the visitors spent the night in the keeper's house. Accommodations were rustic: there was no electricity or plumbing in the house, meals were cooked on a Coleman stove, and participants had to bring their own sleeping bags. The trips have recently been discontinued.

The writer North T. Cairn spent three summers at the lighthouse in the mid-1990s, an experience that she wrote about in her book, *By Monomoy Light.* Cairn described her feelings early in her first summer, as she watched the sun set from an upstairs window in the keeper's house. "When the ragged current of everyday existence was swept away and the quiet came, I could discern the innocence of the natural world bearing down on me, and I knew, without knowing how, that nothing would ever again be quite the same."

By the early twenty-first century, the condition of the buildings was again deteriorating. Because of a lack of funding and the remote location, only minor repairs have been completed in recent years. After leaks in the keeper's house caused some interior damage, the building was partially reroofed in 2005 and a new ventilation system was installed. According to the director of the refuge, Mike Brady, there's major USFWS funding slated for 2010 that will pay for a thorough restoration of the house and tower.

The ferocious blizzard of February 6–7, 1978, cut Monomoy into two islands, North and South Monomoy. South Monomoy is a birdwatcher's mecca, more than 300 species spotted in recent years. Gray seals, once rare in New England, have been breeding on South Monomoy.

Capt. Keith Lincoln offers a variety of cruises on the Monomoy Island Ferry, including a visit to South Monomoy and the lighthouse. See www.monomoyislandferry.com or call (508) 945-5450. The trips depart from the Monomoy National Wildlife Refuge headquarters at Morris Island in Chatham.

For more information on the Monomoy National Wildlife Refuge, call (508) 945-0594 or see www.fws.gov/northeast/monomoy/.

CHAPTER 27

Chatham Light in February 2006. *Photo by the author.*

Chatham Light

1808, 1841, 1877

The present town of Chatham, nestled at Cape Cod's southeast corner, was named for an English seaport and incorporated in 1712. The town remained largely agricultural through much of its history, but an important fishing industry also developed.

Maritime traffic passing the Cape was heavy by the nineteenth century. The waters off Chatham were a menace, with strong currents and dangerous shoals. Mariners talked of a ghostly rider on a white horse who appeared on stormy nights, swinging a lantern that lured sailers to their doom.

In April 1806, nine years after the establishment of the Cape's first lighthouse at North Truro, Congress appropriated $5,000 for a second station at Chatham. About 12 acres of land on a bluff called James's Head was acquired, and a second appropriation of $2,000 was made in 1808. When the station was established in what was then a daisy field, there was about 400 feet of land between the towers and the edge of the bluff. All that land has long since fallen into the ocean.

In order to distinguish Chatham from Highland Light, it was decided that the new station would have two fixed white lights. Two octagonal wooden towers, each 40 feet tall, were erected on movable wooden skids about 70 feet apart. Each tower was topped by an octagonal iron lantern equipped with a system of lamps suspended on iron chains. A one-story, three-room keeper's dwelling, 17 by 26 feet, was also constructed. President Thomas Jefferson approved the appointment of the first keeper, Samuel Nye.

Lt. Edward W. Carpender of the U.S. Navy visited the station in 1838. He noted that one of the original purposes of the lights was to guide vessels across Chatham Bar, which had since filled in. The lights still warned vessels away from the coast and helped traffic navigate past Pollock Rip, a dangerous shoal off Monomoy about eight miles south of Chatham. Carpender suggested that a single fixed red light would suffice at Chatham. He also suggested replacing the three lights at the Nauset station with a single revolving light. Carpender's practical and economical suggestions apparently fell on deaf ears in Washington.

Carpender's report described the 1808 towers as "very much shaken and decayed, so as to make it dangerous to ascend them in windy weather." The lighting apparatus at the time consisted of six lamps and 8½-inch reflectors, with green glass lenses in front of them. Carpender was critical of the keeper.

> *I visited them [the lights] in the late afternoon, and found them in as bad order as they could be—nothing done to them from the previous night; the reflectors, apparently, not having been burnished for a length of time; the glass very smoked; and the lamps neither filled nor trimmed. A sly attempt was made by the keeper to have them prepared through his son; but what were partially done only served to show more plainly the condition of the remainder. If there can be any excuse for this keeper, it is in the dilapidated condition of these towers, requiring a severe tax upon the pride he may possess for a faithful discharge of his duty.*

An appropriation for the rebuilding of the station was requested for the next two years. In late 1841, the Treasury Department announced, "The two light-houses at Chatham . . . being entirely unfit for use, were taken down and rebuilt at an expense of $6,750, out of the general annual appropriation for the present year. They were fitted upon the improved plan, with fourteen-inch reflectors." The two new brick towers, completed in the summer of 1841, were each 30 feet tall. A new brick dwelling was connected to both towers by covered walkways. The contractor responsible for the rebuilding of the station was Winslow Lewis.

Collins Howe, a Cape Cod fisherman who had lost a leg in an accident, became keeper of the Chatham lights shortly before the new towers were built, at a yearly salary of $400. The civil engineer I. W. P. Lewis—Winslow's nephew—visited the station during his important survey of 1842. The brand-new buildings were already in disrepair, as described in a statement made for Lewis by Keeper Howe in September 1842:

> *I expected to have a light-house, and every thing in first-rate order, when these new buildings were put up; but I was mistaken. In the first place, the house is leaky about the roof and windows, every part being badly built as far as I can judge. The cellar and foundation walls are laid on the sand, without any footing to the walls, and so little below the surface, that the rats burrow from outside and infest the cellar. . . . The numerous leaks about my house cause so much dampness, that I find it difficult to preserve my provisions from moulding.*

Howe added that a storm in October 1841 had smashed much of the glass in both lanterns, the result of poor construction. A separate inspection report in 1843 mentioned that the keeper had no fresh water supply and had to borrow water from the well of a neighbor, some distance away. The 1841 buildings somehow survived into the 1870s, and a number of major repairs were completed in 1868–69.

Howe lost his job as keeper in 1845 for political reasons. The next keeper was Simeon Nickerson. Nickerson died in 1848 and his wife, Angeline, took over his duties along with the responsibility of raising four young children on her own. Everything was reported in good order at the time of an 1850 inspection, although the towers and house were again described as leaky.

Perhaps the rats had retreated from the keeper's house, because Collins Howe decided he wanted his position back and tried to have Angeline Nickerson removed. A resident of Chatham wrote a letter to President Taylor about the condition of the station: "I can testify that it has never been in a better condition than since it has been under her charge, nor is there any Light upon the Coast superior to it." President Taylor ruled in favor of Angeline Nickerson, who remained keeper until 1862.

In 1857 the Chatham lights received new fourth-order Fresnel lenses, each showing a fixed white light. The lamps were fueled by lard oil.

A tremendous storm hit Cape Cod in November 1870. Before the storm, the Chatham towers were 228 feet from the edge of the 50-foot bluff. The storm broke through the outer beach, and the erosion rapidly accelerated.

A view of the station, circa 1860s, showing the 1841 towers. *U.S. Coast Guard photo.*

Capt. Josiah Hardy II—born in Chatham in 1822—served as principal keeper from 1872 to 1897, after spending a year as the assistant keeper. Hardy went to sea as a cook at the age of nine, and he had a long career as a sea captain before taking up lightkeeping. A granddaughter of the keeper, Grace Hardy, preserved the logs from Hardy's years at the Chatham Light Station. Transcriptions from the logs are in the collection of the Chatham Historical Society. Many of his entries describe the rapid erosion of the bluff on which the station stood. Here are some excerpts, retaining the original spelling:

December 21, 1874: Wind NNW heavy gales Sch[ooner] draged her anchors to the SW Buoy on the common flats the Shore all along sufferd badly this gale. High tides & heavy Sea. The distance was measured to day from foot of South Tower to the edge of the bank 190 feet, 38 foot in width had been cut off since 1870.

February 8, 1875: The month of February of this year was a cold hard month for Ice Snow & Wind. On the 14th Handkerchief and Shovelful Shoal Light Ships were driven from their Stations by Ice.

September 30, 1876: from tower to Bank 126 feet from East Wall of dwelling 128 feet.

November 21, 1876: to day from the East Wall of Dwelling to Bank 112 feet.

February 28, 1877: the distance from foot of South Tower to the Bank is 95 feet.

Josiah Hardy was keeper 1872–97. *From the collection of Edward Rowe Snow, courtesy of Dorothy Snow Bicknell.*

The authorities took note of the rampant erosion and moved quickly to rebuild the station, across the road and much farther from the edge of the bluff. Two 48-foot conical cast-iron towers were erected in 1877, along with double one-and-a-half-story, wood-frame dwellings for the principal keeper, the assistant keeper, and their families. The new towers were similar to several built in the 1870s and 1880s in New England: five iron rings were bolted together, lined with brick, and topped by an octagonal cast-iron lantern. The towers were virtually identical to the one erected in Portsmouth Harbor, New Hampshire, a short time later.

In his log Hardy recorded the progress of the construction of the new buildings. On July 31, he noted that the old south tower was only 64 feet from the edge. On September 6, the lenses were moved from the old towers to the new ones, and they went into service that night. Workers finished installing the brick lining of the towers a few days later. Hardy and his family moved from the old dwelling to the new one on November 7.

By September 30, 1878, the old south tower was only 26 feet from the edge of the bluff, and it was down to 19 feet by the end of the year. By September 30, 1879, the tower teetered 27 inches from oblivion.

Another two months passed, and a third of the foundation hung over the edge. Around this time some local boys found ancient coins, rumored to be pirate treasure, under the lighthouse. Fishermen placed bets on the exact time that the tower would fall. Finally, at 1:00 p.m. on December 15, the south tower tumbled to the beach below. Fifteen months later, the 1841 keeper's house and the old north tower succumbed.

In his 1946 book, *A Pilgrim Returns to Cape Cod,* Edward Rowe Snow wrote about a visit with a Chatham resident who was acquainted with Josiah Hardy.

> *Mrs. Harding went on with her thoughts. "There's an interesting bit about Chatham Light I have," she reminisced. "One day in the 1880s my husband, Herman, and Captain Josiah Hardy's son, Samuel, were playing near the light, when the veteran white-whiskered light keeper strode over to them. He had just finished calculations for the day, and there was a pleased expression in his face. 'I want you two boys to remember this day as long as you live,' said the captain. 'I have seen as many ships today as there are days in the year.'"*

Hardy retired in 1897 and died in late 1900, survived by his widow and four children. The next keeper was Charles H. Hammond. James T. Allison took over as principal keeper in 1907 and stayed for about 20 years.

By the early 1900s, the Lighthouse Board began phasing out twin light stations as an unnecessary expense. The north light was moved up the coast to Eastham to replace the survivor of the "Three Sisters" in 1923 (see chapter 28), ending 115 years of twin lights at Chatham. The position of assistant keeper was abolished at the same time. A new rotating lens was placed in the remaining tower, along with an incandescent oil-vapor lamp. In 1939 the Coast Guard electrified the light—which had been fueled by kerosene since 1882—and increased its intensity from 30,000 to 800,000 candlepower.

Chatham Light Station, circa 1900. *From the collection of the author.*

George F. Woodman, a veteran of 24 years of service at a number of Massachusetts lighthouses and lifesaving stations, became keeper in 1928. He was a perennial recipient of the superintendent's efficiency star for excellent service. He was still there when a 1937 article reported that the station had more than 1,500 visitors between mid-July and mid-September 1936. No matter how nonsensical the questions (e.g., "Is that the lighthouse?"), Woodman was said to display courtesy to every tourist.

Woodman had the added duty of displaying storm signal flags on a nearby 75-foot tower as needed, as well as storm warning lights at night. At the time of the 1937 article, an assistant was provided to Woodman from December to May. If the assistant was absent and help was needed at Chatham, a keeper would be sent from either Highland or Race Point Light.

George T. Gustavus was keeper from 1941 until his retirement in 1945. Gustavus had previously served at several Massachusetts lighthouses, and he had lost his wife and youngest son in the hurricane of 1938 while at Prudence Island Light in Rhode Island.

Chatham Light was one of the few American lighthouses to remain in service during World War II, which testifies to its importance. During the war, 11 Coast Guard women (SPARS) were chosen for a two-month training course in the new LORAN (long-range aid to navigation) technology. After their training, the women lived for a time at Chatham Light Station, where they operated LORAN equipment. The SPARS were required to have a gun in the LORAN room. The women practiced in a pistol range set up in a building in Chatham, and some of them achieved high marksman status.

In 1969 the Fresnel lens and the entire lantern were removed. Modern aerobeacons producing a rotating 2.8-million-candlepower light were installed, and a new, larger lantern was constructed to accommodate the larger apparatus. Five years later, the old lantern and lens were put on display on the grounds of the Chatham Historical Society's Atwood House Museum on Stage Harbor Road, just a few minutes from the lighthouse.

The light was automated in 1982. It remains an active aid to navigation, and the dwellings have been retained as an active Coast Guard station. In August 1993, a large crowd watched as the top of the lantern was temporarily removed and new DCB-224 aerobeacons were installed.

In recent years, the lighthouse has been "adopted" by Coast Guard Auxiliary Flotilla 11-1. The "keeper" at this writing is Jeff Davis, who took over after Auxiliarist Peggy Fisher's five years in the volunteer role. Davis helps show thousands of people through the tower during open houses held each summer.

The erosion near Chatham Light had slowed in this century, but in recent years a new threat has developed. Hurricane Bob and the ferocious "Perfect Storm" of October 1991 created a new break in the barrier beach east of the lighthouse. The parking lot across the street from the lighthouse was undermined by these storms. The town of Chatham has been implementing erosion control measures, but the time will come, sooner or later, when Chatham Light will have to be moved or follow in the wake of its predecessors.

The lighthouse is not open to the public except during open houses held from spring through fall. For information on open houses and group tours offered by the local Coast Guard Auxiliary flotilla, call (508) 430-0628. A schedule of the open houses is posted at www.lighthouse.cc/chatham/.

A right on Shore Road at the eastern end of Main Street will take you to the parking lot across the street from the lighthouse. The Atwood House Museum, where the old lens and lantern are displayed, is just a few minutes away at 347 Stage Harbor Road. See www.chathamhistoricalsociety.org or call (508) 945-2493 for more information on the museum.

The monument standing near the foundation of the old north light was erected in memory of seven members of the crew of the Monomoy Life-Saving Station, who died attempting to save the crew of a coal barge in 1902.

CHAPTER 28

Nauset Light in February 2006. *Photo by the author.*

The Three Sisters of Nauset

1838, 1892

Nauset Light

1923

The name Nauset (or Nawsett) once applied to a large section of Cape Cod, about 15 miles in length, from Namskeket (now Brewster) to the vicinity of the present-day town of Truro. Nauset was also the name of the tribe of Algonquin Indians that occupied the part of Cape Cod east of the Bass River for many years before the arrival of Europeans. The French explorer Samuel de Champlain described the natives, in 1605, as living in a "great number of little houses surrounding Nauset Harbor."

Over the years, the original Nauset area was split into several towns. Eastham remained largely agricultural; the town's first gristmill was built in 1684. Extensive cranberry bogs provided another industry, and shipbuilding, fishing, and whaling also developed. But despite its large harbor, the town never became a major fishing port. The entrance to the harbor has shifted many times over the years as storms and tidal forces have changed the contours of the outer beach.

In 1836 21 residents of Eastham wrote to the Boston Marine Society asking for a lighthouse on Nauset Beach on the Atlantic shore of the Cape, halfway between Highland (Cape Cod) Light in North Truro and the twin lights at Chatham. Countless vessels had been wrecked on the Nauset Bars offshore.

After being petitioned by the Boston Marine Society, Congress appropriated $10,000 for the new station on March 3, 1837. About five acres of suitable land was purchased for $150 from Benjamin and Sally Collins of Eastham. To differentiate the station from its neighbors, a unique plan was devised.

To distinguish the location from the single light in North Truro and the double lights at Chatham, the authorities decided that there would be three lighthouses at Nauset Beach. Capt. John "Mad Jack" Percival, a Cape Cod native who also commanded the USS *Constitution* for a time, selected the site for the station.

Winslow Lewis, who consistently underbid his competitors, built the original 15-foot triple conical brick towers. The lighthouses, each 15 feet wide at the base and 9 feet wide at the lantern deck, were built in 38 days by a crew consisting of four masons, two carpenters, three laborers, and a cook. One of the masons and one of the carpenters contracted smallpox during the latter half of the construction period.

A small brick dwelling, about 20 by 34 feet with three rooms on the first floor and two in the attic, was also built. The cost of the three towers and the dwelling was $6,549.

The lights were 150 feet apart from each other, arranged in a straight line. The land farther back from the edge of the bluff was uneven, posing construction challenges, so Lewis and company constructed the towers much closer to the edge than was originally planned. Each octagonal iron lantern held 10 lamps with 13½-inch reflectors and exhibited fixed white lights.

Somewhere along the way, the trio of towers acquired their famous nickname, the "Three Sisters of Nauset." The name is frequently said to have originated because the towers looked like three demure ladies in white dresses and black hats.

A local author, Donald B. Sparrow, in his book *A Cape Cod Native Returns: You Can Go Home Again,* offers another explanation. The Three Sisters moniker, according to Sparrow, refers to the three daughters of Henry Y. Hatch, who was keeper from 1851 to 1853. To date, this has not been verified.

The local lighthouse superintendent had hired (at $2.50 per day) a Boston carpenter, David Bryant, to monitor the construction of the

The original "Three Sisters of Nauset" in 1890. *Photo by Henry K. Cummings, courtesy of Nauset Light Preservation Society.*

station. Bryant was dismayed by many aspects of the work—for one thing, he observed masons shoveling sand instead of mortar between the double walls of the towers—and he refused to sign a certificate stating the work had been honorably fulfilled. In an 1842 affidavit, Bryant wrote that he "considered the whole of the work as of the meanest character and description."

Winslow Lewis convinced his friend and champion, Stephen Pleasanton, the fifth auditor of the Treasury, who was in charge of the nation's lighthouses, that the buildings were satisfactory. Bryant was called to the office of the customs collector in Boston and told to sign the certificate of completion. When he asked why he should sign a statement he knew was untrue, Bryant was told that Pleasanton had already accepted the work. "I considered my objections waived by the Government," Bryant wrote. "This man, Bryant," Pleasanton shot back, "will be indicted, and probably punished, for perjury in this case."

Lt. Edward W. Carpender visited the station shortly before the lights went into service. In his 1838 report, Carpender expressed some objections to the presence of three lights.

> They were, doubtless, given this triple appearance to distinguish them from Chatham lights, consisting of two towers similarly arranged. Nauset beach has always been considered a dangerous place for vessels, and many have been wrecked there. To guard against such disasters seems to be the object of these lights. I cannot, however, think that three lights are at all necessary. Any single distinguishable light that can be seen eight or ten miles will answer every purpose. Such a light is a revolving red light. There is no revolving red light, that I know of, on the coast, so that accidents could not possibly occur from its being mistaken. . . .

In his 1843 report to Congress, the engineer I. W P. Lewis (nephew of Winslow Lewis) was highly critical of the station's construction. The bases of the towers rested on the sand with no foundations, and the towers were "laid up in bad lime mortar" and were leaky. Each tower's lower window had been walled over by the keeper because of the damage done by gravel blowing against the windows in storms. Lewis also echoed Carpender's questioning of the need for three lights.

Even the naturalist Henry David Thoreau found the three lighthouses puzzling, writing in his book *Cape Cod,* "They were so many that they might be distinguished from others; but this seemed a shiftless and costly way of accomplishing that object." Despite so many objections, three lights would remain in service for 73 years.

The local lighthouse superintendent inspected the station in 1843, when Henry Horton was keeper. The report noted that the lantern glass had been damaged by the sand, so that the lights were obscured. The oven in the dwelling had been rebuilt in the previous year, but there were problems with the station's water pump, which was "unfaithfully made." A new pump was authorized at a cost not to exceed five dollars.

By the time of an 1850 inspection, Joshua Crosby was keeper and the number of lamps in each tower had been reduced to six. In 1856 all three towers were fitted with sixth-order Fresnel lenses, replacing the old multiple lamps and reflectors.

Nathan Gill's tenure as keeper (1869–83) saw several major changes. In 1873 more powerful fourth-order Fresnel lenses were installed. An assistant keeper was authorized, and by 1876 a second wood-frame dwelling was added to the station after an appropriation of $5,000. Stephen Lewis followed Gill as principal keeper, remaining until 1914.

The Three Sisters fought a long battle with the weather and the gradual forces of erosion. By 1890 the towers stood close to the edge of the bluff. If a three-light station was impractical in 1838, it was even more so in 1892. Even so, three shingled wooden towers, 22 feet high, were built 30 feet west of the old towers in 1892. The lenses were transferred from the old towers to the new ones on April 25, 1892. A small brick oil house was added to the station at the same time.

In the momentous Portland Gale of November 26–27, 1898, it was reported that the force of the storm moved two of the three towers. Almost a month after the gale, Keeper Lewis found the body of a man on the beach, uncovered from the sand by another storm. It was believed the man was one of the nearly 200 people who died in the wreck of the steamer *Portland,* which had sunk off Cape Cod in the great November storm.

By 1911 the cliff had eroded to within eight feet of the northernmost tower, and the Bureau of Lighthouses belatedly decided to change Nauset to a single light. The Three Sisters were moved back from the edge of the bluff. The center tower was given a white light that flashed three times each ten seconds (a sort of tribute to the Three Sisters) and attached to the 1876 keeper's house. The original dwelling was removed.

The single light went into service on June 1, 1911. Not everyone was happy with the change. The *Boston Globe* reported in September 1911 that there were complaints that the single flashing light at Eastham could be confused with Highland Light, which flashed at

The center tower of the Three Sisters served alone 1911–23. *From the collection of Edward Rowe Snow, courtesy of Dorothy Snow Bicknell.*

a different rate. "In thick weather," according to the *Globe*, it was "almost impossible to count the flashes correctly."

In 1918 the two defunct towers—after their lanterns had been removed—were bought for $3.50 by the Cummings family of Attleboro, Massachusetts. About two years later, the lighthouses were incorporated into a summer cottage known as "The Towers" on Cable Road, not far from their original location. The cottage was later used as a dance studio.

By 1923 the remaining Sister was in poor condition. Meanwhile, a few miles to the south, the twin lights at Chatham were reduced to a single light. The discontinued twin from Chatham was dismantled, transported to Eastham, installed on a concrete foundation, and lined with yellow brick. The keeper's house was moved farther back from the edge of the bluff and placed near the relocated tower. The "new" Nauset Light received the fourth-order Fresnel lens from the remaining tower of the Three Sisters. The last of the wooden Sisters was sold to Albert Hall (reportedly for $10) and incorporated into a residence.

The 48-foot cast-iron tower was painted white until the early 1940s, when the upper half was painted red to increase its daytime visibility. Its distinctive image has become a Cape Cod icon, gracing countless calendars, postcards, license plates, and potato chip bags.

Eugene L. Coleman, a veteran of 20 years at various lighthouses, arrived as keeper in 1942. Otis Barton, manager of a combined post office–store in Eastham, greeted Coleman by telling him, "Cap', I think

Eugene Coleman (seen here with his wife, Amanda) was keeper in the 1940s. *Courtesy of Robert Prince.*

you're going to like it here. We have a great climate here. Never gets cold for much of a time. Once in a while we get a below-zero temperature, but, I tell you, there are some beautiful days here in winter."

Four years later, Coleman recalled Barton's words to a newspaper reporter. "Well, that very winter," said Coleman, "it was down to eight below. For two days you'd look out this window and you couldn't see those houses except at noon. Vapor was that thick. It was some cold that winter."

Coleman might not have been impressed with Barton's analysis of the climate, but he was grateful for his hospitality. Just after Coleman arrived at Nauset Light with his wife, Amanda, Otis and his wife invited the Colemans over for Thanksgiving dinner. "It was a wonderful time. Oh boy, what a feed!" Coleman recalled.

After years at island light stations, Amanda Coleman appreciated life on the mainland. "Many's the time, from Christmas to Mother's Day, I haven't seen a woman to speak to," she said. "The hardest part of lighthouse duty is being alone, having no one to talk to."

At the time of the 1946 newspaper article, the Colemans had gone a long time without a radio for entertainment because they hadn't been able to get replacement batteries. There was no electricity in the keeper's house. "We've been promised electric lights," said Amanda. "The big icebox there is run by kerosene. But it's better here. We can go out. We had to learn to drive a car when we got here; we'd never had one. Now we go shopping once a week in Orleans. It was harder in Maine. Three times we almost drowned."

Nauset Light was automated by the Coast Guard in 1955, and the keeper's house passed into private hands. The fourth-order Fresnel lens was replaced by modern aerobeacons in 1981. The characteristic was changed to alternating red and white flashes every five seconds. The old Fresnel lens is now on display at the Cape Cod National Seashore's Salt Pond Visitor Center on Route 6 in Eastham.

In 1981 the keeper's house became the home of Mary Daubenspeck, a freelance writer and editor. She later wrote a book about her years living at the lighthouse, called *Nauset Light: A Personal History.* In it she wrote: "Even in a Nor'easter's seventy-knot gusts, when the house ever so slightly flexes beneath my feet, the presence of the Light just beyond the window lends me a powerful sense of security."

The two towers sold to the Cummings family in 1918 were purchased by the National Park Service in 1965. Ten years later, the third of the Three Sisters was bought by the park service from the Hall family. The Sisters were reunited on a site on Cable Road about 1,800 feet from the beach. For some years, the abandoned lighthouses served as a hangout for teenagers from nearby Nauset Regional High School.

In 1986 the National Park Service announced plans to restore the Three Sisters towers. The idea of relocating them closer to the edge of the bluff was considered, but concerns about erosion and increased traffic on Ocean View Drive prevented that. Instead, the towers remained at their Cable Road location.

A restoration of the Three Sisters was completed in 1989, and the site was opened for tours in the following April. The three towers stand in their original configuration, about 150 feet apart from each other. The center tower—the only one with its lantern room still in place—was fully restored, and the other two towers were partially restored.

Erosion continued to plague the still-active Nauset Light. In just three years, from 1991 to 1994, 30 feet of the bluff disappeared just east of the lighthouse. In particular, the "Perfect Storm" of October 1991 washed great chunks from the cliff and destroyed the stairs to the beach below. By 1994 Mary Daubenspeck could see—for the first time—the ocean from one of the kitchen windows in the keeper's house.

After the Coast Guard proposed the decommissioning of the lighthouse in 1993, hundreds of letters poured into the Boston Coast Guard headquarters requesting that the lighthouse be moved inland and saved. The Nauset Light Preservation Society (NLPS) was soon formed, spearheaded by several local residents—Bill Burt, Hawkins Conrad, Pam Nobili, and Harold Jennings, among others.

In January 1994, the Coast Guard announced that the light would remain active and that it would support the efforts of the NLPS. At a ceremony on April 17, 1995, the Coast Guard granted the society a five-year lease for the lighthouse.

After much debate and consideration of five possible sites by the Cape Cod National Seashore, a new site was chosen for the tower in April 1996. By that time, it stood only 43 feet from the edge of the bluff. A contract with International Chimney Corporation of Buffalo, New York, was signed in September 1996. The team of International Chimney and Expert House Movers had previously moved Highland Light and Block Island's Southeast Light.

Cape Cod dodged a bullet a few weeks later when Hurricane Edouard failed to make landfall, but heavy seas during the storm ate away more of the bluff. The lighthouse stood a mere 36 feet from oblivion.

By early November 1996, the new site had been graded and excavated, a temporary access road to the site had been created, and new footings for the tower and oil house were prepared. The concrete floor of the lighthouse was excavated, and holes were cut in the foundation for the insertion of steel beams. The foundation was cut away from its footings using diamond-tipped circular saws. Meanwhile, the oil house was moved on November 9 to a temporary location in the corner of the Nauset Light Beach parking lot.

Cribbing was installed around the base of the tower and four steel beams were pushed through the foundation. Six interior and four exterior jacks were put in place to raise the 90-ton tower. On November 15, workers endured frigid winds and snow as they lifted the tower and transferred its weight to two heavy-duty dollies, hitched to a truck. The tower was moved to the edge of the road before the end of the day.

The move was completed on Saturday, November 16. As crowds of the curious strained to get a view of the historic event from designated viewing areas, the truck hauled the lighthouse across the road to its new home, 336 feet from the old site.

Over the winter months, a two-course brick foundation was built between the footing and concrete base. The exterior was renovated and painted, and a new exterior railing was installed. The move cost about $250,000 in federal and state funds, and the NLPS spent another $60,000 for the work done on the tower in its new site. The move didn't happen a moment too soon. A red and white stake was placed in the former position of the lighthouse; by early 2003 the stake was only about three feet from the bluff's edge.

After its relocation, the lighthouse remained dark until May 10, 1997, when it was relighted at a gala event attended by about 2,000 supporters. After the ceremony, Hawkins Conrad, president of the society, said, "The emotions felt as we threw the switch were overwhelming. So much accomplished in four years."

After two years of negotiations, Mary Daubenspeck donated the house and the existing site to the National Park Service in early 1998, in exchange for the right to live in the house for another 25 years. A sum of $200,000 in government funds was awarded for moving the keeper's house, renovations to the lighthouse and oil house, and landscaping and maintenance of the site. On October 27, 1998, the house—a precarious 23 feet from the edge of the bluff—was moved to a new foundation near the lighthouse.

Ownership of the lighthouse passed to the Cape Cod National Seashore. A partnership agreement between the National Park Service and the Nauset Light Preservation Society was signed in May 2004. Under the agreement, the NLPS will continue to operate the lighthouse as a private aid to navigation and will be responsible for all maintenance of the tower and oil house.

The NLPS hired J. Goodison Company of East Providence, Rhode Island, to perform an exterior restoration of the tower. The entire exterior was sandblasted, seams were repaired and resealed, and leaks were fixed. The tower was repainted in its traditional color scheme using Wasser High Tech Coatings. Badly rusted handrails on the lantern gallery were replicated and replaced.

Under the leadership of its current president, Bud Griffin, and others, the NLPS continues to make improvements. The tower, with its Italianate detailing and unique color scheme, remains one of the most attractive cast-iron lighthouses on the coast.

Nauset Light is easily accessible by car, and the large Nauset Light Beach parking lot is close by. (In the summer, the Cape Cod National Seashore collects parking fees until 4:30 p.m. each day. Be prepared to pay to park if you arrive before 4:30 p.m.)

The Nauset Light Preservation Society holds lighthouse open houses from May through October. The tours are free, but donations are gladly accepted. For the schedule, check the Nauset Light Preservation Society's Web site at www.nausetlight.org.

For more information or to help with the ongoing preservation of Nauset Light, write to Nauset Light Preservation Society, P.O. Box 941, Eastham, MA 02642, or call (508) 240-2612.

The Three Sisters are accessible via a one-third-mile walking trail from the parking area at Nauset Light Beach. The National Park site is now open to the public and has rangers offering tours from spring to fall.

CHAPTER 29

Highland Light in July 2006. *Photo by the author.*

Highland Light

(Cape Cod Light)
1797, 1833, 1856

When Truro, the second most northerly town on Cape Cod, was first settled as Pamet in 1646, it was part of the larger area then called Nauset. Pamet's name was changed to Truro (after a Cornish town it was said to resemble) when it was incorporated as a separate town in 1709. Truro developed a whaling fleet based at Pamet River Harbor, which comprised nine sloops by the early 1800s.

In its early years, mariners knew Pamet as Dangerfield because of the frequent wrecks off its shores. A treacherous spot called Peaked Hill Bars, a graveyard for many ships, lies about a mile northeast of the lighthouse site. The 64-gun British warship *Somerset*, immortalized in Longfellow's poem *The Ride of Paul Revere*, famously struck the bars in 1778; 21 lives were lost.

In 1792, with these dangers in mind and ever-increasing maritime traffic around Cape Cod, the Massachusetts Humane Society and the Boston Marine Society requested that the governor of Massachusetts ask the U.S. Congress to fund a lighthouse "upon the High Land adjacent to Cape Cod Harbour." There was no immediate action.

Having no luck with their appeal to the governor, the Boston Marine Society appointed a committee of three men in 1796 to draft a petition directly to Congress. The Massachusetts Humane Society and the Salem Marine Society were also included in the petition sent to Congress in February 1796. The petition brought about almost immediate action.

Congress appropriated $8,000 for a lighthouse on May 17, 1796. Tench Coxe, commissioner of Revenue and supervisor of federal lighthouse operations at the time, asked Gen. Benjamin Lincoln—customs collector for Boston and local lighthouse superintendent—to procure a suitable site for the lighthouse by "gift or purchase."

Lincoln, who was also a founding member of the Massachusetts Humane Society, traveled to Cape Cod to select the site. It was the view of mariners that the lighthouse should be built on the Highlands or Clay Pounds of Truro, where the high bluffs—rising nearly 150 feet from the beach—would augment the height and visibility of the light.

Ten acres of land at the Highlands were purchased from a Truro resident, Isaac Small, for $110—$100 for the land and $10 for the "right of passing" over Small's adjoining land. The bluff wasn't the highest in the area, but it appears the deal was made with an eye toward Small's appointment as the light's first keeper.

Government officials knew that since Small already supported himself as a farmer on the adjacent property, he wouldn't be solely dependent on the meager lightkeeper's pay. In a letter Tench Coxe wrote, "The land bought for the site of the Light House was purchased of Mr. Small who owns the adjoining grounds. It is probable therefore, that economy in regard to fencing and salary may be made by appointing him." There were other applicants, but Small won the job.

A 45-foot octagonal wooden tower, the first lighthouse on Cape Cod, was built about 500 feet from the edge of the bluff, where it exhibited its light from 160 feet above mean high water. The light went into service on November 15, 1797.

The contractor who built the lighthouse was Theodore Lincoln, son of Benjamin Lincoln. This stirred a bit of controversy, but Coxe felt that Benjamin Lincoln's "integrity and candor" were beyond reproach. A one-story dwelling for the keeper, 25 by 27 feet, was also constructed, along with a barn, an oil storage shed, and a well. The total cost of the buildings was $7,257.56.

Because of fears that mariners might confuse Highland Light with Boston Light (a single fixed light at that time), some consideration was given to the possibility of a double light at the Cape Cod station. Instead, Lincoln and Coxe determined that the lighthouse would be the first in the nation to have a flashing light. A rotating "eclipser" was designed and built by James Bailey Jr. According to a notice that was issued to the press, the eclipser revolved around the spider lamp (a simple pan of oil with several wicks) once in 80 seconds, and the light would be hidden from view for 30 seconds during each revolution.

When the tower was inspected in December 1797, the lantern's copper dome was already leaky and 12 panes of glass in the lantern had broken because of the "leveling and srinking [sic]" of the wooden tower. Repairs were quickly completed.

The eclipser was also apparently not built well. The weather affected the clockwork machinery, and Small complained that the timing was irregular. The machinery didn't run as long as it was supposed to on a single winding, and Small was required to wind it twice each night. In recognition of this, in 1798 his salary was raised from $150 to $200 yearly.

The poor construction of the tower led to frequent problems. In 1809, Small reported that 12 panes of glass in the lantern had been broken by the wind. There were also complaints that the dim light was often obscured by water vapor rising up from the crashing surf below.

The eclipser continued to behave erratically. It was finally removed in 1812, when the lighthouse received a newly patented Winslow Lewis system of multiple Argand-type lamps and reflectors. The 1797 tower was in such poor condition—"wretchedly constructed," according to the local lighthouse superintendent—that it had to be greatly altered before the new equipment could be installed.

Before Lewis's lighting apparatus could be put into service, the height of the tower was reduced by 17 feet and a new lantern, 10 feet high, was installed. The new equipment was in use by February 1812. Boston Light became a revolving light in 1811, so there was no fear that the two would be hard to tell apart.

Isaac Small was soon complaining that the new lamps required "a great deal more attention and time to tend." Winslow Lewis, a tireless self-promoter who would furnish the lighting apparatus for American lighthouses for the next four decades, fought back in a letter to the superintendent, writing, "Mr. Small's various pursuits will not allow him to pay any attention to the Light House."

Constant Hopkins succeeded Small as keeper in October 1812. Hopkins, who was nearly 70 years old, was—not coincidentally—the brother of Michael Hopkins, an associate of Winslow Lewis in the Boston Marine Society. (Lewis had been a member of the society since 1797, and he would be its president in 1818–20.) Constant Hopkins died less than five years later and was succeeded by John Grocier (or Grozier).

Isaac Small continued farming on the adjacent land. Grocier complained about Small's obtrusive cattle, saying they "brake [sic] the ground up so that it blows away."

An 1828 report by Henry A. S. Dearborn, the local lighthouse super-intendent, stated that the wooden lighthouse was "very imperfect—is easily wracked by the winds, which shakes the lantern so much as to break the glass very frequently." The following year, Dearborn's successor, David Henshaw, recommended the construction of a new lighthouse to Stephen Pleasanton, the man in charge of lighthouses at the Treasury since 1820.

After a congressional appropriation of $5,000 in March 1831, a new 35-foot round brick lighthouse tower was erected close to the site of the original lighthouse. The lighthouse and a new brick dwelling, 26 by 28 feet, were built under contract by none other than Winslow Lewis, at a cost of $4,162. The date the work was completed isn't clear, but it was apparently sometime in 1833.

When Lt. Edward W. Carpender visited during his survey of 1838, there were 15 lamps in use, each with a 15-inch reflector, arranged in two circular series with seven lamps in the upper tier and eight below. Carpender recommended the removal of the reflectors, which blocked the light from the opposite lamps in the circular arrangement. Carpender was also critical of the keeper: "I visited this light a few minutes before sundown, and found the keeper (alarmed at the sight of the revenue cutter) stolen into his lantern to make a hasty rub-up against the expected visit. Time did not admit of the necessary preparations being made before the hour of lighting. But few of the lamps were trimmed. Such chimneys as had been touched were imperfectly cleaned."

In the early 1840s, Highland Light became a battleground between the old guard of lighthouse administration and technology—represented by Winslow Lewis and Stephen Pleasanton—and the new wave of reformers led by the civil engineer I. W. P. (Isaiah William Penn) Lewis, who happened to be Winslow Lewis's nephew.

I. W. P. Lewis had studied civil engineering and entered lighthouse work with the help and encouragement of his uncle. Eventually the two became competitors for lighthouse contracts, and the ambitious I. W. P. sometimes bid below his actual costs to win contracts over his uncle.

In the summer of 1840, the younger Lewis installed a new cast-iron lantern and lighting apparatus at Highland Light. He replaced his uncle's apparatus with a system of lamps and reflectors based on an English model. The lamps and reflectors were more carefully positioned and focused than they had been previously, and they were installed in such a way that they couldn't be easily moved out of proper alignment.

When he began the lantern installation, I. W. P. Lewis found that the tower's window frames, doorframes, and wooden stairs were all rotten and had to be replaced. He also found that the inner brick walls were laid without mortar and that the walls were filled with sand. The tower had no foundation and merely rested on the ground, and the mortar was so bad in the upper part of the tower that 13 feet had to be removed from the top.

I. W. P. Lewis had to rebuild substantially the tower his uncle had built in order to install the new lantern, at a total cost of $5,919. Pleasanton questioned the cost, claiming the work completed was similar in nature to the recent refitting of Delaware's Cape Henlopen Lighthouse at a cost of $3,600.

An inspection by the local superintendent in 1842 described the new apparatus as "in perfect order," showing a "brilliant light."

I. W. P. Lewis, at the request of the Secretary of the Treasury, authored a scathing 1843 report on New England's lighthouses. In the report, Lewis answered Pleasanton's charge that he had overspent at

Highland Light by saying, "The statement there made is not a fair exposition of the truth."

Jesse Holbrook, who became keeper in 1840 at a yearly salary of $350, provided a statement that supported I. W. P. Lewis's assertions regarding the tower and lighting apparatus. The statement was included in the 1843 report to Congress.

> When I took charge of this light, it was fitted with the common lantern, lamps, and reflectors, generally used in all American lights. One of the lamps faced exactly the copper door of the lantern, and the keeper whom I succeeded told me that had always been its position ever since the apparatus was set up. In the summer of 1840, the light-house was refitted with a new lantern of cast iron, glazed with large plate glass five feet by two feet square. . . . Since these improvements were made, the light has been very effective, as generally allowed by all the navigation of the neighborhood. The masters of the Truro and Provincetown packets, plying to Boston, tell me they can see this light and Boston light when half-way down the coast. The tower never has leaked, nor any part of the light-house or lantern, since refitted, and I have much less trouble in keeping the apparatus clean than with that which was removed. This arises from the perfect ventilation of the lantern.

I. W. P. Lewis's report eventually led to the formation of the new U.S. Lighthouse Board in 1852, two years after the death of Winslow Lewis. I. W. P. Lewis, who died in 1855 at the age of 47, has been called the father of American's modern lighthouse system.

Shipwrecks in the vicinity were less frequent after the establishment of the lighthouse, but they were not eliminated. One of the worst wrecks near the station was that of the British bark *Josephus* in a thick fog in April 1849. Two local fishermen went out in a dory in an attempt to aid the crew, but the would-be lifesavers themselves perished in the high seas. It appeared at first that the entire crew of 16 had died, but Keeper Enoch Hamilton returned hours after the wreck to find that two men had washed ashore and were still alive. Hamilton and a companion carried the men to the keeper's house, where they spent the night.

In his 1928 book, *Shipwrecks on Cape Cod*, Isaac Morton Small (grandson of Isaac Small and son of James Small, who also was a keeper) wrote of the *Josephus*, "The terrible circumstances attending the destruction of this ship were so vividly impressed upon my childish mind (I was four years old at the time) that they are as plain in memory as though they had occurred but yesterday." Small stood onshore holding his mother's hand as he watched the two brave fishermen, attempting to save those on the *Josephus*, vanish in the seething sea.

One of the survivors of the *Josephus*, John Jasper, later became the captain of an ocean liner. When his vessel passed Highland Light, he would dip the flag as a signal of respect for Keeper Hamilton.

The naturalist Henry David Thoreau visited Highland Light several times. His book *Cape Cod* combined descriptions from four separate visits to the Cape between 1849 and 1857. The keeper he described was apparently James Small, the son of the original landowner and lightkeeper, Isaac Small. Thoreau found the lighthouse "a neat building, in apple pie order." He wrote:

> *The Highland Light-house, where we were staying, is a substantial-looking building of brick, painted white, and surmounted by an iron cap. Attached to it is the dwelling of the keeper, one story high, also of brick, and built by government. As we were going to spend the night in a light-house, we wished to make the most of so novel an experience, and therefore told our host that we would like to accompany him when he went to light up. At rather early candle-light he lighted a small Japan lamp, allowing it to smoke rather more than we like on ordinary occasions, and told us to follow him. He led the way first through his bedroom, which was placed nearest to the light-house, and then through a long, narrow, covered passage-way, between whitewashed walls like a prison entry, into the lower part of the light-house, where many great butts of oil were arranged around; thence we ascended by a winding and open iron stairway, with a steadily increasing scent of oil and lamp-smoke, to a trap-door in an iron floor, and through this into the lantern. . . . We walked slowly round in that narrow space as the keeper lighted each lamp in succession, conversing with him at the same moment that many a sailor on the deep witnessed the lighting of the Highland Light. His duty was to fill and trim and light his lamps, and keep bright the reflectors. He filled them every morning, and trimmed them commonly once in the course of the night. . . . He spoke of the anxiety and sense of responsibility which he felt in cold and stormy nights in the winter; when he knew that many a poor fellow was depending on him, and his lamps burned dimly, the oil being chilled. Sometimes he was obliged to warm the oil in a kettle in his house at midnight, and fill his lamps over again,—for he could not have a fire in the light-house, it produced such a sweat on the windows. . . .*
>
> *Our host said that the frost, too, on the windows caused him much trouble, and in sultry summer nights the moths covered them and*

*dimmed his lights; sometimes even small birds flew against the thick
plate glass, and were found on the ground beneath in the morning
with their necks broken. . . .*

*The keeper entertained us handsomely in his solitary little ocean
house. He was a man of singular patience and intelligence, who, when
our queries struck him, rung as clear as a bell in response. The lighthouse lamps a few feet distant shone full into my chamber, and made
it as bright as day, so I knew exactly how the Highland Light bore all
that night, and I was in no danger of being wrecked. Unlike the last,
this was as still as a summer night. I thought as I lay there, half
awake and half asleep, looking upward through the window at the
lights above my head, how many sleepless eyes from far out on the
Ocean stream—mariners of all nations spinning their yarns through
the various watches of the night—were directed toward my couch.*

Thoreau also commented on the threat of erosion at the station,
which had been a worry as early as John Grocier's tenure as keeper.

*According to the light-house keeper, the Cape is wasting here on
both sides, though most on the eastern. In some places it had lost
many rods within the last year, and, erelong, the light-house must be
moved. We calculated, from his data, how soon the Cape would be
quite worn away at this point. . . .*

*Between this October and June of the next year, I found that the
bank had lost about forty feet in one place opposite the light-house,
and it was cracked more than forty feet farther from the edge at the
last date, the shore being strewn with the recent rubbish. But I judged
that generally it was not wearing away here at the rate of more than
six feet annually. . . .*

The newly formed Lighthouse Board asked for an appropriation
of $15,000 in 1852 to raise the height of the lighthouse and for the
addition of a first-order Fresnel lens. The funds were not immediately
forthcoming. For the next few years, there was also some discussion
of moving the lighthouse a mile or two, because it was "shut in by the
bluff to the south of it."

Congress appropriated $25,000 in 1854 for the "removal . . . to
a proper site" of the lighthouse at Truro and for the installation of a
steam-operated fog signal. There was even discussion that a relocated
light would make it possible to discontinue the Three Sisters lights
at Eastham, to the south. But rather than relocating the tower, it was
determined that a new, taller lighthouse would be built near the same
location.

An 1855 article in the *Barnstable Patriot,* written by a woman who spent time at the lighthouse with the keeper and his family, told of an incident in the 1833 dwelling built by Winslow Lewis: "We were all seated cozily for dinner . . . when just as the hostess had put her fork into as plump a fowl as ever crowed, there came a rattle, a crash, smash and a cloud of dust which rendered all on the opposite side of the table invisible to me. . . . I looked up and lo! The cause of the catastrophe! A part of the ceiling had fallen down over our devoted board and heads."

A fierce blizzard struck Cape Cod on January 5–6, 1856, doing further damage to the keeper's house. A desperately needed new dwelling was built later that year. A new 66-foot round brick lighthouse tower was built in the following year for $15,000, equipped with a first-order Fresnel lens from L. Sautter and Company of Paris. This powerful lens—about 10 feet high—made Highland Light one of the coast's most powerful lights. The light, the highest on the New England mainland, was for many years the first glimpse of America seen by many immigrants from Europe.

The station also received a coal-burning Daboll fog signal, powerful enough to cut through the frequent thick fog. With the added duties related to the fog signal, the station was assigned two assistant keepers. An additional duplex dwelling was added for the assistants and their families in 1857.

A marine recording station was established at the light station (originally in a room in the keeper's house, and later in a separate building) by 1855, with a telegraph line connecting the station to Boston. An operator would scan the sea with a telescope and record the name of every vessel passing the Cape. The operator telegraphed the information to Boston.

Isaac Morton Small became the marine observer in 1861, at the age of 16. In 1891 Isaac Morton Small wrote a booklet called *Highland Light: This Book Tells You All about It.* The publication described the daily life of the keepers:

> *The routine of their duties is regular and systematic. Promptly, one half hour before sunset the keeper whose watch it may be at the time repairs to the tower and makes preparations for the lighting of the lamps. At the moment the sun drops below the western horizon the light flashes out over the sea; the little cog wheels begin their revolutions; the tiny pumps force the oil up to the wicks and the night watch has begun. At 8 o'clock the man who has lighted the lamp is relieved by No. 2, who in turn is also relieved at midnight by*

No. 3, No. 1 again returning to duty at 4 a.m. As the sun shows its first gleam above the edge of the eastern sea the machinery is stopped and the light is allowed to gradually consume the oil remaining in the wicks and go out. This occurs in about fifteen minutes. As night comes on again No. 2 is the man to light the lamp, the watches are changed at 8, 12 and 4, and so go on as before night after night.

Small also made a plea on behalf of the keepers:

It is written somewhere that keepers must not accept tips from people who visit the light, but of course it does not really mean that, but should be understood that keepers should not solicit tips. When you have climbed to the top floor of that winding stair, and then have reached the ground again, and you are pretty nearly out of breath and exclaim, "My, but that was some climb," you would appreciate the feelings and condition of the keeper who had gone up and down some twenty times during the day. No law requires them to do this, but out of courtesy and your enjoyment they make the trips. Think it over and decide whether you would like to change places with them.

One of the worst storms in New England history struck on November 26, 1898. The storm was later dubbed the "Portland Gale" after the steamer *Portland,* lost with nearly 200 passengers in Massachusetts Bay. At about 10:00 p.m. on the night of the storm, the wind indicator at Highland Light was demolished when wind speeds reached more than 100 miles per hour. A short time later, the windows in the lantern were blown out and the light went out. The storm lasted 36 hours, and wreckage from the *Portland* later washed up along Cape Cod's Atlantic shore. It was a common belief for many years that the wreck of the *Portland* lay near Truro, but the remains were eventually found farther offshore, about midway between Gloucester and Provincetown.

A new first-order Fresnel lens, about 12 feet high and 9 feet in diameter and rotating on 300 pounds of mercury, was installed in 1901 after an appropriation of $15,000, while Stephen D. Rich was keeper. The light was changed from fixed to flashing (a half-second flash every five seconds) to make it more easily identifiable. A temporary light was displayed from an adjacent skeleton tower while the lens was installed. The new lens went into service in October 1901. "Through the darkness," reported the *Boston Globe,* "its beams appear like flashes of lightning in a tempest."

A wireless telegraph station was located at Highland Light in 1904. The station assumed great importance during World War I and was guarded by a detachment of Marines.

William A. Joseph was apparently the keeper referred to simply as "Bill" in a 1921 article in the *Boston Globe*. It seems he had formerly been a train conductor. Growing tired of constant contact with the public, he imagined that a lighthouse-keeping job would give him the solitude he sought. But Highland Light, being a popular tourist attraction, was not what he had in mind. "Bill's life now is one long business of guiding young women up the narrow stairs of the lighthouse," reported the *Globe*, "and explaining to them what it is that makes the wheels go round."

Joseph became the principal keeper in 1923, and he remained in the position until 1947. Probably to Joseph's consternation, a total of 9,517 visitors toured the lighthouse in 1929.

After its conversion to electricity in 1932, the light became the coast's most powerful, at 4 million candlepower. The giant lens was removed in the early 1950s, replaced by modern aerobeacons. The Fresnel lens was destroyed when it was removed, but a fragment of the lens is now on display in the museum at the lighthouse.

Bernie Webber became an assistant keeper under the Coast Guard in April 1946. Bill Joseph sternly informed Webber that the lens had to be covered during the day and the shades in the lantern positively had to be pulled down. If this wasn't done, it was feared that the sun shining through the powerful lens could start fires (a myth). Another thing that made a strong impression on Webber was the foghorn, which could be felt as well as heard. A milk bottle placed on the bluff in front of the horns "would be blown to smithereens" from the blast.

In 1961 the Coast Guard destroyed the assistant keeper's house and replaced it with a modern duplex. The Coast Guard's officer in charge at the time of a 1976 article was Charles Johnson, a native of Springfield, Massachusetts. Johnson reported that the bluff was continuing to erode at the rate of about three feet per year.

The officer in charge from 1978 to 1982 was Petty Officer First Class A. G. "Sandy" Lyle, who moved in with his wife, Jan, and their three children. "It's one of the best pieces of real estate on Cape Cod," said Jan Lyle of the light station, "and we're lucky to be able to borrow it." Her seven-year-old daughter, Christa, added, "My favorite part is going up to the tippy-top of the lighthouse."

The station had a succession of fog signals dating back to 1873, when a first-class Daboll trumpet was established. Lyle activated the

Spectators enjoy a baseball game near Highland Light Station in the early 1900s. *From the collection of Edward Rowe Snow, courtesy of Dorothy Snow Bicknell.*

foghorn when poor visibility prevented him from seeing Province-town's Pilgrim Monument or the Peaked Hill buoy.

Newly married, 21-year-old Chris Ordway moved to the light station in late 1982 with his wife, Laurie. "Every morning," said Chris, "I go out and raise the flag. I look around and breathe the air, and I just realize how lucky we are. Do you know how many people would pay a lot of money to live in a house like this?"

The light's last official keeper was Seaman Patrick Prunty. The biggest drawback of lighthouse life, he said, was the fact that the station was a stop for every tour bus and car full of tourists on Cape Cod. "They knock on the door at two o'clock in the morning and ask, 'Where's the soda machine?'" he said.

When asked for a 1986 article if they had experienced anything unusual at the station, Prunty's wife, Katherine, said they had heard a woman's voice in the keeper's house on two occasions. "It was definitely a lady's voice," she said. "She was talking really fast. In the kitchen, just below the bedroom. I jumped up—the doors were locked."

Patrick Prunty added that on one occasion he was painting inside the tower by himself and left a plugged-in radio playing. There was nobody else around, but when he returned the next morning, the radio had been mysteriously unplugged and smashed on the ground below.

The light was automated in 1986, and Prunty moved to nearby Orleans with his wife, their two children, and their black Labrador retriever named Highland Nor'easter. The station's radio beacon remained in service and the keeper's dwelling remained in use as Coast Guard housing.

When the first lighthouse was built in 1797, it was over 500 feet from the edge of the cliff. By 1885 the distance had shrunk to 336 feet. The bluff continued to erode until, by the early 1990s, the lighthouse stood about 112 feet from the edge. In 1990 alone, 40 feet were lost just north of the lighthouse.

In 1988 the Army Corps of Engineers determined that the most cost-effective way to save the lighthouse would be to move it. Experts said that 100 feet of space would be needed to bring in heavy equipment that would be needed to relocate the tower. Recognizing the desperateness of the situation, a group within the Truro Historical Society began raising funds for the move. In 1991 Congressman Gerry Studds secured legislation requiring that the Coast Guard develop a strategy for saving the lighthouse. The following year, the Coast Guard and Cape Cod National Seashore issued a joint proposal for the relocation of the tower and its development as a public resource in its new location.

Gordon Russell, president of both the Truro Historical Society and the Save the Light Committee, with other volunteers, sent out 30,000 brochures and collected 140,000 signatures on a petition. Bob Firminger, vice chairman of the lighthouse committee and treasurer of the historical society, was another prime catalyst of the project. Local residents and tourists made donations and bought T-shirts and other souvenirs from a trailer near the lighthouse, and the society raised over $180,000.

In 1996 the funds raised by the historical society were combined with $1 million in federal funds and $500,000 in state funds to pay for the move of the 404-ton lighthouse to a site 450 feet back from its former location. The town of Truro donated land for the relocation. The modern duplex dwelling at the station was donated by the Coast Guard to the town and was relocated before the lighthouse move began.

The operation got under way in June 1996, under the direction of International Chimney Corporation of Buffalo, with the help of Expert House Moving of Maryland, the same companies responsible for the successful move of Block Island Southeast Light in 1993. Thousands of sightseers gathered to catch a glimpse of the rare event.

First, a cement floor in the lighthouse was removed and cracks in the walls were patched. The tower has three brick walls with air spaces between them; the spaces in the lower three feet of the tower were filled with grout. The foundation of the lighthouse was excavated, and holes were cut in the masonry for the insertion of support beams and grillage. The steel support beams were themselves supported by duplex beams known as mains.

The entire structure was lifted with a series of 60-ton hydraulic jacks using the Unified Lifting System, which allows for pressure to be placed evenly on the jacks. Once lifted, the tower was mounted on roll beams supported by wooden cribbing. Hydraulic push jacks between the roll beams and the main beams were activated, which pushed the lighthouse along on roller dollies. Each time the tower was moved about five feet, the push jacks had to be repositioned.

A challenge was presented by a 10-foot drop in grade along the relocation route. The problem was solved by the use of a secondary set of jacks in the main beams, which were activated in unison and suspended the tower while roll beams were lowered to compensate for the drop in grade. The lighthouse was lowered in increments and placed on the newly set roll beams.

The relocation was accomplished in 18 days without a hitch. The relocated lighthouse stands close to the seventh fairway of the Highland Golf Links, which has prompted some to declare it the world's first life-sized miniature golf course. "We'll get a windmill from Eastham and put it on number one," the club's greenskeeper joked. After an errant golf ball broke a pane in the lantern room, new, unbreakable panes were installed.

On Sunday, November 3, 1996, Highland Light was relighted in its new location. In the summer of 1998, the lighthouse was opened for visitors; volunteers provided tours. There are now historical exhibits and a gift shop in the keeper's house. Highland Museum and Lighthouse operates the site under a National Park Service concession contract.

The lighthouse got a needed facelift in April 2001. The job, performed by Campbell Construction of Beverly, Massachusetts, entailed sandblasting the lead paint from the interior of the lantern and the tower's stairs, the removal of rust from the exterior ironwork, and the replacement of some railing sections and rusted iron panels. Some cracks in the ironwork were repaired. A new window was installed, and some of the brickwork on the ocean-facing side of the tower was replaced.

The interiors of the lantern and the stairs were repainted, as was the entire exterior of the tower. In addition, a new ventilation system was installed, making visits to the top more comfortable in summer.

☀ **Highland Light is easily accessible off Route 6 in North Truro. The lighthouse is open daily, mid-May through October. You can also visit the nearby Highland House Museum, in a former summer hotel that was once owned by Isaac Morton Small. For more information or to contribute to the ongoing preservation of Highland Light, write to Truro Historical Society, P.O. Box 486, Truro, MA 02666, call (508) 487-3397, or visit www.trurohistorical.org. For information on visiting the lighthouse, call Highland Museum and Lighthouse, Inc., (508) 487-1121.**

CHAPTER 30

Race Point Light in May 2004. *Photo by the author.*

Race Point Light

1816, 1876

Race Point's name comes from the strong crosscurrent, known as a "race," that made navigation around the terminus of Cape Cod a nightmare for mariners. Before the construction of the Cape Cod Canal in 1914, every vessel traveling along the coast between Boston and points south had to negotiate the treacherous bars here. As early as 1808, the merchants and mariners of Provincetown asked for a lighthouse at Race Point.

Funding for a light station was included in a congressional appropriation of $8,000 on April 27, 1816; the same appropriation funded Point Gammon Light in Hyannis on Cape Cod and Petit Manan Light in Maine. Henry A. S. Dearborn, superintendent of lighthouses of Massachusetts, issued a request for bids for the building of the station in July 1816. The original specifications called for an octagonal wooden tower, 20 feet tall, but the plans were soon altered.

A lighthouse at Race Point, Cape Cod's third light station, after Highland Light in Truro and Chatham's twin lights, went into service on November 5, 1816. The rubblestone tower was 25 feet tall and its light was 30 feet above the sea. The tower was joined to the small stone dwelling via a covered passageway connected to the kitchen.

Lt. Edward W. Carpender visited Race Point during his 1838 survey. Recognizing the light's importance, he recommended no reduction in the system of 10 lamps and 13-inch reflectors. It was one of the nation's earliest revolving lights, the result of an attempt to differentiate it from other lighthouses in the vicinity.

Around this time, a sizable fishing community and a saltworks grew up around nearby Herring Cove. The little community, known as "Helltown," was even declared a separate school district in the 1830s. The settlement dwindled later in the nineteenth century.

A tremendous storm swept Cape Cod on October 2, 1841. Provincetown's neighbor, Truro, lost seven vessels and 57 men in the storm. Only two crews from Truro survived. Capt. Matthias Rich, after 12 hours lashed to the wheel, managed to bring his schooner, *Water Witch*, into Herring Cove near Race Point.

Race Point Light Station, circa 1870s, showing the first (1816) lighthouse tower. *National Archives photo.*

I. W. P. Lewis visited the station for his important survey in 1842, when Elijah Dyer was the keeper. Lewis recognized the light's importance, but he found reason to be critical:

> *The light is useful to all vessels leaving Boston, and bound to the eastward, or round the cape, through the South channel; and also as a point of departure for Provincetown harbor, as well as Boston. Its illuminating power is, however, so weak that when a fleet of fishermen are anchored in Herring cove, close by, a stranger would hardly be able to distinguish it from the lights set on board these vessels. A reciprocating light of one good lamp and suitable reflector would be much more efficient than the present apparatus with ten lamps.*

I. W. P. Lewis's uncle Winslow Lewis had devised the lighting system of multiple lamps and reflectors. The younger Lewis reported that the tower was leaky and had no foundation, three panes of glass in the lantern were broken, and the reflectors were out of proper alignment. The keeper's house, he said, was "in very good repair, and most neatly kept."

Another inspection by the local lighthouse superintendent in 1842 noted that the keeper desperately needed a new boat, as the old one "would not withstand a rough sea five minutes." A sum of $65 was requested for a new boat.

There were still 10 lamps in use at the time of an 1850 inspection, when Samuel Cook was keeper. The clockwork mechanism that rotated the lighting apparatus was still running, and everything was "in good order."

A fog bell was installed in 1852. Then, three years later, a fourth-order Fresnel lens replaced the old multiple lamps and reflectors. The 1863 annual report of the Lighthouse Board detailed plenty of activity: "tower partly taken down and rebuilt, new lantern provided, woodwork renewed, kitchen lathed, plastered and newly floored, roofs repaired, chimneys partly rebuilt, grounds graded, &c., fog-bell removed to a position near the dwelling."

In 1873 the bell was replaced by a steam-driven fog signal housed in a new wood-frame building, 12 by 24 feet. With the added duties of tending the fog signal equipment, a second dwelling was built for an assistant keeper in 1874.

The Lighthouse Board's annual report for 1875 described some severe problems: "The tower at this station was originally built of rubble-stone, laid in common lime mortar. The lime disappeared, and the tower became so leaky that it was necessary to cover it with shingles. The shingles are now rotten, as are also the wooden stairs inside, and the tower is so dilapidated that it is necessary to rebuild it. Extensive repairs are also required on the keeper's dwelling."

The needed funds were appropriated, and in 1876 a 45-foot brick-lined cast-iron lighthouse replaced the old stone tower at a cost of $2,800. The new tower is a typical example of a number of cast-iron towers built in the 1870s and 1880s; the design is attributed to Gen. James Chatham Duane, a Lighthouse Board engineer. The Fresnel lens was moved to the new tower and the characteristic was changed from a flashing to a fixed white light. The original keeper's house was torn down around the same time, and a new dwelling was built. A new rainwater cistern was added in 1877.

A kerosene-fed incandescent oil-vapor lamp was installed in 1930. Four years later, the *New Bedford Standard-Times* published an article on the station and its three keepers. William H. Lowther had been the principal keeper since 1915. Lowther had entered the Lighthouse Service as a crewman on the tender *Mayflower* in 1906, and before coming to Cape Cod he had been stationed at Thacher Island off Cape Ann and the Narrows Light in Boston Harbor. Lowther lived at the station with his wife and

Race Point Light Station in the late 1800s. *From the collection of Edward Rowe Snow, courtesy of Dorothy Snow Bicknell.*

their young son, Gerald. Gerald Lowther later recalled his arduous walk of more than two miles on the beach to school each day.

Lowther and his wife lived in Provincetown after retirement. In a 1936 article, Mrs. Lowther said that she saw many wrecks in her years at lighthouses, but there was one that especially affected her at Race Point. "Two men were drowned," she recalled. "I saw everything: the appeals of the men and the shouting and the screeching of the men at the light was so terrible it was in my ears for weeks afterward. I had to go away from the light for a week."

The first assistant keeper at the time of the 1934 article was the Barnstable native James W. Hinckley, who had been at Race Point since 1920. The second assistant was Javan D. York, a veteran of the old Revenue Cutter Service.

In *Famous Lighthouses of New England,* Edward Rowe Snow wrote that Hinckley often carried 15 pounds of groceries from town across the long stretch of soft sand to the light station. He eventually took to riding a horse back and forth to town. In the 1930s, after he succeeded Lowther as principal keeper, Hinckley made the trip much quicker by customizing a Ford into an early dune buggy. The trip that had taken 75 minutes on horseback was shortened to 30 minutes.

Race Point is one of the windiest places on the coast. Snow quoted Hinckley: "The wind often touches a mile a minute. Some of the gusts will blow you several feet, and it's hard going. The sand is bad enough, cutting into your skin, but a combination of sand and snow is almost unbearable."

On the occasion of his retirement on Christmas Day 1937, at the age of 70, Keeper Hinckley expressed the opinion that the government should pay a pension to lighthouse keepers' wives, who "do just as much as the men."

In his 1946 book, *A Pilgrim Returns to Cape Cod,* Snow described a visit with Keeper Osborne Hallett, who was in charge from 1945 to 1955. Over coffee and crackers, Snow and Hallett discussed the wreck of the *Monte Tabor,* which had occurred near Race Point on April 9, 1896. The Sicilian bark was carrying a cargo of salt when it ran into a tremendous storm off Cape Cod. The captain, intending to enter Provincetown Harbor, made a fatal miscalculation and ran right into the Peaked Hill Bars. Surfmen from the local lifesaving stations tried to go to the crew's aid, but the vessel broke apart. Six crewmen soon drifted in on the bark's cabin and were rescued.

The next day, an Italian boy from the crew was found hiding in the bushes near the shore. He told his discoverers that he was afraid he would be killed if discovered; that was what happened to shipwreck

Osborne Hallett was keeper 1945–55. He's seen here with his niece Anne and her mother, circa 1945. *Courtesy of Anne Ames.*

victims on Cape Cod, he had heard. A short time later, the vessel's captain and two crewmembers were found dead, and it was learned they had committed suicide. The captain could not live with the disgrace of causing the *Monte Tabor* to be wrecked, and the two crewmen had apparently followed suit out of loyalty.

Clifton S. Morong arrived as a Coast Guard assistant keeper shortly after World War II. His wife, Shirley, recalled life at Race Point in a 1998 article:

> Water was obtained from a pump connected to a cistern in the basement. The small outside toilet was perched on the side of a sand dune behind the house. A refrigerator was operated by a kerosene powered lamp. . . .
>
> The Coast Guard furnished the station with a jeep that had sand tires. We needed transportation to the boys' school in Provincetown. . . .
>
> For amusement we walked the beach during the day and read at night. Watches were divided by the three crew members.

The Morongs were eventually able to move to the other side of the duplex assistant keepers' house, which was equipped with a full bath. Their frequent beachcombing often led the family to find remnants of old shipwrecks, including a time when the children found a human leg bone in the sand.

The light was converted to electricity in 1957. Three years later, the duplex assistant keepers' house was torn down and the other house was modernized. In its last years as a staffed light station, Race Point was home to a single Coast Guard family.

The Coast Guard's officer in charge in the early 1970s was Thomas Branco, who lived at Race Point with his wife, Charlotte, and their five children. Having one child in kindergarten and the others in older grades meant three round trips to town every day. Years later, the Brancos' daughter Tracy said that a tour operator often brought visitors to see the lighthouse. "He'd drive up and say, 'This is where you'll see the little savages,'" she recalled.

The Brancos had some hardships at the remote station, but the children enjoyed helping to keep the station clean. And they especially enjoyed the gift drops by the "Flying Santa," Edward Rowe Snow, even though the presents usually landed in a thicket of rose bushes. The Branco children cried when it came time to move away, and some of them hid in a cupboard, not wanting to leave. The Brancos went on to live at Highland Light, West Chop Light, and Chatham Light. Thomas Branco retired in 1986.

The light was automated in 1972. The crew of the Coast Guard cutter *Bittersweet* did some maintenance in July 1987; they painted the tower's exterior and replaced some eaves and a porch on the keeper's house. During this period, roving vandals would frequently kick in the cellar door so they could party inside the house.

In 1995 the station was leased to the New England Lighthouse Foundation (now known as the American Lighthouse Foundation). Jim Walker, who became the chairman of the Cape Cod Chapter of the American Lighthouse Foundation (ALF), was a former Coast Guard employee who had been in charge of the crew that closed the station in 1972.

International Chimney Corporation, the same company that has moved three New England lighthouses, repaired the roof of the keeper's house and rebuilt the chimney. Richard Davidson, a contractor from Onset, also did a great deal of work on the house.

Volunteers renovated the interior, and the five-bedroom keeper's house was soon opened for overnight stays. The building now has heat, hot water, flush toilets, refrigeration and a gas stove. Guests must bring their own bedding, and the kitchen is shared with other guests.

Jim Walker reported a mystery in 1996. An American flag appeared on a temporary flagpole, put there by an unknown benefactor. The volunteers took the flag in for the winter and put it out again in spring. It was shredded in a storm, but again, a new flag mysteriously took its place. Walker was grateful to the unknown donor.

The Center for Coastal Studies, a marine mammal research and educational group, leased the fog-signal building. After a $45,000 renovation, the building was dedicated as their new field station in June 1999. The station has also been used for research by the National Seashore and the Cape Cod Museum of Natural History.

Funds were raised in recent years for the installation of a solar electrical system for the keeper's house. Completed and dedicated in October 2003, the system supplemented a diesel-engine electrical generating system. On-site demonstrations show schoolchildren and other visitors how solar power can supply electric energy to the

The restored Race Point lighthouse and keeper's house in May 2004.
Photo by the author.

average family home. At this writing, a wind turbine is being installed to supply additional energy.

A replica door in the tower installed in 2002 was made from wood cut in the same year that the tower was built. Restoration is ongoing, and funds raised through the overnight stays at Race Point have also helped pay for work at other lighthouses cared for by the American Lighthouse Foundation.

Concern over nesting piping plovers on the beach has recently had an effect on access to the station, but the American Lighthouse Foundation and its Cape Cod chapter are working closely with the Cape Cod National Seashore to make sure the overnight stays are disrupted as little as possible.

The light remains an active navigational aid maintained by the Coast Guard, with a solar-powered VRB-25 optic exhibiting a white flash every 10 seconds.

You can park at Race Point Beach and walk about 45 minutes (a little over two miles in very soft sand) to the lighthouse. Sunset at Race Point Beach is one of the Cape's most popular spectacles, and at times humpback whales can be seen from the beach.

For more information on overnight stays and public open houses, write to Race Point Lighthouse, P.O. Box 570, North Truro, MA 02652, call (508) 487-9930, or visit www.racepointlighthouse.net. You can also find out more on the American Lighthouse Foundation Web site at www. lighthousefoundation.org.

CHAPTER 31

Wood End Light in 2001. *Photo by the author.*

Wood End Light

1872

In his book *Cape Cod*, Henry David Thoreau described the harbor at Provincetown, at the tip of Cape Cod. "It opens to the south," he wrote, "is free of rocks, and is never frozen over. . . . It is the harbor of the Cape and of the fishermen of Massachusetts generally." The first two lighthouses in the vicinity, at Race Point and Long Point, were established by 1826. By the 1860s, it was determined that another aid was needed at Wood End, the southernmost extremity of the curving spit of land that protected the harbor.

A white pyramidal day beacon was first erected at Wood End—about a mile from Long Point—in 1864. The decision to establish a light station might have been prompted in part by the wreck of a schooner, the *William H. Atwood* of Wellfleet, near Wood End in November 1871. Congress appropriated $15,000 for a lighthouse on June 10, 1872.

A 38-foot brick tower—originally painted brown—was erected, and the light went into service on November 20, 1872. The square tower, a little over 14 feet wide on each side and topped by a 10-sided, cast-iron lantern, is nearly identical to the second (1875) tower at Long Point. A fifth-order Fresnel lens exhibited a red flash every 15 seconds, 45 feet above the sea. A keeper's dwelling was built about 50 feet northeast of the lighthouse. The first keeper, Thomas Lowe, remained at the station for 25 years.

An 1889 article in the *Boston Globe* described a visit with Keeper Lowe and his wife. Lowe demonstrated for the visiting writer the workings of the clockwork mechanism that rotated the lens. After he lighted the lamp for the night, the party went to the "cozy sitting room" in the keeper's house and Lowe described his interesting pre-keeper life. He had first shipped out as a boy on a fishing schooner from Wellfleet, and he later joined the navy and saw action on the frigate *Ohio* in the Mexican War.

Lowe's travels took him to Sutter's Mill in California at the outset of the Gold Rush in 1849. He had varied success as a prospector, and during this period he took part in the rescue of a party of snowbound settlers. After some time spent farming in southern California, Lowe became a crewman on a clipper ship. Health problems led him to seek employment as a lighthouse keeper.

In spite of the three lighthouses around Provincetown, wrecks still occurred with some regularity. Lowe occasionally had to make hasty trips to town to awaken sleeping citizens to help with the rescue of shipwreck victims. A lifesaving station had been established at Race Point in 1872, and one was finally added at Wood End in 1896, a short distance east of the light station.

In 1896 a new one-and-a-half-story wood-frame keeper's house was built, along with a storage shed and a small brick oil house for the storage of kerosene. New machinery for the revolving lens was installed in 1900. Two years later, a 1,000-pound fog bell and bell tower were added near the lighthouse. Automatic striking machinery enabled the sounding of the bell every 15 seconds.

Eight days before Christmas in 1927, the U.S. Navy submarine *S-4* and the Coast Guard cutter *Paulding* collided a half mile south of Wood End. The submarine was left disabled approximately 100 feet below the surface. About 24 hours later, a diver made contact with six men who were still alive inside the vessel. But heavy weather and the lack of proper equipment hindered the rescue effort, and all 40 men on the *S-4* died. The *S-4* was raised three months later and was used to help devise greater safety measures for future submarines.

During a stretch of severe cold in February 1935, Keeper Douglas Shepherd was marooned at the light station for weeks. The *Boston Globe* reported:

> *Keeper Douglas H. Shepherd of the lonely Wood End Light, on the far-off shore opposite this town, has been ice-bound and imprisoned at his station the past two weeks. He depends upon the Coast Guard to ferry his supplies and mail across the harbor, since it is impossible for him to come into town in his car, owing to the "miniature icebergs" piled all along his route. . . . Keeper Shepherd has struggled vainly to break through the arctic expanse that extends for miles beyond his light. Several times he has attempted it, using axe and crowbar to attack the ice blocks in his path, but each time he has been forced to turn back.*

Ordinarily, Shepherd made a daily trip into town. He had no worries, despite his isolation, as the Coast Guard kept him in touch with the mainland.

James Hinkley Dobbins served as a relief keeper for a period in 1937. His wife, Ruby Kelley Dobbins, and their daughter, Harriet, didn't live at the station. Ruby Kelley Dobbins recalled in her book

A fog-bell tower was added to Wood End Light Station in 1902. *From the collection of Edward Rowe Snow, courtesy of Dorothy Snow Bicknell.*

The Additional Keeper that her husband gave her explicit instructions to "buy all the mousetraps in stock" at a local hardware store before she came for her first visit; the keeper's house was overrun with mice. The Dobbins family had some time for sightseeing in Provincetown and especially enjoyed the traditional town crier, ringing his brass bell and shouting the news of the day.

The light was automated in 1961, and all the buildings except the lighthouse and oil house were destroyed. A new fifth-order lens had replaced the original lens in 1916; that was replaced by a modern optic when the light was automated. The light was converted to solar power in late 1981, making it one of the nation's earliest solar-powered lighthouses. Today a VRB-25 optic exhibits a red flash every 10 seconds.

The Coast Guard licensed the American Lighthouse Foundation (ALF) in 1998 to maintain Wood End Light. Volunteers from ALF painted the tower and reroofed the oil house. The painting of Wood End Light and Long Point Light took eight volunteers two days—and "a lot of cold Coke and hot dogs," according to ALF's Cape Cod Chapter chairman, Jim Walker—to complete. At this writing, there are plans for a volunteer work party to repaint the tower in spring 2007.

You can walk to Wood End across a granite breakwater built in 1911, but waves sometime make the going tricky at high tide. It's a fairly strenuous walk of 30 to 45 minutes each way to the lighthouse. There are limited parking spaces available near the start of the walk, which is an additional walk of around 20 to 30 minutes from the center of Provincetown.

A company called Flyer's runs a seasonal shuttle boat from the Provincetown waterfront to Long Point; from there it is possible to hike to Wood End. See www.flyersrentals.com or call (508) 487-0898.

The lighthouse is also viewable from some of the excursion boats out of Provincetown.

For more information or to donate to the restoration of Wood End Light, write to American Lighthouse Foundation, P. O. Box 565, Rockland, ME 04841, or see www.lighthousefoundation.org.

Long Point Light in 1999. *Photo by the author.*

The 1826 building continued to deteriorate. The contours of the beach that surrounded the lighthouse had changed, leaving it more exposed and vulnerable. In 1873 the Lighthouse Board reported that "a new dwelling is a necessity. . . . the entire structure is in danger of being carried off by a heavy storm." Congress appropriated $13,000 on June 23, 1874, for a new tower, keeper's dwelling, and fog signal.

A square brick lighthouse, 38 feet high, and a one-and-a-half-story wood-frame keeper's house were built in 1875. The lantern held a fifth-order Fresnel lens showing a fixed white light. A 1,200-pound fog bell was also installed at this time on a tower erected north of the lighthouse, along with striking machinery.

The settlement at Long Point had shrunk considerably, but this unusual statement appeared in the 1880 annual report of the Lighthouse Board, while Dunham was keeper: "The keepers have been much annoyed by the stench and flies coming from the fish-oil works located near-by."

Storms in late 1898 and early 1899 washed away much land near the lighthouse, threatening to turn Long Point into an island. The storm of November 26–27, 1898, would be remembered as the Portland Gale because of the sinking of the steamer *Portland* in Massachusetts Bay with the loss of nearly 200 people. Keeper Samuel Soper Smith, who had been at the station since 1888, described the storm to the *Boston Globe* in an 1899 article:

> It looked as if we would be swept away. The buildings shook and cracked ominously under the push of the hurricane, but the greatest danger facing us was that of the waves.
>
> The air was full of water—salt water, blown like fog from the crests of the seas, and this spray, lifted on the north side of the point, blew clear over the land to mingle with the seas on the other side.
>
> The whole scene was white with foam. When the waves struck the rocks around us they burst and fell in sheets away above the breakwater and fairly scooped down the banks of sand as they retreated.

The station's fog bell ran by means of a striking mechanism that had to be hand-wound every few hours. Keeper Smith continued:

> I was sick at the time, the wash of the sea was up around our dwelling and the wind was blowing so fiercely that I doubted my ability to reach the bellhouse. But it had to ring!
>
> I started for the bell tower and reached the raised platform at its base. As I reached it a wave struck me in the breast and hurled me backward. Next minute, however, I climbed to the platform and into

the machinery building and wound it up.

The tide kept rising until at last it was four feet deep all around the house. My wife and a lady friend expressed their fear that our house would be swept away.

I pointed to our outside water tank, an immense cask, nearly filled with fresh water, weighing a ton at least, which stood under the eaves and told them that they need not fear as long as it remained there.

Just as I spoke it lifted, and next minute went around the corner of the house, upright, and it was carried around the sand battery, out of sight to the westward.

The house survived, but parts of the protective breakwater were toppled. The boathouse was stripped of shingles, the cistern was filled with salt water, wooden walkways were swept away, and a woodshed was destroyed. The Portland Gale devastated Provincetown's fishing fleet and destroyed wharves, saltworks, and windmills. The era of Provincetown as a major fishing port had passed, and its day as a resort and arts center was dawning.

The 1899 *Globe* article described the heroism of Keeper Smith's wife during another storm. The keeper was ill on this occasion also, and his wife wouldn't let him leave the house. At the height of the gale, the fog bell stopped working. Mrs. Smith knew that the mechanism's bearings needed oiling. To apply the oil, she had to climb a ladder outside the bell tower to a point about 25 feet above the ground, as the wind howled around her. "With hair and clothing streaming," wrote the *Globe* reporter, "with muscles swelling under the strain, she dragged herself by degrees aloft and applied the oil, with hand wellnigh frozen." The bell was soon sounding its warning again.

In the early 1930s, Keeper A. G. "Ted" Haskins lived at the lighthouse with his wife and three daughters. The Haskins family kept the light station looking attractive, with a garden of dahlias and poppies in the summer.

Their nine-year-old daughter, Mary, had to be taken each morning in a 36-foot powerboat to Provincetown's West End, more than a mile away, where she attended school. The trip was treacherous in rough weather, but the *Globe* reported in February 1932 that Mary had not missed a day of school that year. "The little lighthouse girl must arise at 6 a.m. to have time for breakfast," said the *Globe*, "and get in readiness for her long trip."

In 1933, during one of the common thick fogs in the area, the mechanism that rang the station's fog bell broke down. Keeper

Early-1900s postcard of Long Point Light Station.
From the collection of the author.

Thomas L. Chase rang the bell by hand for over nine hours straight, pulling the rope with his right hand every 30 seconds. After a few hours of sleep he had to sound the bell for several more hours, this time with his left hand.

The fog eventually thinned, but Keeper Chase later said he was prepared to tie the rope to his legs to keep it going if necessary. He said he felt like "a baseball pitcher who has twirled a couple of doubleheaders without rest."

The light was automated in 1952, and the fourth-order Fresnel lens, which had replaced the earlier lens in 1927, was replaced by a modern optic. In 1981 solar panels were installed.

The Cape Cod Chapter of the American Lighthouse Foundation (ALF) has been licensed by the Coast Guard to restore and maintain the lighthouse. The keeper's house and fog-signal building were razed years ago, but the lighthouse remains an active aid to navigation, with a fixed green light and an automated fog signal.

For more information or to donate to the restoration of Long Point Light, write to the American Lighthouse Foundation, P.O. Box 565, Rockland, ME 04841, or visit www.lighthousefoundation.org.

You can see the lighthouse distantly from MacMillan Wharf in Provincetown, and you can walk to it (if you're in good shape) from the town's West End after crossing a breakwater to Wood End at low tide. The lighthouse can also be viewed from various boats leaving Provincetown Harbor, including a ferry to Boston and whale-watch cruises.

A company called Flyer's runs a seasonal shuttle boat from the Provincetown waterfront to Long Point. See www.flyersrentals.com or call (508) 487-0898.

When in Provincetown, be sure to visit the Provincetown Heritage Museum, which has an exhibit on the settlement at Long Point.

CHAPTER 33

Mayo's Beach Light Station in 1898. *From the collection of the author.*

The former keeper's dwelling, now privately owned, in 1996. *Photo by the author.*

Mayo's Beach Light

1838, 1881–1922

Wellfleet, with most of its land within the Cape Cod National Seashore and only about 3,500 year-round residents, is a reminder of the older, quieter Cape Cod. The town's well-protected harbor helped it develop as an important whaling port in the early 1700s, but that industry was curtailed by the Revolution. The town's primary business shifted to fishing and shellfishing, and Wellfleet oysters were eventually shipped all over the world. The town's name comes from a similar location in England that was also known for its abundant oysters.

The town had a growing fishing fleet of about a hundred vessels by the late 1830s, and it was decided that a lighthouse should be erected on Mayo's Beach to aid mariners entering Wellfleet's harbor. There was some disagreement about the need for the light, since Billingsgate Light, established in 1822, already served as a guide into the harbor. Congress nevertheless appropriated a total of $3,000 in 1837 and 1838, and work on the station commenced.

In his important survey of the coast's lighthouses in 1838, Lt. Edward W. Carpender expressed strong reservations about the new light, still under construction when he visited.

> *This harbor is but about four miles long, and when vessels get within Billingsgate Light they are safe as they can be in any part of the harbor. I inquired of the people in Wellfleet the necessity for this light, and the only advantage they promised themselves from it were, in "running a straight course over the flats at high water," and "seeing the shore in winter when the snow was on the ground." . . . Some venerable old fishermen and pilots belonging to the place, whom I also consulted, declared their opinion openly and publicly against the light; and elsewhere on the cape, when the light was mentioned, it raised a smile. Should Government, however, continue of opinion that a light is necessary in this place, then I recommend it should be a tide-light, to consist of one lamp, to be lighted an hour before, and kept lit an hour after high water. But, according to my judgment, it should be entirely suppressed.*

The first lighthouse at the eastern end of Mayo's Beach consisted of a short wooden tower and octagonal lantern on the roof of a brick dwelling containing three rooms on the first floor and two rooms on a small second floor. Joseph Holbrook of Wellfleet was appointed first keeper at a salary of $350 yearly. Ten oil lamps and accompanying 13-inch parabolic reflectors produced a fixed white light 21 feet above mean high water. Four of the lamps shone over the land only and were soon removed.

I. W. P. Lewis's landmark report on the area's lighthouses in 1843 included a statement by Keeper Holbrook, who painted a dire and heartrending picture.

> *The walls of the house are set two feet below the natural surface of the beach, without any other foundation. In consequence of this, the cellar was flooded with water continually; in fact, the tide ebbed and flowed regularly in the cellar. . . . The very wretched manner in which the house was built renders it almost uninhabitable; the walls always and the roof continually leaky. In consequence of this, and being compelled to use the water caught from the roof, which constitutes my only resource, two of my children have died, as I solemnly protest, entirely on account of the unhealthy condition of the house, and from using the stagnant water of the cistern.*

Holbrook said the lantern shook and rattled in high winds. The lamps and reflectors were also bad, he said. All in all, according to the keeper, the lighthouse was erected "in a very shameful manner, and such as no honest man would have done." Lewis concurred, calling the structure "a fair specimen of contract work, and disgraceful to the projectors and agents who erected it." Lewis echoed Carpender's suggestion, arguing that a single lamp would be sufficient for the site.

The problem of the shaky lantern was solved with the addition of a circular brick wall in the cellar, reaching to the timbers that supported the whole structure. A number of other repairs were carried out, and an inspection not long after Lewis's claimed that the lighthouse was "in first-rate order." But that report repeated the observation that "many skillful nautical men continue to entertain an opinion that the light is not wanted in this position."

In spite of all the objections, the light shone on. During Holbrook's first four years at the lighthouse, there were three shipwrecks in the vicinity, including the 270-ton brig *Diligence*. In 1839, Holbrook counted more than 700 vessels passing the lighthouse.

A Fresnel lens replaced the old lamps and reflectors in 1856. A screen was later erected around the lantern to protect it from the birds that flew into it and broke the glass with regularity.

In 1865 a Wellfleet native, William Atwood, who had enlisted at the age of 40 as a private in the Civil War and lost an arm at Fredericksburg, replaced Holbrook as keeper at a salary of $350 yearly. When Atwood died in 1876, his widow, Sarah, became keeper and continued to live at the station with their four children. Sarah Atwood resigned in May 1891. In later years, the children who lived near her on East Commercial Street in Wellfleet knew Sarah Atwood lovingly as Aunt Sarah.

Despite some improvements, the lighthouse remained susceptible to flooding and leaks. A wooden bulkhead, embedded with sand and planted with beach grass, was added in front of the building in 1867. Repairs were completed over the following two years, including the patching of a crack in the tower with cement and the repointing of the dwelling's brick exterior.

The Lighthouse Board's annual report for 1878 stated that the building had been undermined by the sea and recommended that it be rebuilt. An appropriation was secured and work on the new buildings began in 1880, during Sarah Atwood's stay. A cast-iron tower and a wood-frame keeper's house were finished during the following year. The new lighthouse tower was a small version of the cast-iron towers that were commonly built in New England starting in the 1870s, and it was very similar to the tower built about the same time at Ten Pound Island in Gloucester, Massachusetts.

Charlie Turner, who also had a boat shop in Wellfleet, was the keeper for approximately the last 30 years of the light's active life. A dory of his own design was named after Turner, a prominent character in the town.

In his book *Cape Cod Echoes*, Earle Rich described a visit to Turner's boat shop. "Come in, you don't have to knock around here," Turner told the young Rich. "This is a boat shop, not a prayer meeting." A while later, Turner went to a window as the sun was setting, announcing, "She's getting pretty low. Guess I'll call it a day and get over there and get ready to light up for the night." He slipped on his favorite "beach jacket" and headed for the lighthouse for his nightly duties.

The kerosene-fueled lighthouse remained in service until it was discontinued on March 10, 1922. The property was sold at auction on August 1, 1923, to Captain Harry Capron. The lighthouse tower was removed in 1939.

🔅 Today the house and a 1907 oil house remain, along with a foundation ring indicating the former location of the lighthouse. If you visit, be sure to respect the privacy of the owners.

CHAPTER 34

Two late-nineteenth-century views of Billingsgate Light Station.
From the collection of the author.

Billingsgate Light

1822, 1834, 1858–1915

In 1620 the Pilgrims aboard the *Mayflower* made note of a 60-acre island in Cape Cod Bay, about three miles west of the mainland at what is now the town of Eastham and a short distance south of Jeremy's Point in Wellfleet. William Bradford described the island as "a tongue of land, being flat, off from the shore, with a sandy point." Miles Standish and a landing party spent a night on the island, huddled around a fire on the beach.

Much of the area that now constitutes Wellfleet and Eastham, with plentiful fish and shellfish, was dubbed Billingsgate after a famous fish market in London, England. The name was eventually used exclusively for the island. (The British name originally was "Belinsgate," or the "Gate of Belinus," after its founder, Belinus, king of Britain from 380 to 374 B.C.)

Wellfleet's fishing and shellfishing industries were expanding by the 1820s, and Billingsgate Island was the ideal location for a light to guide vessels into the harbor. According to Enoch Pratt's history of Wellfleet, a local captain named Michael Collins deserved much of the credit for convincing the government that a lighthouse was needed at Billingsgate. On May 7, 1822, Congress appropriated $2,000 for the lighthouse.

Suitable land at the island's southern tip was sold to the federal government by Elizah Cobb of Brewster for $100. Winslow Lewis swiftly built a stone keeper's dwelling, 20 by 34 feet. The building was surmounted by an octagonal light tower extending 16 feet above its roof.

The octagonal iron lantern held a system of eight lamps and reflectors that exhibited a fixed white light, 40 feet above the sea and visible for 12 nautical miles. William S. Moore, previously at Bird Island Light near Marion, Massachusetts, was the first keeper, at $350 per year.

Lt. Edward W. Carpender of the U.S. Navy inspected the station during his 1838 survey of the lighthouses in the area. Carpender called it a useful light, but more powerful than was necessary. He recommended that the number of lamps be reduced to six. He noted that the keeper, Abijah Gill, was absent during his visit, and that the reflectors "had the appearance of not having been burnished for some time." The premises were, he reported, in "sufficient order."

Within a dozen years of its construction, the sea undermined the first lighthouse as the island's contours were altered by erosion. I. W. P. Lewis's report of 1843 notes that a second lighthouse had been completed in 1834. A man named Bowker was the builder, working as an agent for Winslow Lewis.

The new structure was a brick dwelling with a wooden tower on the roof. The lantern of the original lighthouse was transferred to the new one, and the new light was 37 feet above mean high water.

The 1834 building, judging by I. W. P. Lewis's description, was inadequately constructed. A protective wall around the lighthouse also earned Lewis's disdain.

> This house was rebuilt about seven years ago, and, in consequence of erecting it without foundations, the entire front wall tumbled down, leaving the interior exposed in view. This defect was repaired, but the whole fabric bears the mark of hasty construction, bad materials, and worse design. . . . [A] bulkhead, of piles stuck five feet deep in the sand, cased inside with two-inch pine plank, was constructed around it, and named a breakwater. If the island should decay by the inroads of the sea, this breakwater would be dismembered at once.

Keeper Abijah Gill, who had been at the station since 1830, told Lewis that the building was leaky and that water and sand flowed through the roof in storms. Eight lamps and reflectors were still in use, and Lewis called the lamps "very bad," adding that the result was a "dim uncertain light in the clearest weather." He concluded by recommending that the lighthouse be entirely rebuilt, and that it be fitted with a single lamp "of a proper form."

An inspection report by the local lighthouse superintendent, also in 1843, had a more positive slant. Except for a few leaks in the roof, everything was fine, according to this report, and no expenses or major repairs were recommended.

It may be worth pointing out that I. W P. Lewis, a civil engineer, was given the task of assessing the less-than-adequate state of the nation's lighthouses by a concerned Congress. He was brutally frank throughout his 79-page report, and he never pulled any punches in his assessments of the work of his uncle Winslow Lewis. The local superintendent, on the other hand, was probably more conservative in his statements, as he wished to sustain positive relationships with those in power.

By the mid-nineteenth century, Billingsgate had a community of 30 homes, a school, and a plant for rendering oil from the blackfish (pilot whales) caught nearby. Pilot whales sometimes stranded themselves in the vicinity of the lighthouse. In his book *Cape Cod,* Henry David Thoreau wrote: "I learned that a few days before this one hundred and eighty blackfish had been driven ashore in one school at Eastham, a little farther south, and that the keeper of Billingsgate Point light went out one morning about the same time and cut his initials on the backs of a large school which had run ashore in the night, and sold his right to them to Provincetown for one thousand dollars, and probably Provincetown made as much more."

An 1850 inspection, when Francis Krogman was keeper, reported the lighting apparatus in good order. The report sounded an ominous note: "The island is washing away very fast."

The second lighthouse was under increasing attack by the encroaching sea by the 1850s. A sum of $2,000 was appropriated for the improved protection of the site in 1854, but it was a losing battle. A storm in the winter of 1854–55 damaged the station, and the chairman of the recently formed Lighthouse Board suggested, in 1855, that it would be more prudent to build a new lighthouse on screwpiles "than to make further attempts to secure the permanency of the present site." He asked for, and received in the following year, an appropriation of $14,000.

The *New York Times* of January 10, 1857, reported that the lighthouse had been undermined by the tide and that the keeper and his family "were obliged to flee to a fish-house, on an island in the neighborhood, for safety." The rebuilding of the station wasn't coming a moment too soon.

Six acres of land for the relocated lighthouse were sold to the government by two men of Eastham. The building of the new tower and dwelling, farther to the north and on higher ground, commenced in August 1857, and the light was reestablished in its new location on September 1, 1858. The new tower was 34 feet tall, and the light's focal plane was 52 feet above mean high water.

Unfortunately, the new buildings—a square lighthouse tower and attached keeper's house, both built of brick—were not built on screwpiles, as the chairman had urged. The rapidly encroaching ocean soon threatened the new station.

Herman Dill became keeper in 1872. In 1873 he wrote in his log that an unusually high tide had flooded the tower to a depth of two inches. On December 21, 1874, he wrote: "We have had quite a heavy blow and a very high tide, the highest for a number of years. [The sea] broke through at the north end of the island, filling the middle of the

Billingsgate Light Station pictured on an early-1900s postcard. *From the collection of the author.*

island full, running up to the south corner of the foundation on which stands the lighthouse, carrying away the walk which leads to the wharf. I could stand on the south corner and jump into four feet of water."

Dill's log entry for February 7, 1875, was bleak: "It has been very Cold here for the last month and the most ice that i ever see in this Rigen. We are almost buried up in it. No salt water to be seen from the island. I have not seen a living man for over a month no prospect for the Better. I do get the blues sometimes to think i can't [get] here from the main so pend up with ice that i can not move in either direction for the ice is 15 feet high in some places."

Dill wrote in November 1875, "I do not know but the Island will All wash away." During bad weather that December, the tower was flooded to a depth of as much as five feet. In March 1876, Keeper Dill was found dead in his boat, afloat in Cape Cod Bay the day after a brutal storm. Many years later, a local resident, Earle G. Rich, wrote that "the day Uncle Herman died" was an expression often heard in Wellfleet for decades.

Thomas K. Payne was keeper from 1860 to 1869 and again from 1876 to 1884. On his last day he wrote the following in the log: "This is our last night on the island as keeper. We are packed up and mostly moved. . . . We have had many pleasant hours but many more very lonely ones. . . . Remember us to friends if any. Good bye."

In 1888 the Lighthouse Board again tried to delay the inevitable by building 1,000 feet of jetties and bulkheads around the island. Three years later, the protective structures were completely buried in sand. In 1904 an additional course of bricks was added around the lighthouse tower and a brick oil house was built. An additional 500 feet of bulkheads were constructed in 1905, but it was a lost cause.

In a 1969 article, Earle G. Rich recalled visiting the lighthouse around 1900, when George Bailey was keeper. When Rich and his brother arrived at the station, Bailey was in the midst of feeding his chickens and a pair of pigs. Rich met the keeper's wife and their two young children, a boy and a girl.

Keeper Bailey had a 34-foot double-ender boat, made on Cape Cod in Orleans, that he used to go to Wellfleet for supplies. The boat was equipped with a 10-horsepower gasoline engine. Rich and his brother were thrilled when the keeper invited them to accompany him on a trip to town. He always tied his boat up at a location in Wellfleet known as Puddle Dock.

As the island dwindled in size, some of the homes were floated across the bay and relocated in Eastham and Wellfleet. The keeper and his family were eventually the only year-round residents. The island was still frequented by plenty of visitors in summer, and it was a favorite place for clambakes.

A prominent Boston surgeon named Maurice Richardson bought what was left of the island in 1897 and constructed a hunting lodge from parts of the abandoned buildings, complete with a high cupola that gave him an advantage over the waterfowl. Richardson sold the island when its area was down to five acres.

By 1915 the foundations of the lighthouse and dwelling were undermined and the tower developed a pronounced list. The keeper was removed, the tower was secured with ropes, and a crew climbed into the lantern to remove all the lighting equipment.

The lighthouse finally toppled in a storm on the day after Christmas that year. A few years later, some of the bricks were salvaged and taken to the mainland. For a while, a light shone from the cupola of a house on the island, then a light on a skeleton tower was erected.

Billingsgate has its share of persistent legends and lore. Some blame a curse for the island's disappearance, claiming that an innocent prisoner declared, "If I am put to death, the island will disappear," shortly before his execution on the gallows. There's also the story of "Lumpkin's Light," a mysterious light that would appear between the island and the mainland, supposedly related to a fisherman who died mysteriously. Then there's the "Sea Witch of Billingsgate," who searched for the souls of lost sailors.

The light was discontinued in 1922 and then reestablished for a time beginning in 1931. By 1942, the island had mostly disappeared, although a trace of it can still be spotted at low tide. Several buoys now mark Billingsgate Shoal.

CHAPTER 35

Sandy Neck Light in May 2004. *Photo by the author.*

Sandy Neck Light

1826, 1857

The eastern tip of Sandy Neck—a half-mile wide, six-mile long, dune-studded peninsula on the north side of Cape Cod—marks the entrance to Barnstable Harbor as well as the approach to the small harbor at Yarmouthport. Both developed as important ports for fishing, whaling, and coastal trade in the nineteenth century. In the days when shore whaling was a major local industry, Sandy Neck was the site of tryworks for the processing of whale blubber. Cranberry harvesting later became the peninsula's chief business. Today it's home to a little cottage community just west of the lighthouse.

Congress appropriated $3,500 for a lighthouse at the eastern tip of the peninsula, a site known as Beach Point, on May 18, 1826. Two acres for the light station were acquired from the town of Barnstable for one dollar, and construction quickly followed. The light went into service on October 1, 1826, and the first keeper—at a yearly salary of $350—was Joseph Nickerson, who stayed for seven years.

The first lighthouse consisted of a wooden lantern on the roof of a brick keeper's house. The lantern originally held 10 lamps and reflectors, exhibiting a fixed white light 40 feet above mean high water and visible for nine nautical miles.

Henry Baxter replaced Nickerson as keeper in early December 1833. He remained until 1844, when he was succeeded by his son, James. Henry Baxter's first entry in the station's log read: "This day moved my famerly [*sic*] and took possession of the lighthouse at Beach Point, Sandineck. Wind NE, Thick weather."

During his stay, Baxter frequently noted severe cold and ice in the harbor, as well as erosion that ate away at the land surrounding the lighthouse. A storm in late October 1837 took six feet of land away on the station's east side. On December 15, 1834, Baxter wrote: "This day a heavy gale from the SW with snow. Came on shore the schooner *Enterprise* . . . and Capt. Sawyer with two women on board. Got them on shore with much trouble. Capt. Sawyer much frost bit. So ends very cold and the ice making fast the schooner, laying in the barr [*sic*] with much ice on her and sails much torn."

In his 1838 inspection report, Lt. Edward W. Carpender recommended the suppression of four of the lamps. "It cannot be that this light requires more lamps than either of the Plymouth [lights]," he wrote. "Those lights are far outside of this, more exposed, and with a vastly heavier trade dependent upon them." Carpender reported that the premises were in good order but expressed the opinion that the combined dwelling and lighthouse posed a risk: if fire should strike one of the structures, both would probably be destroyed. He recommended the rebuilding of the station as two distinct structures.

When the engineer I. W. P. Lewis examined the station in 1842, Henry Baxter was still in charge and the number of lamps had been reduced to six. Lewis proclaimed the light "very necessary and useful," largely because it helped mariners avoid the dangerous bar that extended from Sandy Neck. But he found the lighting apparatus "worn out and dirty" and proclaimed the whole building "another specimen of contract work where the Government have been losers by the operation; the whole construction and materials being equally defective." A wooden bulkhead was under construction to protect the station from the encroaching sea, but Lewis saw the structure as "merely a temporary expedient."

An 1843 report mentioned that shipwreck victims often took refuge at the lighthouse. The keeper, according to the report, needed a new boat; his present one was eight years old and "in great decay."

Thomas P. D. Baxter was keeper from 1846 to 1862. In his 1946 book, *A Pilgrim Returns to Cape Cod,* Edward Rowe Snow described a visit with Baxter's grandson Harry Ryder of Barnstable. Ryder said that his grandfather frequently had visitors at the lighthouse and that the packet boat traveling between Boston and Provincetown often stopped there.

An 1850 inspection report reveals that the lantern had been raised some 8 or 10 feet, and a new system of seven lamps and 14-inch reflectors was in use. The inspection found everything in good order under Baxter, and it noted that erosion had washed away a considerable amount of the sandy shore near the lighthouse.

The original lighthouse was replaced in 1857 by the 48-foot brick tower that still stands, slightly north of the first light's location. The distinctive pair of iron hoops and six staves that surround the central part of the lighthouse were added in 1887 as part of an effort to shore up cracks in the tower.

The waters inside Sandy Neck were often plagued by ice in winter. One cold day, Thomas Baxter was heading to Barnstable in his dory, alternately rowing, pulling, and pushing the vessel through the icy harbor. He caught his leg between the dory and the ice, suffering an injury that led to gangrene and eventually his death in 1862.

Sandy Neck Light Station in the late 1800s. *From the collection of Edward Rowe Snow, courtesy of Dorothy Snow Bicknell.*

Baxter's wife, Lucy Hinckley Baxter, succeeded him as keeper and raised three children at the station. Harry Ryder told Snow, "The picture she often described to us of her having to heat the whale oil in the winter months behind the kitchen stove and carry two oil butts up into the tower at midnight is one we never forgot." In 1867 Lucy resigned and moved her family to Barnstable so it would be easier for the children to attend school. She eventually married a Yarmouth man.

Numerous repairs to the original dwelling kept it inhabitable, but the 1880 annual report of the Lighthouse Board deemed the house "beyond repair." The following year's report announced that the old house had been replaced by a new wood-frame structure, with brick inner walls. The pretty six-room Queen Anne Victorian dwelling still stands.

The station got its second woman keeper, Eunice Crowell Howes, in 1880. She replaced her husband, Jacob S. Howes, who had died after five years as keeper. Eunice Howes remained at Sandy Neck until 1886.

George A. Jamieson, previously at Minot's Ledge Light and Duxbury Pier Light, became keeper in 1897. After a storm in early December 1898, Jamieson discovered that his chicken coop and 40 chickens were gone, apparently washed away to their doom. As it turned out, the coop had washed safely ashore in Barnstable. The chickens were fine, although they did exhibit some strange symptoms that were attributed to seasickness.

In a 1974 interview, Jamieson's daughter—identified only as Mrs. Kenneth Rouillard—described the details of her birth at Sandy Neck. Her father was on his way back to the lighthouse from the mainland when he saw a blanket hanging from the tower. He reversed direction and took his dory back to the mainland, where he fetched a doctor.

> *You see, that was the signal my mother had prearranged with him. It was to tell him that the baby was due. That baby was me. Mother was expecting that spring of 1900 and she had her cousin Elizabeth to keep her company. My father had to make regular trips to the mainland by sailboat in those days for provisions. Of course, there were no telephones, so whenever he went ashore they had worked out the blanket signal. By the time he did get back with the doctor, however, I had already entered this world.*

Mrs. Rouillard recalled that when she reached school age, she was taught by a teacher named Mr. Ferguson, who boarded with the family during the school year. Lessons were held in the small workroom attached to the lighthouse tower. "We had three school desks, one for me and one each for brother and sister. There was a spiral staircase up to the light and Mr. Ferguson had to stand in the area and, as he read, his voice echoed up the stairwell. I'll always remember that."

Keeper Jamieson's wife was sometimes lonely for more company, but she stayed busy caring for her children. She also wrote poetry and painted. The children pitched in by helping with the cleaning and polishing in the

An unidentified keeper and others at Sandy Neck Light Station in the late 1800s. *From the collection of Edward Rowe Snow, courtesy of Dorothy Snow Bicknell.*

lighthouse. Mrs. Rouillard recalled that when the inspector visited, her father always got good ratings.

The Jamieson children had fun being pulled around the grounds by their Saint Bernard dog—they'd hitch up a cart in summer and a sled in winter when there was snow. They also enjoyed swinging over the dunes by hanging onto the ropes on the flagpole. And Mrs. Rouillard remembered walking to the dunes on the outer beach, which was often crowded with seals. "They would see us and begin barking," she said.

Keeper Jamieson helped feed his family by hunting deer and ducks at Sandy Neck. Of course, seafood was a staple. "I can remember my mother preparing eels for supper," said Mrs. Rouillard. "There always seemed to be a lot of those."

Like earlier families at the station, the Jamiesons often fought battles with ice in the harbor in the colder months. On the day after Christmas in 1903, Keeper Jamieson and his brother-in-law had gone into town to purchase provisions. When they were about to get in the boat to return, the keeper's brother-in-law realized he had forgotten something important in town, and he hurried back. In the meantime the weather grew worse, with high winds and snow squalls. Jamieson finally decided that he had to leave without his brother-in-law if he was to get back that day to his wife and children.

During the return trip, a severe squall enveloped the dory as the keeper's wife watched from shore. The boat disappeared from sight, and Mrs. Jamieson feared the worst. She lighted the lamp at sunset, and then paced the floor all night. In the morning, her husband arrived safe and sound in his boat; he had been forced to spend the night at the home of a friend. When she saw her husband approaching her on the beach, Mrs. Jamieson fainted. This incident may have contributed to George Jamieson's decision to quit the Lighthouse Service in 1908 and take a job in the auto industry in Detroit.

Jamieson was succeeded first by James Jorgeson, then in 1909 by Henry L. Pingree. Barnstable Harbor gradually declined in importance, and shifting sands had left the lighthouse in a less advantageous position. In the summer of 1931, when William L. Anderson was keeper, the lighthouse was decommissioned and its lens was moved to a steel skeleton tower 200 feet closer to the tip of Sandy Neck. The new automated light was fueled by acetylene gas and was operated seasonally, from April 15 to October 15. The light was discontinued in 1952.

The lantern was removed from the lighthouse and the property was sold at auction in 1933 to Warren J. Clear. The price was $711 for 1.93 acres and all the light station buildings. A short time later, Francis and Margaret Ellis bought it. Margaret Ellis described life at the light-house in a 1963 article:

We felt quite self-contained in our small domain. Most of our staple provisions had to be brought by boat from the mainland, but there were plentiful clams at our feet for digging, fish were plentiful from the boats and a mile hike up the Neck brought us to marvelous clumps of high-bush blueberries where a pail could easily be filled from one bush, with the little cocker spaniels waiting open-mouthed underneath ready to catch any stray berries that might fall. Later in the season we filled pails from the low bushes heavy with red-purple beach plums, and sometimes, just before we left in the fall, we would come upon a small bog of crimson cranberries hidden in the dune grass.

Refrigeration was always a problem. The Ellises were told that a former keeper once hung sides of meat inside the lighthouse tower, which was very cold in winter. Ice brought from the mainland in summer would be almost completely melted by the time it got to the lighthouse, but the problem was solved when a kerosene-fueled refrigerator was delivered.

The Ellises spent 10 happy summers at the lighthouse. In December 1942, they leased the station to the Coast Guard. For the next two years, the keeper's house was occupied by a Coast Guard beach patrol, reportedly a segregated African American unit. In 1944, after the military use ended, the property was sold to Fred Lang, a radio personality on the Yankee Network.

Edward Rowe Snow visited Lang at the lighthouse during his research for his book *A Pilgrim Returns to Cape Cod.* Lang told Snow that traces of the old tryworks at Sandy Neck could still be seen, and that the ribs of an old shipwreck protruded from the sand about a quarter mile northeast of the lighthouse. Lang also claimed he some-times saw as many as 10,000 ducks at Sandy Neck, and that he had seen deer swim from the peninsula across to Yarmouth.

Lang sold the property to the Hinckley family in 1950. Ken Morton and Kee Hinckley today manage the Sandy Neck Lighthouse property for the family. In 2004 Morton began working with the Cape Cod Chapter of the American Lighthouse Foundation to have a replica lantern installed on the tower in time for its 150th birthday in 2007. The repairs will also protect the interior from water damage when it rains or snows.

The Sandy Neck Lighthouse Restoration Committee eventually became a chapter of the American Lighthouse Foundation, with Ron

Ken Morton, manager of the Sandy Neck Lighthouse property, in May 2004. *Photo by the author.*

Jansson its chairman. Jansson said he had passed the lighthouse in a boat with his grandfather more than 50 years earlier, when he was about 5 years old. He asked, "Why is that lighthouse broken?" His grandfather answered, "I don't know, but maybe when you get older you can fix it."

The restoration committee had a stroke of good luck when it was discovered that the Great Lakes Lighthouse Keepers Association had created a replica lantern for St. Helena Lighthouse in Michigan. The specifications for that lantern were the same as Sandy Neck's, so the Great Lakes group loaned their molds to the restoration committee. It appears that a new lantern—funded totally by private donations—will be installed in 2007. There are hopes that the lighthouse can be relit as a private aid to navigation.

Sandy Neck Light can be seen at a distance from Millway Beach in Barnstable, but it's best seen by boat. The trips offered by Hyannis Whale Watcher Cruises pass close by the lighthouse on their way out of Barnstable Harbor; call (508) 362-6088 or check www.whales.net for more information.

To find out more about the ongoing restoration, write to Sandy Neck Lighthouse Restoration Committee, P.O. Box 147, Barnstable, MA 02630, or to snlrc@hotmail.com.

CHAPTER 36

Duxbury Pier Light during its 2001 renovation. *Photo by the author.*

Duxbury Pier Light

(Bug Light)
1871

This stout, coffeepot-shaped lighthouse, known fondly to locals as "Bug Light," or simply "The Bug," occupies an important niche in lighthouse history as the first offshore cast-iron caisson lighthouse in the United States. Despite its tubby appearance, it's a thing of beauty to the band of plucky preservationists who've saved it from the scrap heap.

Congress appropriated $17,931 on July 15, 1870, for the establishment of a lighthouse to mark a dangerous shoal off Saquish Head in Plymouth Bay, on the north side of the main channel to the harbors of Plymouth, Duxbury, and Kingston. A local resident named William W. Burgess Jr. later described his involvement in the construction of the lighthouse, which was built in shallow water, only two feet deep at low tide.

> In April '71 they decided to build an iron lighthouse . . . on the flats close to the edge of the channel, and my father contracted with the Government Inspector to build it. It was built of iron plates, 10 feet long with flanges on each to bolt them together and form a circle 28 feet in diameter at the bottom. This section was put together in North Dock and a cofferdam built inside of it to float it, and one Sunday we towed it down with the government schooner and our sloop Rose Wood, placed it in position then broke in the cofferdam and sunk it. I got $3.00 for my part of the job, which was looking on.

The lighthouse, 47 feet in height overall, was filled with concrete to a height of 25 feet. The tower contained three levels below the lantern, including two levels that served as living quarters. The lantern held a fifth-order Fresnel lens showing a fixed white light 35 feet above mean high water, first exhibited on September 15, 1871. The first keeper was William Atwood, who stayed until 1878.

In early February 1875, the revenue steamer *Gallatin* was in the vicinity when the captain noticed a signal of distress flying at the lighthouse. The tower was surrounded by so much ice that it was impossible to reach the keeper by boat. The steamer got close enough so that the crew could converse with Atwood, and they learned that he had not been off the lighthouse since December 22 and his supplies of food

The Duxbury Pier Light before the addition of a lower gallery and roof in 1897. *From the collection of the author.*

and water were gone. The keeper and his wife had been reduced to a pint of water a day for several days. Two of the crewmen from the steamer spent two hours cutting through the ice to get a small boat to the lighthouse, and the Atwoods were furnished with supplies.

To protect the structure, 100 tons of stones were placed around the base in 1886, and another 175 tons were added in 1890. A lower gallery and roof were added in 1897. A 700-gallon water cistern was added in 1900, and a fog bell and striking apparatus were installed in 1902.

Keeper Tolman Spencer was fortunate to escape with his life in a harrowing episode in late December 1920. Spencer had gone ashore to visit with his wife, and he left in the afternoon to row back to the lighthouse to light up for the evening while his wife attended a movie. When evening arrived, Mrs. Spencer knew something was amiss when she saw from shore that the light wasn't lit. The Coast Guard at the Gurnet section of Plymouth was alerted, and they sent a man to light the light, while other crewmen searched for the missing keeper.

The Coast Guardsmen couldn't find Spencer, so the keeper's wife went to the police. She went out in a motorboat with two men, vowing to find her husband. Well out in the harbor, they discovered Spencer, who had been unable to make any progress as he rowed with all his might against the increasing wind and tide. He was pulled into the motorboat and immediately collapsed from exhaustion. The keeper and his wife were taken to the lighthouse, and Spencer eventually recovered.

Frank A. Grieder, a Maine native, became keeper in 1930. The Grieders brought their belongings from Maine to Plymouth in a Model A Ford, and the keeper's wife and children took up residence in the Rocky Nook section of the city. In an interview in 2000, Grieder's son, Bill, remembered his father's days as keeper of "The Bug."

> My Dad used to have to row out to the lighthouse. This was before they had outboards. It was in the middle of March, and he was going out. And the Plymouth Yacht Club—I think it was their boat that was out there with two fellows on it. They asked if he wanted a tow, and he said sure. They came alongside and hit him [accidentally] in the bow and knocked him over. He saw the gunwale of the dory and grabbed it and hauled himself in. So they towed him out to the lighthouse. But he was practically a sheet of ice when they got there. And then he had to get up into the tower on the ladder.

> The weather was never the same. You'd go out and a couple of hours later the weather changes and the tide changes.

> The thing that I used to get a big kick out of was when it came in foggy. We had a huge brass bell up on the tower, and it worked like clockwork. You'd wind it up, and it had a big hammer. You'd wind and wind and all of a sudden it'd go "whammo!" and the whole tower would shake. You'd lie there at night and wonder, "How am I going to sleep?" And next thing you know you'd gotten used to it. And when the fog cleared and they shut the bell off, you woke up. You couldn't stand it—"Why is it so quiet?"

> At low tide you could walk around there and pick up lobsters and sea clams. Of course if you were out on the flats you always kept your eye on the tide because it came up quite quickly.

> We used to bring people in there when it was blowing hard and they were a little leery of the weather. They'd tie up on the rail or the steps of the ladder. It could get quite stormy there in Plymouth Harbor.

Fred Bohm, later at Deer Island Light in Boston Harbor, was keeper in the late 1930s into the 1940s. The historian Edward Rowe Snow claimed that Bohm rescued 90 people from drowning in a single year, including 36 Girl Scouts.

One windy night Bohm heard a scream for help. He rushed out to see a woman swimming toward the lighthouse from her capsized boat. Not able to row to her in time, Bohm dove into the water and swam to the woman, who was unconscious by the time he reached her. Bohm brought the woman back to the lighthouse, where she gradually came to. In her struggle to stay afloat she had lost her bathing suit. As she regained consciousness, the woman's first words were, "Where are my clothes?" Keeper Bohm answered, "I don't know, but you're lucky to be alive." Later that night the woman was safely ashore with borrowed clothes.

In December 1942, Bohm and a companion were heading for the mainland in frigid waters to pick up provisions when their boat began to leak. A lobsterman rescued the pair, but Bohm lost two fingers from frostbite.

Harry Salter, a Cape Cod native, became the Coast Guard officer in charge in 1944. Salter later wrote a booklet about his time at the lighthouse, called simply *Bug Light*. He recalled his first reaction when he arrived at the lighthouse: "By no stretch of the imagination would it win any beauty contest." Salter was at the station when the damaging hurricane of 1944 hit, battering the isolated station with 30-foot waves. He described the scene: "The gigantic waves were hammering this stout little light station unmercifully. It shook so bad we had trouble keeping the oil lamps lit. . . . The heavy seas on the east side were striking against the light, then crashing up under the catwalk and tearing away at our boat that we had previously lashed high on the davits."

Salter went out on the deck in an effort to secure the boat. A wave opened a trap door near him and he fell through. Fortunately, another wave drove Salter against the ladder, and he was able to clamber to safety. Salter gave up on saving the boat and watched the hurricane from inside the tower for the next few hours. He and the other crewman on duty surveyed the damage later and found that the boat, the fog-bell mechanism, and the privy—called "our favorite outdoor reading room" by Salter—were all gone.

Walt Harris, the Coast Guard's officer in charge at the lighthouse from September 1962 to September 1963, later recalled that the crewmen had 26 days on the lighthouse followed by six days off, mercifully changed eventually to two weeks on and one week off. The lighthouse was automated in 1964 and the Coast Guard crewmen were reassigned. A modern optic replaced the Fresnel lens. Over the next two decades, the lighthouse fell victim to extensive vandalism, and birds made their home in the interior.

In 1983 the lighthouse was slated by the Coast Guard to be replaced by a fiberglass tower much like the one that had replaced Boston Harbor's old Deer Island Lighthouse. The Coast Guard estimated that a renovation of the lighthouse would cost somewhere between $250,000 and $400,000, whereas a replacement structure would cost $63,000.

Duxbury Pier Light, circa 1960s. *U.S. Coast Guard photo.*

A petition to save the lighthouse was signed by more than 200 Duxbury residents, and concerned local residents soon formed a preservation organization called Project Bug Light. Among those advocating the restoration of the lighthouse was George Davis, the owner of the Plymouth Marina. Davis's father, Frank Allen Davis, was keeper in the World War I era.

Another concerned citizen was a retired Duxbury fire chief, Howard Blanchard, who recalled how the resident Coast Guard crews had once kept the lighthouse in pristine condition. "Many Saturday nights," Blanchard said, "I've gone out there with the Coast Guard and had beans and frankfurts for supper with them. They kept the lighthouse in condition just like a ship. But now it looks like a sunken vessel. It's a derelict."

Aided by Congressman Gerry Studds, Senator Edward M. Kennedy, and State Senator Edward P. Kirby (who spoke of the lighthouse's "magnificent ugliness"), Project Bug Light convinced the Coast Guard to alter their plans. A five-year lease was granted to Project Bug Light. The Coast Guard sandblasted and painted the structure and did some repair work in 1983. Solar power replaced the older battery system.

Project Bug Light raised about $35,000 from donations, sales of T-shirts and bumper stickers, a fashion show, baseball games, and the raffling of a painting. They used the money for repairs to the upper parts of the tower and the interior, including the rebuilding of the roof and the lower gallery. David Silvia, a contractor from Plymouth, completed the work in the fall of 1985.

In the late 1980s, vandals broke into the lantern and left it susceptible to leaks. The weather deteriorated the wood interior so much that all the wood had to be removed, and the iron walls were left bare.

After a few years, Project Bug Light virtually dissolved as an organization, and the five-year lease expired. In 1993 the Coast Guard again talked of replacing the lighthouse with a fiberglass pole, or at least removing the lantern. This time, Dr. Don Muirhead of Duxbury, an avid sailor who was deeply involved in the initial push to save the lighthouse, spearheaded a new preservation effort. In 1994–95, 30 volunteers collectively spent more than 420 hours cleaning, scraping, sanding, and painting. The Coast Guard again did some refurbishing of the lighthouse in 1996.

Dolly Bicknell of Marshfield, Massachusetts, remembers being contacted by Don Muirhead in 1993. "He was trying to save the light once again, as the lease had been allowed to expire," she recalls. "He asked me to become part of Project Bug Light. I was honored to be asked, but not exactly sure just what I could do to help. Soon I found out—I could scrape and paint the lighthouse. The next thing I knew, I was vice president and then president."

Bicknell had some strong memories for inspiration. "My late father-in-law, Alvin Bicknell, used to enjoy taking us sailing out to Bug Light from his home in Duxbury," she says. "Along with many of his friends and neighbors, he was involved with the original group that saved the structure in 1983."

Bicknell's own father was a man who inspired many to preserve New England's maritime treasures. He was Edward Rowe Snow—

This 1983 photo shows the poor condition of the Duxbury Pier Light exterior at that time. *U.S. Coast Guard photo.*

historian, storyteller, treasure hunter, and for more than 40 years, "Flying Santa" to lighthouse keepers and their families. "I remember thinking how pleased my father would have been to know that a group of people was able to save a lighthouse," says Bicknell about the rescue of Bug Light.

Project Bug Light eventually took over responsibility for the care of Plymouth ("Gurnet") Light as well, and the name of the organization was changed to match its mission. Don Muirhead died in 2000, but the volunteers of Project Gurnet and Bug Lights continue to do maintenance at the lighthouse and to raise funds toward the continued preservation of the Bug.

In the fall of 2001, Project Gurnet and Bug Lights hired the Campbell Construction Group of Beverly, Massachusetts, for another major renovation. Joints in the caisson were repaired by caulking and welding, and over 1,200 pounds of rust was removed from the lighthouse. All the paint was removed inside and out, and three new coats of paint were added. Several inches of guano were removed as well.

Duxbury Pier Light, painted dark brown for much of its history, is now red on its lower half and white on its upper half, its lantern and gallery black. It remains an active aid to navigation, with a 250-millimeter optic producing two red flashes every 15 seconds, and an automated fog horn producing a single blast every 15 seconds.

▲ **The Duxbury Pier Light can be seen distantly from the Plymouth waterfront, but it is best viewed from sightseeing cruises out of Plymouth. The Plymouth Harbor Cruise offered by Capt. John Boats passes fairly close to the lighthouse. For information, call (508) 747-3434 or visit www.plymouthharborcruises.com.**

For more on Project Gurnet and Bug Lights, write to P.O. Box 2167, Duxbury, MA 02331, or visit www.buglight.org.

CHAPTER 37

Plymouth Light in April 2006. *Photo by the author.*

Plymouth Light

(Gurnet Light)
1768, 1803, 1843

The seven-mile-long, 27-acre peninsula known as the Gurnet—at the northern border of Plymouth Bay—was visited and mapped in 1605 by the French explorer Samuel de Champlain, who described it as covered with pine trees. The bluff at the eastern extremity of the Gurnet apparently reminded settlers of similar areas back in England. Several headlands in the English Channel are known by the name Gurnet, after a fish of the same name.

Plymouth developed a significant fishing industry, with 75 fishing vessels by the 1770s. Coastal and foreign trade based in Plymouth helped make it one of the major ports of colonial America, and nearby Duxbury and Kingston also became important centers for trade and shipbuilding. The local maritime traffic necessitated a navigational aid at the Gurnet, which is on the approach to the harbors of Plymouth, Kingston, and Duxbury.

The first lighthouse on the high bluff at the eastern end of the Gurnet—the eighth lighthouse in what would become the United States—was authorized by an act of the colonial legislature on February 17, 1768. The structure, built for £660, took the form of a wooden dwelling, 15 by 30 feet, with two lanterns on the roof—one at each end—which made this the site of North America's first twin lights.

The lights were in operation by September 1768. Because of the two lights, each about 86 feet above the water, mariners could not confuse the new station with Boston Light (a single light) to the north.

The station was built on land owned by John and Hannah Thomas. John Thomas, a doctor originally from Marshfield, Massachusetts, had served as a military surgeon. The government didn't initially buy the land. Instead, they paid the Thomases five shillings for the right to build the lighthouse, and John Thomas became the first keeper of the lights.

In the days leading up to the American Revolution, Thomas recruited a regiment of volunteers from Plymouth County. In March 1775, Thomas and his men fortified Dorchester Heights at Boston, which led to the withdrawal of the British. Thomas became a major general and led troops at Quebec. Smallpox spread through his troops, and Thomas died of the disease on June 2, 1776.

Thomas's wife, Hannah, had taken over the duties of keeping the lights at the Gurnet when her husband went to war, along with the responsibilities of raising three children. She was America's first woman lighthouse keeper. It isn't clear exactly when they were extinguished, but the lights were not used for the duration of the war.

In 1776 the towns of Plymouth, Duxbury, and Kingston constructed Fort Andrew on the Gurnet near the lighthouse. It's been commonly written that the British frigate *Niger* fired on the fort a short time later, and that one of the cannonballs pierced the lighthouse building, or possibly even destroyed one of the station's two lights. Research by a local historian, Richard Boonisar, has shown that this is almost certainly not true, although the *Niger* did spend time in the vicinity.

One of the most famous New England shipwrecks happened near the Gurnet in December 1778, when the American brigantine *General Arnold* tried to anchor about a mile from the point and struck White Flats. Seventy-two men on the ship perished in the freezing water. Local residents quickly built a causeway to the ship to rescue the survivors.

The lights were refurbished and returned to service in September 1785. The following year, Hannah Thomas hired a local man named Nathaniel Burgess (or Burges) to serve as lightkeeper.

During a snowstorm in December 1786, a sloop heading for Plymouth from Boston struck a beach near the Gurnet. Two men reached the lighthouse safely, and Burgess sent an assistant—possibly Hannah's son, John—to help the rest of the survivors reach safety. One of the survivors published an account in a newspaper, praising Burgess:

> *Thus, after being wrecked on the shore, and having traveled in the whole, near 7 miles, in a most violent snow-storm for five hours on a desolate beach, through inexpressible fatigue, from wet cold and hunger, some of us having eat nothing for more than 20 hours, we arrived at the friendly house of Mr. Burgess, on the Gurnett, where we received every attention and kindness that compassion and hospitality could afford, until means were obtained for our safe arriving at our own homes.*

In March 1792, Burgess helped two survivors from the wreck of the Liverpool ship *Columbia,* which was wrecked close to the lighthouse. Fourteen others, including the captain, perished in the wreck.

John Thomas, son of Hannah and John, had done much of the work at the station for years by the time he received the official appointment as keeper in 1790. The lighthouse was ceded to the federal government in the same year.

The salary of the keeper at the Gurnet was only $200 yearly because it was deemed a desirable place to live. The fertile land at the station facilitated vegetable gardening, and fish was, of course, readily available. The salaries of the keepers at the Massachusetts light stations at Boston Harbor and Thacher Island were higher— $266.67 yearly.

The original twin-light structure served until June 30, 1801, when it was destroyed by fire. The merchants of Duxbury and Plymouth paid for a temporary structure, which itself was nearly consumed by fire in early 1802. Congress appropriated $2,500 for the rebuilding of the station in April 1802. The local merchants were repaid $270 for their expenses. A new pair of 22-foot-high twin towers was built in 1803, 30 feet apart, exhibiting fixed white lights 70 feet above sea level. The land at the Gurnet was finally bought outright, and the Thomases were paid $120.

John Thomas remained keeper until 1812. The next keeper, Joseph Burgess—son of Nathaniel Burgess—had a 39-year stint. According to an 1896 article, Joseph Burgess, who was known locally as "Uncle Joe," experienced a tragedy during his stay. His 16-year-old daughter, Eunice, fell in love with a soldier at the nearby fort. Her father would not consent to their marriage, and the despondent girl jumped to her death from a large rock near the lighthouse. That boulder was known thereafter as "Lover's Rock."

When Lt. Edward W. Carpender examined the station in 1838, he noted that there were many complaints that the two lights blended into one from a distance and were easily confused with Barnstable's Sandy Neck Light. He recommended replacing one of the lights with a taller tower. Since the 1803 towers were decayed, wrote Carpender, it would be a small sacrifice to demolish them. He called the dwelling an "inferior building" and recommended rebuilding it using brick or stone.

An 1842 inspection report recommended the immediate reconstruction of the station's buildings. The towers were in such poor condition that even Stephen Pleasanton of the Treasury Department, who was in charge of the nation's lighthouses and a notorious penny-pincher, corroborated the urgent need to rebuild in April 1842. "I am afraid they will fall to the ground in the course of the summer," he wrote. When I. W. P. Lewis inspected the station just a short time later, he reported that the old towers were "in the last stages of decay—the lantern and apparatus as rude as can well be imagined." By this time, new towers were under construction.

New octagonal wooden towers, built using post-and-beam construction and joined by a covered walkway, were completed during

Early-1900s postcard view of Plymouth Light Station. *From the collection of the author.*

1843. A spacious new keeper's house was built at the same time. The towers were so close together that the problem of the lights merging when seen from sea remained. The 1870 annual report of the Lighthouse Board pointed out that the lights failed to serve one of the purposes for which they originally were designated—"to serve as a range to clear Brown's Bank." The problem couldn't easily be remedied without building new structures.

Rebuilding was again recommended in the report, but the 1843 twin lights would remain jointly in service at their original locations until 1924. Along the way, the old multiple lamps and reflectors were replaced by sixth-order Fresnel lenses, which were later upgraded to fourth-order lenses.

William Sears had a 20-year stay as keeper that ended with his resignation in the spring of 1881. Milton H. Reamy, previously the assistant keeper at nearby Duxbury Pier Light, succeeded Sears. Alfred G. Eisener, previously at Thacher Island and Cuttyhunk Light, became keeper in 1894. A newspaper article in 1896 reported that visitors were allowed to tour the station for two hours each day, except Sundays and holidays.

A 1904 article by Arthur Hewitt described a visit with the keeper at that time, Willis Higgins:

> *I pictured Higgins, the keeper, cleaning one of his lanterns, made*
> *friends with the patrolmen of the coast, caught more fish in the*
> *channel in an hour than one generally gets in a month, watched*

*the porgy seiners and lobstermen, and thoroughly enjoyed this
almost deserted spot.*

*Higgins and I often chatted. We disagreed on only one subject.
I wanted Higgins to be photographed in the knockabout clothes he
usually wore—he called them his undress uniform—but he vetoed
this each time, and immediately donned the full regalia of the United
States Lighthouse Establishment. . . . He was a representative of the
United States Government, and wished to be treated as such.*

A fog-bell tower, with a 1,500-pound bell and automatic striking
machinery, was added to the station in 1907. A first-class Daboll fog
trumpet eventually replaced the bell, and a new building was erected
for the related equipment.

The importance of the station decreased as maritime commerce
fell off in Plymouth, but it later grew in importance again after the
1914 opening of the Cape Cod Canal led to more shipping traffic in the
vicinity. By the 1920s the twin light stations established on the East
Coast were being phased out. In 1924, as part of this effort, the northeast light at the Gurnet was discontinued and torn down, ending 156
years of twin lights on the site. The single light was given a new characteristic, a single flash alternating with a double flash every 20 seconds.
The surviving 39-foot shingled tower is the nation's oldest freestanding
lighthouse tower built only of wood.

Frank Allen Davis, previously in charge at Tarpaulin Cove Light,
became keeper in 1925. The Davis family, with three children, occupied
the west side of the keeper's house, while an assistant keeper, Hubert
Needham, lived in the east side of the house with his wife. Davis made
the pages of the *Lighthouse Service Bulletin* on November 1, 1929, for
rescuing two men from an overturned sailboat, and for rendering
assistance to several people whose motorboat had run aground.

Davis's wife, Olive, drove a Model T Ford several miles to Duxbury
daily to take her children to school. Olive always carried a special
wrench in her purse. The tool was used to tighten drive bands in the
car; sand getting into the engine often made them slip. Once, on the
way back from a meeting of the Eastern Star social club, the car got
stuck in the sand. "I just took off my shoes, tucked my gown out of
the way and walked home," Olive later recalled.

Olive Davis also had the duty of raising storm-warning flags near
the lighthouse as needed. She was paid $11 monthly by the federal
government for performing that important service.

The Davis family hunted ducks and geese on the Gurnet, and the
keeper's son, Frank Arthur Davis, became a licensed lobsterman at the

age of nine. By the time he was 10, Frank was sailing his own boat and hauling his own lobster traps. He loved growing up at the Gurnet, later comparing his early life to the lives of Huck Finn and Tom Sawyer. "From the time I could walk," he said, "I had boats, fishing, hunting, and the run of the entire area. In the summer, I could play in the clumps of bushes and scrub cedar trees on the beach; the sand dunes were my mountains. I was king of the marshland and beach—creeks were my great rivers of the world."

James Hinkley Dobbins served as a relief keeper in 1937. His wife, Ruby Kelley Dobbins, remembered their stint at the Gurnet in her book *The Additional Keeper*. She recalled a visiting circus employee who brought a pair of performing bull terriers that "sang" and "talked." She also described the drive to the light station with Olive Davis:

> *The trip was difficult, to say the least. Sometimes the road was so narrow it seemed the car couldn't go through, then there were places where the tide overflowed the road. And set up along the way were huge constructions of swamp grass and driftwood called duck blinds where hunters came to camp overnight to duck hunt.*
>
> *But the scenery was breathtaking. On one side the bright blue ocean stretched clear to the horizon; on the other side we could watch activities of ships and sailboats and cruisers, some commercial, others pleasure boats. It seems people came from all over the country to enjoy the dune beaches for swimming, picnicking, and just plain relaxation.*

When the Coast Guard took over control of lighthouses in 1939, Keeper Davis joined that service. At the start of World War II, he was ordered to extinguish the light, as well as the lights on some local buoys.

The old dwelling was destroyed and a new four-bedroom ranch house was built to house the Coast Guard crew in 1962. Paul Christian, now of Portland, Oregon, spent boyhood summers close to the Plymouth Light Station. Families on the Gurnet—especially the children —often socialized with the Coast Guardsmen at the lighthouse. "Our house abutted the Coast Guard property," Christian recalls. "When we were kids, most of us would go to the station at night and watch TV. One of the station guys even started baseball games between the Gurnet kids and Saquish [a nearby beach] kids."

Paul's father, Bud Christian, recalls that during the Kennedy administration there was a national emphasis on physical fitness. The officer in charge at the light station wanted to get his crew in shape, so every morning he would get them up early and they would all jog around the Gurnet's dirt roads.

Al Readdy, a Coast Guard keeper in 1951, polishes the fourth-order Fresnel lens. *Courtesy of Al Readdy.*

Part of what made the Coast Guard personnel so important to the Gurnet and Saquish residents is that they provided the only link to the outside world, according to Paul Christian. "During the time that I was growing up on the Gurnet in the '60s and the early '70s, the Coast Guard had the only telephone to the mainland," he says. "People from the Gurnet and Saquish would come up to the station and ask if they could use the phone. The alternative was to drive on the beach to Duxbury to the nearest phone. Also, the Coast Guard had the only 'full-time' electric power. Some people would go to the station to do their laundry."

Susan Sevigny of Plymouth spent summers with her grandparents on the Gurnet. "I remember watching TV at the Coast Guard station or sitting around and watching them play pool," she says. "We all got involved in the softball games or playing Frisbee, no matter what our ages were. My time to come in at night was when the lighthouse came on. Then they changed the lighthouse so it was shining 24 hours a day. My grandmother had to buy us all watches."

The Coast Guard announced plans to automate and destaff the light in the mid-1980s, and many local residents objected. The light station still provided an important communications link to emergency services. Boatswain's Mate First Class Joseph Robicheau, the officer in charge, was an emergency medical technician, and the only mobile firefighting equipment on the Gurnet was at the station. Robicheau enjoyed life at the station with his wife, Leanne, and their two young daughters. "I really don't find anything out here that difficult," he told a reporter. "You do experience some hardships, but if you like it, it is not really a hardship."

The light was officially automated on October 1, 1986, when a modern optic replaced the fourth-order Fresnel lens. On the day of automation, Robicheau told the *Quincy Patriot Ledger,* "I'd stay here forever if they'd let me." The family continued living at the light station for some months after automation, until housing was located closer to Robicheau's new assignment in Boston.

Dolly Snow Bicknell of Project Gurnet and Bug Lights at the lighthouse in April 2006. *Photo by the author.*

In 1989 the station was leased by the Coast Guard to the Massachusetts Chapter of the U.S. Lighthouse Society. A related organization, the Friends of Plymouth Light, was formed as well. Volunteers lived in the 1963 ranch-style keeper's house, and the property was opened to overnight visitors. Bill and Debbi Ricci were married at the lighthouse and as caretakers made many improvements to the property during their stay there. In the group's newsletter, Debbi Ricci described the joys of lighthouse life: "We are becoming skilled at foraging and our diet now includes wild blackberries, bluefish, chowder made from sea clams, mussels, and steamers. . . . We have watched fireworks from the best vantage point in town, thunderstorms and their resulting rainbows, and the warmest, sunniest summer we can ever remember. Each new event just adds to the excitement of living at a lighthouse, a dream only a few people share."

The lease for the lighthouse later reverted to the Coast Guard. With the tower only 45 feet from the edge of the bluff, which was eroding at the rate of at least a foot a year, there was discussion of moving the lighthouse back in 1997, but neighbors complained that trucks would damage the fragile dirt roads on the Gurnet and that the lighthouse would be too close to their homes.

After discussion between residents and the Coast Guard, the 13-ton tower was moved approximately 140 feet on a system of rollers and blocks in December 1998, at a cost of $200,000. The move was managed by the Coast Guard's Civil Engineering Unit Providence and performed by Northern Construction Service of Hingham, Massachusetts, with the help of D and K Building Movers of Scituate, Massachusetts. The new location is near a spot that Gurnet residents had long used as second base during their Saturday-night baseball games.

Project Gurnet and Bug Lights, a group responsible for the restoration of Duxbury Pier ("Bug") Light near Plymouth, acquired a lease for the lighthouse in May 1999. The father of the group's president, Dolly Bicknell, was the popular New England historian and storyteller Edward Rowe Snow. Snow was also famous as the "Flying Santa" to lighthouse keepers for more than 40 years. The Gurnet holds a special place in Dolly's memories.

I remember flying over the lighthouse in a small plane with my dad when he was the Flying Santa at Christmastime. Also, my father used to lead a group of people—the Harbor Ramblers—on adventures around New England. One of my very favorite trips as a child was by beach buggy to Gurnet Light. We traveled in an open-air army-type vehicle that held perhaps 30 people, and it would bounce and jostle its way on the sandy beach. What fun it was!

At the end of the ride we would all pile out and explore the Gurnet area, including the Coast Guard building where I was allowed to play pool with the Coast Guardsmen. Of course, then there was the wonderfully bumpy ride home, back over the sand—not the road that we use now.

Volunteers have painted the lighthouse in recent years, and a window was replaced in 2001. In addition, rugosa roses and bayberry bushes have been planted to guard against erosion.

The light, 102 feet above mean high water, remains an active aid to navigation, with a sequence of three white flashes every 30 seconds. It was converted to solar power in 1994. A red sector warns mariner of dangerous Mary Ann Rocks, and there's an automated foghorn sounding two blasts every 15 seconds.

Automobile access to the Gurnet is limited to residents, but an open house is held in late May each year by Project Gurnet and Bug Lights as part of the Opening of the Bay festival in Duxbury. For more information, write to Project Gurnet and Bug Lights, P.O. Box 2167, Duxbury, MA 02331, or visit www.buglight.org.

An added attraction at the open houses is the opening of the nearby Gurnet Point Lifesaving Station, owned by Richard Boonisar. Boonisar has amassed an impressive collection of artifacts of the U.S. Life-Saving and Lighthouse services, including an early 1940s surfboat.

The lighthouse can also be seen distantly from the Plymouth Harbor area and from sightseeing cruises leaving Plymouth. You can see the old fourth-order Fresnel lens from the lighthouse at the Hull Lifesaving Museum in Hull, Massachusetts.

CHAPTER 38

Scituate Light in April 2006. *Photo by the author.*

Scituate Light

1812

This is the fifth-oldest lighthouse tower in New England, and the oldest extant lighthouse tower and keeper's house combination in America. The lighthouse's life as an aid to navigation was relatively brief, but it's had a long and healthy reincarnation as a historic and pictureque attraction.

Members of the Plymouth Colony, along with newcomers from England, settled the area we now know as Scituate, on Boston's South Shore, in 1627. The town was incorporated in 1636. Its name comes from an Indian word for "cold brook" and refers to a brook that runs into the harbor.

Scituate had developed a significant fishing industry by the late eighteenth century, owing to its small but protected harbor, sheltered by Cedar Point to the north and First Cliff to the south. Entering the harbor was difficult because of shallow water and mudflats.

Jesse Dunbar, a shipmaster, and other local citizens petitioned the town's selectmen for a lighthouse in 1807. The selectmen convinced the federal government to appropriate $4,000 in 1810 for the building of a lighthouse at the harbor entrance, about a dozen miles south of Boston Light. The light would also serve to guide coastal traffic past the dangerous Cohasset Rocks offshore. Some consideration was given to First Cliff, but Cedar Point was chosen for the location.

Land for the station at Cedar Point was taken from Benjamin Barker by eminent domain. Barker obviously wasn't pleased with the taking of his land, and he later denied passage through his adjoining property and feuded with the first keeper.

Three men from the nearby town of Hingham—Nathaniel Gill, Charles Gill, and Joseph Hammond Jr.—built the lighthouse at a cost of $3,200, completing it two months ahead of schedule in September 1811. The 25-foot-tall tower was accompanied by a one-and-a-half-story keeper's house, an oil vault (12 by 18 feet), and a well.

The Boston Marine Society was concerned that the new light be easy to differentiate from other lights in Boston Bay. In October 1811, a committee of the society met to discuss the situation with the local lighthouse superintendent Henry Dearborn. (This was the senior Henry Dearborn; his son, Henry A. S. Dearborn, succeeded his father as customs collector and local lighthouse superintendent in 1812.) They asked that the light not be put into service until the following March, after sufficient discussion of its characteristic.

The society recommended that an eclipser be installed to make Scituate Light a flashing light, which would differentiate it from Boston Light. The committee also recommended obscuring some of the range of the light. The Marine Society pointed out that their suggestions would save $174 in oil annually, but the plan was never adopted.

Instead, Scituate Light went into service as a fixed white light in April 1812. (According to some sources, it went into service on September 19, 1811, but a "Notice to Mariners" issued in January 1812 indicates that it was to be lit on April 1, 1812.) Boston Light was changed to a revolving light around the same time, after the new equipment was installed by Winslow Lewis. The decision puzzled some mariners.

In any case, Scituate's fixed light remained in service. The first keeper—appointed in December 1811—was Simeon Bates, who stayed at the lighthouse until his death in 1834 at the age of 99. Bates and his wife, Rachel, had nine children, including two daughters, Rebecca and Abigail. These two sisters would become heroic figures in the history of American lighthouses.

During the War of 1812, British warships frequently raided New England coastal towns. On June 11, 1814, British forces plundered and burned a number of vessels at Scituate. Keeper Bates fired two shots from a small cannon, angering the captain of a British warship as it departed.

Less than three months later, around September 1, Keeper Bates and most of his family were away, leaving 21-year-old Rebecca and 15-year-old (or, according to some accounts, 17-year-old) Abigail in charge. The sisters were horrified to see a British warship anchored in the harbor. In a magazine article many years later, Rebecca was quoted:

> I knew the ship at a glance. It was the La Hogue. "Oh Lord," says I to my sister, "that old La Hogue is off here again. What shall we do? Here are their barges and they'll burn our vessels just as they did afore."
>
> You see there were two vessels at the wharf loaded with flour, and we couldn't afford to lose that in times when the embargo made it so hard to live. We had to boil pumpkins all day to get sweetening for sugar.
>
> There were the muskets of the guard. I was of a good mind to take those out beyond the lighthouse and fire them at the barges.

I might have killed one or two, but it would have done no good for they would have turned around and fired on the village.

"I'll tell you what I'll do," says I to my sister, "Look here, you take the drum and I'll take the fife." I was fond of military music and could play four tunes on the fife—Yankee Doodle was my masterpiece. . . . "What good'll that do?" says she. "Scare them," says I. "All you've got to do is call the roll. I'll scream the fife and we must keep out of sight; if they see us they'll laugh us to scorn."

The British thought the sound of the fife and drum signaled the approach of the Scituate town militia, and they hastily retreated. Thus was born the legend of Scituate's "Lighthouse Army of Two."

The Bates sisters lived to be quite elderly. The Reverend George E. Ellis, overseer of Harvard College and a distinguished historian, obtained a signed statement from Rebecca attesting to the truth of the story. Rebecca sold copies of the affidavit for ten cents apiece, always asserting the veracity of her story in spite of doubters. Some have pointed out that records show that the British ship *La Hogue* was clearly elsewhere at the time of the alleged events, but it's certainly possible that the Bates sisters were confused about the identity of the vessel.

David Ball of the Scituate Historical Society has done extensive research into the story and believes it is likely true. The "Army of Two" has inspired several children's books, and the story has a firm place in the hearts of lighthouse buffs and Scituate residents. The fife played by Rebecca is still on display in the keeper's house.

In 1827 Marshall Lincoln, a contractor, was hired to add a 15-foot brick extension and a new lantern to the tower to increase the light's visibility. When the work was completed, a fixed white light was displayed from the lantern, while a red light was shown from the lower windows. Eight lamps and reflectors produced the red light; seven lamps and reflectors produced the white light. Red glass placed against the windows gave the lower light its color.

Lt. Edward W. Carpender questioned the need for the double light in his 1838 report:

> *It is not apparent why this should be a double light, when a single one would answer all the purpose. There is no other red light in Boston bay, so that, by having this a single red light, it is not possible that it should be mistaken. Accordingly, I recommend its conversion into a single red light. . . .*
>
> *Arranged as the lights now are, the lower only twenty feet above the level of the sea, and made in the manner it now is, it is not possible they should be of much service. To know them, you must*

*approach near to them; for, being only fifteen feet apart, they blend
at a short distance, and appear like a single light.*

In his report Carpender also found fault with Keeper Zeba
Cushing, who had succeeded Simeon Bates.

> *I visited this light by the middle of the forenoon; the keeper absent,
> to be gone until the middle of the afternoon; not a lamp touched, the
> reflectors looking as if they had not been burnished for a length of
> time, and the glass smoked. Perhaps no place on the coast requires
> a better light than Scituate; not so much on its own account, for the
> port is small, and cannot have much trade, but on account of the
> navigation between it and the mouth of Boston harbor. . . .*
>
> *The keeper, at his own expense, has been allowed to build an
> addition to the Government dwelling. I mention this, not only as it
> is without precedent, but because the keeper has the reputation of
> intrusting the care of the light to his tenant, which may be one
> reason, among others, why this light has such a low reputation.*

The double light was still in use when a new lantern and new
lighting apparatus were installed under the direction of Winslow Lewis
in the spring of 1841. Interestingly, Lewis had written in 1817, "The
utility of this light has been questioned by the most experienced
navigators on this part of the coast."

The lantern was fitted with 11 lamps in two tiers, with 14-inch
reflectors, and the lower light was fitted with four lamps and 14-inch
reflectors.

Winslow Lewis's nephew, the civil engineer I. W. P. Lewis, examined the station during his important survey of 1842. The younger
Lewis roundly criticized his uncle's recent work, calling the lamps "all
leaky and burnt out" and the reflectors "out of plumb." The woodwork
in the tower was "all more or less rotten," and the interior was covered
with ice in winter and moss in summer.

Keeper Ebenezer Osborne, who had been appointed in January
1841 at a salary of $350 per year, provided a litany of complaints for
I. W. P. Lewis's report:

> *The lantern is glazed with plate glass . . . five lights of this glass
> have been broken by frost or heat.*
>
> *The lamps are Hemmenway's patent, and nine out of the eleven
> are so much burnt, and so very leaky, that I have great difficulty
> in keeping them in order. I have to wedge up the glass holders with
> wood, to keep them in their places, and all the wick turnscrews leak*

in their sockets. The lantern vibrates so much in a gale of wind as to rattle the glass chimneys out of their places; the stove pipe from the lower light passes through the floor of the upper lantern, and has broken by its heat three panes of glass.

Both I. W P. Lewis and Osborne described many defects in the keeper's dwelling. "The house is much decayed," wrote Lewis, "all the framework being more or less rotten." The tide ebbed and flowed right through the house's cellar, and as much as three feet of water flooded the cellar in spring tides. Osborne called the house "miserable, leaky, smoky, and uncomfortable," and he noted falling plaster and leaky windows. He also complained that he wasn't allowed a boat.

Lewis noted that, despite the double light at Scituate, mariners had repeatedly mistaken it for Boston Light. Some had run aground at Minot's Ledge, four miles to the north, because of this common problem. Lewis called for significant changes:

> *This light-house is useful merely in a local point of view. The small amount of tonnage owned at Scituate may be, and is undoubtedly, benefited by the convenience it affords in showing the entrance to the harbor; but, to the navigation of Boston bay, this light is, and always has been, a positive injury, and the cause of several heart-rending shipwrecks. The distinction of a red and white light here is altogether useless, and a wasteful expense, for the reason that the red light is only visible upon a close approach that would lead to casualties. . . .*
>
> *This light should be reduced to a simple beacon of one lamp, instead of fifteen now used. It would then fall into its proper mark, and not be likely to cause such accidents as heretofore.*

Minor improvements were made, but the authorities held off the construction of a new tower. They had a new lighthouse in mind, not at Cedar Point, but offshore at Minot's Ledge. Stephen Pleasanton, the fifth auditor of the Treasury in charge of the nation's lighthouses, wrote, "Instead of building a new Keeper's house the present year I would prefer to have the old one repaired, as I am somewhat in hopes that Congress may be induced to make an adequate appropriation for the contemplated light on Minot's Ledge."

Construction on the first Minot's Ledge Lighthouse began in 1847, and the tower was first lit on January 1, 1850. Scituate Light remained in service, with a fixed red light. James Y. Bates, grandson of the first keeper, became keeper in August 1849.

With the new light offshore, it seemed that Scituate Light's days were numbered. But the first Minot's Ledge Lighthouse was destroyed in a storm on April 16, 1851, and the light at Cedar Point regained a measure of importance.

The light at Scituate was changed from red to white in October 1854. The lighthouse received a new Fresnel lens in 1855, and some measures were undertaken to slow erosion at the station in 1857.

A second tower at Minot's Ledge, built sturdily of granite, went into service on November 15, 1860. Thomas Richardson had become keeper at Scituate in late 1856. In his book *Famous Lighthouses of New England*, Edward Rowe Snow described the apparent end of Scituate Light's years as an aid to navigation.

> *On the night of November 14, 1860, Keeper Thomas Richardson lit the Scituate lamps for the last time, as the following evening Keeper Wilder out at the new Minot's Light tower was scheduled to illuminate his tower for the first full night's glow. With the intention of making the occasion live in the memory of his son Edward, ten years old, he decided to awaken the boy when it was time to turn the tower light off.*
>
> *Half an hour before dawn on the morning of November 15, 1860, Richardson aroused his son and told him his plan. Hardly realizing what it was all about, and grumbling because of the early hour, the lad stumbled into his clothes and followed his father out through the covered way to the still lighted tower. As the first red streaks of dawn appeared in the eastern sky, the lad looked out at Minot's Ledge Light, the successful rival of the old Scituate beacon, and a minute later put out forever the beam which had guided Scituate sailors and fishermen into the harbor since 1811. That same evening Edward Richardson and his father silently watched Minot's friendly glow flashing out across the water. The career of Scituate Light had ended.*

According to an 1890 newspaper article, a small light was hung in the lighthouse for some years "for the guidance of Scituate herring fishermen." Then the federal government had a 630-foot breakwater built at Cedar Point between 1885 and 1890, which made the harbor a more secure place of refuge. Years later, a second 450-foot jetty was added, extending southwest from the base of the first jetty.

A light was exhibited from a lamp on a spar at the breakwater's end beginning on June 10, 1891. The light was shown from a skeleton tower after the spar was carried away by high seas in early 1904. The kerosene-fueled light exhibited a fixed red light, 31 feet above the sea.

Keepers were assigned to the jetty light and lived in the old Scituate Light keeper's house. The first keeper was John E. O. Prouty, at $120 yearly. For a number of years, the keeper was a harbor pilot,

Scituate Light during its period of abandonment, circa early 1900s. *From the collection of the author.*

J. Frank Cushman. Cushman operated an ice cream parlor in the west side of the keeper's house for a time.

In 1924 a new acetylene automatic light was installed, and a keeper was no longer needed. Since 1958 an automatic electric beacon has been on the breakwater; the tower was last replaced in 1984.

The lighthouse tower, which had its lantern removed, had been long abandoned and was referred to as a "picturesque ruin" by one writer. The local chapter of the Daughters of the American Revolution launched a petition drive to restore the tower in 1907 and presented the petition, with 600 signatures, to their representative in Congress. It appears no action was taken until 1912, when Selectman Jamie Turner and his wife, Jessie, learned that the property was to be auctioned the very next day. Jessie Turner took a train to Boston with a $1,000 check from the town's treasurer. Her efforts put a hold on the auction proceedings.

Scituate residents appealed to Senator Henry Cabot Lodge, and the sale was delayed. Among those who eventually contributed to the purchase price of $4,000 was William Bates, grandnephew of Abigail and Rebecca Bates. The sale to the town of Scituate became official in 1917.

One of the most dramatic events in the history of Cedar Point occurred in a blizzard featuring 80-mile-per-hour winds on March 16, 1956, when the 441-foot Italian freighter *Etrusco* ran aground near the lighthouse. The Coast Guard rescued the 31 crewmen by breeches buoy, a system consisting of a ring and a canvas sling suspended from a pulley running along a rope from the ship to shore. The ship

The freighter *Etrusco* grounded near Scituate Light on March 16, 1956. *From the collection of the author.*

remained at Cedar Point until the following December, when it was floated off at high tide after much of the rock around it was blasted away. Many thousands of people visited Scituate Light that year to see the gigantic stranded vessel.

The town had a replica lantern created and installed in 1930. Some improvements were made to the lighthouse and keeper's house, but by the 1960s the house was again in disrepair. Kathleen Laidlaw of the Scituate Historical Society informed the board of selectmen that the town was required to maintain the property in good condition under the tenets of the 1917 sale. The town agreed to appropriate $6,500 for repairs.

In 1968 custody of the site was awarded to the historical society. Today contributions and rent paid by the residents of the keeper's house pay for the upkeep of the property.

A 1968 article in the *Boston Herald Traveler* provided a glimpse into the lives of Tom and Jean O'Neil, the caretakers at that time. Part of the deal was that they would serve as tour guides during four open house dates in the summer. The historical society took care of any needed repairs, and local Scouts tended the garden.

Some have claimed that the ghosts of Rebecca and Abigail Bates haunt Scituate Light. Fife and drum music, they say, can be heard blending in with the wind and waves. Residents of the keeper's house have seen no ghosts, but Jean O'Neil said she thought she heard "sounds like a fife and drum in the fireplace chimney."

In 1989 the Cedar Point Association received funding for a new Lighthouse Park. The lighthouse was relighted in July 1991, after 131 years in darkness, although the light was visible from land only. At the relighting ceremony, Kathleen Laidlaw said, "The lighthouse has become almost the symbol of Scituate. The light will bring it back to life."

A local resident, Herb Jason, using a ball from Nantucket's Sankaty Head Light as a model, crafted a new 27-inch diameter ventilator ball for the top of the lantern. In August 1994, Scituate Light's comeback climaxed when the nation's eleventh-oldest lighthouse was relighted as a private aid to navigation. An acrylic 250-millimeter optic displays a flashing white light visible for about four miles.

George Downton, a U.S. Navy veteran and retired Proctor & Gamble engineer, moved into the keeper's house with his wife, Ruth, in 1986. The couple weathered the devastating "Perfect Storm" of October 1991, and they were credited with minimizing the damage to the property. The popular Downton died in early 2000; at this writing, Ruth Downton still lives in the keeper's house.

In the summer of 2000, David Ball and the Scituate Historical Society began raising funds for the development of educational panels to be placed in the covered walkway between the tower and keeper's house. The American Lighthouse Foundation became the first organization to sponsor a panel in the walkway, and others quickly followed suit. Today the formerly barren walkway is essentially a small museum, with panels on the history of the lighthouse and surrounding area.

By the early twenty-first century, it was realized that nearly 180 years of harsh New England winters had caused the bricks in the upper portion of the lighthouse tower to deteriorate. In early 2004, spalling of the brick faces was clearly visible from the ground. At a town meeting, the historical society asked for funds for emergency repairs, and consultants were brought in to examine the tower. Core samples were taken, and it was determined that the outer layer of bricks needed to be replaced.

ESI Waterproofing and Masonry Restoration of Boston performed the restoration of the tower in 2004. The $125,000 needed for the project came from the Massachusetts Bay Transit Authority as part of a mitigation agreement with the town. By June 2005, the tower was repainted and was looking as good as—or better than—new.

Scituate Light is easy to reach by car, and there's a large, free parking lot. Bear in mind that the keeper's house is a private residence. The tower is normally closed to the public, but there are several open-house dates each year. The historical society will also provide tours of the walkway and tower by appointment.

For more information, write to the Scituate Historical Society, P.O. Box 276, Scituate, MA 02066, call (781) 545-1083, or visit www.scituatehistoricalsociety.org.

Minot's Ledge Light in 1998. *Photo by the author.*

Minot's Ledge Light

1850, 1860

It's not the tallest or the oldest lighthouse in Massachusetts, and few would claim it's the prettiest. But this rugged, waveswept tower has probably sparked more imaginations—and possibly more romances—than any beacon in the state.

Minot's Ledge—about a mile offshore, near the line between the South Shore towns of Cohasset and Scituate—is part of the dangerous Cohasset Rocks, formerly known as the Conyhasset or Quonahassit Rocks after a local Indian tribe. It's said that the Quonahassit people would visit the ledges and leave gifts of arrowheads, beads, and various trinkets, in an effort to appease the spirit they believed resided in the rocks. If the spirit became angry, they thought, it would bring destructive storms to the tribe.

The origin of the name of Minot's Ledge isn't clear. According to the historian Edward Rowe Snow, it was probably named for George Minot, who owned T Wharf in Boston in the mid-1700s. Snow believed that a ship owned by Minot might have been wrecked on the ledge.

In August 1838, the Boston Marine Society appointed a committee of three to study the feasibility of a lighthouse on the ledge. The committee reported in November 1838: "The practibility of building a Light house on it that will withstand the force of the sea does not admit of a doubt—the importance of having a light house on a rock so dangerous to the navigation of Boston, on which so many lives, & so much property has been lost is too well known to need comment."

The Marine Society repeatedly petitioned Congress for a lighthouse between 1839 and 1841, with no positive results.

Scituate Light, established in 1812, was intended to help mariners avoid the dangers in the area, but there was widespread feeling that it actually made matters worse; mariners often confused the light at Scituate with Boston Light, and disaster resulted. I. W. P. Lewis made reference to the problem in his 1843 report to Congress.

For a long series of years, petitions have been presented to Congress, from the citizens of Boston, for erecting a light-house on these dreadful rocks, but no action has ever yet been taken upon the subject. One of the causes of frequent shipwrecks on these rocks has

been the light-house at Scituate, four miles to the leeward of the reef,
which has been repeatedly mistaken for Boston light, and thus caused
the death of many a brave seaman and the loss of large amounts of
property.

Lewis's report listed more than 40 vessels that had been lost on
the ledge from 1832 to 1841. He asserted, "A light house on this reef is
more required than on any part of the seaboard of New England."

The ledge remained unmarked, and vessels continued to have
trouble negotiating the area. On February 12, 1847, a brig from New
Orleans struck the rocks in the vicinity of Minot's Ledge. Luckily,
the ship was able to make it to Boston with nine feet of water in
its hold.

Less than a month later, Congress finally appropriated $20,000
for a lighthouse on the ledge; an additional $19,500 would eventually
be needed for the completion of the project, including $4,500 for the
lighting apparatus. The site selected was the rock known as the Outer
Minot. Many people believed a granite tower similar to the waveswept
lighthouses of the British Isles to be the proper solution, but Capt.
William H. Swift of the Corps of Topographical Engineers deemed it
impractical to build such a tower on the small (about 25 feet wide),
mostly submerged ledge.

Instead, Swift planned an iron pile lighthouse, a 70-foot-tall spidery
structure with piles drilled into the rock, on the theory that waves
would pass harmlessly through the structure. The cost-conscious
lighthouse administrators of the day appreciated the fact that a tower
of this type would be far less expensive than one made of stone.

Work began in the summer of 1847. A schooner transported
workers and materials to the site, and the workers slept on the vessel
each night. A drill, which required four men to operate, was supported
on a wooden platform. The contractor on the project was Benjamin
Pomeroy.

James Sullivan Savage, who had built Boston's Bunker Hill
Monument, oversaw the drilling operations. The drilling equipment
was twice swept off the ledge in 1847, and it took nearly two full
seasons to complete the drilling.

The octagonal keepers' quarters (14 feet in diameter) and
wrought-iron lantern (11 feet wide and 6 ½ feet high) were built atop
nine 10-inch-diameter piles, cemented into 5-foot-deep holes drilled in
the ledge and braced horizontally by three sets of iron rods. The iron
pile were manufactured at Cyrus Alger's ironworks in South Boston;
Alger was a well-known maker of cannons.

In his book *Cape Cod*, Henry David Thoreau described passing the lighthouse while it was still under construction in 1849:

> *Here was the new iron light-house, then unfinished, in the shape of an egg-shell painted red, and placed high on iron pillars, like the ovum of a sea monster floating on the waves. . . . As we passed it at half-tide we saw the spray tossed up nearly to the shell. A man was to live in that eggshell, day and night, a mile from the shore. When I passed it the next summer it was finished and two men lived in it, and a light-house keeper said that they told him that in a recent gale it had rocked so as to shake the plates off the table. Think of making your bed thus in the crest of a breaker! To have the waves, like a pack of hungry wolves, eyeing you always, night and day, and from time to time making a spring at you, almost sure to have you at last.*

Less than three months before the light went into service, at the height of Ireland's great famine, the 200-ton Irish brig *Saint John* was heading for Boston with more than a hundred immigrants. A Boston newspaper reported what happened as the ship encountered a devastating gale:

> *Capt. Oliver . . . states that he made Cape Cod Light about 5 o'clock Saturday evening, Scituate Light near 1 o'clock Sunday morning, then stood away to the northward, to clear the land, for about three hours. Then, it being about daylight, he tacked the ship and stood S.S.W. Weather very thick, he came inside of Minot's Light House, and there saw a brig lying at anchor, just inside of breakers, at a place called Hooksett Rock, tried to wear up to the brig, but found he could not fetch up, and threw over both anchors, which dragged. He then cut away her masts, and she drifted on to Grampus Ledge, where she went to pieces.*

It was impossible to launch the lifeboats in the turbulent sea, and most of the passengers drowned. There were only a few survivors; 99 passengers and crew died in the worst disaster ever in the vicinity of Minot's Ledge.

The lighthouse was finished in late 1849. It was lighted for the first time on January 1, 1850, with 15 lamps and 21-inch reflectors in two tiers exhibiting a fixed white light. It was the first lighthouse in the United States to be exposed to the ocean's full fury.

The first keeper—at $600 yearly—was Isaac Dunham, a Massachusetts native who was previously keeper of Pemaquid Point Light in Maine. There were usually two keepers on duty at a time; Dunham's assistants included his son, Isaac A. Dunham, and Russell Higgins of Cape Cod. Dunham didn't believe the structure was safe. Only a week after the light went into service, he wrote in the log (original spelling retained): "Clensd the Lantern for Liting in a tremendous Gale of wind. It seames as though the Light House would go from the Rock."

In April 1850, Dunham wrote:

> *April 6—The wind E. blowing very hard with an ugly sea which makes the light real like a Drunken Man—I hope God will in mercy still the raging sea—or we must perish. . . . God only knows what the end will be.*
>
> *At 4 P.M. the gale continues with great fury. It appears to me that if the wind continues from the East and it now is[,] that we cannot survive the night—if it is to be so—O God receive my unworthy soul for Christ sake for in him I put my trust.*

On July 2, Dunham wrote that his son, when leaving the tower, had to swing from a rope and drop into a waiting boat. "It would have frightened Daniel Webster," he wrote.

In his book *The Story of Minot's Light,* Edward Rowe Snow wrote that Dunham's pet kitten was so agitated by life in the unsteady tower that it jumped from the watchroom gallery to its death in the waves below. Fearing for his life, Dunham requested that the tower be strengthened, but Captain Swift assured everyone that it was perfectly safe.

Unconvinced, Dunham resigned after 10 months as keeper. His two assistants also resigned. Dunham had offered to stay on if he could live most of the winter on shore as a "relief man," but his offer was refused. There were no immediate applicants for the keeper positions, so the authorities resorted to advertising in the newspapers.

The second keeper was John W. Bennett, a veteran of 25 years at sea and a former first lieutenant in the British navy who was described by the local lighthouse superintendent as "a man of courage as well as character." The yearly salary of the principal keeper was raised to $1,000, and the salary of the assistants was raised from $360 to $550.

Bennett was confident at first, but he soon came to believe the lighthouse was unsafe. After a storm in the late fall, Bennett contacted the local superintendent, Philip Greely, who sent a committee to examine the structure. Visiting on a calm day, the committee concluded that the tower would withstand "any storm without danger." The keepers were unconvinced.

A drawing of the first (1850) Minot's Ledge Lighthouse. *From the collection of the author.*

Bennett installed a thick rope hawser extending from the tower to a rock about 200 feet away. A basket or sling was suspended from the rope, with the idea that the keepers could use it as an escape route in emergencies. Bennett apparently did leave the lighthouse via the hawser in times of heavy seas.

A 640-pound fog bell was installed in late October 1850, to be sounded in times of "fog and snow storms, or other thick weather."

A visitor in late 1850 wrote that the lighthouse swayed two feet in each direction in a storm. Bennett and his assistants increasingly lived in fear of their lives as stormy weather became more frequent with the onset of winter. Assistant Keeper Samuel Gardiner described a December storm in a letter to Bennett, who was away:

During your absence we have had a very heavy gale and tremendous sea from the N.E. such a one as there has not been seen since the Light House has been built. . . . The house was shaking very bad from 9 am until 4 pm. The watch bell was constantly ringing and it was almost impossible for us to stand on our feet. There was a barrel of water standing in the cellar which was half emptied by the shaking of the house. . . . The piles beneath us are now one solid mass of ice nearly as big as a three barrel cask. As for the ladder, that cannot be found. . . . I assure you sir that it was the most awful situation that ever I was placed in before in my life, and I begin to think that the many stories which were told about it before I came were mostly true. At any rate it was much worse than ever I imagined it could be, and now sir you cannot think [it] strange that we are not contented to remain here for the paltry sum of one dollar a day . . . If we were sure of the wages being raised there would be some encouragement, but we are not willing to risk our lives for the present pay any longer. We do not wish to make you uneasy about our leaving, but we hope you will secure others as soon as possible who do not set such value on their lives as we.

A few days later, Bennett wrote to Greely, "My firm belief is that unless something is done and that without procrastination to secure the edifice more firmly it cannot stand and I fear something awful will happen."

During a desperate night, Bennett wrote the following message:

> These last forty-eight hours have been the most terrific that I have witnessed for many a year. . . . The raging violence of the sea no man can appreciate, unless he is an eye witness. . . .
>
> The rods put into the lower section are bent up in fantastic shapes; some are torn asunder from their fastenings; the ice is so massive that there is no appearance of the ladder; the sea is now running at least twenty-five feet above the level, and each one roars like a heavy peal of thunder; the northern part of the foundation is split, and the light house shakes at least two feet each way. I feel as seasick as ever I did on board a ship.
>
> Our lantern windows are all iced up outside, although we have a fire continually burning; and it is not without imminent peril that we can climb up outside to scrape it off, which I have done several times already. I have a dread of some ship striking against us, although we have kept the bell constantly ringing all night. Our water is a solid mass of ice in the casks, which we have been obliged to cut to pieces with an axe before we could obtain any drink.
>
> Our situation is perilous. If anything happens before day dawns on us again, we have no hope of escape. But I shall, if it be God's will, die in the performance of my duty.
>
> P.S. I have put a copy of this in a bottle, with the hope it may be picked up in case of any accident to us.

Meanwhile, Dunham, the former keeper, wrote to Stephen Pleasanton, in charge of the nation's lighthouses, in early January 1851. Dunham said he was enjoying life at his North Bridgewater home "mutch better than on that Rock." Dunham reiterated his fears that the tower would soon fall if nothing was done.

Greely, apparently tiring of the constant flow of dire predictions from the present and former keepers, wrote to Pleasanton:

> The keepers are not very judicious, and are quite too much disposed to consider themselves heroes, and I do not know as if it is possible to prevent them or anybody else from "magnifying" their office and telling exaggerated and frightful stories. . . .
>
> I have always said to you that, in my judgment, the Light House is perfectly safe . . . but I have thought it was best to get

*an appropriation from Congress to be expended in strengthening
the House . . . and I have recommended also, in strong terms, an
increase of the Salaries of the Keepers.*

Captain Swift felt compelled to respond to the widespread fear
that the tower would fall. On January 18, 1851, a long letter from Swift
was published in the *Boston Daily Advertiser.* He wrote, "Time, the
great expounder of the truth or the fallacy of the question, will decide
for or against the Minot; but inasmuch as the light has outlived nearly
three winters, there is some reason to hope that it may survive one or
two more."

Swift did express some worry about the escape hawser installed
by Bennett, calling it a "gross violation of common sense. . . . It needs
no Solomon to perceive that the effect of the sea upon this guy is precisely that which a gang of men would exert if laboring at the rope to
pull the light-house down."

After a storm struck the Boston area on March 16, 1851, the
Pittsfield Sun reported, "Minot's Ledge light house stood the racket
bravely; and . . . it may confidently be expected that the edifice will
withstand the elements hereafter." The heavy seas smashed the dory
and forced the keepers to spend nearly four days in the storeroom,
below their living quarters, living on uncooked meat and bread until
the seas died down.

During a visit to Boston just after the March storm, Assistant
Keeper Joseph Wilson, a 20-year-old native of England, told a friend
that he would stay at the lighthouse as long as Bennett remained in
charge. Wilson also said that in the event of a catastrophe, he would
stay in the tower as long as it stood. He was confident of his ability to
reach shore if the tower should fall.

There was another gale on April 9, and Greely reported, "The
structure was not the least injured in the storm." The keepers' boat
was lost, and Greely promised to furnish a new one "forthwith."

On April 16–17, 1851, a colossal storm brought high seas to the
Boston Harbor area, turning Boston into an island, washing a schoolhouse and a seawall off Deer Island in Boston Harbor, sweeping away
several houses in Cohasset, and flooding much of the area. This gale
would be immortalized as the Minot's Light Storm.

Bennett had gone to Boston to see Greely about procuring a new
boat on Monday, April 14, and was unable to return to the lighthouse
on Tuesday because of heavy seas. Two young assistant keepers,
Joseph Wilson and Joseph Antoine, a 25-year-old native of Portugal,
were on duty.

The light was seen to burn through the night on Tuesday, and the tower was last seen from shore, clearly standing, about 4:00 p.m. on Wednesday. Scituate residents reported that the light was last seen burning about 10:00 p.m. on Wednesday night. At some point, as the seas grew more turbulent, Antoine and Wilson dropped a note in a bottle into the waves below. The note, found the following day by a Gloucester fisherman, read:

> *The lighthouse won't stand over to night. She shakes 2 feet each way now.*
> *J.W. + J.A.*

The tide reached its height around midnight. At about 1:00 a.m., residents onshore heard the frantic ringing of the fog bell at the lighthouse, possibly being sounded as an alarm or call for help.

The central support apparently broke first; a man onshore reported that the tower had a decided list by Wednesday afternoon. The outer supports all snapped by the early hours of Thursday morning. Evidence suggested the two men left using the escape hawser before the lighthouse fell.

Bennett went to the shore about 5:00 a.m. He saw fragments of the lighthouse lantern washing ashore, along with bedding and some of his own clothing. He also found an India rubber life jacket, which looked as if it had been worn by one of the assistant keepers, but was apparently torn from his body by the force of the seas. Two miles of beach were eventually littered with furniture and fragments of the wooden parts of the lighthouse.

The body of Joseph Antoine was found at Nantasket Beach in Hull. The remains of Joseph Wilson were found the following October by John Bennett on a small island called Gull Rock, about a mile southwest of Minot's Ledge. His position on the island indicated that he may have reached it alive but died of exposure before morning. Wilson's skull was fractured, suggesting that he had fallen or had been struck by wreckage from the lighthouse.

Captain Swift visited the ledge on April 22, 1851, and he made a sketch of the few bent pilings that remained fastened to the rock. Some of the tower could be seen on its side in the water.

There was much debate about where blame should be assigned for the disaster. It's worth noting that there were originally plans to install additional bracing on the lower part of the tower, but Swift decided against it because he believed the braces would create added surface for the seas to push against and thus make the tower less safe.

The *Boston Transcript* recalled Swift's letter defending the safety of the structure, calling it an "ungenerous sneer at the fears which had been expressed by Mr. Bennett." But a later article in the same newspaper cited a longtime shipyard worker from Cohasset who firmly believed that it was the heavy, frozen hawser that pulled the lighthouse down.

The Boston Marine Society held an emergency meeting a few hours after the lighthouse's demise, to devise some plan to reestablish a light at the ledge as quickly as possible. The towboat *R. B. Forbes* was sent to display a light, but another storm on April 20 forced the boat to return to port. John Bennett visited the ledge on April 24, and a 31-foot spar was placed as a warning to mariners.

A short time later, a small lightship, stationed at Brandywine Shoal in the Delaware Bay since 1823, was anchored at the ledge. John Bennett was put in charge of the vessel. The lightship crew had a famous pet for a time; their Newfoundland dog was renowned for fetching floating bundles of newspapers dropped off by passing ships. A new lightship, built for about $27,000 at Somerset, Massachusetts, served at the station from 1854 to 1860.

Congress appropriated $80,000 for a new lighthouse "of granite, iron, or a combination of both" in August 1852, and a survey of the ledge was soon completed. The survey revealed that it would be impossible to build a tower with a diameter greater than 22 feet without going below the low water line. That diameter wasn't sufficient for the proposed tower. It was determined that the diameter would be 30 feet, meaning that much work would have to be done underwater. Additional appropriations totaling $244,000 were needed before the work was completed in 1860.

General Joseph G. Totten of the Lighthouse Board designed the second Minot's Ledge Lighthouse. As the famed engineer Gen. John Gross Barnard later stated, "It ranks, by the engineering difficulties surrounding its erection, and by the skill and science shown in the details of its construction, among the chief of the great sea-rock light-houses of the world."

Lt. Barton S. Alexander of the Army Corps of Engineers, a Kentucky native and West Point graduate, made some modifications in the design and was superintendent of the project. A friend once described Alexander as "a man of massive stature, with a head and heart in full proportion to his body." In his later career, Alexander became a brigadier general and worked on fortifications in New York Harbor, Boston Harbor, and the Maine coast.

Alexander first landed at the ledge in May 1855. He later described his initial impressions: "The stumps of the broken iron piles of the old lighthouse first attracted my attention. They had a melancholy appearance; they told of disaster, and the determination to remove them was involuntary. The wreck of the old lighthouse was visible under water, as we stood on the rock, and I determined to remove it also."

On June 20, 1855, workers arrived to clear the ledge of mussels and to loosen the wedges around the stumps of the old tower. On July 1, Alexander brought a hammer and chisel to the ledge and made a benchmark at the highest part of the ledge. In the following days, the crew marked the ledge to indicate how it would be leveled.

Only 130 hours of work were completed at the site in 1855. The work on the foundation could take place only at low tide at times of calm seas, and the season lasted only until September 15.

Labor at the site began in earnest on April 1, 1856, with the cutting of the uneven ledge into a series of levels. The foundation holes from the original lighthouse were utilized in the positioning of nine wrought-iron piles, which would serve to bolt the tower to the ledge. A 20-foot-high scaffold was erected to provide safety for workers. A total of 157 hours was worked on the ledge in 1856.

The project had a setback on January 19, 1857, when the iron scaffolding was destroyed during a storm. Alexander was discouraged. "If wrought iron won't stand it," he said, "I have my fears about a stone tower."

Alexander was relieved when it became apparent that the damage was caused by a ship—the bark *New Empire*—that hit the ledge, not by the waves. The rocks themselves were damaged by the collision, and the work had to start all over again. A visitor described a typical workday for the *New England Magazine:*

> *Captain Alexander had constructed two large, staunch row boats, naming one* Deucalion *and the other* Pyrrha,—*for he was a droll fellow, full of dry wit. The* Deucalion *was painted red, and this was more especially for his own use, while the* Pyrrha, *a green painted craft, was to carry the men. We would watch the tide from the cove, and just as soon as the ebb had reached the proper stage we would start out with it, and at the moment a square yard of ledge was bare of water out would jump a stone cutter and begin work. Soon another would follow, and as fast as they had elbow room others still, until the rock would resemble a carcass covered with a flock of crows.*

When one of the workers asked what the names *Deucalion* and *Pyrrha* meant, Alexander explained that *Deucalion* was a giant of Greek mythology who would pick up giant stones and toss them out of his way, and *Pyrrha* was his wife, who ate them.

Conditions were unfavorable during the working season in 1857, and only 130 hours of labor were completed. The foundation pit was nearly completed, and four stones of the foundation were laid. The conditions in the following year were more favorable, and the lowest stone of the tower was laid on July 11, 1858. The first six courses of the tower were laid in that year, and 208 hours of work were completed on the site.

The painstaking cutting and assembling of the granite took place at Cohasset's Government Island, attached to the mainland. A team of oxen moved the blocks to a vessel that took them to the ledge. Each block was dovetailed to its neighbors on either side, and the blocks were doweled to each other with iron pins. Strong Portland cement was used to adhere the blocks to each other.

Not a single man was seriously injured in the course of construction, although waves swept the workers off the rocks many times. Despite the fact that all the workers were required to know how to swim, a Cohasset diver, Michael Neptune Brennock, was hired to act as a lifeguard. When a wave hit, the men learned to hold on tightly to a steel bolt or rope until the danger passed. While the crews were working on the ledge, there was always a boat nearby with three crewmen to pick up anyone who was washed from the rock.

Once a stonecutter named Reed didn't hear the call of "Roller coming!" He was suddenly in the water 40 feet from the ledge, stunned and going under. Brennock was instantly on the scene. As the lifeguard held tight to Reed, the other workers got a line to the men and tragedy was averted.

Another man who took part in the building of the tower was Capt. John Newell Cook of Cohasset. On the occasion of his death in 1896, it was reported that Captain Cook had designed the derrick that was used to lift the granite blocks into place in the tower, but for some reason he had never received the credit he deserved.

On October 2, 1858, the cornerstone was laid and an official dedication was held at Government Island. Mayor Frederick W. Lincoln of Boston introduced Captain Alexander, who said: "So may it stand, that 'they who go down to the sea in ships' may see this signal fire burning brightly to warn them from the countless rocks that echo with the rage that oft swells from the bosom of old ocean."

The great orator Edward Everett followed Alexander: "Well do I remember that dreadful night, when a furious storm swept along the coast of New England. . . . In the course of that tremendous night, the lighthouse on Minot's Ledge disappeared . . . and with it the two brave men who, in that awful hour, stood bravely at their posts. We have come now, sir, to repair the desolation of that hour."

The year 1859 saw the masonry finished to the top of the thirty-second course, 62 feet above the water. The last stone was laid on June 29, 1860, five years minus one day after Alexander and his workmen first landed at the ledge. The final cost of $300,000—including two keepers' houses onshore—made it one of the most expensive lighthouses in United States history.

The lantern and a second-order Fresnel lens were put into place, and the lighthouse was first illuminated on November 15, 1860. Its light was 84 feet above mean high water. The power of the light shown by the lightship that had served in the interim was described by the *Boston Post* as "farthing candles" compared to the brilliance of the new light.

Built of 1,079 blocks (3,514 tons) of Quincy granite (chosen because it was "finest of grain, toughest, and clearest of sap"), the tower has stood through countless storms and hurricanes, a testament to its designer and builders. The first 40 feet are solid granite, topped by a storeroom, living quarters, and workspace. Below the lantern is a watchroom and space for the machinery that rotated the lens. The height from the ledge to the very top of the lantern is 114 feet.

The poet Henry Wadsworth Longfellow, whose many visits to Portland Head Light in Maine inspired his poem "The Lighthouse," visited Minot's Ledge Light in 1871. Longfellow was hoisted to the doorway in the tower on a chair, and that method of entry was thereafter known as "Longfellow's chair." He wrote: "We find ourselves at the base of the lighthouse rising sheer out of the sea. . . . We are hoisted up forty feet in a chair, some of us; others go up by an iron ladder. . . . The lighthouse rises out of the sea like a beautiful stone cannon, mouth upward, belching forth only friendly fires."

Surprisingly, visitors to the tower were quite common. Records indicated 710 visitors in 1861 and 496 in 1865. In 1937, 357 people toured the lighthouse. The youngest was Mary Ellen Keith, who was carried to the top of the tower in August 1869 at the age of nine months.

Joshua Wilder, the first keeper of the 1860 tower, remained for only about a year. He was followed by James Tower of Newton, Massachusetts, who was in charge from 1861 to 1874. When Tower died in 1888, the *Boston Globe* reported, "The hardship of such a life seriously injured his health, and he gave up his position there and returned to Newton, where for the past 13 years he has held the situation of janitor in the public library."

Levi L. Creed was an assistant keeper under Tower, and he became the principal keeper in 1874. Some people worried that the new tower would ultimately topple in a storm, like its predecessor, but in a letter to the *Boston Globe* in April 1876—25 years almost to the day after the original tower was destroyed—Creed reassured the public after a particularly bad storm.

I have the honor to report that during the gale of the 4th and 5th insts., the sea for hours dashed over the height of thirty feet above the dome; everything above the oil room was on the move, even the lens itself trembling violently. The sea broke on the ledge with such tremendous force as to displace a section of the rock, weighing in my opinion some four or five hundred pounds. Altogether it the most terrible gale I have seen during my residence in this light, some nine years. The sea continued to break clean over the lighthouse for ten hours after the gale abated.

Another ex-keeper in the late nineteenth century said that during storms, when high waves struck the tower, seawater would enter through the vents in the lantern, dripping down the interior walls. Anything movable would move about the floors, and anything breakable had to be secured. Still, keepers felt that the tower would survive any storm.

Frank F. Martin, after a brief stint as an assistant, succeeded Creed as principal keeper in 1881. Joseph Fratus, an assistant under Martin, was at the lighthouse for two tremendous storms in November and December 1885. After the first storm, which reached its peak on Thanksgiving Day, one of the keepers told a *Boston Globe* reporter that the tower didn't just shake—as it always did in storms—but actually swayed. Paint on the interior walls cracked and came off in sheets, and dishes rattled on the shelves.

The December gale left the tower completely coated with ice. Fratus, who had traveled at sea since he was a boy, had never seen "such a heavy sea in such shoal water." Albert Burdick, who had been an assistant for 12 years, said he had never seen such heavy seas. The *Boston Globe* reported: "The light burned perfectly throughout the storm, but the work of watching it was very uncomfortable as the watch-room was cold and wet, owing to the heavy coating of ice. Captain Fratus is firm in the belief that no storm can destroy this structure."

Milton Herbert Reamy, a native of Rochester, Massachusetts, who previously served a total of 10 years at Duxbury Pier Light and Plymouth Light, was the principal keeper from 1887 to 1915. A writer for the *Boston Herald* interviewed Reamy in 1888, and he was described as "on the youthful side of 40, with a curling bronze-hued beard and a clear, sharp eye."

Roscoe Lopaus, a second assistant keeper, served 20 years under Reamy. The keepers lived part of the time with their families onshore in two duplex houses at Government Island in Cohasset, but they spent most of the time inside the tower. From 1887 until around 1900, there was a third assistant assigned to the station, making four keepers in all. The station's initial third assistant was George L. Lyon, who in 1889 moved on to a long stay at Egg Rock Light north of Boston Harbor.

At the time of the 1888 *Herald* article, two were on duty at a time, each spending 14 days at the lighthouse followed by 14 days off. Bad weather and sea conditions often delayed the changing of the keepers, and it was not rare for them to spend a stretch of several weeks at the tower.

When it was time to switch keepers and the sea conditions were relatively calm, the men on duty would fly a red "liberty flag" to signal the keepers onshore that it was safe to make the trip. "I will say," said Reamy, "that one of the most disagreeable things about service at the light is the task of going to it and coming away."

Life in the tower, especially in winter, was more than some men could stand. "The trouble with life here," Reamy once said, "is that we have too much time to think." Legend has it that one keeper quit because he missed corners too much, as the tower had nothing but curving walls.

An 1892 article in *Harper's Young People* provided more details of life at Minot's Ledge:

> *The life tells terribly on the keepers. More than one has so far lost his mind as to attempt his own life, and several were removed because they became insane. In the summer, however, the keepers take turns going ashore. . . . Visitors often come off to the light. The tower is always well supplied with water, fuel, and food. The library of fifty volumes is often changed, the medicine chest is replenished, and the Light-house Inspector and the Light-house Engineer visit them at frequent intervals.*

The writer Gustav Kobbe traveled to the lighthouse in the winter of 1893 aboard the tender *Geranium* for an article in *The Century Magazine*. Because the sea conditions were too rough for the use of the ladder, Kobbe was hoisted to the doorway of the tower on the end of a loop attached to a line held by the keeper.

Kobbe stayed at the tower for a time as the guest of Keeper Reamy. It was so cold inside the tower that Kobbe slept fully clothed, covered with sheets and blankets, "and even then had difficulty in keeping thoroughly warm." In the morning, he washed using icy water from the well in the tower's base, and he was greeted with a hot breakfast. "Good food and a pipe of good tobacco are the only luxuries that tend to ameliorate life in this tower," Kobbe wrote.

Kobbe was shocked when he first heard the thunderous sound of heavy seas striking the tower. Waves have been known to sweep over the top of the lighthouse, and Reamy claimed that a wave of 176 feet hit the tower on Christmas Day in 1909. Besides their own voices, all the keepers heard in winter were the sounds of the sea and the clang of the fog bell.

Not surprisingly, like many isolated lighthouses, this one has its ghost stories. Kobbe wrote:

> Strange noises have been heard in the oil-room—sudden rattling of cans and clinking of glass, as if someone were at work there. Stories are also current of the mysterious filling of the lamp and cleaning of the lens and lantern. . . . One night, as the midnight watch was drawing to a close, the keeper in the watch-room, who had been brooding over the destruction of the old tower, quite unconsciously leaned forward and rapped with his pipe. A few minutes later he was startled to hear an answering rap from below.

Legend claims that to this day, in dark and stormy weather, sailors hear a voice coming from the tower crying in Portuguese (Joseph Antoine's nationality), "Keep away!" According to one keeper, many Portuguese fishermen studiously avoided coming close to the lighthouse.

Another article in a publication called *Old Ocean* in 1894 described a visit to the shore station on Government Island. The children of the keepers informed the visitors that their fathers had worked out a system of communication between the lighthouse and the shore, signaling with the dip of a lantern or the motions of a flag. By this time, the men were spending three weeks at the tower followed by one week off.

In 1894 Capt. F. A. Mahan, an engineer with the Lighthouse Board, suggested a new system for lighthouse characteristics. Under the new plan, every lighthouse in the nation would be given a unique numerical flash. As a trial of the new system, on May 1, 1894, Minot's Ledge Light was given a new 12-panel rotating second-order Fresnel lens and a distinctive characteristic 1-4-3 flash—a single flash followed by an interval of three seconds, then four flashes separated by one second, then another interval of three seconds of darkness followed by three flashes again separated by one second.

Someone decided that 1-4-3 stood for "I love you," and Minot's Ledge Light was soon popularly referred to as the "I Love You Light," an appellation that has inspired numerous songs and poems. When the light malfunctions, complaints are invariably received until the 1-4-3 signature can be restored.

Milton Reamy's son, Octavius, succeeded his father as keeper in 1915. The younger Reamy watched as American destroyers left Boston Harbor during World War I. Naval reservists were stationed at the tower during the war.

Octavius Reamy guessed that waves had cleared the top of the tower probably 10,000 times in its existence. Once a wave struck with such fury that the clockwork mechanism that turned the lens was stopped. Reamy left Minot's Ledge in 1924, when he was transferred to the slightly less turbulent Graves Light.

One of the assistants around 1917 was Winfield Scott Thompson Jr. Many years later, Thompson's daughter, Carol Hyland, recalled visiting the men at the lighthouse with her mother. "We took the newspaper out to the light," she said. They also took pies and cakes that her mother had baked.

According to Hyland, her father and the other keepers once encountered German sailors coming up the tower's ladder during the war. A bucket of coal was dropped on them, and the Germans left.

Hyland recalled her mother's being very lonely at the shore station. Every night she'd take her three children to a window where they could see the flash of the lighthouse in the distance. "Do you know what that means?" she'd ask. "It means I love you and good-night."

Pierre Nadeau, a native of Canada who came to the United States and joined the Revenue Cutter Service in 1913, became a second assistant keeper in the early 1920s. A brief newspaper clipping, circa 1924 or 1925, tells us the following: "Pierre Nadeau, second assistant keeper at Minot's Light, has been commended to Lighthouse Department for keeping light going three nights without sleep, while storm held Keeper Tornberg and First Assistant Fitzpatrick on shore, where they had gone for supplies."

Keeping the kerosene-fueled light operating at Minot's was not an easy task even with two or three keepers on duty, and Nadeau's feat of single-handedly maintaining the light for three nights during a storm is worthy of note. Unfortunately, further details of this episode appear to have been lost to the passing decades.

A tragedy led to the end of Pierre Nadeau's lighthouse-keeping career. On August 10, 1925, the Nadeaus' three-year-old daughter, Doris, drowned after slipping from a seawall in Cohasset. This apparently occurred while the family was staying at the assistant keeper's house onshore at Cohasset's Government Island, and Pierre Nadeau was at the lighthouse at the time.

Per Frederick Tornberg—a native of Sweden who was educated in Germany—was principal keeper from 1924 until 1936, when he left for the tranquil light station at Annisquam, Massachusetts. Fred Calabretta of the Mystic Seaport Museum interviewed Molly Tornberg Orr, Keeper Orr's daughter, in 1990.

Molly was six when the family arrived at Cohasset, and she said they were "just aghast at the beauty" of the area. She recalled her first visit to the lighthouse, when she was eight years old. Manuel Figarado (or Figueiredo, in some accounts), a local fisherman who frequently transported the keepers to and from the tower, provided a boat ride for Molly, her mother, and her younger sister, Betty.

> *My mother would pick us up one at a time under the armpits and push us to the ladder and say, "Go!" and we'd grab hold of a rung and start the climb. Betty was first, I was second, and my mother last. About a third of the way up there was a rung that was loose—it turned in your hands—and I tell you my terror was so great that I considered dropping off into the Atlantic Ocean. I thought it would be much easier to die than to go on with what I was doing. But my father was up above encouraging us, "Don't look down, look at the ladder, come on up." And he grabbed each one of us and pulled us in the door as we got to the top, and this was six and eight years of age, you know.*

Molly's favorite room in the tower was the kitchen. "It was cozy and warm, and had a nice little stove and the cupboards were all built around—they were round cupboards, and there was a gorgeous banjo clock hanging there, and I just thought it would be the best place in the world to play house."

The way down from the tower back to the boat was as terrifying for Molly as the climb up had been. "And so Betty and I were tucked into this chair and tied in, and then it was pushed out the door swinging on a davit. And we were lowered to the boat. Well, I think my fear that time was just about as great as when I got hold of that moving rung on the ladder—you know, to be swinging in midair."

Molly Tornberg Orr recalled that there was no electricity at the shore station on Government Island, and that much of the house was cold. The children had the job of polishing the kitchen stove in preparation for visits of the inspector, Capt. George B. Eaton. "My mother told us if we didn't keep our rooms clean and everything spit and polish, Captain Eaton might turn us out of her home," Molly remembered.

By the 1920s, the keepers were spending 10 days on shore between 20-day stints at the lighthouse. Much of Keeper Tornberg's time away from the lighthouse was occupied by the maintenance of the house at Government Island. While on shore, the keepers also had to tend four small local harbor lights, which they visited by boat.

In February 1936, Tornberg and Manuel Figarado were on their way to the tower when their boat became trapped between two ice floes about 600 feet from the ledge. The seams on the boat split and it began to fill rapidly with water. Anthony Souza, the assistant keeper on duty, witnessed the men's plight and telephoned for help. Coast Guard crews from Hull and Scituate soon arrived and rescued the two men.

George H. Fitzpatrick was principal keeper from 1936 to 1940. A newspaper article described the life of Fitzpatrick and the assistant keepers, Anthony Souza and Otis Walsh. Because it was difficult to get regular deliveries of food to the lighthouse, the men relied largely on canned goods. During one bad stretch of weather, they were down to their last can of tomatoes before a tender arrived with supplies.

A well in the lower part of the tower, filled twice yearly by the lighthouse tender, held the water supply for the keepers. One day, while a party of young women toured the tower, one asked what the

Minot's Ledge Lighthouse in high seas. *Photo by Edward Rowe Snow, courtesy of Dorothy Snow Bicknell.*

well was for. Otis Walsh tried to convince her it was the keepers' bathtub. "It goes down 40 feet," he told her. The woman paused and replied, "You must be out of luck when you drop the soap."

By 1940 Fitzpatrick and two assistants were spending 20 days in the tower followed by 10 days off. During one bad storm, Fitzpatrick reported that every fourth wave was higher than the tower. His wife and their 15-year-old daughter lived onshore. Even during severe storms, Mrs. Fitzpatrick said she never worried about her husband. Having a telephone at the lighthouse helped the keepers stay in contact with their families.

The light was automated—and converted to electric operation for the first time—and the keepers were removed in 1947. Coast Guardsman Allison Gregg Haskins was in charge of the automation project. In a 1960 letter to Edward Rowe Snow, Haskins said that the second-order lens was carefully dismantled in September 1947 and was stored in a room in the tower pending further notice. A third-order lens was put into service. Some time later, officials of the Boston Museum of Science expressed interest in the old lens. Before it could be transported to the museum, vandals entered the tower and smashed sections of the lens. As a result, it was reportedly disposed of.

A power cable from shore—installed in 1964 to replace a battery system—was damaged in a storm in February 1971, and batteries were again used until the light was converted to solar power in 1983.

A renovation of the tower was carried out in 1987–89. The lantern was lifted off by helicopter and subsequently cleaned, and some of the damaged upper granite blocks were removed and replaced. The Gayle Electric Company of New Jersey, under contract to the Coast Guard, performed the work. The light was relit on August 20, 1989, and it continues to flash its famous 1-4-3 as an active aid to navigation.

In 1992–93, the remaining keeper's house at Government Island was restored for $200,000, money that was raised by the nonprofit Cohasset Lightkeepers Corporation. The house contains two apartments upstairs and a hall for community use downstairs.

Today you can visit Government Island to see a replica of the lantern atop some of the granite blocks removed during the renovation. Part of the third-order Fresnel lens once used in the lighthouse is on display inside the replica lantern. A fog bell is also on display, restored by a local fisherman, Herb Jason, and his grandson John Small. Herb Jason had rescued the bell several years earlier, when it was about to be used for scrap.

In 1997, a group of local residents began a campaign to erect a granite memorial to Joseph Antoine and Joseph Wilson. The memorial was finished and dedicated in 2000 on Government Island.

⚑ **You can see Minot's Ledge Light from Government Island in Cohasset and other points onshore, but it is best viewed by boat. Special lighthouse cruises may occasionally provide closer views. For information, contact Friends of the Boston Harbor Islands, (781) 740-4290, www.fbhi.org, or Boston Harbor Cruises, (617) 227-4321, www.bostonharborcruises.com.**

CHAPTER 40

Long Island Head Light in 2002. *Photo by the author.*

Long Island Head Light

1819, 1844, 1881, 1901

Long Island, the longest and largest (214 acres) of the 34 islands in Boston Harbor, has seen myriad uses; it's been home to a resort hotel, military fortifications, cottages occupied by Portuguese fishermen, a hospital, and even a missile base. The island has a healthy dose of legend and lore. Some claim it's haunted by the "Woman in Scarlet," the ghost of the wife of a British soldier. The woman was reportedly killed by cannon fire in 1776 and buried in a red cloak.

From its inauguration in 1716 into the early nineteenth century, Boston Light served as the only lighthouse for vessels approaching Boston. In 1818 a committee of the Boston Marine Society noted the large number of vessels that passed close by Long Island as they entered the harbor from Broad Sound. The committee sent their recommendation for a lighthouse on Long Island Head to Congressman Jonathan Mason.

Congress wasted little time, appropriating $11,500 for the lighthouse in March 3, 1819. Henry A. S. Dearborn, collector of the Port of Boston and local lighthouse superintendent, requested that a committee of the Boston Marine Society be formed to designate the site for the new lighthouse, and a meeting was held in March 1819 to appoint the committee. One of the five men appointed was Winslow Lewis, who gained prominence as the builder of many early lighthouses and as the primary supplier of lighting apparatus for many years.

A site was selected by early April. The island's first lighthouse was a stone tower 20 feet tall, topped by a 7-foot-tall lantern with a soapstone roof. It was built high on the hill at Long Island Head, at the northern end of the island, with its light 109 feet above the sea. The keeper's dwelling, also built of stone, was attached to the tower. The house had two rooms and an attached kitchen on the first floor and two rooms in the attic. A fixed white light was produced by a system of 10 oil lamps and reflectors. The light went into service on October 9, 1819, and the first keeper was Jonathan Lawrence.

Lawrence was a local man who had served in the Army during the War of 1812. At the Battle of Fort Erie in August 1814, Lawrence was struck by a bullet that grazed his head, entered his shoulder, and exited through his back.

One Sunday in April 1821, Lawrence spotted a sailboat in distress near the island. He quickly descended the hill and launched a small boat. With the help of a man from nearby Rainsford Island, Lawrence rescued three survivors who were clinging to the overturned sailboat. Two other passengers had already drowned.

Lawrence died at the age of 45 in September 1825, apparently of complications from his war wounds. The next keeper was Charles Beck. In his book *Famous Lighthouses of New England,* Edward Rowe Snow informs us that Beck was still in charge in 1845 when the writer James Lloyd Homer visited and observed that the keeper had the added duty of running a signal tower for harbor pilots, hoisting a black ball as a signal when pilots were needed for an incoming vessel. This system was apparently in use from the earliest days of the lighthouse.

In his important survey of the area's lighthouses in 1838, Lt. Edward W. Carpender reported that there were 11 lamps in use in the lighthouse with 13½-inch reflectors. Carpender recommended the removal of five of the lamp-reflector pairs and the rearrangement of the remaining ones to improve the light's visibility.

I. W. P. Lewis visited during his examination of the coast's lights in 1842. By that time, the number of lamps had been reduced to nine, with 16-inch reflectors, attached to two circular iron frames. Lewis reported that the tower was leaky and the walls were cracked with frost. He added the following criticisms:

> *This light was erected here to serve as a leading mark for vessels entering Boston Harbor through Broad Sound, and its position is well adapted for the purpose; but the arrangement of the apparatus is in direct opposition to this purpose, the light being reflected in six different directions, and nearly all around the horizon. The lantern is of the rudest description, and a considerable portion of the light lost by obstruction from the frame work. One lamp of a proper form is sufficient for this locality.*

A separate inspection in 1843 by Levi Lincoln, collector of the Port of Boston and local lighthouse superintendent, mentioned that the wooden parts of the tower were decayed, and that the lantern glass had been cracked and broken by a severe winter. In fact, the entire tower, which had a shallow foundation, seemed to have moved as the ground froze and thawed.

A new cast-iron lighthouse—the first of its type in the United States—was built the following year. It was similar in appearance to two other New England lighthouses built a short time later, at Juniper Island, Vermont (1846), and Monomoy Point, Massachusetts (1849). A Boston newspaper described the new lighthouse on May 4, 1844:

> *A cast-iron lighthouse, to be placed on the old site on Long Island Head, has just been completed by the South Boston Iron Company. It is cast in sections of about seven feet each in height, and twelve feet in diameter at the base, and six feet at the top. It is furnished with an iron deck, projecting on the outside so as to furnish a walk round the lantern twenty inches in width finished with a railing. The lantern is made of upright wrought iron bars to receive the glass, having sixteen sides of four feet by sixteen inches, and is surmounted by a cast-iron dome or roof, making the whole height thirty-four feet. In the centre is a cast-iron pipe, extending from the bottom to the summit, which serves as a smoke flue for the stove, and around which winds a circular staircase of cast iron.*

In 1857 a fourth-order Fresnel lens, producing a fixed white light, replaced the old lamps and reflectors. The tower was lined with brick around the same time. A number of repairs were carried out in 1863, including the replacement of the tower's watchroom floor.

P. B. Small was keeper in October 1865, when the schooner *Joseph Fish*, carrying 1,200 barrels of petroleum, was rammed by another vessel while anchored near Long Island Head. Small reported that the schooner caught fire and was totally destroyed.

A tremendous storm on September 8, 1869, knocked the chimney off the keeper's house and damaged the roof. A skylight window was blown in and the station's fence was damaged. Not long before that, lightning had struck and damaged the boathouse. Necessary repairs were quickly carried out.

Military use of Long Island began at least as early as the American Revolution, when the American army erected a redoubt near the later site of the lighthouse for the purpose of driving the British fleet out of the harbor. A Civil War training camp called Camp Wightman was established in Long Island in 1861. The Ninth Regiment Massachusetts Volunteer Infantry was the first regiment to be quartered at the camp. The men of the "Fighting Ninth" were nearly all Irish, and they carried the Irish flag into battle along with the state and U.S. flags. Camp Wightman closed with the end of the war, but in 1867 Fort Strong was relocated from East Boston to the island. The fort was greatly enlarged in the 1870s.

A new cast-iron lighthouse was built in 1881, along with a new wood-frame keeper's house. The new tower was typical of the ones

Long Island Head Light Station, circa 1870s, showing the second (1844) lighthouse. *U.S. Coast Guard photo.*

built at many New England locations around that time, consisting of several iron cylinders bolted together.

A *Boston Globe* article in February 1895 described a tugboat visit to Long Island Head to deliver newspapers to Keeper John B. Carter during a severe freeze that slowed harbor traffic. The keeper told his visitors, "I have a cow and some fowl and I don't care how hard it blows. My daughter has her piano, and we manage to take lots of comfort here, gale or no gale."

The 1881 tower remained in use for less than twenty years. Fort Strong was enlarged again around 1900, and it was decided that the light station should be relocated to a position where it would not be "exposed to injury by the firing of guns in the new sea coast battery."

A 52-foot cylindrical brick lighthouse was built in the new location. The keeper's house, oil house, and other outbuildings were moved rather than rebuilt. According to the Lighthouse Board's annual report of 1901, the 1881 iron tower was sold at auction, presumably for scrap. The following year's annual report announced that a boathouse had been added to the station, and that the tower's color was changed from unpainted red brick to white.

On January 8, 1918, Edwin Tarr—who had become keeper in 1906—died while sitting in his chair facing the harbor. A few days later,

Tarr's funeral was held in the keeper's house. A sleet storm arrived during the service. When the pallbearers emerged with the casket, they found the steep hill coated with a sheet of ice.

As the four men attempted to carry the casket down the path, one of them slipped and lost his grip. The coffin fell to the ice and began to slide on its own. The men, seeing no other option, jumped on the coffin in an attempt to slow it down, and they rode it down the hill like a toboggan. The coffin came to rest just at the head of the wharf and further catastrophe was averted. One of the pallbearers, a soldier at Fort Strong, related the incident to Edward Rowe Snow, who immortalized the macabre story in *The Islands of Boston Harbor*.

After Tarr's death, various custodians attended Long Island Head Light until 1929, when it was converted to automatic acetylene gas operation. The keeper's house and other outbuildings were removed at some point after automation.

After extensive use during World War I, Fort Strong was eventually abandoned; some of the fort's structures still stand in disrepair.

In 1982 the Coast Guard discontinued the lighthouse. That decision was reconsidered in 1985 and the tower was renovated, a solar-powered optic was installed, and the light became active again. It remains an active aid to navigation, with a modern 250-millimeter optic producing a white flash every 2.5 seconds.

The lighthouse received a major renovation in the summer of 1998, carried out by the Campbell Construction Group of Beverly, Massachusetts. The tower and lantern were repainted, and some of the original brick, mortar, and ironwork were replaced.

A bridge to Long Island was built from the city of Quincy in 1951, but it is off-limits to the general public. There has been talk of making Long Island Head publicly accessible by boat.

Long Island Head Light can be viewed from any of the boats leaving Boston's Long Wharf for Georges Island, and from many of the other scenic cruises in the harbor leaving Long Wharf and Rowe's Wharf. The Friends of the Boston Harbor Islands organization offers a variety of sightseeing cruises that pass the lighthouse; see www.fbhi.org, or call (781) 740-4290 for information.

The lighthouse can also be seen across the harbor from the public walking trail around the perimeter of Deer Island, which is accessible from the town of Winthrop.

CHAPTER 41

Top: The 1897 range light station, showing the keeper's house and the rear range light. *Bottom:* The 1903 range light station. *National Archives photos.*

Spectacle Island Range Lights

1897–1913

Broad Sound Channel Inner Range Lights

1903–1950s

Boston Harbor's 105-acre Spectacle Island received its name because the shape of the island is said to resemble a pair of eyeglasses. For hundreds of years, native people came to the island to fish and gather clams. Early European settlers harvested the island's lumber, and in 1649 planting rights were granted for sixpence an acre.

Spectacle Island served as a quarantine station for a time in the 1700s; all immigrants coming from Ireland were detained in case of smallpox. Two summer hotels on the island enjoyed success for a period, but illegal activities led to a police raid in 1857. A plant for rendering dead horses and cattle began a few years later, and a garbage reclaiming plant, where trash was burned for oil, was opened.

The island also served as a trash dump for the City of Boston from the 1920s until 1959. The landfill added many acres and changed the island's shape over the years.

The 1892 annual report of the Lighthouse Board made a strong case for the establishment of range lights, a set of lights that mariners can keep lined up one behind the other as they proceed, on Spectacle Island: "Boston is one of the most important commercial cities in the country. Its harbor is without sufficient aids to navigation. Among those needed are range beacons on Spectacle Island to mark the center of the dredged channel from State Ledge toward the city and to mark the turning point into the channel for vessels coming up from Nix's Mate."

On March 2, 1895, Congress appropriated $9,350 for a range light station. A Lighthouse Board notice in June 1897 described the newly established lights:

On May 20 a fixed red reflector light was established in each of the two towers recently erected on the north side and easterly point of the northerly part of Spectacle Island, south side of President Roads, Boston Harbor. Each tower is a white, octagonal, pyramidal, shingled structure with a small window on the northwesterly side, from which the light is shown. The focal plane of the front light is 29 feet above the water and 13.3 feet above the base of the tower, and of the rear light 54 feet above the water and 23 feet above the base of the tower. The rear tower stands 379 feet SE.½ S. in rear of the front tower. . . . The lights mark a range line to guide NW. ½ N. from the line marked by the South Boston Range Lights up the main channel to Boston.

Winfield L. Creed was the first keeper, and he stayed until 1926. In 1902 new pairs of range lights were authorized on both Lovell's Island and Spectacle Island in Boston Harbor. The addition of a second pair of range lights made Spectacle Island home to four working lighthouses, which was certainly unusual for an island of its size. A sum of $13,000 was appropriated for the new Spectacle Island beacons, and they were built in the spring of 1903 and first lighted on April 10, 1903.

The lights established on the island in 1903, together with the Lovell's Island Range Lights, guided vessels through the newly improved Broad Sound Channel, also known as the Boston North Channel, which connected with the President Roads shipping channel.

The 1903 lights on Spectacle Island were called the Broad Sound Channel Inner Range Lights. The new lighthouses were located very close to the 1897 range lights on the northeast part of the island. The two wooden towers were 337 feet apart, and they both held fourth-order Fresnel lenses manufactured by the Chance Brothers in Birmingham, England.

The front light was 53 feet above the water and flashed white every five seconds. The rear light was 70 feet above the water and displayed a fixed red light, produced by a red chimney over the lens. The towers were painted red initially, but the 1904 report of the Lighthouse Board reported that the color had been changed to white.

In 1904 the 1897 range light towers were moved about 15 feet to the south and placed on new masonry foundations. The towers' colors were changed to white on their upper and lower thirds and red on their middle thirds.

A new wood-frame six-room keeper's house was erected for the Broad Sound Channel Inner Range Lights, 65 feet from the rear tower. Photographs from the time show two keepers' houses for the two pairs of range lights, and payroll records indicate that, for a time, there was a principal keeper and an assistant keeper caring for the four lights.

A 1909 inspection revealed that the water collected in a 2,000-gallon cistern was unsatisfactory because of the high amount of smoke from the rendering plant on the island. The inspector recommended frequent cleaning of the cistern.

In 1913 the government announced plans to discontinue the Spectacle Island Range Lights. The Pilot Commissioners and the Boston Marine Society objected, thinking that the 1903 Broad Sound Channel Inner Range Lights were being extinguished. It was soon made clear that the lights in question were the 1897 range lights, made obsolete by changes in the shipping channel. The lights were discontinued on July 15, 1913. After that, the Broad Sound Channel Inner Range Lights were generally referred to as the Spectacle Island Range Lights.

John Lelan Hart, a native of Rockland, Maine, who had formerly served at Boston Light, became keeper in 1926. When he retired in 1938 at age 68, Hart said that although he had spent his life on the sea or near it, he had "never really enjoyed it."

The Broad Sound Channel Inner Range Lights were deactivated in the 1950s. According to the historian Edward Rowe Snow, the last keeper at Spectacle Island was reportedly murdered at the outbreak of World War II.

In 1914 John Lindberg, a former assistant keeper of Graves Light, moved to Castle Island with his family to tend this fog signal. Lindberg became chief engineer on the Nantucket Lightship, leaving his wife in charge of the fog signal. When it became foggy, Helen Lindberg would throw a switch in a closet that activated the signal. She remained keeper of the signal until 1948, which made her the last civilian "lamplighter" in the Boston Harbor area.

Spectacle Island is now jointly owned by the City of Boston and the Massachusetts Department of Conservation and Recreation. The Island Alliance and National Park Service assist with the management of the island. The island's basic shape has once again been modified in recent years using dirt from Boston's massive Big Dig project, a restructuring of the city's highway system. The island has a visitor center, two sandy beaches, a café, and a marina. There are five miles of walking trails and a panoramic view from the island's 157-foot-high summit.

There are no lighthouses today on Spectacle Island, but it's a site worth visiting. Passenger ferry service is provided from Boston, and interisland connections are provided to Georges and Thompson islands. Visit www.bostonislands.org or call (617) 223-8666 for details.

CHAPTER 42

Top: An early-1900s postcard view of Deer Island Light. *From the collection of the author. Bottom:* Deer Island Light in September 2006. *Photo by the author.*

Deer Island Light

1890-1982

Deer Island in Boston Harbor, south of the town of Winthrop, has a
varied and often sordid past. The 210-acre island served as an internment camp for Indians in 1675 during King Philip's War. Later, it was
the site of a quarantine station where many immigrants died, a hospital, an almshouse, a fort, and a state prison. Today the island is home
to a massive sewage treatment plant for the Boston area. Deer Island
ceased being an island in the 1930s, when Shirley Gut, which previously
separated it from Winthrop, was filled in.

In 1832 the Boston Marine Society petitioned Congress for $3,000
for the placement of an unlighted stone beacon at Deer Island Point,
at the north side of the entrance to Boston's inner harbor and about
500 yards south of the island's southeasterly point. This marker served
as a navigational aid for almost 60 years.

In the annual reports for 1884 and 1885, the Lighthouse Board
stated the following: "A light and fog-signal at this point are particularly
desirable, because of the narrow and devious passages."

Congress appropriated $35,000 for the lighthouse on August 4,
1886. A suitable location was selected near the southern extremity of
the spit extending from Deer Island, near the old day beacon. During
the design process, it was realized that the initial appropriation was
not sufficient, and an additional $6,000 was obtained.

The cylindrical caisson base for the lighthouse, 33 feet in diameter
and 30 feet high, was sunk four feet into the gravel and clay of the
spit, in about 6 feet of water. The caisson was filled with concrete, with
some space left for a basement and cisterns. The cast-iron superstructure built on top of the caisson had four levels between the lantern
and basement, including living quarters. The lighthouse was painted
brown except for the lantern, which was painted black.

The new light went into service on January 26, 1890, with a fixed
white light interrupted by a red flash every 30 seconds, 57 feet above
mean high water. The lens revolved by means of a clockwork mechanism that had to be periodically wound by hand. A fog bell was
mounted on the lower gallery deck, with striking machinery that produced a single blow every 10 seconds.

The station was assigned a principal keeper and an assistant. John Farley was the first principal keeper, and Michael J. Curran was the first assistant. Wesley A. Pingree—formerly at Boston Light—arrived as an assistant in 1893 and became principal keeper in 1895. His stay of six years was one of the longer stints in the station's history.

The *Boston Globe* presented a portrait of lighthouse life in August 1893, when Everett F. Boyd was in charge and Pingree was his assistant. The men shared the watches at night: one kept watch from sunset to midnight, and the other from midnight to sunrise.

Boyd lived at the lighthouse with his wife and eight-year-old daughter, and Pingree was single. The Boyds' bedroom on the second level showed a woman's decorating touch with its knickknacks and ribbons, according to the reporter. "A chamber in a home ashore," he continued, "couldn't have been prettier to the eye or cozier to the mind."

The assistant's bedroom—on the third level—was plainer, with two cots, two chairs, a bookcase, and some pictures. The kitchen, on the first level, included a stove, a sink, and rocking chairs. The neat basement was perfectly dry, with wood piled in one corner, some coal in the chute, and cans of kerosene packed in boxes. An iron plate on the floor, when lifted, revealed the cistern that held the station's water supply. Rainwater was caught on the gallery roof and piped below into the cistern. "The taste is good," wrote the reporter, "barring a hint of cement."

The *Globe* reporter's visit came during some rough weather in the harbor, which he described: "Sitting in the kitchen of the lighthouse and looking out through the splashed glass it was a grand scene. You could hear the howl of the wind, but couldn't feel it, you could hear the dash of the waves, but there was not a shiver of the iron tower with its lining of brick."

Frank Sibley, who later served as a *Boston Globe* correspondent during World War I, spent much time at the lighthouse during several summers in the 1890s, and he was possibly the writer of the 1893 article. (No byline was included.) Sibley became acquainted with Florence Lyndon, daughter of the keeper of Long Island Head Light across the harbor, and the two were married in 1893.

Wesley Pingree's father, Henry, was keeper of Boston Light from 1894 to 1909. In 1895 Wesley Pingree married Josephine Horte, whose father, Albert, had been keeper of Boston Light in 1893–94. According to the historian Edward Rowe Snow, Wesley and Josephine spent their honeymoon at Deer Island Light.

Wesley Pingree was in charge during the famous Portland Gale of November 1898. Many vessels were wrecked in the storm, including the steamer *Portland,* which was carrying nearly 200 people from Boston to Portland, Maine. Pingree later described his experience of the storm to Edward Rowe Snow: "At two o'clock in the afternoon the ocean was as smooth as glass. At five p.m. it had started snowing and the wind was coming up. A little later the Bangor boat went by but returned to the harbor, as the sea was rapidly getting worse. At 7 p.m. the *Portland* came down the channel, and the other boat, anchored in President Road, whistled a warning to her. At this time the waves were hitting so high that I was lashing my dory fast to the light."

Pingree rode out the storm inside the lighthouse, keeping watch all night. The station's dory and a ladder were lost, the bell tower was washed away, kitchen windows were smashed, three feet of water collected in the basement, and the cistern filled with seawater. All told, 141 vessels were wrecked and 456 lives were lost in the Portland Gale, one of the worst storms in recorded New England history.

Even in calm weather, there were often mishaps with the heavy maritime traffic near the lighthouse. Secretary of Commerce William C. Redfield commended Elmo C. Mott, the assistant in 1915, for rendering assistance to the disabled powerboat *Alice.* The boat was towed to the lighthouse and the 11 men on board were provided with food and shelter.

Joseph McCabe arrived as assistant keeper in June 1908. He made the pages of the *Globe* in March 1913, when he purchased a piano and had it delivered to the lighthouse to "break the monotony of the lonely life in the isolated tower." Less than three years later, McCabe, who rented a room in East Boston when he wasn't at the lighthouse, became engaged to Gertrude Walter, a resident of that community. The couple planned a wedding on Easter Sunday, but it wasn't to be.

On Saturday, February 19, 1916, McCabe left the lighthouse to meet his fiancée on Deer Island, where they wrote out wedding invitations together. When he was ready to return, McCabe found that ice around the island had trapped his boat. He decided to borrow a pair of rubber boots and walk across the spit to the lighthouse. He was followed by his friend Wesley Pingree, who was by then an employee of the pumping station on Deer Island, and Pingree's 15-year-old son, Philip.

As he jumped forward to make it past a gap in the spit, McCabe lost his footing and disappeared into the turbulent waters of the harbor. The *Globe* reported that Philip Pingree made a desperate effort to save McCabe, who put up "a valiant but vain fight for his life against the intense cold and swift currents." Employees from Deer Island rushed to the scene in a dory, but it was too late. The body of Joseph McCabe, who was 28 years old, was never recovered.

Judson Small, one of three lightkeeping brothers (Tom and Arthur were the others), was assistant keeper at Deer Island Light in the 1920s under Merrill B. King, the principal keeper. King was alone in the lighthouse during a tremendous storm two days after Christmas in 1930. As high tide approached late in the afternoon, 40-foot breakers punished the station. King secured everything to the best of his ability and prepared a lifeboat for launching in case he had to make a fast escape. He managed to ride out the storm and kept the light burning through the night, going many hours without sleep until his assistant was finally able to return from shore leave.

Tom Small, who was keeper at the Narrows Light when it burned down in 1929, became keeper at Deer Island in 1931. Small had a pet that gained fame as "the climbing cat of Deer Island Light." Edward Rowe Snow reported that Small's cat would leap into the water, emerge with a fish in its mouth, climb the ladder, and eat the fish.

The caisson base of the lighthouse was battered repeatedly in storms. It was patched and banded for reinforcement around 1902, but by 1937 it was in such rough shape that a circular protective wall was built around the lower part of the structure.

A view of Deer Island Light in the 1930s, taken by a friend of Keeper Tom Small. *From the collection of Edward Rowe Snow, courtesy of Dorothy Snow Bicknell.*

Fred Bohm became the last civilian keeper in the 1940s after leaving the Spectacle Island Range Lights, about two miles to the southwest in the harbor. During the first year and a half of World War II, Keeper Bohm not only had to tend the light, but also was required to patrol the area and watch for German submarines. After Bohm left, Coast Guard crews looked after the lighthouse.

In spite of the protective wall around the base, the lighthouse continued to deteriorate. The roof over the lower gallery had to be removed in 1965. According to the last Coast Guard keeper, Pedro Marticio, the crew abandoned the lighthouse during a storm on February 19, 1972, at precisely 6:30 p.m.

At the time the press was calling it the worst nor'easter in 40 years. We had lost all power, when a wave broke in the plate glass windows and frames and washed down into the engine room. There were three of us on board during the storm. The Coast Guard cutter Pendant *was dispatched to shoot us a line and pass us a pump.*

When Boatswain Mate Chief John Butler, officer in charge of the Pendant, *saw the tower starting to tip, he informed Boston, and in turn they told me to abandon station. The* Pendant *rammed its bow into the tower and my crew and I jumped on board. When he backed into deep water he got broadsided by a wave that almost capsized the 65-foot tug.*

By the late 1970s, it became apparent that the lighthouse had deteriorated to the point that it was unsafe. The Coast Guard estimated that repairs could cost up to $400,000. The Massachusetts Historic Commission decided that Deer Island Light was not eligible for the National Register of Historic Places, a determination that paved the way for the old lighthouse's destruction.

Beginning on June 14, 1982, the tower was dismantled by a work crew from the cutter *White Heath*, which took about six weeks in all. During this period a lighted buoy served as a temporary aid to navigation. A white fiberglass tower set atop a concrete cap on the original caisson replaced the familiar landmark. The tower was built in England at a cost of $100,000 and was designed to withstand winds of 110 miles per hour.

There were complaints that the white tower blended in with the background of Deer Island. Meanwhile, in March 1983, Great Point Lighthouse on Nantucket was destroyed in a storm. The Coast Guard decided to replace it with a fiberglass tower, so they moved the Deer Island tower to Nantucket. A 33-foot brown fiberglass tower replaced the white one at the Deer Island site in September 1984.

The automated light on the "matchstick" tower continues as an active aid to navigation; a VRB-25 optic produces an alternating red and white flash every five seconds, with a focal plane height of 53 feet.

The present Deer Island Light is easily seen from many of the sightseeing cruises in Boston Harbor and from the public walking trail around the perimeter of Deer Island, accessible from the town of Winthrop.

CHAPTER 43

Two views of the Lovell's Island Range Light Station. *Top photo courtesy of U.S. Coast Guard; bottom photo from the collection of the author.*

Lovell's Island Range Lights

1903-1939

The peaceful air of Lovell's Island, now within the boundaries of the Boston Harbor Islands National Park Area, belies its long, busy past. About six miles from the Boston waterfront, the island of around 60 acres is approximately three-quarters of a mile long and a quarter mile in width. The island takes its name from Captain William Lovell, an early settler of nearby Dorchester.

The island's proximity to the main shipping channel into Boston has dictated its uses through the last three centuries. It was briefly employed as a quarantine station in the 1600s, and in the early twentieth century the island became home to Fort Standish.

The U.S. Lighthouse Board recognized the important location of Lovell's Island. A buoy depot was relocated to the island from Cohasset, on Boston's South Shore.

The man in charge of the buoy depot for four years in the 1870s was Winfield Scott Schley. He would later gain wide fame as the leader of the mission to rescue Adolphus Greely's Arctic expedition, and as commander of the U.S. Navy's "Flying Squadron" during the Spanish-American War. An 1898 article recalled the Schley family's life in a "small, trim house under the shoulder of the green hill at Lovell's, on the edge of a wide waste of sand bridged over by a rough plank walk."

The depot provided an exciting playground for Schley's young son, Tommy, with "long tubes of whistling buoys for boys to crawl up, bell buoys to climb and hit, and no end of fun." Best of all was the view from the wharf. The channel was only 300 feet wide, and all large vessels headed in and out of Boston had to pass close by. Hundreds of vessels could be seen on a typical day.

In the early 1900s, a new shipping route to Boston from the outer harbor was established, which necessitated a new system of navigational aids to direct traffic to the inner harbor. Congressmen Joseph A. Conry and William C. Lovering of Massachusetts were instrumental in obtaining appropriations for range lights on Lovell's Island and on Spectacle Island, across the channel. A sum of $10,000 was appropriated for the Lovell's Island Range Light Station on June 28, 1902.

The station was built in 1902–03. Two light towers were erected on the northern end of the island, known as Ram's Head. The conical, shingled wooden towers were 40 feet (the rear light) and 31 feet (the front light) tall, and 400 feet separated the two. A seven-foot-high wooden walkway connected the lighthouses, the six-room keeper's house, a woodshed, and a small brick oil house.

The station went into service on April 10, 1903. Both towers held fourth-order Fresnel lenses. The rear light exhibited a red flash every five seconds, and the front light's characteristic was fixed red. When mariners heading toward Boston from the Sound Channel of Broad Sound lined up the rear light directly above the front light, they were assured they were in the center of the shipping channel.

The range lights had only two keepers in their 36-year history. The first was Alfred G. Eisener, who was born in Bremen, Maine, in 1849. After about two decades of seafaring life, Eisener joined the Lighthouse Service in 1882. He spent all his lightkeeping years in Massachusetts: eight years at Thacher Island, four at Cuttyhunk, and nine at the Plymouth station before his transfer to Lovell's Island.

Eisener was considered a top-notch keeper and was a perennial recipient of the commissioner's efficiency star. Inspired by his reading of Kipling, Eisener moonlighted as a poet and author. He wrote a novel, apparently based on his own experiences at sea, called *Dan, or the Gale of Seventy-Three*.

Here are a few excerpts from the keeper's log at Lovell's Island kept during Eisener's stay (courtesy of Jim Claflin of Kenrick Claflin and Sons Antiques, and Jeff Shook of the Michigan Lighthouse Conservancy):

> *October 2, 1911: Sch[oone]r. M. H. Read ashore on Rams Head. Crew taken off.*
>
> *January 13, 1913: Very high tide. Place overflowed. 3 to 6 feet of water between towers. 6 in. water in cellar of house.*
>
> *January 14, 1913: Bailed water out of cellar. Water pipes froze.*
>
> *February 16, 1913: Inspected 3:50 p.m. Fences carried away in January gale. . . . Station otherwise in good condition except painting that will have to be done in the spring.*
>
> *July 16, 1917: My son here today after an absence [of] 14 years. My daughter & granddaughter also.*
>
> *October 1, 1918: Lights to remain unlighted until further orders are received.*
>
> *November 11, 1918: Great War practically ended today. Armistice signed November 11, 11 a.m.*
>
> *January 1, 1919: Lighted the lights for the first time since September 30, 1918.*
>
> *June 30, 1919: This page closes my lighthouse life, consisting of 35*

years of service, beginning at Cape Ann, ending at Lovell's Island, Mass.—Alfred G. Eisener.

On the occasion of his retirement in 1919, Eisener voiced some fairly strong opinions about government treatment of lighthouse keepers to the *Globe* when he retired:

> *I have always believed that less restrictions and more leniency should be given men in charge of lighthouses. They have the responsibility, and in my opinion they should be given more authority over their own affairs.*
>
> *They cannot live as other government employees live, work seven or eight hours and leave this job for the other 16 hours. The lighthouse man must stay right there with the goods all the time, or nearly all.*
>
> *I hope the salaries of the men who keep lighthouses will continue to advance until they compare favorably with those who hold similar positions, and living conditions continue to improve until life on them will consist of just a little more than mere existence.*

Succeeding Eisener as keeper was Charles Jennings, a native of Provincetown, Massachusetts, who had previously served at Thacher Island, Monomoy Point, and Boston Light.

We know a great deal about Jennings's years at Lovell's Island, thanks to a delightful 1989 volume published by his son, Harold, called *A Lighthouse Family.* Harold was born about two years after Keeper Jennings and his wife arrived at the station. He recalled that the family had a large garden near the keeper's house, along with chickens, ducks, and turkeys. The turkeys were a variety called bourbon reds, bought through the poultry section of the Sears, Roebuck catalog.

When he started his formal education, young Harold went to the school in the town of Hull, a short distance to the south. Tom Small, keeper of the Narrows ("Bug") Light, not far from Lovell's Island, had a young son about Harold's age. The two families rented a house in Hull, and the mothers took turns staying with the children. Late on Fridays, they'd catch a ride on an army boat back to the island. On Sundays, one of the fathers would row the group back to Hull.

In the next few years, Harold went to school successively at South Boston, East Boston, and Salem. Eventually, the state sent a tutor to the island, and Harold had private lessons for his fifth- and sixth-grade years. "This wasn't good," wrote Harold in *A Lighthouse Family,* "because I missed having someone else to play with and I was alone a lot of the time. Also, I could hear my dad working about and this was distracting."

Harold also recalled visits from the Flying Santa. William H. Wincapaw, a pilot from Maine, started this tradition in 1929, dropping presents from his plane at lighthouses as a show of appreciation for keepers and their families. "As a lad," Harold wrote, "it was great to see Santa leaning out the plane door in his red suit waving a Christmas greeting, and then run after the package which would contain pencils, paper, coloring and story books, candy, gifts for the ladies and cigarettes for dad." The historian Edward Rowe Snow, who lived in nearby Winthrop and became a good friend of the Jennings family, became involved in the 1930s and continued the flights until 1980. (A nonprofit organization, the Friends of Flying Santa, carries on the tradition today.)

The parade of passing ships was a constant delight. When the Provincetown ferry would pass by on its way into Boston each evening, Harold would blow a police whistle three times, which would be answered by three blasts of the ship's steam whistle. He could even carry on a conversation with the passengers on the ferry, about 500 feet away, by yelling to them.

While digging in his garden, Keeper Jennings would occasionally find an old, tarnished coin. The oldest of these European coins dated to 1600.

Once, a relief keeper came to the island so that Jennings could leave for a vacation. Jennings showed the other man a couple of the coins he had found and jokingly pointed to the garden, saying, "That's where the treasure is buried." On his return, Jennings discovered a much larger hole in his garden. The relief keeper, it was said, retired a short time later. "You can take it from there," wrote Harold.

There was no electricity on the island, but the Jennings family had kerosene lamps for reading and a crystal radio set for entertainment. Eventually, Keeper Jennings built a wind generator from a kit advertised in *Popular Mechanics*. This provided enough power for three lightbulbs in the house. "We all knew at this time," wrote Harold, "how Thomas Edison felt when he lit his first lightbulb." A windstorm destroyed the system's propeller, and it was soon back to kerosene lamps.

One of Harold's biggest thrills was accompanying his father into the lighthouses to "light up" at sunset. As a young boy, Harold was constantly reminded to keep his fingers off the polished brasswork and painted woodwork. But he showed an interest in the workings of the light, so his father taught him how to fill the kerosene reservoir and to trim the wicks.

Harold's early training as a "wickie" would prove useful. In 1939 Keeper Jennings fell ill with high blood pressure and kidney problems. His wife tended the lights for a while, until Harold quit high school at

Edward Rowe Snow
with Keeper Charles
Jennings at Lovell's
Island in January 1937.
*From the collection of
Edward Rowe Snow,
courtesy of Dorothy
Snow Bicknell.*

the age of 18 so he could help out. He served as keeper for two months, earning a salary of $55 per month.

For years the range light station had shared the island with the army's Fort Standish. In the late 1930s, the government decided to expand the fort, and the light station was discontinued to make room. The Jennings family moved to a farm in Maine, but Charles had a brief retirement, as he died about a year later. Harold eventually moved to Cape Cod, and in his later years he became involved in the preservation of Nauset Light. He died in 1996.

Meanwhile, the buoy depot on Lovell's Island was relocated to Chelsea, Massachusetts, in 1921. George Kezer, a veteran lighthouse keeper, was in charge of the depot at the time of the relocation. The house where he and his family lived on the island was floated on a scow to Chelsea, with the family inside and their old horse alongside.

After the fort saw much use in World War II, Lovell's Island was declared surplus property by the federal government in the 1950s. It was purchased in 1958 by the Metropolitan District Commission for use as a public park.

Today, Lovell's Island is managed by Massachusetts Department of Conservation and Recreation and has the harbor islands' only official swimming beach. Trails and old asphalt roads lead past the ruins of Fort Standish. The only vestige of the range light station is the little brick oil house, now without its roof.

🔆 **The island is accessible via a shuttle boat from the harbor's transportation hub, Georges Island, which can be reached by ferry from Boston, Hull, or Quincy. For more information on visiting the Boston Harbor islands, see www.bostonislands.org or call (617) 223-8666.**

CHAPTER 44

Narrows ("Bug") Light as it appeared on an early-1900s postcard.
From the collection of the author.

Narrows Light

(Bug Light)
1856–1929

Boston's outer harbor is dotted with islands and crisscrossed by sand-bars that make it a potential nightmare for mariners. One meandering spit extends more than a mile from Great Brewster Island to the southwest, ending near the southeast end of Lovell's Island. The spot marks the entrance to the Narrows Channel, once the main route into the inner harbor. Charts as early as 1778 show an unlighted beacon at the end of the spit.

On August 3, 1854, Congress appropriated $15,000 for a proper lighthouse. The light would also serve to warn mariners of treacherous Hardings Ledge, four miles to the southeast. Captains would line up Narrows Light with Long Island Head Light to know they were clear of the ledge.

Harrison Loring was hired to build the lighthouse, which resembled a large bug on seven iron stilts—hence its popular nickname, "Bug Light." The hexagonal wooden dwelling on a screwpile foundation had a galvanized iron roof. There were three rooms on the first floor, a small bedroom on the second, and a lantern on the roof. It wasn't the most hospitable place to live; the only heat came from the kitchen stove, and ice covered the windows in winter.

A sixth-order Fresnel lens exhibited a fixed red light, about 35 feet above sea level and visible for seven nautical miles. There was also a fog bell with striking machinery on the side of the lighthouse, which struck a single blow every 20 seconds in times of poor visibility. Nathaniel R. Hooper was the first keeper. He stayed until 1871, minus a brief absence in 1861–62.

A vessel ran into the lighthouse in 1863, but the building was soon repaired. An ice-breaking structure was added and was subsequently swept away by the sea; it was rebuilt in 1867. It consisted, according to the annual report of the Lighthouse Board, of "oak piles secured with girders ballasted with stone, planked all over, shod with iron, and painted with red lead."

James Turner, who was rumored to have been a pirate and mur-derer, was said to be an early keeper. Turner was a lobsterman known around the harbor as the King of Calf Island, as he often wandered the sandbars connecting the Narrows Light to the outer islands, including

Calf. Turner's name doesn't appear in the payroll records for the lighthouse, but he may have served as an unofficial assistant or temporary keeper.

In the 1940s, the local historian and storyteller Edward Rowe Snow learned from a local fisherman that Turner was believed to have buried treasure on one of the outer harbor islands. Snow subsequently found an ancient book in a cellar on nearby Middle Brewster Island. Pinpricks above certain letters on a page in the book spelled out a clue when read backward: "GOLD IS DUE EAST TREES STRONG ISLAND CHATHAM OUTER BAR." Snow and his brother Donald, with the help of a metal detector, eventually found a small chest full of coins on Strong Island off Chatham on Cape Cod, an event that made national news.

In 1891 a new, wider gallery was built around the dwelling. At the same time new outer stairs were added. A 600-gallon water tank was installed in 1900.

An 1895 article in the *Boston Globe* described a visit to the lighthouse via tugboat after a February blizzard, chiefly to deliver a stack of newspapers to Keeper Samuel Liscom. The keeper said it was one of the worst winters he had seen.

> *This is by far the worst battle of ice against vessel that I have ever witnessed. Craft of all kinds, steam and under sail, pass under my very door, sometimes so close that I could toss a biscuit on board. But the water is deep about the bar, and in thick weather the clang of our bell gives warning to the hardy mariner who ventures down to the deep in ships and depend upon the light keepers to warn them of danger.*
>
> *During the blizzard we have managed to keep comfortable, but nothing more. Years ago, when the bar was to the northeast of the lighthouse, the lower floor was often flooded to the depth of a foot, as the great combers would break and force their way through crevices or doors.*

Gershom C. Freeman followed Liscom as keeper in 1895. A housekeeper, a Mrs. Tenney, moved into the lighthouse, and her young son made a boat trip to Georges Island and then on to Boston every day for school. The housekeeper told Edward Rowe Snow about being at the Narrows Light during the destructive Portland Gale of 1898. She said that the stones striking the structure's iron legs sounded like strange music, as every leg had a slightly different pitch. The icebreaker was destroyed by the storm and shingles were blown from the dwelling.

Shipping mishaps near the lighthouse were not uncommon. During a thick snowstorm in early December 1907, a power fishing dory went aground on the spit with four men aboard. It was reported that the men were saved by the quick actions of a lobsterman living in a cabin on Great Brewster Island.

Malcolm N. Huse was keeper in August 1915, when the vessel *Nautilus* went aground nearby at Lovell's Island. Huse went to the aid of those on board, and just two days later he assisted three persons on board a motorboat that had run out of fuel. Secretary of Commerce William C. Redfield officially commended Huse for his good deeds.

Three brothers—Arthur, Judson, and Tom Small—all served as keepers in the light's last decades. Once, in a winter storm while Arthur Small was keeper, an Italian fishing boat went ashore on the bar near the lighthouse. Small managed to get a line out and pulled two of the men to safety in the lighthouse, but the third man perished.

Around noon on June 7, 1929, Keeper Tom Small was near the end of a weeklong project involving the removal of paint from the outside of the structure with a blowtorch. A spark ignited a fire in the roof, and within 15 minutes the entire lighthouse was in flames. Small managed to throw a few belongings into a rowboat and narrowly escaped with his life as debris fell around him. According to the *Lighthouse Service Bulletin,* the falling fog bell missed him by a few inches.

Officials at a quarantine station on Gallop's Island phoned the Hull fire department. There was no fireboat in Hull, so Boston was called. By the time a fireboat made the seven-mile trip, it was far too late to save the lighthouse. There was some fear that several barrels of oil might ignite, but they fell into the water and an explosion was averted.

Luckily Small's wife and eight-year-old son—who lived at the lighthouse in the summer months—were visiting friends in South Boston. There was one happy note in the fire's aftermath. Near the end of June, a party of engineers dredging near the site recovered Jimmy Small's little bank containing two dollars in pennies. The savings were soon returned to the boy.

Immediately after the fire, the crew of the tender *Mayflower* placed a gas-operated lighted bell buoy at the site. The base of the lighthouse stayed standing for a while, and an automatic light and fog bell were placed on top of it. Today an automatic light on a small steel skeleton tower stands near the former location of "Bug Light."

The modern skeleton tower near the site of the old Narrows Lighthouse can be seen distantly from George's Island, the destination of daily harbor cruises from Boston's Long Wharf during the summer. For more information, visit www.bostonharborcruises.com or call (617) 227-4321.

CHAPTER 45

Boston Light in July 2004. *Photo by the author.*

Boston Light

1716, 1783

Boston Light, aptly dubbed the "ideal American lighthouse" by the historian Edward Rowe Snow, holds a place of honor among our nation's beacons. This was the first light station established on the North American continent, and the last in the United States to be automated. It's also our only light station that still retains an official keeper. Seasonal public tours provide the public with the opportunity to experience this cultural treasure up close, and few attractions in New England can approach the thrilling panorama of the harbor and city as seen from the lighthouse's lantern.

There were simple lighted beacons in the harbor before the first lighthouse. The primary function of the early beacons was not navigational, but rather to warn of approaching enemy vessels. It's recorded that there was a beacon on Point Allerton in Hull as early as 1673. The beacon was a simple structure supporting an open iron basket or grate in which "fier-bales of pitch and ocre" were burned.

Fitz-Henry Smith Jr., author of *The Story of Boston Light*, believed there might have been an unlighted day beacon on the island we now know as Little Brewster before the lighthouse was established there, since early records refer to it as "Beacon Island." The rocky island—about a mile north of Hull and about eight miles east of Boston—is only about 600 feet long and at most 250 feet wide, its total area being only one acre above the mean high water mark. The highest elevation of about 18 feet is at the eastern end of the island, where the lighthouse is located.

Boston's deep and spacious harbor led it to become the commercial center of America in colonial days. At that time, all large vessels had to enter the harbor between the Brewster Islands in the outer harbor and Point Allerton in the town of Hull.

Clough's *New England Almanac* of 1701 hinted at the need for a lighthouse at the entrance to the harbor. Early in 1713, a prominent Boston merchant and selectman named John George, representing the business community of the city, proposed to the General Court the "Erecting of a Light Hous & Lanthorn on some Head Land at the Entrance to the Harbour of Boston for the Direction of Ships & Vessels in the Night Time bound into the said Harbour." (John George didn't live to see the lighthouse established, as he died in November 1714. His widow later married the Reverend Cotton Mather.)

A committee headed by Lieutenant Governor William Tailer planned for the lighthouse. After visiting several of the harbor islands and conferring with the area's most experienced shipmasters, Tailer reported that the best site for the lighthouse was "the Southernmost Part of the Great Brewster called Beacon Island." Several islands in Boston's outer harbor are collectively known as the Brewsters, after the Elder Brewster of the Plymouth Colony. Beacon Island, now known as Little Brewster, is attached to Great Brewster by a sand bar.

On July 23, 1715, the General Court of Massachusetts passed the Boston Light Bill. It read, in part: "Whereas the want of a lighthouse erected at the entrance to the harbor of Boston hath been a great discouragement to navigation by the loss of the lives and estates of several of his majesty's subjects; for prevention thereof—Be it enacted . . . that there be a lighthouse erected at the charge of the Province, on the southernmost part of the Great Brewster, called Beacon Island, to be kept lighted from sun setting to sun rising."

The islands known as the Brewsters are close to the Point Allerton section of the town of Hull, southeast of Boston; the town voted to grant the needed land to the province for a lighthouse. The first lighthouse was financed by a tax of a penny a ton on all vessels coming into the harbor, and the same amount for vessels leaving the harbor. Smaller coasting vessels paid only two shillings as they left the harbor. Fishing vessels and small vessels transporting lumber and other building materials locally were taxed five shillings yearly.

A stone tower was built at a cost of £2,385. The exact dimensions aren't known, but it's believed the tower was at least 50 feet tall. The first keeper, 43-year-old George Worthylake, lighted the lighthouse on Friday, September 14, 1716.

No description of the original lighting apparatus survives, but Arnold Burges Johnson wrote in his book *The Modern Light-House Service* that it was "first lighted by tallow candles." The keeper was supplied with "Oyl Week and Candles" in November 1716; it's possible that the lantern originally held both candles and oil lamps.

Worthylake, who was brought up on Georges Island (previously known as Pemberton Island) in Boston Harbor, moved to the light station with his wife, Ann, and their daughters, Ruth and Ann. An African slave named Shadwell lived at the lighthouse as well. Worthylake also maintained a farm on Lovell's Island, closer to Boston.

Worthylake was paid £50 a year, which was raised to £75 in 1717. He made additional money as a harbor pilot for incoming vessels, and he also kept a flock of sheep on Great Brewster Island. Fifty-nine of his sheep were caught on the long sand spit off Great Brewster during a 1717 storm; they drowned when the tide came in.

On November 3, 1718, Worthylake went to Boston to collect his pay. On his way back he stopped at Lovell's Island, where he and his wife and their daughter Ruth boarded a sloop heading for Boston Light. A friend, John Edge, accompanied them. Witnesses later said that the party were seen to eat and drink "very friendly" while aboard the sloop, "tho not to excess."

The sloop anchored near Little Brewster Island a few minutes past noon, and Shadwell paddled out in a canoe to transfer the party to the island. Young Ann Worthylake and a friend, Mary Thompson, watched from shore. Suddenly, the two girls on shore saw "Worthylake, his wife & others swimming or floating on the water, with their boat Oversett." The canoe—possibly overloaded—had capsized, and all five people drowned. George, Ann, and Ruth Worthylake were buried beneath a triple headstone in Copp's Hill Burying Ground in Boston's North End.

Benjamin Franklin, 12 years old at the time, was urged by his brother to write a poem based on the disaster. The young Franklin wrote a poem called "The Lighthouse Tragedy" and hawked copies on the streets of Boston. Franklin later wrote in his autobiography that the poem was "wretched stuff," although it "sold prodigiously."

Robert Saunders, a former sloop captain, became Boston Light's second keeper on a temporary basis, until a new permanent keeper could be chosen. Saunders apparently drowned only a few days after taking the job; no details of the incident survive. John Hayes, an experienced seaman described as an "able-bodied and discreet person," became the next keeper.

Hayes asked for a gallery to be installed around the tower's lantern room so that he could clean the glass of ice and snow. He also noted the need for some kind of fog signal, asking that "a great Gun may be placed on the Said Island to answer Ships in a Fogg."

A cannon, America's first fog signal, was placed on the island in 1719. Passing ships would fire their cannons when passing nearby in times of fog, and the keeper would reply with a blast from the light station.

The cannon, cast in 1700 and possibly relocated from Long Island in the inner harbor, served on Little Brewster Island for 132 years. In the early 1960s, the cannon was moved to the Coast Guard Academy in New London, Connecticut. In 1993, it was returned by helicopter to Little Brewster, and the venerable fog cannon sits today on a new carriage inside the base of the lighthouse tower.

A fire broke out in the lighthouse lantern on January 13, 1720, caused by the oil lamps falling on wooden benches. Hayes's wife roused the keeper and informed him of the fire, and Hayes quickly ran up the stairs of the tower with two pails of water. He later reported that the "fire was too violent to be subdued," but he "saved many things belonging to the Light House."

It cost £2,100 to repair the damage, and Hayes's salary was withheld until he was absolved of the blame. Hayes was still keeper when a storm in 1723 brought record high tides to the area that damaged the lighthouse and the island's wharf.

John Hayes retired because of advancing age in 1733. Robert Ball, an Englishman whose stay of about 40 years would be the longest stint of any keeper in the station's history, succeeded him. Ball was assisted by a slave known as Samson, who died in 1762 and was buried on Rainsford Island in the harbor.

The keeper still doubled as a harbor pilot during Ball's stay. Ball complained that other enterprising individuals were taking many of the piloting jobs, which he felt rightfully belonged to him. The court pronounced Ball the "established pilot" for the harbor and announced that anyone else painting his boat to resemble Ball's would be fined five pounds, to be paid to Ball. Ball seems to have made out well financially; he eventually owned three of the harbor islands—Outer Brewster, Calf Island, and Green Island.

The tower was repaired and encased in "Good oak Plank" in 1734, and 12 iron hoops were added around the exterior for added strength.

The *Boston Gazette* of March 24, 1735, reported an incident that echoed the 1718 tragedy. A sudden gust of wind had upset the lighthouse boat. Three persons were "providentially saved," but a man named John Kerigan drowned in the accident.

A bad fire gutted the lighthouse in 1751, and for a time the light was shown from a 40-foot spar. After repairs totaling £1,170, including the replacement of the original wooden lantern with one made of iron (with a copper roof), a higher duty was imposed on local shipping.

The early lighthouse was struck by lightning on several occasions, including an instance in June 1754 when lightning "tore off shingles from several places on the outside." The installation of a lightning rod was delayed because of the objections of some "godly men" who thought it "vanity and irreligion for the arm of flesh to presume to avert the stroke of heaven," according to a 1789 article. Practicality eventually won out and a lightning conductor was installed.

More repairs to the lighthouse were in the works when the American Revolution intervened. In July 1775, Boston Harbor and the

Boston Light, circa 1720s. *From the collection of the author.*

lighthouse were under the control of the British. On July 20, American troops under Maj. Joseph Vose landed at the lighthouse and took lamps, oil, and some gunpowder and burned the wooden parts of the tower. After leaving the island they had to outrun an armed British schooner, and two Americans were wounded. An eyewitness described "the flames of the lighthouse ascending up to Heaven, like grateful incense, and the ships wasting their powder."

As the British worked to repair the tower, 300 American soldiers under Maj. Benjamin Tupper landed at the island on July 31. They easily defeated the British guard and again burned the lighthouse. As they tried to leave, they found their boats stranded, for the tide had gone out. This gave British vessels time to reach the scene.

The Americans finally managed to launch their boats as the British fired on them. American troops at Nantasket in Hull helped by firing a cannon at the British boats, landing a direct hit on one. This turned the tide of battle and the Americans escaped with only one soldier having been killed. Gen. George Washington praised the men: "The General thanks Major Tupper and the Officers and Soldiers under his Command, for their gallant and soldierlike behaviour in possessing themselves of the enemy's post at the Light House, and for the Number of Prisoners they took there, and doubts not, but the Continental Army, will be as famous for their mercy as for their valour."

At the end of their occupation of Boston Harbor during the war, the British lingered in the harbor for some months. As they left the area on June 13, 1776, one of their final acts was to set off a timed charge on the lighthouse island, completely destroying the tower. The remains of the metal lantern were used to make ladles for American cannons.

In June 1783, a committee of the Boston Marine Society addressed the lack of a lighthouse. The commissary general of Massachusetts, Richard Devens, was authorized to build a new lighthouse on the original site.

The new 60-foot (75 feet to the top of the octagonal lantern), conical rubblestone tower was designed to be "nearly of the same dimensions of the former lighthouse." It has sometimes been claimed that part of the original tower was incorporated into the new one, but there appears to be no evidence to support this assertion.

Thomas Knox was the first post-Revolution keeper. He stayed in the position for 27 years, also serving as a harbor pilot. Two of his brothers were also harbor pilots. Knox's father owned Nix's Mate Island in the harbor, and Thomas inherited ownership when his father died in 1790.

The light station was ceded to the federal government in 1790. With the change, Knox lost his title as Boston's official "branch pilot." Governor Hancock assigned that designation to another man, but Knox continued to work as a pilot. In 1794 Knox's yearly salary as keeper was set by the federal government at $266.67, which was raised to $333.33 in 1796.

In an article published in 1789, Knox described the lighting apparatus as four lamps, each holding a gallon of oil, and each having four lights. The lamps were divided into four sections that each operated

Boston Light, circa 1780s. *Courtesy of National Archives.*

independently. There were complaints that the light was too dim when seen from the sea, and the lamps produced a great deal of smoke.

In 1807 Winslow Lewis, a member of the Boston Marine Society, began experiments with lighthouse illumination. He patented his system of Argand lamps (more efficient and less smoky than the old lamps) paired with parabolic reflectors in 1810. He first demonstrated his system in the cupola of the State House in Boston.

Lewis's system was subsequently installed at Boston Light in May 1810. Six whale-oil–fueled Argand lamps were installed in two parallel rows, about 15 inches apart. A parabolic reflector was placed behind each lamp.

The lighthouse had exhibited a fixed white light, but in 1811 machinery was installed that enabled the light to revolve. This, in theory, made it easier for mariners to differentiate Boston Light from the new light established at Scituate a few miles down the coast. In reality, many wrecks resulted from confusion between the lights.

The Boston Marine Society urged the adoption of Lewis's apparatus in all American lighthouses, and he was subsequently awarded a contract for that purpose. This system remained in use in the United States into the 1850s, long after much of the rest of the world had adopted the use of the more efficient Fresnel lens invented in France in 1822.

In June 1809, the local lighthouse superintendent, Henry Dearborn, found three perpendicular cracks in the tower, extending for almost its entire height. Six iron hoops were added around the tower for extra support. One band was removed in the early twentieth century; five aluminum bands are in place today.

Jonathan Bruce followed Knox as keeper in 1811. Bruce and his wife, Mary, watched from the island on June 1, 1813, as the British ship *Shannon* battled the American frigate *Chesapeake* during the War of 1812. The *Chesapeake* was swiftly defeated, but not before the mortally wounded Capt. James Lawrence uttered the immortal words, "Don't give up the ship!"

Lt. Edward W. Carpender inspected the station in 1838, while David Tower was the keeper. Carpender described the lighting apparatus as 14 Argand lamps and parabolic reflectors—varying from 13½ to 16 inches in diameter—arranged on opposite sides of an oblong frame or chandelier. The entire apparatus revolved, completing a revolution every three and a half minutes. Keeper Tower complained that the lantern leaked, which sometimes caused the rotating mechanism to stop and forced him to turn the apparatus by hand.

Like his predecessors, Tower doubled as a harbor pilot. Carpender noted that this practice took Tower away from the lighthouse frequently at night, and he recommended that keepers be forbidden by law to take on any pursuits that removed them from their station during the hours that they should be concerned, above all, with the lighting of the lamps.

Apparently owing in large part to recommendations made by Carpender, Winslow Lewis installed a new lantern in 1839, along with new 21-inch reflectors from England. The engineer I. W P. Lewis, Winslow's nephew, visited Boston Light for his 1843 report to Congress. He was critical, calling the tower "loose and leaky" and noting that the wooden stairway was so rotten "as to be unsafe of ascent." The two-story house, with four rooms on each floor, was in good repair, as was a new boathouse.

David Tower died in 1844 after a brief illness. That same year, a new cast-iron spiral stairway with a wrought-iron railing was installed; the stairway is still in use today. Iron doors and window frames were also installed.

Joshua Snow followed Tower as keeper. Around this time, an unusual enterprise was in operation on Little Brewster Island—a "Spanish cigar factory," staffed by young girls from Boston. The cigars the girls made were labeled as "Cuban" and were sold to unsuspecting locals. The authorities soon broke up the illegal business. Snow left in December 1844, apparently dismissed after only a few months on the island.

Tobias Cook of Cohasset, Massachusetts, was the next keeper, staying until 1849. Following Cook as keeper was William Long of Charlestown, Massachusetts. An 1851 inspection was somewhat critical of Long, noting that he didn't light up at sunset or put out the light precisely at sunrise. The tower was in need of whitewashing, and the copper lightning conductors were broken and neglected by the keeper.

In *Famous Lighthouses of New England,* Snow included some passages from the 1849–51 diary of Keeper Long's daughter, Lucy:

> *Monday. October 29—In the afternoon I went over to the island, on returning saw the body of a man on the bar, supposedly washed from the wreck of the vessel, lost on Minot's Ledge.*
>
> *Mon. Dec. 31—A snowstorm in the morning. George came over to wind up the clock, and I cleaned the light, at night I light the light.*
>
> *Monday, Aug. 26—Pleasant weather, this morning Albert came down in his boat.*

Albert was Albert Small, a harbor pilot. Despite much competition, Small won the hand of Lucy Maria Long in marriage. His proposal came at the top of the lighthouse, and the two were wed in 1853.

Boston Light Station, circa late 1800s. *From the collection of Edward Rowe Snow, courtesy of Dorothy Snow Bicknell.*

A 1,375-pound fog bell, operated by clockwork machinery, replaced the old cannon in 1851. Zebedee Small was keeper from 1851 to 1853, followed by Hugh Douglass (1853–56). During Douglass's stay, the rotation of the lens was speeded up to a revolution every one and a half minutes.

A Gloucester native, Moses Barrett, saw much change during his time as keeper (1856–62). The Lighthouse Board suggested in 1857 that the tower be rebuilt at a cost of $71,000, but improvements were made instead. In 1859 the tower was raised to its present height of 89 feet and a new lantern was installed along with a 12-sided second-order Fresnel lens. The giant lens—about 11 feet tall and 15 feet in circumference—rotated by means of a clockwork mechanism that required frequent winding. A single lamp inside the new lens replaced the system of multiple lamps, and round "bull's-eye" panels on the lens produced a flash each time they passed in front of the light source. The lens went into operation on December 20, 1859.

In the same year, the tower was lined with brick, a spacious brick entryway was added to the tower, and a new duplex keeper's house was built. Beginning in 1861, Boston Light was assigned a keeper and two assistants.

Barrett witnessed one of Boston Harbor's worst tragedies on November 8, 1861, when the 991-ton ship *Maritana* ran into Shag Rocks in the outer harbor during a heavy snow squall in the predawn hours. The ship, with 39 people aboard, had been heading for Boston from Liverpool. Around 8:30 a.m., the ship broke in two, and the captain was killed.

Keeper Barrett signaled the town of Hull, and a pilot boat soon sent a dory to Shag Rocks. A dozen people survived, but 27 died in the wreck. During the following spring, the captain's wife journeyed to Little Brewster Island to receive her husband's watch and other belongings that Barrett had been holding for her.

Thomas Bates took over as keeper in July 1864 and remained until his death in April 1893. The light station was the scene of many happy gatherings during the Bates area. Frequent sing-alongs took place, with the accompaniment of Assistant Keeper Edward Gorham on accordion. "When the Roll Is Called Up Yonder" and "Crossing the Bar" were special favorites.

On January 31, 1882, Keeper Bates, along with an assistant and a local fisherman, rescued the crew of the *Fanny Pike*, which had run into Shag Rocks.

A brick cistern was added in 1884 in a building near the tower. The cistern held 21,800 gallons of rainwater for the keepers and their families. A second keeper's house was added in 1885, located at the opposite end of the island from the lighthouse. Two houses had become a necessity with three keepers and their families living on the island.

A Daboll compressed-air fog trumpet replaced the bell in 1872. It remained in use until 1887, when a steam-driven siren replaced it. In the late nineteenth century, students from the Massachusetts Institute of Technology conducted experiments with fog signals at Boston Light, trying to perfect a signal that would penetrate the so-called ghost walk, an area about six miles east of the lighthouse where no sound could penetrate. Despite the students' best efforts, even the largest horn could not penetrate the ghost walk.

Henry L. Pingree was keeper from 1894 to 1909. Pingree's son, Wesley, who was an assistant keeper at Deer Island Light in Boston Harbor, married Horte's sister, Josephine.

An auxiliary light was added to the station in 1890—a fixed white light was exhibited from a small wooden building. The light was designed to help mariners avoid dangerous Hardings Ledge. If they strayed too far from the channel to either side, they would see a red light.

Charles Jennings, a Cape Cod native previously stationed at Monomoy Point Light, became keeper in 1916 at a yearly salary of $804. In his book, *A Lighthouse Family*, Charles's son, Harold, described a celebrated rescue his father performed:

On February 3, 1918, the USS Alacrity, *a Coast Guard patrol boat, ran aground in the ice a few yards from the station. The tide was ebbing fast and it wasn't long before the vessel lay over on her side. This made it impossible for the crew to launch their lifeboat. Dad and the assistant keeper saw their plight and began figuring out how to rescue the crew. They reasoned that if they tried to get a dory through the ice cakes, they would be crushed. Dad remembered that in the boathouse there was some gunpowder and firing caps that were used in the old cannon, originally used as a fog signal at the light. The assistant keeper got a coil of rope that could be used. They set the fuse and pushed the gunpowder down the barrel. They made a hard ball in the end of the rope. The remaining coil lay next to the cannon. The fuse was ignited and when the gun fired, the rope followed the ball out to the ship. It was not quite on target so they tried again with no success. Now they had to launch the dory and take a chance that the ice did not close in on them. After a couple of trips, carrying the crew and gear, the rescue was a success. This was the last time the fog cannon was fired at Boston Light.*

Jennings, who received a commendation from the secretary of Commerce for the rescue of twenty-four men from the *Alacrity,* moved on to be the keeper of the range lights at Lovell's Island in 1919.

John Lelan Hart was keeper from 1919 to 1926. In 1921 Hart and his assistant, William J. Howard—who later gained fame as a lifesaver at Wing's Neck Light—were credited with saving the life of the second assistant keeper, whose boat had capsized. Hart was involved in several more rescues during his stay.

Maurice A. Babcock, formerly at Thacher Island, Bird Island, and Gay Head, was principal keeper from 1926 to 1941. In 1934, members of the Bostonian Society and the Massachusetts Historical Society held a ceremony on Little Brewster honoring the twenty-five keepers of Boston Light. Fitz-Henry Smith, author of a history of the lighthouse, unveiled a tablet bearing the names of the keepers. The modest and taciturn Babcock was invited to speak. Here is the entire text of his speech: "Well, ladies and gentlemen, I am not much of an orator, but I enjoy keeping the light burning for the ships coming in, and the fog signal sounding. I thank you."

The Babcocks' children boarded in the nearby towns of Winthrop or Hull so they could attend school, and they spent their vacations on Little Brewster. On one occasion, Keeper Babcock rowed through dangerous ice floes to Hull to pick up his son Bill during a February vacation. The keeper's wife watched her husband fight off giant ice cakes as he headed for Hull. She lost sight of him for an agonizing two hours. Finally she caught sight of the returning dory, with her husband rowing and their son fending off the ice. "After I had given them a good scolding," she later said, "I sat them down to a hot supper and we had a pleasant holiday." Bill Babcock later carried on the family tradition, becoming a keeper at Graves Light in Boston Harbor.

The Babcocks were on the island for the devastating hurricane of September 21, 1938, which struck New England without warning. As the winds picked up late that afternoon, Keeper Babcock had to crawl on his hands and knees to reach the lighthouse. A dock at the island was wrecked by the storm. Babcock and one of his assistants spent the night in the lighthouse lantern, making sure the light stayed lit. Babcock's log entries, now at the National Archives, make note of the storm but mention nothing of his own extraordinary efforts.

In late 1939, Keeper Babcock lost part of a finger in an accident with a motor on the island. He spent a few weeks in Boston recuperating. In a newspaper article during that period, he said that he had never driven an automobile and had no intention of doing so. By boat

The unveiling of a tablet at Boston Light on December 2, 1934, which lists the station's keepers. *Left to right:* J. Lelan Hart, keeper 1919–26; Charles Jennings, keeper 1916–19; Maurice Babcock, keeper 1926–41, and Fitz-Henry Smith, author of *The Story of Boston Light. From the collection of Edward Rowe Snow, courtesy of Dorothy Snow Bicknell.*

he could reach Boston's South Station in 50 minutes, much faster than the trip by car from Hull. "We do our shopping for groceries just as anybody else does," he told the reporter. "The only difference is that we are farther from the store. We lay in larger supplies than most people, on account of the distance. We can't trot out to the chain store if we happen to forget the coffee."

As mentioned earlier, the young Benjamin Franklin composed a poem describing the death of Boston Light's first keeper, George Worthylake. Not a single copy of the poem was known to exist until 1940, when Maurice Babcock Jr., son of the keeper, found a tattered copy in the pocket of a rotting leather jacket in the ruins of an old house on Middle Brewster Island. The copy could not be proved to be authentic, so no value could be placed on it.

The find by the young Babcock was publicized in news media throughout the country. Here's part of the poem as printed on the copy:

Quick the prow is upward borne
George in Ann's arm is thrown
Husband, wife and child together
To the chilly waves have gone.

Frenzied clasp of wife and daughter
Bears the sturdy swimmers down
Save the boat upon the water
Nothing of their fate is known.

Friends of the Babcocks threw the family a farewell party on the island on the day of the keeper's retirement in November 1941. Just after their retirement to the town of Marion, Massachusetts, Babcock's wife told the *Boston Post:* "For 23 years we have been away from civilization. Now we'll join civilization again. And we are both glad and sorry. You don't surrender a 23-year routine without regret. But, all in all, we're glad to be back in the world again."

The Coast Guard took over the management of the nation's lighthouses in 1939, and civilian keepers were given the option of remaining civilians or joining the Coast Guard. Ralph C. Norwood, an assistant under Maurice Babcock, enlisted in the Coast Guard and became the next keeper in 1941. Norwood's grandfather was Albert Norwood, keeper of Wood Island Light in Maine and father of 12.

The 1930s had been exciting years for the Norwoods. In 1932 Josephine Norwood, Ralph's wife, was expecting their seventh child. (She would have nine children by the time she reached 27.) During a spring storm, Josephine believed the birth was imminent and a doctor was summoned from Hull.

It took an hour and a half for the boat to land at the island in heavy seas. As it turned out, Georgia wasn't born until a week later in calm weather, but the headlines from the night of the storm forever stamped Georgia as the "Storm Child."

The writer Ruth Carmen based a novel called *Storm Child* on the story. The book, a highly fictionalized version of the Norwoods' story, even included a tidal wave destroying the lighthouse. Georgia and her parents were showered with publicity, and they traveled to New York City to appear on the nationally broadcast *We the People* program.

Hollywood subsequently came calling to make a movie version of *Storm Child,* and five-year-old Georgia was slated to play herself. Described as "smiling and sunny-curled," Georgia was to be the "Bay State's own Shirley Temple."

The movie never happened. "I would not separate the children," said Josephine. "Each one was as precious as the other and they all needed my supervision." Apparently Georgia agreed, reportedly saying, "I don't want to go to Hollywood. I want to go back to Boston Light."

The legend of the Storm Child lived on just the same. Georgia's son, Willie Emerson, later wrote a book called *First Light,* which relates the true story of his mother's birth and life at Boston Light. "The days spent on Boston Light were busy ones," Josephine told her grandson for his book, "with eleven of us to cook for. . . . As we never knew when inspection of the houses, tower and fog signal would be held, it was a matter of course to have the beds made, the dishes done, and the sweeping and dry mopping done by ten o'clock. Of course our children were brought up to help with the work. Then they had their time to swim, go fishing, walking over the bar at low tide, or go rowing."

In the 1930s, there were three families and as many as 19 children living on the tiny island. The school-aged Norwood children lived with their mother in Hull during the school year, but they always looked forward to their glorious summers on the island. "You never relaxed until they were all safely in bed at night," said Josephine. She once rigged a leash attached to the clothesline for her young son Bobbie, but "Georgia felt sorry for him and untied him."

Ralph Norwood's daughter Priscilla Reece later remembered that her father would go to Hull once a month for groceries. "Sometimes he would take one of us kids with him," she recalled, "and the grocers would feel sorry and give you a cabbage or something." Attempts to maintain a vegetable garden on the island met with little success, as the soil was poor. The Norwoods, of course, always had plenty of

Georgia Norwood, daughter of Keeper Ralph Norwood. *From the book* Storm Child.

seafood. The children would harvest the plentiful crabs, periwinkles, and mussels from the shores of the island. The older children made money by lobstering.

Summers were lively, filled with rowboat races and pie-eating contests with the children who summered on nearby Great Brewster. Games of all sorts were played, even baseball—in the water was an automatic out. Life was generally harmonious, although Maurice Babcock Jr. did get a punch in the nose once from one of the Norwood girls. He had trespassed onto the Norwoods' part of the island. Bruce Norwood said years later, "I've never been in another place that felt like the home Boston Light was."

The Norwoods left the island in 1945. One of Ralph and Josephine's sons, Gail, later became a lightkeeper in Nova Scotia, making four generations of keepers in the family.

Boston Light was extinguished during World War II, and it went back into operation in July 1945. The light was converted to electricity in 1948, and shortly after that the clockwork mechanism that rotated the lens was replaced by an electric motor. The second-order Fresnel lens remains in use today.

A child was born on the island in March 1950 to Mary Ellen Lavigne, wife of Joseph E. Lavigne, the Coast Guard's principal keeper. When the baby's birth was imminent, low tide prevented the keeper from launching a boat to get his wife to the mainland. A doctor was rushed over from Pemberton Point in Hull in a Coast Guard boat, and Joseph Jr. was delivered at 7:30 a.m. Mary Ellen was later taken to Quincy City Hospital to recuperate. Joseph Jr. was the couple's first son and their fourth child.

In 1960 it was decided that the smaller 1885 seven-room keeper's house would suffice for the island's Coast Guard personnel. The 1859 duplex dwelling had badly deteriorated. A 1949 inspection reported that the ceiling in the kitchen was falling down and there were rat holes in the house. The Coast Guard razed the structure in the spring of 1960. After this, Coast Guardsmen lived at the station without their families.

Boatswain's Mate First Class William "Mike" Mikelonis was the Coast Guard keeper at Boston Light for several years beginning in 1962. The Coast Guard staff at that time spent two weeks on the island and one week off.

Mikelonis and other keepers over the years have enjoyed great fishing off the ledges. When Mikelonis retired in 1967, he said he had caught more than 1,000 striped bass, two of them over 50 pounds.

Mikelonis shared the island with two assistants and a shaggy black dog named Salty, one of a long line of Boston Light dogs. Salty was succeeded by Salty II, and later by Farrah (named during the era of *Charlie's Angels*), a friendly mutt who lived for 13 years on Little Brewster. Farrah would whine and shake when taken to the mainland. Once, at low tide, Farrah wandered over to Great Brewster Island, and 11 puppies resulted from her short trip away from home. Farrah died in November 1989, and her final resting place is a marked grave not far from the cistern building.

A later dog was named Shadwell in honor of the slave who drowned with the first keeper. Cats have also lived at the station, including a frisky black cat named Ida Lewis, after America's most famous woman lighthouse keeper.

Petty Officer Paul Dodds, a local man from Hull, became the officer in charge in early 1984. Dodds recalled sitting on a seawall as a boy, gazing at the lighthouse. By this time, Boston Light's fame as a National Historic Landmark (designated in 1966) was bringing more visitors to the island. Dodds was told that the island's historic significance was the only reason keepers were retained, instead of automating and destaffing the station.

During their stay, Dodds and Fireman Patrick Doherty painted the boathouse and converted the upper story into a gym, installed new doors, and supervised the installation of a new fuel line. The men split 12-hour watches, maintained the buildings and grounds, and called weather reports to the Coast Guard station at Point Allerton.

Joe Larnard of Newburyport, Massachusetts, was another of the Coast Guard's keepers in the 1980s. Profiled in *People* magazine, Larnard said the view of the city was tantalizing. "We know we're missing out," he said, "so we stop looking. It's like being in a ship at sea, only we're on a rock that doesn't roll." Larnard also alluded to the often-told tales of hauntings on the island. "I used to think the ghost stories were true," he said, "what with the wind and all."

Some people have reported weird happenings on Little Brewster over the years. Russell Anderson was a Coast Guard keeper in 1947. One day, his 22-year-old wife, Mazie, was walking along the shore. She heard footsteps close behind her, but saw no one when she turned around.

That night as she tried to sleep, Mazie felt a presence in the room. Later she heard what she described as "horrible maniacal laughter" coming from the boathouse. On another night she heard the same sound coming from the fog signal house. This time a little girl's sobbing voice followed, calling "Shaaaadwell!" over and over.

Mazie Anderson related this story in an article for *Yankee* magazine many years later. She said that on one occasion the fog-signal engines started themselves and the light mysteriously went on by itself. Mazie saw an unfamiliar figure outlined against the lens. Soon she again heard the man's laughing voice and the girl's sobbing cries. It wasn't until years later that Mazie Anderson read that the Boston Light slave's name was Shadwell—the name repeated by the little girl's voice.

Petty Officer First Class Dennis Dever, the Coast Guard officer in charge in the late 1980s, had a few odd experiences. While working in the station's boathouse, he liked to have his radio tuned to a rock station. Often, with nobody else in the boathouse, the station would change itself to a classical station. Dever said he and other Coast Guard crew attributed events like this to "Old George"—Worthylake, that is.

One day Dever was in the kitchen of the keeper's house looking out the window at the tower, and he clearly saw a man in the lantern room. This was alarming, as the only other person on the island was his assistant in the next room. From a distance, it appeared that the figure at the top of the tower was wearing an old-fashioned keeper's uniform. Dever rushed to the tower and went up the stairs, but he found the lantern room empty.

Reports of mysterious figures seen in the tower and in the keeper's house continue to the present day. A number of people have described the ghostly figure of a woman in a white nightgown at the top of the tower.

By 1989 the Coast Guard had automated almost every lighthouse in the United States, and Boston Light was scheduled to be the last in this process. Harry Duvall, an automation expert for the Coast Guard, started preparation for the process but voiced misgivings. "Automation can't maintain the building," he told a *Boston Globe* reporter.

It looked as though Dennis Dever, a Maine native, would be the light's last keeper, and he relished the honor. "When sailors crossed those open seas and saw the lighthouse, they knew they'd made it.

The keepers kept that light going. That is what compels me," he told a reporter. In addition to his regular duties, Dever kept busy by creating two scarecrows designed to keep gulls off the dock, planting flower and vegetable gardens, and designing a Boston Light T-shirt.

Local groups—including the Friends of the Boston Harbor Islands and the Boston Harbor Association—protested the change to Congress and the Coast Guard, fearing that an abandoned station would fall to ruin. With the help of Massachusetts Senator Edward M. Kennedy, the plans to destaff the station were changed.

In October 1989, it was announced that the Senate Appropriations Committee had put specific language in the Coast Guard budget that would compel the Coast Guard to "retain staffing at Boston Light during fiscal year 1990 and conduct a review of its ownership, maintenance, and staffing."

In 1990 Historic Boston and the Massachusetts Department of Environmental Management commissioned a stewardship plan and preservation guidelines for the station. As a result of the study, much work was done on the island in the 1990s, including replacing trim on the keeper's house and repainting all the buildings.

Little Brewster Island was hit hard by the "Perfect Storm" of October 1991 and a December storm in 1992. Extensive damage to the buildings was repaired, but the storms also exacerbated concerns over the erosion of parts of the island, especially at the east end near the lighthouse.

Boston Light became the last lighthouse in the United States to be automated on April 16, 1998. A Coast Guard crew continued to perform all the other traditional keepers' duties, except for turning the light on at sunset and off at sunrise. The light currently operates 24 hours a day.

Sally Snowman and Jay Thomson, both Massachusetts natives, met during Coast Guard Auxiliary training in 1993. Once, when they were in a boat passing Boston Light, Sally remarked that she had always fantasized about getting married there. Jay immediately replied, "Let me know when you want to do it." A year later they decided to set the date.

On October 8, 1994, Jay and Sally went out to Little Brewster Island on a friend's 32-foot sailboat named *True Love*. The 22 guests arrived on one sailboat and two powerboats. After the ceremony the tower was opened for guests to climb. "I think the tower tour was as much the highlight of the trip as the wedding," said Sally.

Coast Guard Auxiliary (volunteer) personnel have worked on the island since 1980. Just a month after their wedding, Sally Snowman and Jay Thomson went back to Little Brewster to do their first light-house duty as Auxiliarists. Researching Boston Light's past became a passionate pursuit. The book *Boston Light: A Historical Perspective*, published in 1999, was the culmination of five years of research by Sally and Jay. The almost 300-page book is the most extensive volume ever published on America's first light station.

The Auxiliary personnel at Boston Light are now referred to as Watchstanders, and a program was established for their training in 2000. In September 2003, Sally Snowman was appointed as the new civilian keeper of Boston Light—the first civilian keeper since 1941 and the first woman keeper in the lighthouse's long history. The active-duty Coast Guard personnel who had been assigned to the island were relocated to meet the needs of Homeland Security.

National Park rangers are also present during the days the island is open from June to October. The rangers are there during the day only, whereas the Watchstander Program requires that participants stay overnight on the island for four- to seven-day stretches.

You can see Boston Light distantly from the shores of Hull, Revere, and Winthrop. The lighthouse can also be seen from sightseeing cruises, including some of those offered by the Friends of the Boston Harbor Islands. Call (781) 740-4290 or see www.fbhi.org for details.

Ranger-guided tours leave from the Moakley U.S. Courthouse at Fan Pier in the South Boston Seaport District. Parking is available and the pier is easily reached by public transportation. Reservations are strongly recommended. The trips run from June to early October, Thursday through Sunday. Call (617) 223-8666 or check www.bostonislands.org for the latest schedule. The trips last three and a half hours; more than an hour is spent on Little Brewster Island.

CHAPTER 46

Graves Light in July 2004. *Photo by the author.*

Graves Light

1905

Austere and weather-beaten, Graves Light might appear to the uninformed observer to be a more ancient structure than Boston Light, its neighbor in Boston's outer harbor. Surprisingly, it's actually one of Massachusetts' youngest lighthouses.

The ledges called the Graves, by the way, are not named—as some believe—for a resemblance to gravestones, or because of a high incidence of fatal shipwrecks in the vicinity. They were named for Rear Adm. Thomas Graves, who came to America from London in 1628 and was an early settler of Charlestown, Massachusetts. Graves himself, as early as 1634, noted the danger to navigation the ledges presented.

In 1843 the engineer I. W. P. Lewis recommended that a buoy be placed in the vicinity of Graves Ledges. The erection of a spindle on the ledges was considered, but Maj. C. A. Ogden of the Army Corps of Engineers examined the ledge in 1853 and found that there didn't appear to be "base enough to build a more permanent beacon." Ogden instead suggested a bell buoy.

An iron bell buoy was placed near the ledges in 1854. It was later replaced by a whistling buoy beyond the northeast end of the ledges, described in 1905 by the *Boston Globe:*

> *The lone sentinel is a huge fabric of steel plates, with the mechanism so arranged that the billows, which heave it this way and that, force the air through an aperture at the top, making the most weirdly mournful and bloodchilling sounds. An old sea dog on one of the harbor boats said that its sorrowings in bad weather, which touched every shade of grief, from a weary, heartbreaking sigh to a terrifying, far-carrying shriek of despair, used to make him creepy with mind pictures of all the dead of all the years snatched from life by all the shipwrecks since the first finding of Boston Harbor.*

A new entrance into Boston Harbor, near Graves Ledges, was improved in the early twentieth century so that larger ships could enter the harbor. Before then, the main entrance to the busy harbor was through the Narrows, between Point Allerton in Hull and the outer harbor islands, which joined the President Roads channel farther inside the harbor.

In 1902 Congress appropriated $75,000 for a lighthouse and fog signal, and Governor Crane of Massachusetts signed a deed conveying 435,400 square feet at the ledges to the federal government. The project ultimately cost $188,000, meaning a second appropriation of $113,000 was required in April 1904.

At first the lighthouse was to be located on the most northeasterly ledge, but no suitable spot for a foundation could be found. The site was changed to a larger rock, about two-thirds of the length of the ledges to the southwest.

Construction took place from 1903 to 1905, and Royal Luther of Malden, Massachusetts, was in charge. Col. William S. Stanton, engineer for the Second Lighthouse District, oversaw the operations. First, the granite blocks for the tower were cut at Rockport on Cape Ann in early 1903. A temporary wharf and temporary quarters for the workers were built at the Lovell's Island buoy depot in the harbor. A small steam vessel provided transportation for workers and materials between Lovell's Island and the Graves.

Work at the Graves began in June 1903. A shanty for the workmen, constructed of hard pine, was erected on a high ledge southwest of the lighthouse site and was accessed by means of a 90-foot walkway. The shanty had living quarters, a storeroom, a blacksmith shop, and a kitchen, and up to 40 men lived there in the summers of 1903 and 1904.

An area on the ledge was leveled by blasting, and a landing stage was prepared. The schooner *A. J. Miller* transported the granite to the site, beginning on August 11, 1903. The foundation was laid just 4 feet above the low tide mark, and the lower courses were bolted 3 feet deep into the rock. By the time the summer of 1903 was over, the first 42 feet of the tower was completed, the blocks put into place with the aid of a hoisting engine and derrick.

Royal Luther of Malden, Massachusetts, seen here at right, was in charge of the construction of Graves Light. *From the collection of Edward Rowe Snow, courtesy of Dorothy Snow Bicknell.*

The tower is just over 30 feet in diameter at the base, and the lower stones—held to each other with strong bolts—are 7 feet thick. The lower

A postcard image of Graves Light soon after it was built. *From the collection of the author.*

42-foot section of the tower was filled with concrete, with a space left for a cistern.

While the tower was under construction, interior ironwork for the lighthouse was being prepared in Boston, interior woodwork was fashioned at a facility in Portland, Maine, and a huge first-order Fresnel lens was being created in Paris, France. The summer of 1904 saw the lighthouse reach its ultimate height—not including the lantern—of 88 feet, with a total of 882 granite blocks in 44 courses.

During the last stage of work in 1905, which was delayed for some time by bad weather, the tower was lined with enameled brick. The lantern, gallery, and lens were put into place. A granite oil house was built 90 feet south of the tower, reached by crossing a footbridge, and a wharf was built near the tower, protected by 2,000 tons of riprap.

On the night of September 1, 1905, the first keeper, Elliot C. Hadley, lighted what was then the most powerful lighthouse in the state's history. The gigantic lens rotated on 400 pounds of mercury. A Lighthouse Board report stated: "At so exposed a site the height necessary for the lantern above the heavier masses of spray, the consequent geographic range, its location so far seaward, the service of the light to the large commerce of Boston and modern ships of deep draft, make it perhaps the most important light north of Cape Cod."

The total height of the tower—lantern included—is 113 feet. The focal plane of the lens, exhibiting a double flash every six seconds, is 98 feet above mean high water. The light was initially rated at 380,000 candlepower. It was later upgraded to 3.2 million candlepower, and it was for many years the most powerful light in New England.

The station's fog signal went into operation on November 23, 1905, with a Daboll trumpet powered by oil engines and air compressors installed in duplicate. The trumpet projected from the tower just below the lantern.

The entrance door to the tower was at the top of a 30-foot ladder, which made entry difficult in rough weather. The first story was the landing and storage space, the second was the engine room containing the fog-signal equipment, and the third floor was the kitchen. The fourth and fifth levels contained the keepers' beds and a library. Handgrips were built into the outside of the lantern, which made the treacherous job of cleaning the outside of the glass a little easier.

Two of the floors and all the walls were finished with enameled bricks. The handrails on the stairways were mahogany, and the rest of the woodwork was oak. A newspaper article described the rooms in the lighthouse as "reminiscent of cheery, compact little cabins on a smart steamer."

The 1,500-gallon water cistern in the bottom of the lighthouse was filled twice yearly by a lighthouse tender, and food was delivered regularly. The keepers augmented their diet with lobsters caught in their own traps around the ledges.

Keeper Hadley—previously stationed at the Massachusetts light stations on Thacher Island and Plum Island—was credited with saving two men whose canoe had overturned near the ledges in the fall of 1910. Hadley launched his dory into heavy seas and was able to reach the men. He took them to the lighthouse and even provided them with clothes, since all their belongings except their bathing suits had gone to the bottom of the harbor.

Another time, Hadley saved four fishermen whose engine had died near the Boston Lightship as they drifted helplessly into the ledges at the Graves. He was also credited with the rescue of two men and a woman from a swamped sailing dory. When it was reported that the dory had been sighted near the Graves but the occupants were missing, a lighthouse official said, "Rest easy. Hadley'll get them."

In 1910 Hadley described the conditions in storms, which generally weren't as much of a problem as the practice shots fired at nearby forts.

> I've looked up at solid water rushing in towards the ledges. . . . I don't know how far up the solid water comes. I've been knocked down by it on the wharf beside the light, and opening a window to look out more than halfway up the tower, I've had as much as three buckets-full dashed in my face. Sometimes, the seas go clean over the magazine [oil house] set at the end of the bridge. They never shake the tower. That stands as firm as the ledges. The only vibration it gets is from heavy firing at the forts, once when the gun goes off and again when the shot strikes. . . . The way we found out first was by having all our dishes broken.

Four keepers were originally assigned to the station, two on at all times. One of the early assistants was Hadley's son, Elliot C. Hadley Jr. The two Hadleys alternated two-week stints at the lighthouse with the two other assistants. The Hadleys lived a few miles away, in the Point Shirley section of Winthrop, and the trip to the lighthouse via dory was arduous in rough weather, sometimes taking as much as two hours. When the area around Point Shirley was frozen in winter, the lighthouse tender *Mayflower* was used to transport the keepers.

In December 1916, First Assistant Keeper Harry Whin was alone at the lighthouse and running short on supplies when a ferocious storm struck. Whin had already been on the station for more than 70 days and was weeks overdue to be relieved. He was reduced to eating almost nothing but fish and smoking rope and tea leaves in his pipe. He described the storm in a letter to the historian Edward Rowe Snow of nearby Winthrop:

> *The wind must have reached more than 100 m.p.h. It turned to snow, then sleet, then rain and fog; the engines had to run day and night to keep the fog horn going; the light had to run at night even though you couldn't see the light 100 yards from the station; the water pump that cooled the engines kept freezing. [It was] located down at the wharf. I had to climb that ladder up and down to thaw out that pump. This lasted for five days and nights!*
>
> *[On] Christmas Eve . . . I lowered the station boat on the ice and pushed her into open water, headed for Nahant Rock and provisions! My boat developed a leak. I started bailing, my cap in one hand and a tomato soup can in the other. I finally got ahead of the leak and started the engine. . . . [Got] some supplies and tobacco— they got all wet on my return trip; had to dump it all. Returned to the station about 5 a.m.—drifted quite a distance. Took me 5 hours to get back!*

The principal keeper returned the following day, and Whin subsequently submitted his resignation from the Lighthouse Service.

Octavius H. Reamy was an assistant under Hadley and later returned as principal keeper in the 1920s. Reamy was in charge of the station on September 1, 1935, when Edward Rowe Snow brought 65 people for a celebration of the lighthouse's thirtieth birthday. Among the assembled guests was Maurice Babcock, principal keeper of Boston Light.

During their tour, the visitors learned that the keepers had, by this time, been furnished with radio equipment and a telephone to keep them in contact with the outside world.

Assistant Keeper George H. Fitzpatrick (left) and Keeper Octavius Reamy, circa 1935. *From the collection of Edward Rowe Snow, courtesy of Dorothy Snow Bicknell.*

A severe storm two months later, in November 1935, moved giant stones, some weighing three tons, and deposited them near the lighthouse. "Never before," observed the *Lighthouse Service Bulletin,* "since the tower was built, had the sea been powerful enough to move these rocks."

Several wrecks have occurred near the Graves, including three during the tenure of Llewellyn Rogers, the last civilian keeper. In April 1938, the 419-foot British freighter *City of Salisbury,* recalled as the "Zoo Ship" for its cargo of zoo animals, struck an uncharted rock about one-half mile from the Graves. The vessel's cargo also included rubber and tea. There was no loss of human life. It was reported that three honey bears and several hundred rare birds from India and Ceylon were rescued successfully, but many monkeys and snakes died later from the effects of the accident. The ship became a tourist attraction for a few months before it finally split in two and sank.

Llewellyn Rogers was also at the lighthouse in 1936 when the steamer *New York* crashed into the excursion vessel *Romance,* which was carrying more than 200 passengers. The *Romance* sank in 20 minutes, but no lives were lost. Rogers witnessed another disaster on January 21, 1941, when the fishing schooner *Mary E. O'Hara* struck a barge anchored near the lighthouse. The men on the schooner climbed the icy rigging in a desperate effort to stay alive as the vessel slowly sank, but only five of 24 on board survived. It was the third-worst shipwreck in Boston Harbor's history.

The Coast Guard took over the operation of the station in the early 1940s. During the Coast Guard era, there were generally two keepers on duty at all times; each man spent two or three weeks at the lighthouse followed by a week off.

Coast Guardsman Larry Bowers was stationed at Graves Light from 1961 to 1963. Like other keepers before him, Bowers experienced some mighty storms. "We had one storm when I was on board with waves coming over the top of the light," he later recalled. "The waves knocked out the window on the first deck and killed the generator."

Bowers enjoyed scuba diving around the ledges, and he sometimes explored the wreck of the *City of Salisbury*. He even fashioned pieces of brass and copper from the wreck into a belt buckle.

Visits from a buoy tender, which brought water and fuel, were welcomed at the waveswept location. "Except," according to Bowers, "one time when they pumped fuel into the water tank. No fun on that one. Number-two diesel takes a long time to get out of a cistern. We had to pump it dry, and clean it, whitewash it, and bleach it. Still didn't help much. We only used that tank in emergencies."

Lou Reich, who was stationed at Graves Light in 1965, later recalled, "There was a lot of sanding and painting to be done to keep the iron railings from rusting." The foghorn was hard to forget. "A person can actually get used to sleeping through a night where the fog horn was blasting all night long," said Reich. "Not at first, but after a while."

An organization called Save Our Shores joined forces with the Coast Guard to refurbish the lighthouse in the summer of 1971. The light was automated in 1976 and the keepers were reassigned. There had been problems in the 1970s with the mercury that served as a bearing for the rotating lens.

Pedro Marticio was the last Coast Guard keeper. "I was there for two tours of duty," he said later. "I closed it down the first time due to a mercury spill, and after the light was decontaminated, I went out for another year." The enormous Fresnel lens, replaced by modern equipment when the light was automated, now sits in storage at the Smithsonian Institution.

Weather and vandalism have taken their toll. The old walkway has been destroyed by storms, and vandals have caused thousands of dollars in damage. The fog-signal house was swept away by the "Perfect Storm" of October 1991. The badly damaged landing platform was repaired in 1993. The original oil house still stands.

The light was converted to solar power in the summer of 2001, which eliminated the need for a submarine power cable. Graves Light remains an active aid to navigation, with two white flashes every 12 seconds and an automated foghorn.

You can get distant views of Graves Light from the shores of Winthrop, Nahant, and Hull. There are opportunities for special lighthouse cruises that will provide closer views. For information, call Friends of the Boston Harbor Islands, (781) 740-4290, or Boston Harbor Cruises, (617) 227-4321, or see www.bostonharborcruises.com.

CHAPTER 47

Top: The first (1856) Egg Rock Lighthouse. Bottom: The second (1898) lighthouse. Both from the collection of the author.

Egg Rock Light, Swampscott, Mass.

Egg Rock Light

1856, 1898–1922

Prominent Egg Rock, a little less than a mile northeast of the town of Nahant, resembles a whitish-gray whale rising out of the ocean. The three-acre island—about 80 feet high—can be seen from many locations north of Boston, from Winthrop to Marblehead. It's a familiar sight to the throngs who crowd the local beaches in summer, but probably very few have any inkling that a lighthouse once graced the rock.

Alonzo Lewis of nearby Lynn was a historian, poet, and civil engineer. He had a great deal to do with the establishment of a road from Lynn to Nahant and the building of a breakwater and road along Lynn Beach. Lewis described Egg Rock in his 1855 volume, *The Picture of Nahant:* "The gulls lay their eggs here in abundance, whence the rock derives its name. The approach to this rock is dangerous except in calm weather, and there is but one good landing place, which is on the western side. Its shape and color are highly picturesque. Viewed from the north, it has the semblance of a couchant lion, lying out in front of the city, to protect it from the approach of a foreign enemy."

Swampscott, a neighbor of Lynn and Nahant, had a fleet of about 150 fishing vessels by the mid-nineteenth century, and it was Swampscott's fishermen who first clamored for a lighthouse. Nahant also had a fishing fleet and was growing in popularity as a summer resort. As maritime traffic increased in the area, Alonzo Lewis was among those who advocated a lighthouse on Egg Rock. Congress initially appropriated $5,000 for a lighthouse in 1850, but the project was delayed, apparently owing to difficulties in obtaining title to the site.

In 1851 the brig *Exile* tried to pass between Egg Rock and the mainland, as the captain mistook the island for one of the islands farther north off Marblehead. The vessel was wrecked when it struck a nearby ledge. According to Lewis, in 10 years 11 vessels had been wrecked and nine lives lost near Egg Rock.

Funds for the lighthouse were reappropriated in August 1854, but still construction stalled. Thirty presidents of Boston life and property insurance companies signed a petition to Congress in 1855, and the project finally moved forward in August of that year.

Ira P. Brown, a local contractor, built Egg Rock's first lighthouse at a cost of $3,700. The foundation was laid in 1855, but bad weather and rough seas late that year caused the project to be suspended until the following year. At the end of September, some of the workers were stranded on the island for more than three days, their supplies dwindling. A Nahant resident, Dexter Stetson, had gained a reputation as an expert builder in 1851 when he erected the town's Village Church. During the building of the lighthouse, Stetson became acquainted with the foreman and eventually participated in the construction process. Stetson went on to become one of the nation's most renowned lighthouse builders. He was responsible for the building of the second (extant) Cape Hatteras Lighthouse and Bodie Island Lighthouse in North Carolina.

The project was completed in the summer of 1856. A lantern was installed atop a stone dwelling, 32 feet square. The stone for the building was cut from the island itself. A fifth-order Fresnel lens produced a fixed white light, 86 feet above the sea, first exhibited on September 15, 1856. The light was changed to red a year later in reaction to the wreck of the schooner *Shark*, whose captain had mistaken Egg Rock Light for Long Island Head Light in Boston Harbor.

The first keeper was George B. Taylor of Nahant, who lived at the lighthouse with his wife and five children, along with chickens, goats, a tame crow, and a dog named Milo. An 1860 newspaper article described the dwelling, which had three good-sized rooms on the first floor and two small rooms upstairs, all "substantially but plainly finished." Keeper Taylor, according to the article, kept a small garden and raised vegetables "of really California dimensions." His beets were "hard to beat by any gardener on the more favored shore."

Taylor's wife and children were described as contented and attached to their home on the rock. It was a quiet place in winter, but visitors were plentiful in summer; as many as 300 stopped by in August. The sight of the Taylor children jumping from rock to rock unnerved the newspaper reporter, but their parents assured him that they had never had an accident, except for the time one of them fell from the doorstep.

One of the most famous of all lighthouse pets was Milo, the Taylors' huge Newfoundland–Saint Bernard mix. One day Keeper Taylor was shooting waterfowl on the island. He shot a loon, which fell to the ocean. The bird was wounded, but not mortally. Milo swam in pursuit, but the loon took off and flew a short distance. Every time Milo would close in, the bird would take off again. Taylor watched the chase from shore until the dog and bird disappeared from sight. Milo wasn't seen again that day. The next day, he was seen swimming from Nahant, where he apparently had spent the night. He swam safely back to his home at Egg Rock.

Saved, Sir Edwin Henry Landseer's portrait of Milo, the hero dog of Egg Rock.

Local fishermen enjoyed playing a game with Milo. They would lash two or three good-sized cod to pieces of wood and set them adrift. The dog would retrieve the floating prizes, sometimes as far as a mile from the island, and take them to the Taylors for dinner.

In foggy weather Milo also served as a kind of fog signal, barking at vessels as they approached Egg Rock. Taylor claimed his dog was as useful as the light. No details of the episodes seem to have survived, but Milo was also credited with the rescue of several children from drowning around the island.

The dog's fame spread across the Atlantic. An English artist known for portraying animals, Sir Edwin Henry Landseer, painted Milo's portrait, depicting a small child lying atop the animal's enormous paws. The model for the child was reportedly Keeper Taylor's young son Fred. The painting, titled *Saved,* became internationally famous.

Keeper Taylor lost his job for political reasons in 1861. He lived in Nahant for many more years, working as a lobsterman. Thomas Widger of Swampscott, the second keeper, lived on Egg Rock for a decade. Widger and his wife had three sons born on the island during their years there, as well as two daughters born ashore in Swampscott.

The Widgers continued to maintain the island's small garden, with cabbage and asparagus among the chief crops. An older son rowed his younger sister to shore each day for school, and the Widger children enjoyed playing on the island with the family's dog, pigeons, chickens, and pigs.

In December 1865, with his wife about to give birth, Keeper Widger rowed his dory to shore and enlisted the help of a Swampscott midwife. As they started the return trip in heavy surf, the dory capsized and threw the pair overboard. The woman refused to go any further. Keeper Widger rowed alone back to Egg Rock, and a son, Abraham, was born a short time later. After a few days, a doctor arrived in calm seas and pronounced mother and son healthy.

Abraham Widger, interviewed at the age of 80, recalled his early offshore life. "We never gave the neighbors any trouble," he said. "They were too far away on shore."

Henry N. Richardson became keeper in 1871. He made a surprising entry in the station's log in April 1873: "A severe rainstorm. Keeper went ashore to get some groceries and got caught in the storm; was detained away four days on account of the rough seas. The wife kept the light all trimmed and burning bright and clear. Keeper was drunk ashore all the time."

Richardson's daughter, who was 12 years old in 1873, later claimed that she was the one who kept the light going during her father's absence. She also said her father signaled her from East Point in Nahant several times each day in an effort to keep her courage up, which seems to indicate that the comment about being "drunk ashore" was merely a joke. In May 1873, Richardson wrote in the log: "Eben Phillips caught a cod off the rock & gold ring in it, 18k with H.L. marked on it."

The unlucky Mr. Phillips had already sold the cod when the ring was discovered inside. Here's another colorful entry from the pen of Keeper Richardson (original spelling retained): "July 25, 1877: 2 ladies and Mr. Deny upset landing, Mr. Horton rescued them. The house needs repairing all over, the lightning rods aint good for nothing, and the smoak stack bin off a year."

While Richardson was keeper, two sons of the former keeper Taylor spotted a distress signal on the island and rowed out to see what the problem was. It turned out that Richardson had lost his boat and was marooned. He had begun constructing a new boat. The Taylor boys took him back to the mainland, where he soon procured another boat.

Charles Hooper, a Civil War veteran, was keeper from 1874 to 1883. Hooper recorded a visit by Cdr. George Dewey, who inspected the station in October 1875. This was during the admiral-to-be's two-year stint as an inspector in the Second Lighthouse District. Dewey rated Keeper Hooper's work as "excellent."

After a brief stay by George Wadleigh, Charles Dunham—a Civil War veteran who had spent time as a keeper at the Thacher Island twin lights off Rockport—became keeper. In December 1884, Dunham wrote in the log, "Could not get ashore, and so no Christmas presents." The gloomy entries continued through the winter. Some examples:

January 17, 1885: Terrific westerly winds in the evening, and jars the clock so that it stops, at any rate it stops, whether the wind does it or not.
February 16: Terrific easterly winds and very heavy sea. Night the rain beats badly at the east chamber windows. Seas break across the island.
February 19: Surrounded by ice in the forenoon.

The weather cleared enough in March for the keeper to make a trip ashore with his 17-year-old daughter, Dora.

March 2, 1884: Dora and I went to Nahant today for corn, oats and shorts and to send monthly reports and to get our mail. There was quite a streak of the polar regions about this forenoon in the form of large blocks of ice around the island, and between the station and the shore.

Keeper Dunham recorded some happy news in two later entries:

May 28, 1885: Girl baby born on Egg Rock to Mr. and Mrs. Charles Dunham.
November 26, 1885: Thanksgiving day and lots of grub on the island, Found valuable Chesapeake retriever pup awaiting me ashore, the gift of Mr. George B. Inches.

The pup was dubbed "Rock" and was eventually passed on to the next keeper. The local writer Charles Lawrence visited the island several years later and said that the dog had "grown into an old and very grumpy canine."

Dunham's daughter Dora later recounted some memories of Egg Rock in a letter:

There were many crazy stories about the Egg Rock people. I have many times been on the street, both in Nahant and Lynn, and would hear, when passing, "There goes the Egg Rock girl," and heads would be turned, as if I were a natural curiosity, not expected to know anything, or have any feelings.
I enjoyed life there, as I love the sea, but it was monotonous for my mother, who did not row, and so could not get ashore, as one person had to be on the island all the time. She had only one vacation in the

6 ½ years she lived there. At that time I stayed with my father and when he had a few days off, my mother and I remained.

There's a story involving a keeper of Egg Rock Light that has been passed down through the years, but it isn't clear if the story has any basis in fact. According to the story, the wife of one of the nineteenth-century keepers died in the early winter. The island was surrounded by ice, so the keeper couldn't take his wife's body to the mainland. Instead, he laid the body in an outbuilding, where it soon froze solid.

In the early spring, when the ice had cleared enough, the keeper rowed his wife's body to the mainland. A funeral was held that day. After the funeral, the keeper visited with an old childhood sweetheart. He hastily proposed marriage, and the same preacher who had performed the keeper's first wife's funeral just hours earlier performed a hasty wedding ceremony. The keeper was back at Egg Rock with his new wife before nightfall, according to the legend.

In 1889 the lantern was raised and a new wooden deck and railing were built. George L. Lyon, a Lynn native who was previously an assistant at Minot's Ledge Light, became keeper in the same year. Lyon grew up during Lynn's heyday as a center of shoe manufacturing and learned that trade as a boy, but he became interested in other pursuits. A large and athletic man, Lyon loved the sea and was on a lifesaving crew on Lake Erie by the age of 21.

The artist and writer Charles A. Lawrence of Lynn visited Egg Rock in 1891 with a newspaper reporter, Walter Ramsdell, a future mayor of Lynn. Lawrence described Lyon: "Bronzed and blue-shirted, his yellow beard suggested the Norseman of old. I would not have been surprised to see him raise a drinking horn from somewhere and shout, 'SKOAL!' But instead, he cupped his big hand and shouted as we fumbled at the mooring line while the dory rose and fell. . . . The keeper smiled—how comforting was that smile, as we tossed heavily in the wash of that wolfish sea!"

After several tries, the party landed on the island safely and proceeded to the lighthouse. The keeper's mother, who was nearly 90, and her visiting granddaughter greeted the visitors. They also met the station's housekeep-

George L. Lyon was keeper at Egg Rock 1889–1911. *Courtesy of Lighthouse Digest.*

er, Ada Foster, who was 15 at the time of their visit. During a tour of the lighthouse, the keeper jokingly told Lawrence, "Lots of people ask us what makes the light red, and we tell 'em it's the red oil. Some of 'em don't get it, and they say, 'Oh, that's it. I never knew.'"(The light was actually made red by the placement of a red glass chimney around the lamp.)

A 1905 article in the *Boston Globe* gives us more detail about this fascinating man. In the summer, Lyon grew tired of people asking him if he longed for life on the mainland and took to wearing a sign on his back that said, "No, thank you, I am not the least bit lonesome." He was an avid reader, especially of scientific and technical books. Also among his favorite subjects was the realm of psychic phenomena. This was apparently sparked by an incident when he was at Minot's Ledge Light. While in the watchroom, he felt something brush his cheek and heard his name, "George," spoken in his ear. The voice was that of a favorite aunt, and he learned later that the aunt had died at the same hour he had heard her voice.

Keeper Lyon was a carpenter, boatbuilder, an expert marksman with a rifle, and an authority on firearms and explosives. He developed a well-equipped machine shop in the island's boathouse. His mechanical aptitude enabled him to repair the dory engines of many local fishermen, and he invented a new type of crankshaft for boat engines that saved on gasoline. He was among the first to experiment with the use of a steam winch to haul lobster traps. He took a correspondence course in mechanical drawing, and he built and raced his own dories.

Lyon's crowning achievement at Egg Rock was the building of a landing stage on the island. With this arrangement, a boat would be hoisted out of the water onto a deck, and then hoisted again into the boathouse. A powerful hand winch was used for both hoists.

Lyon was responsible for countless rescues in the vicinity of Egg Rock during his 22 years there. One day in August 1895, Lyon was on his way to Marblehead to visit relatives and passed near a fleet of dories. The seas were heavy, and four of the dories were overturned by the waves. Lyon, with the assistance of a friend who stayed at the wheel of his boat, rescued the occupants of three of the dories and took them to Marblehead.

A sudden squall on August 12, 1905, upset a dory near Egg Rock and sent five men into the waves. The men had been clinging to the overturned boat for two hours when Lyon spotted them and headed out in his boat. Two of the men were barely conscious when they were pulled into Lyon's boat, but all five men were taken safely to the police station in Nahant.

The scene virtually repeated itself in May 1906. Four men were fishing near the island in a sailboat, which capsized in heavy seas. The men had been in the cold water for three-quarters of an hour and were nearly drowned when Lyon reached them in his power dory. A lifesaving crew arrived moments after Lyon rescued the men, and the crew took the four men ashore for medical attention. Early in September that same year, the keeper rescued four men, three women, and a baby who were aboard a motor launch that had become disabled and was drifting helplessly off Nahant. According to a newspaper account, the boat would have smashed against the rocks if Lyon hadn't arrived in time.

On another occasion, on a foggy and stormy night, Lyon heard cries for help and discovered two young men from Nahant trying to land their small boat on the island. The keeper directed the men until he was able to get close enough to grab the bow of the boat and pull them to safety.

Landing on the island was never easy and was frequently treacherous. Lyon later said that in his early years, before he got used to the place, he lost at least one boat every year. Once, Lyon and Ada Foster had just returned from the mainland with groceries. The keeper was standing on the landing by the bow of the boat when a rogue wave swept both boat and keeper through the air to the rocks about 50 feet away. Lyon was lucky to escape with only a bad cut on his hand.

Another time, as he returned from a trip to Boston, heavy surf prevented the keeper from landing. The young housekeeper shouted to him over the waves, reassuring Lyon that the light would be lit and the chickens were in. He retreated to Nahant, but returned to the lighthouse as soon as the conditions allowed, about 2:00 a.m. There was at least one other occasion when rough weather prevented Lyon from landing and Foster spent the night at the lighthouse alone. She had learned all the duties of the keeper, and the light never failed.

The 1905 *Globe* article described a dramatic incident during the previous winter. Lyon was severely ill with the flu for several days, and during that period his power dory broke loose from its lashings in a storm and was hanging precariously from a boom over the ocean. The keeper and his housekeeper had to muster all their strength to haul in the boat, which was encrusted in ice. The keeper himself was described as a "frozen manikin" by the time he was able to return to his sickbed.

By the time of a 1910 article, Lyon said that he had probably saved the lives of at least 200 people. He couldn't help everybody, though, as he explained:

Blass you, if I was to go out every time anybody appeared to be in trouble, some days I wouldn't get a chance to eat my meals. I let them work two or three hours and then as likely as not they get their engine started again. I keep an eye on them with the glass and if it's getting dark or coming on to blow or if the women are getting sick then I go out and get them. Of course they get scared at the least little chop, not knowing what rough water is, and think they're going to the bottom. I've brought in, I guess, some pretty frightened women and some pretty sick men.

Once, after the keeper saved a group of five men, they took up a collection and presented a not-so-generous reward of 85 cents to their savior.

Lyon had a Newfoundland dog with the strange name of O-who. O-who loved to fetch sticks thrown by the keeper into the waves, and he rode along and "assisted" in some of the rescues around the island. Charles Lawrence called O-who a "sailor at heart." The dog was succeeded at Egg Rock by a family of black cocker spaniels.

Lyon didn't keep as many animals as some of his predecessors, but he did have several goats for a time. He also kept chickens. When word got out that some of his chickens had mysteriously vanished, a cartoonist at the *Lynn Daily Evening Item* drew a sea serpent snatching the birds from the rock.

After numerous repairs to the original building, the lighthouse was entirely rebuilt in 1897. Some sources erroneously claim the first lighthouse was destroyed by fire. This misunderstanding may have stemmed from the fact that the workmen's shanty was destroyed by fire during construction.

The contractor for the new building was John McDuffie. A 19-year-old local resident named Joe White was in charge of bringing materials out to the island in a dory, and it was said that over the course of the project he made the round-trip more than 300 times. White once went ashore to get badly needed food for the workers during a stretch of foul weather, and he made an extremely difficult landing on his return. "Joe does not know what fear means," commented the foreman.

The new lighthouse consisted of a square brick tower, topped by an octagonal lantern and attached to a six-room, wood-frame dwelling, 30 by 32 feet. The dwelling had a more substantial cellar than the first building, which had offered only limited storage space for food below the first floor. The fixed red light, 90 feet above the water and 32 feet above the ground, went into service in February 1898.

In 1901 an experimental submarine fog-signal station was added to the island. A large bell was suspended from a buoy 50 feet below the surface of the ocean. The bell was sounded from a powerhouse on Egg Rock, using an electric current. The signals were intended to be picked up by ships equipped with proper receiving equipment. Submarine bells were eventually used at some locations, such as lightship stations.

Keeper Lyon and his housekeeper, Ada Foster, developed a friendship that grew into romance over the years. Charles Lawrence wrote that Ada blossomed from a slender girl and developed a "robust physique that enabled her to bear a hand at the winch in hoisting the boats, an accomplishment which in no wise detracted from her fine skills as a cook and entertainer."

After leaving Egg Rock in 1911, Lyon became keeper at Graves Light in Boston Harbor, then at Nobska Point Light at Woods Hole on Cape Cod. The keeper and Ada planned to marry, but Ada died before the marriage could take place, while Lyon was at Nobska Point Light.

Malcolm N. Huse, Andrew S. Nickerson, and James Yates followed Lyon as keepers in quick succession. During World War I, the light was dimmed out of fear of enemy submarines in the area. Around this time, a telephone cable connected the lighthouse to the mainland. The lighthouse tender *Mayflower* would stop by and leave one of its crew on the island to watch the light for a week at a time. It became a popular pastime for some of the young women in the area to call the lighthouse and chat with the men to help them pass the lonely hours. The life of one of those men might have been saved by the phone calls, as several young women convinced him to stay at the lighthouse during a bad storm instead of making a risky trip to shore.

In early 1919, an automatic acetylene-gas–operated light was placed in the tower, and the characteristic was changed to flashing white. In late 1920, it was announced that the buildings on the island—except for the lighthouse tower—would be sold, provided the high bidder could move them off the island. The first round brought only two bids, the highest being $100. The bid was rejected and the sale was delayed.

Then, on April 17, 1922, a crew from the tender *Mayflower* dismantled the lighting apparatus and the light was discontinued. The government sold the buildings at auction at the end of May for $160. The buyer, John Cavanaugh, planned to move the dwelling to the Hough's Neck in Quincy, south of Boston. A crew was hired to move the structure onto a barge. In preparation the dwelling was separated from the tower. The house was jacked up and placed on rollers and was moved about 50 feet before disaster struck.

The keeper's house at Egg Rock slid into the ocean in October 1922. *Courtesy of Lynn Historical Society.*

In October 1922, as the crew slowly moved the building, a cable snapped. The house slid down the rocks and hung precariously at the edge of the ocean. There were several workmen inside the dwelling at the time, but they managed to break windows and escape to safety. A life-saving crew from Nahant arrived shortly after the disaster.

There was some hope that the building could be saved and moved to shore in sections, but it collapsed into the sea a few days later, after some of the lumber was salvaged. For some time, remains of the dwelling washed up on local beaches.

The brick lighthouse tower stood until 1927, when it was destroyed. All the remaining wooden structures on the island were burned at that time. The state of Massachusetts took over Egg Rock and maintained it as a bird sanctuary.

In 1933 Charles A. Lawrence summed up the appeal of the scene when the lighthouse was still there:

> Picture a summer day, or one in early fall, when the ocean is mostly calm, and at low tide the rocks present attractions known to those who like to search for them. The wholesome, healthful fare. The cordial hospitality, the antics of the numerous pets, the lovely skies, and the exquisite play of color upon the changing face of the ocean. And then, following a sunset that words can never describe, the soft dimness of the twilight, the lights springing up along the shore, and the flashing beacons visible from Thachers, Bakers, and Marblehead to the north; and Minot's, spelling its splendid telegraphy upon the southern sky, while the slow circle of Boston Light makes its round— can you imagine a more fascinating place?

🔆 **The best views of Egg Rock are from Nahant Beach and from Lynn Shore Drive in Lynn. There are no landing facilities, and the island is not accessible to the public.**

CHAPTER 48

Marblehead Light in September 2004. *Photo by the author.*

Marblehead Light

1835, 1896

The North Shore town of Marblehead, settled in 1629, is a sailing
mecca with many eighteenth-century homes and narrow, winding
streets. Blessed with a large, deep harbor, Marblehead grew up as a
fishing town and, like neighboring Salem, also developed significant
foreign trade. The harbor is situated between the main peninsula of
the town and Marblehead Neck, a separate peninsula extending to the
east. The neck is connected to the rest of the town by a long sandbar,
now a causeway.

On August 30, 1831, Eleazer Graves and other citizens of Marblehead petitioned the town's selectmen, requesting that a lighthouse be
erected "on the point of Neck at the entrance to the harbour and to see
if the town then assembled will petition Congress for that purpose."
David Henshaw, collector of the Port of Boston and the local lighthouse
superintendent, was not convinced the neck was a proper location. A
committee in Marblehead answered, "it is not our intention to enter
into the strife of bargaining for said point of Neck, our only object is
to have the best spot selected; we have a good harbour and we wish
to make it easy of access to the care and weather beaten mariner."

Congress appropriated $4,500 for the lighthouse on June 30, 1834.
It was finally agreed that the northern tip of Marblehead Neck was the
most suitable location, and about four acres of land were bought from
Joseph W. Green and Ephraim Brown for $375. The light station was
constructed and put in operation on October 10, 1835.

A 23-foot white tower and a keeper's cottage, attached to the
tower by a covered walkway, were built near a small fort. The tower is
described as brick in I. W. P. Lewis's 1843 report, but other sources
describe it as stone. The small dwelling had three rooms, a kitchen
on the first floor and two rooms in the attic. The 10 lamps inside the
octagonal lantern burned whale oil, and the fixed white light was
exhibited from 53 feet above mean high water (57 feet according to
some sources).

The first keeper—at $400 yearly–was Ezekiel Darling, a native
of Duxbury, Massachusetts, and former chief gunner on the USS
Constitution. He had first gone to sea at the age of eight or nine, and

he was wounded in the War of 1812. Darling didn't receive a pension because he was considered "disfigured, but not disabled."

Darling was in charge when the engineer I. W. P. Lewis examined the station. The keeper provided a statement for Lewis's report to Congress in 1843: "The tower is leaky about the window casing, there being no recess in the brick for the window frames. The lantern sweats considerably, and formerly I wiped up large quantities of water accumulating from this cause. I now admit as much air as the state of the weather will permit, which in some degree remedies this evil. . . . The dwelling-house is very damp, and the water comes through the walls. The chimneys are all smoky."

Darling described improvements and additions he had made to the house, and he mentioned that he had cultivated a garden on the station's three acres. Lewis praised Darling in his report. "Perfect order, cleanliness, and apparent comfort," he wrote, "reign throughout the whole establishment, much to the credit of the keeper." Lewis offered the opinion that the ten lamps in use could easily be reduced to a single lamp "of a suitable character."

Another inspection report was submitted in 1843 by the local superintendent, who said the tower, lantern, and lamps were in the best possible order. Darling was again praised for his "remarkable care, attention, and order."

A sixth-order Fresnel lens replaced the old system of multiple lamps and reflectors in 1857. An article from that year provides us with more detail about Darling:

> He is a man of small stature, but of a wiry and well-knit frame, showing that when in his prime he must have been capable of great endurance. . . .
>
> In the duty appertaining to this position he has often distinguished himself. He once rescued some shipwrecked mariners from the Devil's Back, and in the spring of 1843 took charge of a dory with four gallant Marblehead men, put off in a tremendous sea, and brought ashore the officers and crew of the brig John Hancock, which was dashed to pieces on Tinker's Island in a violent easterly storm, when the snow drifted eight to ten feet deep. For this act he received a medal from the Humane Society. There are few men among us who can show a finer record of gallant deeds than Captain Darling.

By 1860 Darling was about 70 and almost blind, and he had to retire after 25 years as keeper. Jane C. Martin, a Marblehead native said to be the only woman lighthouse keeper on the East Coast at the time she was appointed, succeeded him. She had previously assisted her

The first (1835) Marblehead Lighthouse, with its original "birdcage-style" lantern. *U.S. Coast Guard photo.*

father, Ambrose Martin, at nearby Baker's Island Light.

John Goodwin succeeded Martin in 1862 and remained for a decade. The 1868 and 1869 annual reports of the Lighthouse Board show much activity, including many repairs to the dwelling and boathouse and the rebuilding of the privy.

James S. Bailey became keeper in 1872. The old brick dwelling was in increasingly poor condition despite the numerous repairs, and Bailey was in charge when a new two-story, wood-frame house—typical of many keeper's houses built in New England around that time—was completed in 1878.

According to an 1889 article in the *Boston Globe*, Bailey had saved the lives of 17 people in the vicinity of the lighthouse. On one occasion, the keeper went to the aid of six men whose schooner was in a dire situation during a winter gale. By the time Bailey reached them, the men were clinging to the rigging to avoid being swept into the icy harbor. In the process of rescuing them, Bailey was injured when his boat was thrown by the waves. He got the men safely to shore and cared for them for several days. Bailey later asked the wealthy Philadelphia owners of the schooner for compensation for the food he had given the stranded men. He was refused on the grounds that nobody had ordered him to feed them.

Another time, Bailey spotted a small boat in trouble in the harbor. He rowed out in his dory and found that one of the two men from the boat was already in the water. According to the *Globe*, the man's "bald pate was all that could be seen." The keeper dove in and pulled the drowning man to safety, and he was later rewarded with a medal from the Massachusetts Humane Society for his brave action.

The *Globe* article described another instance, in which Bailey saw two drunken men "dancing in a rowboat." They both landed in the harbor, and the keeper rowed out and saved them. Upon reaching dry land, the men argued about which of them had caused the accident, and each of them begged Bailey to throw the other one back into the water.

Keeper Bailey said he would never accept financial reward for saving human life: "It is a duty for me to save my fellow men, and as long as I am able to wield an oar and keep my eyesight, I shall never refrain from undertaking the trip over the waves that may be the means of saving life."

By the 1870s, large summer cottages were springing up all around the lighthouse. By 1880 the first small tower was obscured by houses and could not be seen at sea. In 1883 a light was hoisted to the top of a tall mast near the lighthouse. (Some sources claim the mast was 100 feet tall, but in photos it appears shorter.) This arrangement bought some time before a taller lighthouse was finally built.

After a brief stint by Albert M. Horte, who replaced Bailey in 1892, Henry T. Drayton—a former lightship sailor—became keeper on May 1, 1893. Drayton and his wife raised eight children in 35 years at Marblehead Light, and five of their children were born at the station. The Draytons' son Lawrence grew up to be keeper at Plymouth Light, Massachusetts. Their youngest daughter, Mary, later recalled that her father often had difficulty with the lantern on the mast, as the light would frequently go out when it was hoisted into position.

The 1893 annual report of the Lighthouse Board made a case for a new, taller tower. An appropriation of $45,000 was requested for the construction of a brick tower, around 100 feet high, and the request was repeated the following year. Funds were appropriated, and a contract was awarded in June 1895 for the building of a new lighthouse, but it was not to be a brick tower. Instead, a 105-foot cast-iron skeleton tower was erected by Chamblin, Delaney, and Scott of Richmond, Virginia, at a cost of $8,786.

It isn't clear why the authorities decided on this type of tower, but the lower cost was undoubtedly a major factor. This is the only lighthouse of its type in the New England states; the nearest similar tower is at Coney Island, New York. There are several of the same type in the mid-Atlantic region, and a few more in Florida.

The structure has a square footprint and is an example of a standard design that began with Sanibel Island Lighthouse in

The wife and daughter of Keeper Henry Drayton are seen here hoisting an "Efficiency Flag," awarded to the best-kept light station in the district. *Courtesy of the Drayton family.*

The Marlbehead Light Station in the early 1900s. *From the collection of the author.*

Florida in 1884. The lighthouse is composed of eight cast-iron pilings—resting on eight concrete foundation disks—connected by supports, with a central iron cylinder that contains a spiral stairway. There are 127 steps to the landing below the lantern level.

The light was exhibited from a temporary wooden tower while the lighthouse was under construction. When first constructed, the new tower's lantern held a sixth-order Fresnel lens and a kerosene-fueled lamp, and it exhibited a fixed white light 130 feet above mean high water. The light in the new tower was first illuminated on April 17, 1896. The characteristic was changed in 1922 to fixed red (to stand out against the lights of the town) and was changed again in 1938 to fixed green.

The new tower was painted "metallic brown," the lantern and gallery black. It retains the same color scheme today, despite requests from various parties for it to be painted a "prettier" white. The brown color shows up best against the tower's surroundings.

Keeper Drayton held on to the skeleton key that opened the first lighthouse even after the tower was demolished. Many years later, his descendants donated the key—along with a brass oilcan—to the town for display.

In 1966 Mary Drayton Dewey recalled many aspects of her early life at Marblehead Light Station. The Neck was a center of activity in summer, but it was lonely in winter, she remembered.

> *It was a half-mile to our nearest neighbor in the winter and another half-mile to the next neighbor. There were just those two during the winters. During the summers, of course, there were lots of people. But during the winter there were no other children. I just*

played with my brothers, and we went sliding or skating on the pond. That was our only amusement. We had no electricity, just kerosene lights. When I was a junior in high school my brother built his first radio—about 1920.

Mary recalled the keeper's house as comfortable, with hot-water radiators in every room and running water from the town. Downstairs were a living room, dining room, kitchen, and pantry, and there were four bedrooms and a bath upstairs.

The Draytons kept a cow for milk, and they also had chickens, pigs, and a large garden. Keeper Drayton went to Boston once a month to pick up supplies, including barrels of flour, sugar, and beans. Twice yearly, a government supply boat arrived with kerosene and other supplies for the light.

Mary took a ferry to Marblehead to attend school. When the weather was bad, she'd hide under the captain's slicker. In winter the nearest ferry landing was pulled up and Mary had to walk a mile to catch the boat.

For much of the Draytons' tenure, the road to Marblehead Neck was passable only at low tide. When Mrs. Drayton felt the birth of a child was imminent, she'd tell the older children as they left for school that they'd better tell the doctor to come. When the tide was low, the doctor would make his way to the Neck with a horse and buggy. Everything worked out fine. "We never had much sickness or suffering," said Mary. "I guess when you're living in such a remote place the Lord takes care of you."

The family never had a horse and wagon or any kind of motor transportation until one of Mary's brothers bought a motorcycle with a sidecar in 1923. The keeper had a dory, kept in the station's boathouse. During World War I, the boathouse was converted to living quarters for navy personnel who kept watch on the nearby waters. "They used to come in and play cards and so on," recalled Mary.

A telephone was installed in the boathouse for military use, and the phone remained when the war ended and the navy men left. The light was converted to electricity in 1922, but according to Mary, the power lines bypassed the keeper's house.

Drayton retired in 1928. He was followed as keeper by Russell B. Eastman (1928–30) and Edwin C. "Sparky" Rogers (1930–38). Rogers and his wife had four children, three of whom were born during the family's years at the lighthouse.

The Rogerses' son Edwin was six years old when the family moved to the station. In 1999 he related one of his favorite memories during a visit to the lighthouse: "See that ball [the ventilator ball] up on the top of the tower? I once climbed up there to sit on top of that. My mother came out of the house looking for me and found me up there. My father had to climb up and get me down."

Harry S. Marden became keeper in May 1938. Just four months later, the worst hurricane in New England history belted the coast. The storm was far more disastrous along New England's south-facing coast, but it was still a serious situation farther north. The light went dim as the lighthouse lost its electric power. Keeper Marden, thinking quickly, drove his car next to the lighthouse and connected the car's battery to the lighthouse's wiring. He spent the night in the tower and managed to keep the light going until morning.

The station was used by the U.S. Army during World War II and was off-limits to the public between 1941 and 1946. The light was extinguished during the war.

Chandler Hovey, a Marblehead Neck resident and a prominent yachtsman, purchased the land around the lighthouse and donated it to the town in 1947. The last residents of the keeper's house (1947–54) were Joseph Barry, superintendent of the town's parks, and his wife, Beryl Dupar Barry. The keeper's house was torn down in June 1959, but a brick oil house remains standing along with the lighthouse. The light was automated in 1960, and the old Fresnel lens was replaced by a modern optic.

The town of Marblehead now has a license to care for the tower, while the light is still maintained as an active Coast Guard aid to navigation. In recent years, the Marblehead Rotary Club has decorated the tower with white lights in the Christmas season, and with red, white, and blue lights around the Fourth of July.

On Sunday, September 8, 2002, local residents gathered at Chandler Hovey Park to enjoy a celebration of the light station's history. A highlight of the "rededication" was the unveiling of a new plaque near the tower, outlining some of the history of the light and its keepers.

☀ **Over the years, a shade pavilion and benches have been added to Chandler Hovey Park. The park is almost always busy in good weather, with visitors watching sailboats, flying kites, watching the ocean, or enjoying a sunset.**

It's easy to drive to the park after taking Ocean Avenue across the causeway to Marblehead Neck. The lighthouse can also be seen from occasional lighthouse cruises offered by various organizations, including the Friends of the Boston Harbor Islands; see www.fbhi.org or call (781) 740-4290 for information.

CHAPTER 49

Derby Wharf Light in September 2004. *Photo by the author.*

Derby Wharf Light

1871

Half-mile-long Derby Wharf—for many years the hub of Salem's fabled maritime trade—dates back to 1762 and reached its present length by 1806. The wharf is named for the man responsible for the construction of its original portion, Elias Hasket Derby, a leading ship merchant of the late 1700s who is considered America's first millionaire. As many as 15 tall warehouses and dozens of businesses once stood along the sides of the wharf.

Across the street from the foot of the wharf is the 1818 Custom House, a striking example of federal architecture. Nathaniel Hawthorne worked as a clerk for a time in this building just before he achieved his greatest success as a novelist in the mid-1800s.

For years, the twin lights at Baker's Island—about three miles east of the entrance to Salem Harbor—had sufficed to guide vessels into port, but the Lighthouse Board announced in 1869 that "three small lights" were required to "complete the lighting of this harbor." The once-great port of Salem was in its decline as a center for overseas trade by this time, but there was still plenty of local maritime traffic, and Salem was considered an important harbor of refuge for vessels passing along the coast.

Congress appropriated $30,000 for three lights on July 15, 1870. The other two lights built under the appropriation were Salem's Fort Pickering Light and Hospital Point Light in Beverly. The lights at Fort Pickering and Derby Wharf formed a range; incoming mariners would line up the two lights to make sure they were in the main shipping channel into the harbor.

The square brick lighthouse—originally painted red—was built for $3,000. The tower is about 14 feet tall to the lantern level, and each face of the tower is 12 feet across. A fifth-order Fresnel lens exhibited a fixed red light from 25 feet above mean high water. The light on the wharf was first lighted on January 17, 1871. The Lighthouse Board's annual report announced, "A permanent building of brick has been erected, and the light, which was exhibited from an old building near by, has been removed to it."

Because of its proximity to the city, the lighthouse always had a caretaker rather than a resident keeper. There were only six caretakers in the lighthouse's history, the longest stint of service being John Lynch's 20 years beginning in 1885.

A tall, distinctive cast-iron chimney pipe was added to the tower for ventilation in 1886, but changes to the lighthouse have otherwise been minimal. A schooner crashed into the wharf around 1892 and damaged the railing around the lantern, which was quickly repaired.

It became difficult to walk to the lighthouse as the wharf deteriorated, so a wooden walkway was added from the higher part of the wharf right to the lighthouse door in 1905. The following year, a fourth-order lens replaced the original one. In 1910 it was downgraded to a sixth-order lens. Meanwhile, the characteristic was changed multiple times from fixed to flashing and back again.

The Naumkeag Steam Cotton Company built a new, large facility near Derby Wharf about 1915. The Salem harbormaster and others complained that the lights of the mill made it difficult to distinguish the light from the lighthouse when entering the harbor at night. There was discussion about reconstructing the lighthouse, but it doesn't appear any major changes were made around that time other than the conversion of the light to automatic operation, using acetylene gas, in October 1917.

The last keeper before the automation of the light was William M. Osgood, who walked to the lighthouse each morning and evening from his home on Summer Street. During the disastrous Salem fire of 1914, Osgood was occupied with saving his own home. His wife took the keys and lit the lighthouse for the evening, and it was reported that she was barely able to escape the wharf before the flames swept in. From that time until the light was automated, Osgood had to reach the lighthouse using a rowboat.

Derby Wharf continued to fall into ruin and was used as a dumping ground for scrap metal and as a storage facility for railroad cars for some years. Large sections of the wharf's stone walls collapsed over time, which allowed much of the earth fill to be washed away, and the timber cribbing of the wharf had largely disappeared because of decay.

The National Park Service initiated the restoration of the wharf in 1937. The Salem Maritime National Historic Site was the first national historic site

Derby Wharf Light, circa 1960s.
U.S. Coast Guard photo.

Salem's 1818 Custom House stands across from the foot of Derby Wharf. *Photo by the author.*

in the national park system. Today the historic site includes nine acres of land and 12 buildings on the waterfront, as well as a downtown visitors' center.

The light was electrified in 1930. The Coast Guard deactivated it in 1977, and ownership went to the National Park Service in 1979. The abandoned lighthouse deteriorated from neglect and vandalism. Local citizens formed a group called the Friends of Salem Maritime; their goals were to restore the lighthouse and to convince the Coast Guard to relight it. Some restoration was done, and the light was relighted in 1983 as a private aid to navigation, with a solar-powered optic flashing red every six seconds.

The National Park Service again renovated the lighthouse in 1989, with an $8,000 grant from the Massachusetts Historical Commission. Along with the painting of the tower, some of the brickwork was repointed, glass was replaced, a floor drain was installed, and the lightning rod was grounded.

The lighthouse sadly still suffers from vandalism, and the lantern glass is frequently cracked or broken. It remains an active private aid to navigation, with a 155-millimeter optic exhibiting a red flash every six seconds.

🔆 **The walk to the lighthouse at the end of Derby Wharf is easy and pleasant. The *Friendship*, a replica of a three-masted 171-foot Salem trade vessel of the late eighteenth century, is docked at Derby Wharf and is open to the public. For more information on the *Friendship*, call (978) 741-8100. Also nearby at Pickering Wharf is the schooner *Fame*, a replica of a successful privateer from the War of 1812.**

For more information on Derby Wharf and the other historic attractions of the Salem National Historic Site, write to the National Park Service, Salem National Historic Site, 174 Derby St., Salem, MA 01970, or visit www.nps.gov/sama/.

CHAPTER 50

Fort Pickering Light in January 2006. *Photo by the author.*

Fort Pickering Light

(Winter Island Light)
1871

Winter Island, at the entrance to Salem's inner harbor and attached to the mainland by a short causeway, figures prominently in nearly four centuries of the city's history. The 20-acre island became a fishing settlement following Salem's establishment in 1626. The road leading to the island was one of the city's first streets, and Salem's first tavern was located here. A shipyard on the island also flourished; the famed 32-gun frigate *Essex* was built here in 1799.

Fortifications were added to the island by 1643. In its early days, Winter Island's fort was named Fort William after the king of England; it was changed in 1704 to Fort Anne after the queen. In 1799 it was renamed Fort Pickering in honor of Colonel Timothy Pickering, a Salem native who served as secretary of state under President Washington. Remnants of the fort, rebuilt in the Civil War era, still stand near the lighthouse.

Salem's harbor is the second deepest and largest in Massachusetts, which led to the city's development as a center for maritime trade. The port had its heyday from 1750 to 1810, when ships left for thousands of voyages to China, Japan, and other Asian destinations. The harbor's importance declined after the War of 1812, but there was still plenty of maritime traffic.

A congressional appropriation of $30,000 on July 15, 1870, paid for new lighthouses at Hospital Point in nearby Beverly, at Derby Wharf in Salem's inner harbor, and at the southeastern corner of Winter Island. With the addition of the new lights, mariners would line up Fort Pickering and Derby Wharf lights after passing Baker's Island on their way into Salem Harbor.

Fort Pickering Light, built of cast iron and lined with brick, had a fifth-order Fresnel lens that exhibited a flashing white light 28 feet above the sea. The light went into service on January 17, 1871. It was one of the earliest—and smallest—examples of the conical cast-iron towers that would remain in vogue from the 1870s into the early 1900s.

The lighthouse, painted brown or red for much of its history, was built slightly offshore. The wood-frame six-room keeper's house was farther back on the island. A wooden walkway, about 52 feet long, led to the tower. The walkway had to be rebuilt at least twice, in 1879 and in 1904, after it had been destroyed by ice.

John Harris, an Ipswich native and Civil War veteran, became keeper in December 1882. On the occasion of his retirement in 1919, when he was 75 years old, it was reported that Keeper Harris had been absent from the lighthouse for only five nights in 37 years. He ventured only occasionally into the city, about two miles away, for supplies. Harris shared the keeper's house with his wife, Annie (Davis). Their son, Arthur, lived with them until he entered the army.

In all of Harris's years as keeper, not a single vessel was wrecked at Winter Island. The light shone faithfully every night, even in the worst storms. The *Boston Globe* interviewed keeper Harris in 1919. "When I went to the island," he said, "it was nothing but a lot of pasture land, but now there is a nice house there, and I have improved the place so that there are walks laid out and lawns planted, and it really is a very beautiful spot, especially in summer."

Harris seldom rode his horse, which had reached the ripe old age of 28 in 1919, into the city. Until his retirement, he never saw the streets of Salem after dark, and he never rode in a car. "It seems as though we have been out of the world for a long time, " he said, "and it will take some time for us to learn how to act among people." On the very night he retired, Harris attended his first motion picture. Years before, he had attended a re-creation of the Battle of Gettysburg. That display, he said, "couldn't beat the movies by a long shot."

"I feel that I shall miss the quiet and freedom," Harris told the *Globe*. After decades living with no immediate neighbors on Winter Island, upon retirement the Harrises moved to a house at the busy corner of Federal and Rust streets in Salem. They left the light station in early January 1919, but their retirement was brief. Annie Harris died only seven months later, and John died the following April.

Winter Island Light House, Salem Harbor, Mass. looking East

Postcard view of Fort Pickering Light, circa early 1900s. *From the collection of the author.*

By 1920 a sixth-order Fresnel lens was in use in the lighthouse, with an incandescent electric light. An oil lamp served as a back-up in case power was interrupted.

A Coast Guard airplane hangar was constructed on Winter Island in 1934, and an air station was relocated there from Ten Pound Island in Gloucester. The Coast Guardsmen lived temporarily in the keeper's house until new quarters could be built. It appears that Coast Guard personnel also took over the responsibility for the lighthouse at that time.

In January 1935, a blizzard imprisoned thirty men in the house until a plow could get through. Their heating fuel had just about run out as the temperatures dipped to 12 below zero. The hangar and combined living space were soon completed. The keeper's house later became the officers' club for the Coast Guard station.

Coast Guard Air Station Salem was officially commissioned in February 1935. The station assumed new importance during World War II, when its planes were on the lookout for German submarines along the coast. On October 21, 1944, the station was designated the first air and sea rescue station on the eastern seaboard.

The Coast Guard left Winter Island in 1969, and at the same time an offshore buoy replaced the lighthouse. With no one watching out for it, the old tower soon fell into disrepair. The great blizzard of February 1978 undermined the foundation and left the tower in a precarious position. Some feared it wouldn't stand through another winter. The storm also took the door right off the lighthouse, and it remained underwater for several years.

A group of concerned citizens and businesses formed the Fort Pickering Light Association in the early 1980s, and the association worked with the city's Winter Island Commission to initiate the restoration of the lighthouse. They fished the door out of the harbor and put it back in place. The foundation was shored up with new concrete, much of it paid for by donations.

The project culminated when the lighthouse was relighted in 1983 as a private aid to navigation. It was converted to solar power in April 1994, after going dark for six months when the power cable was severed. The light continues to operate today, with a modern 300-millimeter optic producing a white flash every four seconds.

The lighthouse received another facelift in 1999. The American Steeple Corporation, which had previously restored Boston's famous Old North Church, completed $13,800 worth of repairs and painting.

▲ **A visit to Fort Pickering Light makes a pleasant trip in combination with nearby Salem Willows Park, a great spot for picnicking and strolling by the water. For more on Winter Island, call (978) 745-9430 or visit www.salemweb.com/winterisland/.**

CHAPTER 51

Hospital Point Light Station in August 2006. *Photo by the author.*

Hospital Point Light

(Hospital Point Range Front Light)
1872

The promontory called Hospital Point, in the town of Beverly on Boston's North Shore, derives its name from a smallpox hospital built there in 1801. The hospital, used as a barracks in the War of 1812, burned down in 1849.

Beverly served as a center for privateering during the Revolution and is often regarded as the birthplace of the U.S. Navy; the *Hannah*, the first ship commissioned by the navy, sailed from here in 1775.

After the war, Beverly remained an active port for both trade and fishing for many years. But it was the maritime commerce of Salem, rather than Beverly, that led to the establishment of a lighthouse at Hospital Point. The Lighthouse Board requested funds "to complete the lighting" of Salem Harbor in 1869, and $30,000 was appropriated by Congress on July 15, 1870, for that purpose.

The appropriation paid for lighthouses at Salem's Derby Wharf and Winter Island (Fort Pickering), and at Hospital Point on the north side of the channel to Salem Harbor. The town of Beverly transferred about two acres of land for the light station to the federal government.

The two lights in Salem were put into service in 1871, and a temporary light was exhibited at Hospital Point beginning on May 1 of that year. By the following year, a 45-foot-square brick lighthouse and adjacent two-story, Queen Anne Revival–style keeper's house were completed. The keeper's house still stands, with major additions made in 1947 and 1968 and much of its original trim removed. A brick oil house, built in 1902, also still stands. A garage was added to the station in 1942.

The lighthouse was provided a three-and-a-half-order Fresnel lens, a rare size in New England. A condensing panel was installed in front of the lens. Because of this panel, the light diminishes in intensity if a mariner veers from the main channel. The panel is considered unique in American lighthouses.

After the establishment of the light station, Hospital Point became known as a sort of local lovers' lane. As a local newspaper reported in the early 1900s, "Many a Beverly maid's heart was lost and found on the rocks beneath the faithful light."

During the presidency of William Howard Taft (1909–12), a large home at Woodbury Point, on the shore between Hospital Point and

This view of Hospital Point Light Station appears to have been taken just before the light went into service in 1872; the lens is not yet in place. *From the collection of Edward Rowe Snow, courtesy of Dorothy Snow Bicknell.*

Beverly Cove, became the summer White House. A newspaper item of August 24, 1909, reported that the president's son Charley—about 12 years old at the time—had visited the lighthouse: "He climbed the lighthouse in order to look out on to the water and when he reached the top he complained of being sick. The little fellow was assisted to the ground floor . . . and he felt much better."

On May 1, 1927, the lighthouse officially became the Hospital Point Range Front Light. A rear range light, created by adapting discarded lightship equipment, was installed in the steeple of Beverly's First Baptist Church, a mile away. The light, seen through a window in the steeple, is 127 feet above mean high water. The additional light was lined up by incoming mariners with the front range light as an added guide to Salem Harbor.

The Hospital Point Range Rear Light shines from the steeple of Beverly's First Baptist Church, a mile from the lighthouse. *Photo by the author.*

The steeple was the only part of the church to survive a disastrous fire in 1975. Don Decker, a former Coast Guardsman who once serviced several lighthouses in the Salem and Beverly area, says that his least favorite light to service was the one in the church steeple. The steeple was a

Hospital Point Light's 3½-order Fresnel lens. *Photo by the author.*

favorite nesting site for pigeons, making it a very unpleasant place to visit, according to Decker.

Arthur Small, whose wife was killed at New Bedford's Palmer's Island Light in the hurricane of 1938, became keeper at Hospital Point in 1939, after he had recovered from his own injuries. During World War II, Keeper Small maintained a shore patrol in the area. He had the added duty of checking the lights at Derby Wharf and Fort Pickering in Salem. The keeper's house was enlarged during the war to provide barracks for 20 Coast Guardsmen.

The lighthouse was automated in 1947, and since then this tidy lighthouse station has been home to the commander of the First Coast Guard District and his or her family.

Rear Adm. William B. Ellis and his wife, Dorcas, lived at the lighthouse for a time in the 1960s. Dorcas Ellis told the *Boston Traveler,* "One night the beacon went out, and I felt as though I should put a lantern in the tower, as they did in the old days. But a repair team from the Salem station came over and repaired it immediately."

Another resident of the station was Rear Adm. Richard A. Bauman, who retired in 1983. Bauman was a lighthouse aficionado who had climbed 680 lighthouses in the United States, leaving his calling card posted in most of them.

Rear Adm. Vivien S. Crea, a former helicopter pilot who became the first woman in command of a Coast Guard district, was a recent occupant of the light station. In 2004 Crea went on to become the commander of the Coast Guard Atlantic Area and commander of the Maritime Defense Zone Atlantic.

Rear Admiral Crea, a lighthouse buff who appreciated the opportunity to live at a historic light station, especially enjoyed the traditional visits of the Flying Santa, courtesy of the nonprofit organization Friends of Flying Santa.

Hospital Point Light remains an active aid to navigation, as does the rear range light. Though the lighthouse is easy to drive to, the grounds are not open to the public, with the exception of one day early in August each year, when an open house is held as part of the weeklong Beverly Homecoming celebration. A good but fairly distant view can be found from Salem Willows Park in Salem, and some cruises in the area pass nearby.

CHAPTER 52

Baker's Island Light in July 2004. *Photo by the author.*

Baker's Island Light
1798, 1816, 1820

The historian Edward Rowe Snow wrote that 55-acre Baker's Island was named for an early seventeenth-century visitor who was killed on the island by a falling tree. There doesn't appear to be a record of such an incident, but it is a fact that in 1640 a man named Robert Baker was killed by a falling piece of lumber as a ship was being built on the mainland in Salem. It isn't clear why—or if—the island was named for this unfortunate man.

The island, about three miles east of the entrance to Salem's harbor, was first granted to Salem in 1660. For a time in the 1670s, the island was rented to John Turner, the builder of Salem's celebrated House of the Seven Gables.

Salem was already a well-established port for foreign trade by the late 1700s, but there were no major aids to navigation to help mariners past the islands and rocks outside the harbor. Aiming to fill this void, on May 25, 1791, the Salem Marine Society voted for a committee of three men to "Aract a Backon on Backers Island." A few weeks later they voted to spend the sum of £20 to erect an unlighted beacon. It was soon realized that additional funds were needed, so a public subscription paper was circulated in July 1791: "From the many accidents that has happen'd & frequent Mistakes made by Vessels coming into this Port in the Night & in thick weather for want of a Land Mark to ascertain Bakers Island so call'd we the Subscribers agree to give for the Purpose of building a Beacon on the Northernmost Part of Sd Island the Sums by us Subscribed . . ."

Seventy-one persons signed and contributed an additional £89. On July 28, according to the Reverend Dr. William Bentley, "the intended Beacon was raised by a large & Jovial party." The conical beacon was 57 feet tall, painted red, and topped by a two-foot-diameter black ball. The foundation stones, said Bentley, were "very miserably laid." Nevertheless, for the next five years the tower served as an important daytime guide to Salem Harbor.

The Salem Marine Society proceeded to establish buoys to improve local navigation, but by 1792 they set out to convince the local lighthouse superintendent, Gen. Benjamin Lincoln, and the U.S. Congress that a lighted aid was sorely needed. The inadequacy of the day beacon was proven by the wrecks of three vessels in 1796, in which 16 lives were lost. The Marine Society sent a letter to Congress: "much of the property and many of the lives of their fellow citizens are almost every year lost in coming into the harbour of Salem for want of proper lights to direct their course. . . . This calamity can, in the opinion of this society, be prevented only by erecting a lighthouse on the northern end of Bakers Island."

On April 8, 1796, President Washington signed a congressional appropriation of $6,000 for a lighthouse. General Lincoln visited the site in June and expressed misgivings. There were already twin lights at Thacher Island to the north and Plymouth to the south, as well as a single light at Boston Harbor in the middle and another single light in the planning stages at Cape Cod. Lincoln worried that the light or lights at Baker's Island could be confused with one of the other stations, so he proposed a two-story building with three lights arranged along a 50-foot span on its roof. This proposal was apparently regarded as impractical, and it was eventually agreed that two lights would be adequate at Baker's Island.

Ten acres of land for the station were ceded to the federal government, and Solomon Blake, a contractor from Boston, constructed the lighthouse in 1797 for $3,674.57. A committee of five Salem master mariners prepared sailing directions that were published in December, and the two lights went into service on January 3, 1798.

Two towers were located on top of a two-story wood-frame keeper's house, about 40 feet apart, at either end of the building. The structure was declared "very plain" by the Reverend Dr. Bentley. The south light was 95 feet above mean high water, and the north light was 78 feet above.

The first keeper was Capt. George Chapman of the Salem Marine Society. He served until 1815, when he was about 75 years old. Chapman later became blind, a condition that was blamed on the brightness of the lighthouse lamps.

Salem's peak as a port came in the late 1700s into the early 1800s, when as many as 10 ships unloaded each week at the city's wharves. Vessels from Salem journeyed to far-flung ports in China, India, Japan, and Australia. On the ships' return, pilots stationed on Baker's Island would board the incoming ships and navigate to the wharves.

Joseph Perkins, who received a federal commission as a pilot in 1791, was on Baker's Island during the War of 1812. One day he was alarmed to see the American frigate USS *Constitution* being pursued by a pair of British vessels, the *Tenedos* and the *Endymion*. Perkins rowed out in his dory, boarded "Old Ironsides," and deftly guided the frigate to the safety of Marblehead Harbor.

Perkins succeeded Chapman as keeper in 1815, and he witnessed a number of shipwrecks during his years on the island. He weathered a severe storm in early August 1815. A newspaper reported that the gale was "extremely severe at Bakers Island; nearly every square of glass on the Western side of the Light house, and in the Lanterns, was demolished." It was estimated that about 100,000 panes of glass were broken by the storm in Salem, and damage to local crops was "not a trifling calamity."

A "Notice to Mariners" issued by the Massachusetts lighthouse superintendent Henry A. S. Dearborn in late June 1816 announced that the lights would be extinguished for two months while the station was altered. In place of the two lights, there would be a single fixed light, three feet lower than the lower of the two original lights.

During a snowstorm in the predawn hours of February 24, 1817, the ship *Union* smashed into the island's rocky shore with a cargo of pepper and tin, much of which was strewn on the beach. The Reverend Dr. William Bentley visited Perkins at the lighthouse in August 1817. He described the visit in his diary, which was later published.

> *The wrecks of the pepper vessel and coaster lay on the shore still visible. We saw the lights in good order. The patent lamps with metallic reflectors behind and glass panes convex before were sufficient to save much of the oil.*
>
> *Captain Perkins has a garden enclosed, three cows, six pigs, and was cutting hay for the winter. Keeps rabbits and sheep. Has many conveniences about his house in a state much beyond what was formerly seen.*

Mariners claimed that having only one light made it difficult for them to distinguish Baker's Island from Boston Light, a fact that was proven by an increased number of wrecks, including that of the *Union*. There were also complaints that the light was too low and too dim, a problem caused by heavy condensation on the lantern glass. A letter in the *Salem Gazette* of May 29, 1818, urged a return to two lights:

> *It is the design of a light-house, we conceive, to be permanent. Any alteration in it defeats the very purpose for which it was intended— for how are we to be guided by that which is itself continually liable to change?*
>
> *This alteration in the lights has excited we believe very general dissatisfaction, and has been the cause of frequent and heavy losses, not only in this but in other seaports. That our complaints have not been wholly unfounded, appears from the simple fact, that within a year,*

*three vessels have been lost on Baker's Island. Of one of these, the
Union, a fine ship, just returned from India, with a cargo upwards of
eighty thousand dollars, the loss we believe was entirely owing to a
mistake of the lights; the alteration having been made after the ship
had sailed, and the master not knowing, nor having the slightest
suspicion of any deception in the usual marks for running.*

*But according to the representatives of Mr. Perkins (the keeper), as
well as other competent judges, the lights themselves are bad—much
worse than they were before the alterations. . . . Formerly, as we
understand it, there were two lights, one lower than the other, having
the keeper's house between. At present, there is only one and this
situated a considerable distance from the dwelling house. . . . In the
words of "A Mariner," "the two lights . . . were a mark of safety, and
always a guide preferable to the compass."*

*We hope . . . and trust that something will shortly be devised to
correct this mischief, and if we cannot have two lights, at least have
one that can be seen.*

In 1820 the Salem Marine Society and the people of Salem,
Marblehead, and Beverly petitioned the government for the return of a
second light. The station was reverted to two lights in the summer and
fall of 1820 after an appropriation of $9,000 (the sum included funds
for a lighthouse at Ten Pound Island in Gloucester).

A new 47-foot conical stone tower and the refurbished shorter
(26-foot) octagonal stone tower, both with octagonal iron lanterns,
were lighted in October 1820. Somewhere along the line, the two
towers—about 40 feet apart from each other—picked up the nickname
of the "Ma and Pa" or "Mr. and Mrs." lighthouses.

Near the end of March 1825, Keeper Nathaniel Ward and his assistant, a Mr. Marshall, left the mainland in a small flat-bottomed boat
laden with wood and other supplies, heading for the island. A storm
and heavy seas prevented their safe return. Ward was later found dead
on the shore of the island; Marshall died in the boat. According to a
newspaper account, Ward was 49 years old and left a large family "in
indigent circumstances."

Ambrose Martin followed Ward as keeper at a salary of $300 yearly,
raised to $400 in 1829. Martin's daughter, Jane, who learned to help her
father tend the station, later became keeper at Marblehead Light. One
son, Joseph G. Martin, became a prominent stockbroker in Boston,
and another, Samuel, became a harbor pilot.

Another of the keeper's sons, Elbridge Gerry Martin, 13 years old
at the time, made the local newspapers in November 1827 when he

shot an eagle, with a wingspan of nearly seven feet, on the island. The bird was presented to the East India Museum in Salem.

In 1833 two sons of Keeper Martin were in a boat about six miles east of the island when they saw what appeared to be a sea serpent of incredible length. This was during a period when sea-serpent sightings along the New England coast were frequently front-page news. In this case, as the Martin brothers grew closer, it became plain that the "serpent" was actually a long chain of "blackfish"—pilot whales—that scattered when the boat grew too near. From a distance, they resembled a single undulating creature. The *New Bedford Mercury* asserted that this explanation would "to most minds put to rest conclusively the existence of the Sea Serpent."

Martin was still keeper when the engineer I. W. P. Lewis visited during his survey of 1842. At that time, the taller tower was equipped with 15 lamps and 14-inch reflectors, and the shorter tower had 10 lamps with 13-inch reflectors. Lewis described both towers as leaky and rotten, and the interiors as plagued with ice in winter. Both towers, he said, required a thorough repair. The dwelling, according to Lewis, was "old and crazy" and uncomfortable in winter, and it needed to be replaced. Lewis stressed the importance of the station and praised Keeper Martin:

> The double light here is . . . of high importance to a port where so many valuable ships annually enter and depart from, and should be maintained in the most perfect state of efficiency. Such, however, is far from being the case. No light-house of its class in Massachusetts is so poorly provided for in respect to the quality of the apparatus, which was old when introduced here, and now completely worn out. The keeper is deserving of the greatest praise for the extreme neatness and order of the whole establishment, which is second to none in this particular. A good apparatus, therefore, in such hands, would be well cared for, and is absolutely required in so important a locality; and seventeen winters' residence in a house little better than a barn entitles a faithful public servant to a comfortable dwelling in his old age.

Martin echoed Lewis's criticisms in a statement, and he added that he had trouble with livestock owned by a neighbor, Ephraim Brown. It seems the animals wandered onto the light-station grounds because of the lack of a proper fence or wall. "One of his horses killed my cow last June, worth $50," Martin wrote.

Martin added that there was no boathouse and no place to store fuel, and that he had not had a boat since one was lost in a storm in

1841. The keeper's right to use the only landing place on the island was disputed by Brown, who owned most of the island's property.

Somewhere along the line, possibly as a result of Lewis's report, the shorter tower was encased in an octagonal wooden frame. New lanterns and Fresnel lenses were installed on both towers in 1857. The annual report of the Lighthouse Board claims that a new dwelling was built at the same time, but the Baker's Island Lighthouse Preservation Society believes that the older of the two existing houses survives from 1816; the house has been altered and enlarged over the years. A fog-bell tower was erected sometime before 1868. A wood-frame assistant keeper's house was added in 1873, and a new fog-bell tower replaced the original one in 1877. The year 1894 saw the addition of a brick oil house and a 122-foot boat slip.

In the 1860s, the Lighthouse Board announced its intention to increase the distance between the two lights to create a more advantageous range that would enable mariners to line up the lights and avoid dangerous rocks on their way through the main channel to Salem. The neighbor owning the land needed for this change was unwilling to sell, however, and the plan never came to pass.

A former harbor pilot, Charles J. Williams, was keeper from 1861 to 1871. He was followed by George Hobbs of Salem, who stayed until 1874. The assistant keeper beginning in 1872 was Walter Scott Rogers of neighboring Beverly. When he was 17, early in the Civil War, Rogers had enlisted in the army and was wounded at the battle of Spotsylvania.

When Rogers took the assistant position, he was in poor health and weighed only 101 pounds. He became the principal keeper when Hobbs left, and life at the station apparently treated him well—he had gained 115 pounds by the time he left for West Chop Light on Martha's Vineyard in 1881. He returned in 1892 for an 11-year stint as keeper. In 1894 he recorded as many as 500 visitors to the light station in one day.

Rogers reported in February 1875 that the harbors of Salem and Beverly were frozen solid as far as Baker's Island. When the ice broke up, it piled as high as 15 feet. In early March, Rogers wrote that "wild ducks from the ocean," displaced by the ice, "sought shelter under the lee of the keeper's house." Rogers also experienced many bad storms during his stay, including the momentous Portland Gale of November 1898, which moved some of the nearby buoys from their positions.

During a particularly bad stretch of fog in October 1876, Baker's Island's fog bell was sounded for 72 straight hours. Later there were often problems with the bell-striking mechanism, and the keepers sometimes had to strike the bell with a hand-held hammer. In July 1879, a storm struck the area, and lightning destroyed the fog-bell tower. The storm killed 30 people in the Boston Bay area. The bell tower was rebuilt in October and new striking machinery was installed.

The Massachusetts Humane Society awarded Eugene Terpeny, an assistant keeper, a medal in 1894 for his role in saving the lives of the crew of the wrecked schooner *Hero* in October of that year. During a fierce storm, Terpeny and another man had launched a boat from the island and saved six men from the schooner, which was sinking fast.

The late 1800s were a time of change for the rest of the island. Dr. Nathan A. Morse of Salem bought the island, except for the light-house, in 1887. The following year, he opened a 75-room hotel called the Winne-Egan (said to be "beautiful expanse of water" in an Indian language). For a time, Keeper Rogers had a part-time job on the side, harvesting and cutting ice from the island's pond to fill the hotel's iceboxes. The Winne-Egan hotel burned down in 1906, and the island became the exclusive domain of the cottage owners.

Beginning in 1902, the Lighthouse Board pleaded with Congress for funds to install a powerful new fog signal to replace the station's bell. The board pointed out that 482,470 tons of cargo entered Salem in 1901. The value of the coal delivered at the port for the year was more than $1.6 million. The board also stressed that Salem remained an important harbor of refuge. The plea was repeated yearly until Congress appropriated $10,000 on June 30, 1906.

Fog-bell tower at Baker's Island, circa late 1800s. *From the collection of the author.*

A powerful new siren replaced the old fog bell, officially going into service on July 12, 1907. A brick building was added to house the related equipment, including two 20-horsepower oil engines. A neighbor observed the reactions of a horse and cattle at the light station on the occasion of the first trial of the siren. Most of the animals hightailed it for the other side of the island. A single cow, apparently enamored of the sound, mooed her rapturous reply until the siren ceased.

Early-1900s postcard view of Baker's Island Light Station. Notice the foghorn to the right of the taller lighthouse. *From the collection of the author.*

The complaints of island residents after the new signal went into operation were vehement. In September 1907, officials of the Lighthouse Board cruised to the island to observe experiments designed to lower the volume. Rear Adm. George C. Reiter, chairman of the Lighthouse Board, said he had no power to abolish the signal, but he would do what he could to lessen its effect on residents. Eventually, the signal was aimed at the sea through a megaphone, so that it was barely audible on the island.

Keeper Rogers retired to a farm in Rowley, Massachusetts, in October 1911. A newspaper story at the time of his retirement stated that Rogers had assisted in 21 wrecks during his years at Baker's Island, and he had saved the lives of six men. He had furnished more than 400 meals for shipwrecked mariners.

Elliot Hadley, previously the first keeper of Graves Light in Boston Harbor, served as the principal keeper at Baker's Island from 1911 to 1918. Hadley used a horse-drawn vehicle described in DeWitt D. Wise's book *Now, Then, Baker's Island* as a "springless, two-planked gig" to get around the island. His children were the last to attend school on the island, in a small building near the principal keeper's house.

Hadley and his wife, Grace, were active in the affairs of the island and the city. When a disastrous fire broke out in Salem in June 1914, Hadley helped move patients from Salem Hospital to safety.

During World War I, a Naval Reserve unit was stationed on the island to keep watch for German submarines. The men were quartered in a house near the light station and, later, in the former schoolhouse on the station grounds.

The last civilian keeper on the island was Arthur L. Payne. Keeper Payne served from 1918 to 1943, the longest stint of any keeper in the station's history. Payne also was appointed constable for the island in 1918, and he brought the first automotive transportation to the island—a Commerce truck in 1921, and later a Briscoe touring car.

Like the keepers before him, Payne kept a sharp eye out for vessels in trouble. Secretary of Commerce William C. Redfield officially commended Payne in August 1919 for going to the aid of two women whose boat had been wrecked and for towing a disabled motorboat with eight passengers from a point three miles off Baker's Island into the harbor at Manchester. In 1931 he was again commended, along with Assistant Keeper Ernest A. Sampson, for rescuing two men who were stranded on a rock after their boat was lost. Ten days after that, on April 20, Payne put out a grass fire that had gotten out of control at a cottage on the island.

Almost the entire population of the light station fell ill with the flu in early 1920. Keeper Payne, Assistant Keeper Elmo C. Mott, his wife, and their baby all had severe symptoms. The authorities had to send medical assistance to the island, along with two men to tend the lights and fog-signal equipment.

Officials proposed the discontinuance of the smaller of the two lighthouses in 1922. In contrast to what had happened in 1816, nobody in the Salem area voiced any strong objections. The smaller lighthouse was discontinued on June 30, 1926. John Robinson, a mechanic at the lighthouse depot in Chelsea, Massachusetts, spent 10 days on the island overseeing the installation of new equipment in the taller tower. When the lens pedestal was removed, Keeper Payne found an 1847 penny that had been hidden beneath it.

A crew from the lighthouse tender *Azalea* began dismantling the smaller tower two days after its light was extinguished. By October 30, the lighthouse was gone.

The fog siren remained in use until it was replaced by an air horn in 1959. In July 1967, the fog signal sounded for a record 324 hours and 20 minutes, or nearly half the month. One island resident said, "It doesn't bother us because you get used to it."

Payne, called by Edward Rowe Snow a "brave, deserving lighthouse man who faithfully performed his duty to the end," retired in 1943 and was followed by a succession of Coast Guard crews. After his retirement, Payne remained on the island and was elected president of the Baker's Island Association in 1945.

The Coast Guard erected a lookout tower east of the lighthouse during World War II, and a detachment kept a constant watch for German submarines. The men began nightly patrols of the island's shores, unaware of the presence of much poison ivy. According to DeWitt Wise, Arthur Payne came to the rescue and treated the itchy Coast Guardsmen.

The Coast Guard stationed two keepers and their families on the island. In 1967 the only winter residents on the island were Coast Guard keeper Randall Anderson, his wife, and their baby; and Coast Guardsman John Krebs and his wife. "In the wintertime, you're all alone, really alone," said Krebs. "It's awesome in a storm." The only company the families had was "a lobsterman now and then."

The light, which was converted to kerosene in 1878 and then to electric operation in 1938, was automated in 1972. A Coast Guard crew arrived to remove the Fresnel lens, which floated on a bed of mercury, as part of the automation process. They were overcome by mercury fumes and had to be removed by helicopter. The lens is now on display at the Maine Lighthouse Museum in Rockland, Maine.

In 1988 the Baker's Island Association, which manages the island, was granted a 30-year license to use and preserve the two keepers' residences. The houses are presently occupied by islanders during the summer.

For a time, the familiar alternating red and white flash of the light was changed to a simple white flash. In 1974 the power of the light was increased and the flash was restored to alternating red and white every 20 seconds.

In 1993 the Coast Guard made repairs to the lantern and the generator house. Three years later, a $250,000 restoration project began. The contractor hired by the Coast Guard, Marty Nally of nearby Manchester-by-the-Sea, found that some stones from near the top of the tower had fallen out, and that the foundation was nearly crumbling.

Despite its deteriorating condition, Nally was impressed with the construction methods. "These days we would use lasers to line up bricks at the proper angle to do work like this," he told the *Salem Evening News*. "I can't imagine how they did it back then." A Coast Guard architect, Marsha Levy, who formulated the plans for the restoration, added that the lighthouse's construction is more sophisticated than most built around the same time.

Nally and his crew used mortar similar to what was used when the tower was first built, and the exterior was coated with a rough stucco material that accentuates the bumpy stone construction. Nally fell in love with the lighthouse and island during the restoration, and he later published a children's book about the experience called *My Dad Fixed the Lighthouse.*

In the summer of 2000, the Coast Guard converted the light to solar power and renovated the fog-signal building. The brick was removed from the sealed windows and replaced with glass. The fog signal was removed from the top of the building and was placed on an adjacent concrete pad.

In 2002, under the provisions of the National Historic Lighthouse Preservation Act of 2000, the light station was made available to a qualified new owner. In late April 2005, it was announced that U.S. Secretary of the Interior Gale Norton had recommended that ownership be transferred to the Essex National Heritage Commission (ENHC). A committee of the National Park Service (NPS) had chosen the ENHC as the most qualified applicant.

The only other applicant was the Baker's Island Lighthouse Preservation Society (BILPS), made up of island residents. BILPS challenged the decision of the NPS in court, but a federal judge upheld the original decision in late October 2006, apparently clearing the way for transfer to the ENHC.

The Baker's Island Association, founded in 1914, manages the island. Landing is not permitted on the island except by residents and their guests.

The lighthouse can be seen distantly from points in Salem (including Salem Willows), Marblehead, and Manchester-by-the-Sea, but it is best viewed by boat.

For information on special lighthouse cruises that may pass close to the lighthouse, call Friends of the Boston Harbor Islands, (781) 740-4290, or see www.fbhi.org; or Boston Harbor Cruises, (617) 227-4321, or wwwbostonharborcruises.com.

Helicopter Services Boston offers a variety of tours that include lighthouses in the Boston area, the North Shore, and Cape Ann. Call (617) 737-2427 or visit www.bostonhelicopter.com.

CHAPTER 53

Ten Pound Island Light in July 2004. *Photo by the author.*

Ten Pound Island Light

1821, 1881

Tradition tells us that Ten Pound Island, on the east side of Gloucester
Harbor, received its name from the amount of money paid to the local
Indians for the property by the early settlers. This commonly told tale
is disputed by the Cape Ann historian Joseph Garland, who wrote in
The Gloucester Guide that it was more likely named for the number of
sheep pens (also known as pounds) on the island, which was reserved
in the early days for "rams onlie."

To help mariners find their way into Gloucester's inner harbor, and
to help them avoid a dangerous ledge to the southwest of the island,
Congress appropriated $9,000 in May 1820. (The appropriation also
covered a new lighthouse on Baker's Island, near Salem.) The State of
Massachusetts and the selectmen of Gloucester ceded the land for the
light station to the federal government.

A 20-foot conical stone lighthouse tower was built, along with a
stone dwelling. The light was in service by October 1821, with a fixed
white light exhibited from 39 feet above mean high water.

Just a few weeks after the light went into service, Capt. John
Skolfield was sailing a vessel to Boston with a cargo of wood during a
heavy snowstorm. He was unaware of the new light in Gloucester
Harbor. Mistaking the light for the one on Baker's Island, Skolfield
became disoriented and was unable to make landfall until six days
later, when he arrived at Martha's Vineyard. The cargo was lost in the
storm, as was the ship's water supply.

Amos Story, a Gloucester native, became keeper in 1833 for $350
yearly. In 1842 Story provided a statement for I. W. P. Lewis's report
to Congress, and the picture he painted wasn't pretty:

> *The tower and dwelling are both built of rough-split stone, with a
> wall around the same. Both buildings leak, in consequence of bad
> work and defective mortar. Where the mortar pointing has cracked
> off, a stream of dry sand runs out from between the joints. The floor
> of the dwelling-house has rotted away, so that I have been obliged to
> nail battens over the openings. The lantern leaks and sweats. There
> were formerly ten lamps, but four have been discontinued. . . .*

The leaks around the windows of the dwelling-house are so bad that we are obliged to set a tub to catch the water whenever it rains hard. The wood work, frames, &c, of the windows, are rotten.

Lewis was highly critical of the station's construction, and he recommended the reduction of the light to a single lamp. Some repairs were soon completed, and a subsequent report stated that the dwelling was "in comfortable repair."

An inspection report in 1850 pronounced the whole establishment "as clean as it possibly can be." The report praised Keeper George A. Davis, who took charge in October 1849: "This present keeper has been brought up on the ocean, and keeps his ship in fine order, and everything in its proper place."

In the summer of 1880, the acclaimed American artist Winslow Homer boarded with the keeper at Ten Pound Island. Homer painted about 50 scenes of Gloucester Harbor during that summer.

A new 30-foot conical cast-iron lighthouse tower, lined with brick, was built in 1881, along with a wood-frame keeper's house. The light's characteristic was changed in 1889 from fixed white to fixed with a more intense flash every five seconds. In 1905–06, there was much activity: a new boathouse, a fuel house, a barn, and an oil house were built.

Maritime traffic in Gloucester Harbor was always heavy, and wrecks were not infrequent. A snowstorm on February 4, 1882, with winds nearing 60 miles per hour, drove a New Brunswick schooner onto the island's shore. The same storm wrecked the schooner *Bunker Hill* in the harbor.

The three-masted schooner *Ella M. Storer*—heading to Gardiner, Maine, from New York City—was driven ashore by high winds in the

Ten Pound Island Light Station, showing the first (1821) tower with its original "birdcage-style" lantern. *U.S. Coast Guard photo.*

harbor near Dolliver's Neck, during a storm in December 1914. All aboard, including the captain's wife, escaped in a lifeboat. They rowed across the harbor to Ten Pound Island, where Keeper James Bailey hospitably received them.

The light was decommissioned in 1956. The fifth-order Fresnel lens was replaced by a modern optic installed on the old fog-bell tower, later moved to a skeleton tower. The Fresnel lens is now at the Maine Lighthouse Museum in Rockland, Maine.

The wife of Keeper Edward Hopkins spelled out this greeting for "Flying Santa" Edward Rowe Snow by nailing newspapers to the ground. *From the collection of Edward Rowe Snow, courtesy of Dorothy Snow Bicknell.*

The keeper's house and outbuildings (except for the oil house, which survives) were reduced to rubble. Ownership of the island reverted to Gloucester from the federal government.

By the mid-1980s, the lighthouse was covered with graffiti and the oil house had lost its roof and door. The Lighthouse Preservation Society initiated renovation of the tower in 1987.

The $45,000 necessary for the restoration came from the city, a federal grant, and a grant from the Massachusetts Historical Commission, along with funding from the Bank of New England and money raised by the Lighthouse Preservation Society. Hilgenhurst Associates did the design work, and K & K Painting Company of Maryland repaired the tower. The work took more than two years to complete.

Massachusetts Senator Edward M. Kennedy announced the federal grant: "It [Ten Pound Island Light] has seen the stately schooners and the historic vessels that make their way to sea every day for over a century and watched over the Gloucester fishermen who braved the wind and waves to make their living. For some of those brave souls this . . . vista of Ten Pound Island was their final vision of land."

The lighthouse was relighted as an active aid to navigation on August 7, 1989, Lighthouse Bicentennial Day, in a ceremony complete with fireworks. The oil house was restored in 1995.

🔆 **Ten Pound Island Light can be seen from many points along the Gloucester waterfront, including the area around the famous fisherman statue. Closer views are available from various tour boats that pass through the harbor.**

CHAPTER 54

Eastern Point Light in July 2004. *Photo by the author.*

Eastern Point Light

1832, 1848, 1890

Eastern Point's pretty white lighthouse in its rough and rugged setting has long been a popular destination for photographers and sightseers. For nearly two centuries, a light here has guided "those who go down to the sea in ships" safely into harbor. It's been an invaluable sentinel in one of America's most historic old fishing ports.

The Eastern Point section of Gloucester—at the east side of the entrance to the city's harbor—has been home to farms, a quarry, a Civil War fort, and opulent estates.

A cluster of oak trees served as a landmark at Eastern Point for some years before a lighthouse was established. In 1829 the trustees of the Boston Marine Society voted: "it is the opinion of this Society, that the erection of a monument, on Eastern Point Cape Ann, would be highly usefull to navigation in Boston Bay—the old Land Marks of Trees being nearly decayed & gone—"

After Congress appropriated $2,000 and suitable land was purchased for $100 from George Burnham, an unlighted day beacon was placed at Eastern Point by the end of 1829. Gloucester inhabitants had petitioned Congress for a lighted beacon, but President Andrew Jackson at first opposed the project—possibly because Gloucester residents had voted against him (453–77) in the 1828 presidential election.

With ever-increasing fishing traffic using the harbor, it became obvious that a proper lighthouse was sorely needed. Congress authorized $5,000 for the light station in March 1831, and President Jackson signed the appropriation.

Rather than building a new tower from scratch, the authorities decided to convert the stone day beacon into a lighthouse. The contractor, Samuel Friend, added a wrought-iron lantern with a copper dome to the structure.

The makeshift lighthouse, 30 feet tall, was first lighted on January 1, 1832. Ten lamps, fueled by whale oil, showed a fixed white light 58 feet above mean high water. The first keeper was a local fisherman, 58-year-old Samuel Wonson, with a salary of $400 yearly. Wonson and his wife, Lydia, lived in a tiny brick dwelling that contained two rooms and an attached kitchen on the first floor and two small rooms upstairs.

I. W. P. Lewis's 1843 report to Congress provides a good description of the original lighthouse:

> Tower of rubble masonry, thirty feet high, laid dry, and pointed with lime mortar inside and out; base resting on the surface of a ledge; staircase, and all wood decayed and rotten; soapstone roof, loose and leaky; the whole structure requires to be rebuilt. . . .
>
> No ventilation whatever—the keeper having boarded over the dome of the lantern in the inside, and whitewashed it to diffuse the light.

Lewis recognized the importance of the location, but he believed that too many lamps were in use. "This harbor is a favorite resort of the mackerel fishermen, and other small craft; two hundred sail often run in there, in the course of a few hours, to escape the approach of a gale. There is also a considerable amount of tonnage owned at this place, employed in foreign voyages. One lamp only of a proper form is required here, instead of ten now used."

In a statement for the report to Congress, Wonson added more harsh detail to Lewis's description of the lighthouse:

> It is built of rough-split stone, laid dry, and pointed inside and out; the deck is soapstone; the tower leaks in every direction; the walls inside are covered with ice in winter, and green mould in summer; the window casings are loose in the walls, and rotten besides; the door frames and sills are also rotten; the posts of the lantern only run down one foot in the walls, and in gales of wind it is wrenched and shaken so as to break the glass; the scuttle frame is entirely rotten; the rain blows in under the deck of the lantern, and runs through the walls.

Wonson also complained that the lantern—only six feet in diameter—was too small to allow him to stand comfortably while trimming the lamps. An inspection report by the local superintendent a short time later pointed out that the stone tower was "erected for a monument, and entirely too small for a suitable lantern."

Eastern Point Light Station, circa 1870s, showing the 1848 lighthouse. *U.S. Coast Guard photo.*

With the arrival of the railroad in Gloucester in the mid-1800s and a great influx of immigrants, the fishing business exploded into one of the world's largest, and Eastern Point Light assumed even greater importance. Between 1830 and 1910, 779 vessels out of Gloucester were lost at sea, resulting in the loss of 5,305 lives. One can easily imagine the relief the Gloucestermen must have felt upon sighting Eastern Point Light after long months spent far away on the fishing grounds.

A new, 34-foot brick lighthouse was built on the original foundation for $2,550 in 1848. The contractor hired for the job was Winslow Lewis, who had built many of the nation's lighthouses and had designed the lighting apparatus used in most. Lewis was 78 years old when he built the new Eastern Point Light; he lived only two more years.

The second lighthouse became known as the "ruby light." Its fixed red light, produced by French red plate glass surrounding 11 whale oil lamps and 15-inch reflectors, went into service on November 3, 1848.

In 1857 a fourth-order Fresnel lens was installed along with a new lantern, which increased the visibility of the light from 11 to 13 nautical miles. During the same year, a fog bell, operated by hand-wound machinery, was added. The station was assigned an assistant keeper because of the extra duties related to the fog bell, and for some years there was also a second assistant.

The fog bell tower was destroyed by a storm on September 8, 1869, and for a while the bell was hung on a temporary frame where the keepers struck it by hand as needed. The striking machinery was soon repaired, and a new bell tower was erected in 1877.

1870s engraving showing Keeper Charles Friend in the lighthouse lantern. *From the collection of the author.*

A new keeper's dwelling was built in 1879, while Charles Friend was keeper. The building was later enlarged to become duplex housing for a principal keeper, an assistant keeper, and their families. Another assistant keeper's house, with a gambrel roof, was added in 1908.

On October 1, 1882, the light's characteristic was changed from fixed to flashing red. The revolving fourth-order lens was turned by a clockwork mechanism that had to be periodically wound by the keepers.

A whistling buoy was installed near Eastern Point in 1883 to provide additional warning and guidance to the harbor. Some summer residents objected to their quietude being shattered. Elizabeth Stuart Phelps, a well-known local writer, claimed she suffered from a "nervous ailment" that was aggravated by the sound of the buoy. The Secretary of the Navy ordered the buoy removed from May to October.

Elizabeth Phelps later married the Reverend Herbert Ward, and the *Boston Record* reported, "Since her marriage Mrs. Ward is much better, and the officer who had to remove the buoy has put it back with the assurance that next summer he will have no orders to disturb it."

The third and present lighthouse at Eastern Point was built in 1890 on the same foundation as its predecessors. The 36-foot brick tower was attached to the keeper's house by a covered walkway.

A 4,000-pound bell went into operation in 1897, run by a powerful Shipman steam engine. Within the next four years, a telephone line, the city water supply, and electricity reached the station, and a new boathouse was built.

The 2,250-foot breakwater in front of the lighthouse—consisting of 231,756 tons of Cape Ann granite—was built for $300,000 between 1894 and 1905. The breakwater was constructed to protect the harbor, as well as to keep vessels from hitting dangerous Dog Bar Reef.

Before the breakwater was completed, it sometimes proved a menace to navigation. The two-masted schooner *Flo F. Mader,* from Lunenberg, Nova Scotia, struck the breakwater at about 2:30 a.m. on December 5, 1902. The weather was deteriorating, and the captain—unaware of the unfinished breakwater—had decided to turn into Gloucester Harbor. The vessel was a total loss, but all aboard were rescued by a crew from the Dolliver's Neck Lifesaving Station. The men were housed by Keeper George E. Bailey (in charge from 1892 to 1926) at the light station.

At the end of the completed breakwater, a new light called Gloucester Breakwater Light was established. The keepers at Eastern Point Light had the added duty of keeping this light, an especially dangerous task when ice covered the granite blocks.

George E. Bailey was still keeper in September 1922 when tragedy struck the station. Assistant Keeper Frank Parsons was painting the keeper's house when he fell from the staging to his death on the rocks below. Parsons, who left a wife, had been in the Lighthouse Service for less than five years.

A severe storm in March 1931 dislodged blocks from the breakwater and severed the cable to the breakwater light and fog signal. The outer section of the boat slip was also washed away in the gale.

Carl Deland Hill and Francis R. Macy were the keepers during World War II, when the Coast Guard and lighthouses were put under the jurisdiction of the U.S. Navy. Both men had become chief boatswain's mates after the Coast Guard took over lighthouses in 1939. Each family had six rooms in the duplex house, and the men alternated one long day on with one long day off.

At the time of a 1975 article, the Coast Guard's officer in charge was Boatswain's Mate First Class Lon D. Reed, who was assisted by a young machinery technician. In addition to keeping the light in good repair, the men monitored distress calls, maintained a radio beacon, sent weather reports to Boston and Gloucester, displayed storm warning flags as needed, activated the foghorn when necessary, and kept up the buildings and grounds.

The great blizzard of February 6–7, 1978, its winds gusting to 70 knots, sent seas crashing against the eastern side of the buildings. Much damage was done to several buildings and much of the station's machinery, and the garage was nearly destroyed. Repairs were completed to the breakwater light in 1981.

Michael Mone was the Coast Guard keeper in the early 1980s. He and his wife, Sheila, loved the station, but it wasn't always peaceful. "Anything can happen," Michael told *Woman's World* magazine. "Sometimes we have to retrieve boats that have been torn from their moorings and return them to their owners. Or we might help the Coast Guard patrol boat locate an overdue fishing vessel."

Michael Mone described one night when the seas were so high a vessel was actually driven over the 35-foot-high breakwater. The Mones' four-year-old son, Timothy, said, "This place is swell, but sometimes it gets spooky." Sheila added, "I always have to assure him there are no such things as ghosts."

One of the last Coast Guard keepers was Boatswain's Mate First Class Rick O'Rourke, who lived at Eastern Point in 1983–84. His ex-wife, Christine Plattner, has written of their stay:

> *My memories of life at the light are wonderful: the exciting winter storms with waves wildly crashing over the breakwater; the trail of fishing boats leaving the harbor every dawn; the artists from the Rocky Neck artist colony painting scenes of the lighthouse on warm summer days; welcoming visitors from around the world into our home for a tour of the lighthouse; collecting stray lobster buoys that washed ashore after a storm; eating lobster that my husband caught in his traps; listening to the fog bell moaning on foggy nights; and more and more and more. What a life experience! We loved it!*

The last Coast Guard keeper was Chris Benton, who lived at the station with his wife, Lee. Eastern Point Light was automated in September 1985, and about twenty neighbors attended a ceremony marking the change. A descendant of the first keeper, Carroll Wonson, was given the honor of being the last person to turn on the light manually.

The Coast Guard retained the station for family housing. From late 1989 to early 1992, Scott W. McClain, a second-class electronics technician, lived with his family at the station. They were there for the infamous "Perfect Storm" on the day before Halloween in 1991. Scott's wife, Gaynetta McClain, recalls the storm:

> When the tide really rolled in, we began to realize what trouble we were in. We lived on the east side of the lighthouse, near the garage. The waves were crashing into the side of the house and darkening the kitchen windows. My husband drilled holes in the walkway to the light tower to keep it from collapsing from the weight of the water that was crashing into and flooding it. Around 10:00 p.m., we were removing items from the cellar and moving them to higher ground because we heard the morning tide was to be worse. We moved our most valuable items to the second floor and waited for lower tide to try to walk out of there with our two little girls, ages five and one. About midnight, we took our chance to go. We rode out the rest of the night at the yacht club.
>
> The following morning was devastating! A summer house below the lighthouse had been half washed away. There were mattresses, books, art, and furniture all over the Coast Guard property and the summer house property. The seawall was over half gone, and it was one of the most heart-wrenching things we did when we called the summer neighbors to inform them that their house was half gone. The fence around the lighthouse was gone, and the garage sustained damage to the back, which faced the ocean. There was a sidewalk that led up to the deck porch to our side, and it looked as if there had been an earthquake that twisted and bent the concrete out of the ground. We were really caught off guard at the velocity and power of it all. To this day, it remains the most frightening experience of my life.

A later resident was Chief Petty Officer John Bostel, a New Jersey native who moved into the station in September 1995 with his wife, Carol, their two sons, and a perky dachshund named Lacey.

The worst storm the Bostels experienced at Eastern Point was during the winter of 1995, shortly after they moved in. The winter gale sent waves into the yard and against the garage, and it buried Bostel's

Gloucester Breakwater Light in August 2006. *Photo by the author.*

truck beneath seven-foot snowdrifts.

Bostel and his sons appreciated the great fishing at the station—all they had to do was go out on the rocks in the backyard to catch striped bass. Bostel witnessed many people catch cod, flounder, and even sharks near the station.

Life at Eastern Point Light was usually peaceful and quiet, but it was quite different in summer, when flocks of tourists arrived. Despite the "No Trespassing" signs at the gate to the light station, people would walk right in. Some picnicked in the yard, others peered into the windows. Carol Bostel reported that a visitor once walked right into the house without even knocking.

New Hampshire had (until May 2003) its Old Man of the Mountain, and Eastern Point has "Mother Ann." The shape of a reclining woman can supposedly be seen from certain angles in the rocks next to the lighthouse. The whistling buoy offshore is sometimes called Mother Ann's Cow.

🗼 **Eastern Point Light remains an active aid to navigation, displaying a white flash every five seconds, 24 hours a day. The road to the lighthouse is marked "private," but the public is allowed to drive directly to the station. There's an adjacent parking lot, but the grounds of the light station are closed to the public. You can walk on the breakwater for excellent views of the lighthouse.**

CHAPTER 55

The Thacher Island Twin Lights in July 2004. *Photo by the author.*

Thacher Island Twin Lights

(Cape Ann Light Station)
1771, 1861

European visitors to 50-acre Thacher Island—less than a mile offshore from the nearest mainland point at Rockport's Loblolly Cove, off the east side of Cape Ann—date back at least to Samuel de Champlain in 1605 and Capt. John Smith in 1614.

The island was named for Anthony Thacher, an Englishman whose vessel, the *Watch and Wait*, was wrecked in a ferocious hurricane near the island in 1635 on the way to Marblehead from Ipswich. Thacher later described the dreadful wreck: "Now look with me upon our distress, and consider of my misery, who beheld the ship broken, the water in her, and violently overwhelming us, my goods and provisions swimming in the seas, my friends almost drowned, and mine own poor children so untimely (if I may so term it without offence), before mine eyes drowned, and ready to be swallowed up, and dashed to pieces against the rocks by the merciless waves, and myself ready to accompany them."

Thacher and his wife, Elizabeth, were the only survivors of the wreck in which 21 people died. Four of Thacher's children from an earlier marriage perished in the wreck, and his cousin the Reverend Joseph Avery (often referred to as John Avery) drowned along with his wife and six children.

In 1637 the General Court awarded Anthony Thacher the island "at the head of Cape Ann" to recompense him for his losses, and he appropriately dubbed the island "Thacher's Woe."

The island remained in the Thacher family for 80 years. It was eventually bought back by the Massachusetts government from three men of Gloucester at a cost of £500, for the purpose of establishing a light station.

By the summer of 1771, there were ten light stations in operation in the American colonies. North of Cape Cod there were only three: at Boston, Plymouth, and Portsmouth. All the lighthouses built to that point by the colonial governments were constructed to mark the entrances to ports. The lighthouses built on Thacher Island in 1771 were the first erected primarily to mark a dangerous spot—the Londoner Ledge, a 90-foot-long obstruction southeast of the island—rather than a harbor entrance. They were also the last lighthouses built under British rule in the colonies.

The petition asking for the lighthouses on Thacher Island was presented to the General Court by John Hancock, who owned ships on Cape Ann. The preamble of the act passed on April 26, 1771, for the establishment of the light station reads as follows:

> Whereas the headland of Cape Ann projects itself into the main ocean in such manner as to form two deep bays—one, to the northward, commonly called Ipswich Bay; and another, to the southward, called the Massachusetts, or more commonly, Boston Bay—that there are two very dangerous ledges of rocks which lay off from the headland which, for want of some guide, frequently prove fatal to vessels; and it being generally thought that a lighthouse, or lighthouses erected on Thachers Island, or the mainland of Cape Ann, would be very serviceable to the navigation and commerce of this province and be a means of preserving the lives and estates of a great number of His Majesty's subjects by directing the distressed in stormy and tempestuous weather into a safe harbour.

Dues were collected from local shipping to pay for the lighthouses. Two stone towers, 37 feet tall (to the base of the lanterns) and about 860 feet apart, were lighted for the first time on December 21, 1771. The diameter of the identical towers was 18 feet at the base, and the thickness of the walls was 4 feet at the base. The twin lights soon gained the nickname "Ann's Eyes."

The first keeper, Capt. James Kirkwood, and his two assistants kept cattle and sheep on the island. Eighteen months after taking the keeper position, Kirkwood complained to the General Court of Massachusetts that he and his assistants had not been paid. "The island being at some distance from the mainland," he wrote, "and much exposed to hard gales of wind and extreme cold in the winter which together with the lighthouses and dwelling not being quite finished make it a very uncomfortable habitation, and attended with great difficulty."

The General Court ordered that Kirkwood be given his pay and reimbursed for work done on the island. Local patriots, however, accused Kirkwood of being unpatriotic, and he was branded a Tory. In 1775 minutemen arrived at the island and removed Kirkwood, who fled to Canada.

The station remained abandoned until the close of the Revolution. Samuel Huston was hired as keeper (by Secretary of the Treasury Alexander Hamilton, per order of President Washington) in 1784, along with two assistants. The men got the station in order, but the lights remained dark until 1793.

In June 1790, the light station was ceded by the state of Massachusetts to the federal government. Joseph Sayward was keeper in 1793 when the twin lights were relighted. His pay was $400 yearly, but it was reduced to "266 ⅔ dollars" by order of President Washington. This was apparently because the island was thought to be an advantageous place to live, since there were cattle and a vegetable garden to provide food.

In 1810 the south tower became the scene of a test of new lighting apparatus designed by Winslow Lewis of Boston—a system of multiple Argand oil lamps and parabolic reflectors. Henry Dearborn, the local lighthouse superintendent, observed the twin lights from a distance and pronounced the new light to be like "a brilliant star" in comparison to the old one in the north tower. In 1812 Lewis was contracted to outfit all American lighthouses with his apparatus.

Sayward was still in charge during the War of 1812, when British soldiers landed at the island and pilfered potatoes from his garden. After the war, Sayward's son was offered the chance to replace his aging father as keeper, but he considered the offer of $250 yearly to be inadequate. The next keeper was a Cape Ann native, Aaron Wheeler.

Winslow Lewis built a new one-story, two-room brick dwelling, 20 by 34 feet, in 1816, at a cost of $1,415. The house still stands with its many modifications, including the addition of a second story. Improvements to the lighthouses, including the installation of new iron lanterns on both towers, were completed in 1828.

Austin Wheeler, possibly a distant relative of Aaron, became keeper in early 1834. Three years later, Austin was succeeded by his brother, Charles, at a yearly salary of $450. The brothers hailed from nearby Pigeon Cove, a center of Cape Ann's burgeoning granite industry.

Winslow Lewis installed new lanterns and a new lighting apparatus in May 1841. The work entailed taking down some of the stonework near the tops of both towers, rebuilding the towers with brick, and installing new soapstone decks.

A tremendous storm hit the area just six months later, destroying 14 of 16 vessels at Pigeon Cove Harbor. The glass in the lanterns of both towers was loosened, and some of it was broken. According to I. W. P. Lewis, who inspected the station in 1842, only the fast action of Keeper Wheeler saved both lanterns from total destruction. Wheeler used pieces of lead to reinforce the panes of glass, and he later "puttied the whole very carefully" to stop leaks.

In his 1843 report to Congress, I. W. P. Lewis bluntly criticized the recent work of his uncle Winslow Lewis: "These lanterns, with their lamps, &c. cost $5,360, and were erected as specimens of 'modern improvements.' They reflect little credit on their projectors, and less light than is needed by the navigator." There were 11 lamps in each tower at the time, and I. W. P. Lewis felt that 18 were called for. He felt the use of a single lighthouse at the location would suffice.

I. W. P. Lewis described both lighthouse towers as leaky, the masonry being "in a bad state." He saved his praise for an 1840 two-story wooden dwelling, which he called the "best house in the district." Keeper Wheeler was using the old 1816 dwelling as a schoolroom and storehouse.

Wheeler's wife died in 1845, leaving him with seven children. Lightkeeping jobs were susceptible to the political winds in the mid-nineteenth century, and Wheeler—a Whig—was frequently criticized, probably unjustly, by political opponents.

Wheeler pleaded his case to a newspaper in 1849. Among his many positive contributions above and beyond the keeping of the lights, Wheeler had invented and put into service a new lighthouse lamp that kept oil from solidifying in the winter. He had made many improvements on the island, including clearing land, erecting a fence, and planting apple and pear trees, grapevines, blueberries, blackberries, and quince. He also had aided the survivors of shipwrecks several times, sometimes at risk to his own life.

Despite his pleas, Wheeler was replaced by William Hale in August 1849. Wheeler headed to California a few months later, enticed by the Gold Rush. Hale, a former sailor, got high marks in an 1850 inspection, which reported that the towers had been recently whitewashed inside and out, new lamps had been installed in the south tower, and the dwelling had been newly papered inside.

Lancelot Kelly Rowe succeeded Hale as keeper in 1853. That year an agent of the Portland Steam Packet Company wrote that a fog bell on Thacher Island "would be of immense benefit to the whole eastern coasting interest." A fog bell was soon installed. Later that same year, Rowe's wife, Nancy, gave birth to a baby daughter, christened Belle Thacher Rowe.

The Fresnel lens, invented by the French physicist Augustin Fresnel in 1822, provided a lighting system that was far more efficient than the old multiple lamps and reflectors. Tests showed that a flame backed by a reflector lost about 83 percent of its light, but a light source inside a Fresnel lens—bent into a narrow beam by multiple prisms—lost only about 17 percent of its light.

The new invention was swiftly adopted in Europe, but the United States lagged behind, largely because of the continued influence of Winslow Lewis. With the formation of the U.S. Lighthouse Board in 1852, American lighthouses started to catch up with their European counterparts.

The Thacher Island south tower and the 1816 dwelling, circa late 1800s. *From the collection of the author.*

The new Lighthouse Board noted in 1852, "This is a very important light-station, and the lights require to be increased in power and range." Still, by 1857, Thacher Island, Boston Light, and Cape Canaveral Light in Florida were the only American lights still using the old-style apparatus.

In 1857 the Lighthouse Board pronounced that the Thacher Island twin lights, occupying "a prominent position, with many dangers to the navigator . . . would be greatly benefited by having two lights of the first order in place of the present ones."

To exhibit the improved lights properly, it was decided that new, taller towers were in order. Congress appropriated $81,417.60 for this purpose in March 1859. Twin towers, 124 feet high, were completed in 1861. New Hampshire granite was used instead of Cape Ann granite, which drew much criticism from locals. A new wood-frame keeper's dwelling was built near the north tower at about the same time; the house was destroyed by fire in the 1950s.

The twin lighthouses were fitted with enormous first-order Fresnel lenses that cost $10,000 each. The new towers, with their lights 166 feet above mean high water, were first illuminated on October 1, 1861.

James Collins Parsons was keeper during the construction of the new towers, and Albert Giddings Hale took over in 1861. Hale had recently been ill with typhoid fever, and his doctor advised him that the life of a lighthouse keeper would speed his recovery. He may have recovered from his illness, but taking part in the rescue of shipwreck victims on multiple occasions probably sapped Hale's strength. The Hales left Thacher Island in 1864, and Alexander Bray became the new principal keeper.

Bray—a Civil War veteran—and his wife, Maria (Herrick), were both descended from old Gloucester families. Bray had been an assistant keeper since 1861, and it was reported that he was the first man to light the new lens in the south tower.

Maria Bray was described as a woman of unusual literary abilities. She contributed articles to the local newspapers and wrote short stories, and for a time she served as the editor of a literary magazine called *Magnolia Leaves*. During her time on Thacher Island, Maria developed an interest in the classification of marine plant life. She assembled an important collection of sea mosses and algae and became a recognized authority on the subject. She also learned to perform all the lightkeeping duties of her husband.

On December 21, 1864, one of the assistant keepers fell ill with a fever. Keeper Bray and another assistant left for the mainland to take the ailing man to a doctor. They left Maria in charge of the station. According to one version of the story, the only person with her was her 14-year-old nephew, Sidney Haskell. (Maria Bray's obituary credits two other keepers' wives with helping to keep the station operating during the storm.)

A heavy snowstorm blew in later that day, making it impossible for Alexander Bray to return to the island. Maria Bray and Sidney Haskell braved the high winds and heavy snow to light the lamps in both towers. Each tower had 148 steps to the top, and Maria had to repeat the trip three times that night to keep the lamps supplied with oil and the lantern-room panes free of soot.

A second night passed before Alexander Bray could return to the island, and not once did Maria allow either light to go out. It was a happy Christmas as the Brays were reunited. The Brays left the island in 1869.

The Lighthouse Board's annual reports for 1867–69 list many repairs and improvements to the towers and dwellings. In addition, a new 12-by-24-foot engine house was built for a hot-air-engine fog signal, with an Ericsson engine trumpet. The new fog trumpet was more powerful than a signal that had been established in 1861. The extant 32-by-32-foot fog-signal building was built in 1887.

Because of the many duties involved with the two light towers and the fog signal, Thacher Island in the early 1870s was home to five keepers and their families. More living space was needed, so a new one-and-a-half-story wood-frame house was built near the south tower in 1876. Weather has always been a major factor in life here, and getting to and from the island was frequently a challenge. On October 20, 1891, an assistant keeper named John Farley lost his life as he attempted to land at the boatslip in heavy seas.

Despite the lights and fog signal, wrecks still occurred in the vicinity. In 1876, freighter carrying 800 tons of coal struck a submerged wreck in a storm. The citizens of Cape Ann saved on their fuel bills that year, as they salvaged 500 tons of coal from the ship. Two assistant keepers, Albert Whitten and Elliot Hadley, were recognized for their bravery in the rescue of four men from the wreck of the *Lottie* on August 24, 1893. The schooner had run aground in a thick fog.

A railroad system was installed on the island in the late 1800s, and it was gradually extended until it was more than 500 feet long by 1900. The railroad was used to bring fuel and supplies to the station's buildings.

An underwater telegraph line first connected the island to the mainland in 1876, but the system was dismantled after the Spanish-American War. Then, in the name of national defense, a telephone line was installed in 1902.

Assistant Keeper George Kezer with his sons Thatcher and Harlan. *Courtesy of Barbara Kezer.*

Several children were born to keepers' families at Thacher Island over the years, including Bertha Whitten, born to Assistant Keeper Albert Whitten and his wife in 1891. Thatcher Warren Kezer was born on the island in 1900. He later claimed that his father, Assistant Keeper George Kezer, took so long trying to fetch the doctor to the island for his birth that little Thatcher was waving to them from the boat ramp by the time they returned.

Addison Franklin Tarr served longer than any other keeper, from 1881 to 1912. In an 1890 newspaper article, Tarr expressed some resentment of tourists who failed to treat him with respect. "What would some of these people think if I hailed their carriage, took a ride about their place, criticized everything, and ended by giving them hardly a 'thank you?'"

Early in his stay, Tarr rowed his young daughter, Mary, to Loblolly Cove in Rockport every day so she could attend school. The boat trip was followed by a two-mile walk to the Cove Hill Primary School.

There were as many as seven children living at the station in the early 1900s, along with one child at the nearby Straitsmouth Island Light Station. The state refused to build a school on the island, but it finally agreed to pay a teacher to live there. The teacher, a young woman, didn't stay very long. She met and subsequently married Edwin Tarr, a son of the keeper and an assistant keeper himself. The couple moved to Boston Harbor, where Edwin served as keeper of the Long Island Head Lighthouse.

After that, most of the children boarded on the mainland during the week so they could attend school. When the children were ready to return to the island for the weekend, they would walk back and forth at a designated spot at Loblolly Cove, and one of the fathers would row to shore to pick them up.

John Cook, a veteran of the Spanish-American War, served as an assistant under Addison Tarr beginning in 1911. Cook's wife, Emma, was known for her beautiful singing voice, and the couple often hosted parties for visiting friends.

Fog is by no means uncommon in the area. During one particularly bad stretch of fog in July 1959, the foghorn sounded for 211 consecutive hours. On a nasty night in 1919, President Woodrow Wilson was returning from the Versailles Peace Conference on board the SS *America* when the ship ran into rain and fog near Thacher Island. The fog signal was sounding, but the ship kept heading straight for the rocks. Years later, Maurice Babcock, who was the third assistant keeper at the time of the incident, described what happened next.

I was standing watch in the signal house, keeping the old foghorn going. Through the rain, I made out the outline of a big ship with what seemed to be a convoy ahead—and they were heading straight for the island. We could hear signals from them as though they were trying to get an answer from someone. Our horn was going like mad all the time, and I guess they must have heard us finally, because suddenly they backed up. It wasn't until dawn, when we could see the big ship offshore, that we knew it was the President's boat, bound for Boston.

Like other tall, powerful lighthouses, the Thacher Island lights sometimes confused seabirds. On New Year's Eve 1921, William Daggett, an assistant keeper, discovered that several geese had flown right into the lantern of the north tower, shattering two thick panes of glass. Three geese were found dead inside the lantern, and two more were discovered at the base of the tower the following morning. Needless to say, the families had goose for New Year's dinner that year.

The government first proposed the discontinuance of the north light in 1912. Complaints put off the inevitable for another 20 years, but on February 1, 1932, the north light was extinguished, seemingly forever. Thacher Island had been the last twin-light station on the coast. There were, at one time, seven twin-light stations and one triple-light station, all on the Atlantic coast.

A submarine cable provided power for the south light, which was intensified to 160,000 candlepower with the addition of four 250-watt incandescent electric lamps. On May 3, 1932, it was reported that the master of the steamship *Falmouth* saw the newly intensified south light from a distance of 44 miles, an unusually great distance for any lighthouse.

George Seavey was the principal keeper from 1933 to 1945, and he was in charge when the Coast Guard took over the operation of the nation's lighthouses in 1939. The Coast Guard sent a crew to demolish an old navy watch station on the island in 1948. They left after burning the structure down, but smoldering embers started a fire that quickly spread. The families feared that the fire would reach the fog-signal station, where it could ignite an explosion because of the compressed steam. A squad of firemen and Coast Guardsmen from the mainland were needed to extinguish the flames, and disaster was narrowly averted.

Richard Lord was one of the Coast Guard keepers in the early 1960s. Lord and his wife moved to the island with a young child, and two more children were born to the couple during their three years at the station. The two other crewmen at the time were Richard D'Entremont, who lived with his wife and three daughters, and Officer in Charge Charles Riker, who lived on the island with his wife. The sum of $77.10 per month was allotted for food, but it cost Lord only about $40 each month to feed his family with groceries bought at Hanscom Air Force Base.

Lord fondly recalls his lighthouse-keeping days. He built a walk-in chicken coop and bought 12 laying hens, and the family's food supply was also augmented by plenty of cod, striped bass, and mackerel caught around the island. Sand sharks were caught and used as bait in lobster traps.

George and Dottie Carroll of the Thacher Island Association. *Courtesy of Dottie Carroll.*

The Coast Guard keepers got along very well with their mainland neighbors, but Lord remembers a retired admiral with a view of the island who would sometimes call to complain that the flashing characteristic of the south light was slightly off.

In 1967 federal officers brought Joseph Barboza "The Animal" Baron, who had testified against organized crime figures, to Thacher Island for safekeeping, along with his wife and child. Baron was termed a "known killer" by the Suffolk County district attorney, and his testimony had led to indictments against a score of crime figures.

Baron complained of the primitive living conditions on the island. The secret of his whereabouts was soon out, so he was moved to a rented estate on Gloucester's Eastern Point. He was eventually relocated to California under the witness-protection program. One Coast Guardsman later reported that Baron was a "hell of a nice guy." Nice guy or not, Baron was shot to death on a San Francisco street about eight years later.

The wives and children of the Coast Guard keepers moved to the mainland when Baron was brought to the island, and the island remained a "stag" station after that. A 1969 article described life for the Coast Guard keepers at Thacher Island. Seaman James Davis, a 20-year-old native of Rhode Island, lived on the island with one other Coast Guardsman for two weeks followed by a week at home in Gloucester with his wife and infant son. Seaman Davis's wife, Pamela, was allowed to visit for a day on weekends during the summer only.

The other Coast Guardsman at that time was 19-year-old Engineman Second Class John Wigger of South Carolina. Their only company consisted of three dogs—a black mongrel, Rastus; a collie, Angel; and a German shepherd, Duchess—and two cats, Pat and Mike. Mike surprised everyone by giving birth to five kittens.

The General Services Administration announced in April 1970 that the north tower had been designated excess property and would be disposed of. Town officials were concerned, and a committee was established for the preservation of the site. In 1972 the entire northern part of the island—about 22 acres in all—was transferred to the

Bureau of Sport Fisheries and Wildlife, now known as the U.S. Fish and Wildlife Service. The town eventually leased this section of the island, and in 1976 the Thacher Island Town Committee (TITC) was formed to maintain the property.

In 1980 the south light and the fog signal were automated and the last Coast Guard crew vacated the island. The first-order Fresnel lens was removed from the south tower; it's now on display at the Coast Guard Academy Museum in New London, Connecticut.

Ned Cameron and other concerned citizens of Cape Ann formed the Thacher Island Association, a nonprofit fund-raising arm of the TITC, in 1981. The first man chosen for the job of on-island caretaker was Russell Grubb, a retired bank employee. Grubb eventually assembled a menagerie of sheep, goats, a dog, and a cat to keep him company.

After three years on the island (he returned a couple of years later for two more years on the island), Grubb gave way to a succession of other resident caretakers. The winter keepers for some years were Armand and Betty Desharnais. George and Dottie Carroll, a retired couple, had a six-year stint as summer caretakers (May to October) beginning in 1987, and they are still very active in the Thacher Island Association. Dottie once told the *Boston Globe* that she and George got along happily on the island. "After 45 years, you have to," she said. George added, "There are two lighthouses on the island. Sometimes, she's in one and I'm in the other."

In 1989 the long-abandoned north lighthouse tower was restored with U.S. Fish and Wildlife Service funds, along with money raised by the Thacher Island Association and the Lighthouse Preservation Society. The tower was opened to visitors, offering a panoramic view of the area. The north light was also relighted as a private aid to navigation. Its yellow light, now solar powered, makes Thacher Island once again the only operating twin-light station in the United States.

For several years the Thacher Island Association ran a boat to the island from T Wharf in Rockport, and rooms in the assistant keeper's house were made available to overnight visitors. The landing ramp was damaged by storms in 1991 and 1992, and the island was without tourists until 1994, when repairs were completed. In the harsh winter of 1995, the landing ramp was completely washed out.

In 1998 U.S. Representative John F. Tierney secured $250,000 for a new boat ramp as part of a spending bill passed by Congress. This funding, combined with money raised by the Thacher Island Association and the Rockport Town Committee's revenue-sharing funds, provided for a new 120-foot ramp, which was completed in the fall of 2000.

Thacher Island in 2001. *Photo by the author.*

In the spring of 2000, a new Coast Guard "Keeper Class" buoy tender was launched, the *Maria Bray,* named for the heroic wife of the Civil War–era keeper Alexander Bray. On its way to its home port in Mayport, Florida, the vessel stopped for a ceremony near Thacher Island. Members of the Thacher Island Association were on board as Cdr. David Foley related the incredible tale of how Maria Bray kept the lights going through the December storm in 1864. A wreath was placed in the ocean in her honor.

On January 3, 2001, Interior Secretary Bruce Babbitt designated Cape Ann Light Station on Thacher Island a National Historic Landmark, making it the ninth light station—and one of fewer than 2,500 sites nationwide—to receive this designation. Paul St. Germain, president of the Thacher Island Association, said, "This is a great honor for Rockport and an opportunity for us to attract private and public grants for our ongoing preservation efforts for this historic site."

The Thacher Island Town Committee, in partnership with the Thacher Island Association, now maintains and operates the island under agreements with the Coast Guard and the U.S. Fish and Wildlife Service, which still owns 22 acres at the northern section of the island.

The Coast Guard transferred its 28-acre section of the island to the town of Rockport in 2001. With the transfer, the town took over responsibility for the maintenance of the south tower, in addition to the continued upkeep of the north tower. Coast Guard aids-to-navigation personnel continue to maintain the solar-powered light in the south tower.

In May 2002, the Campbell Construction Group was contracted to replace the roof and repaint the assistant keeper's dwelling. Repair work also included replacing rotted wooden components of the building and repointing brickwork and chimneys.

The restoration of the principal keeper's house is in progress at this writing and is expected to be completed in 2007. The island caretakers will live in the principal keeper's house. This will double the space available for overnight visitors in the assistant keeper's house, which will also house a visitor center and interpretive exhibits. Much remains to be done to complete restoration of all the station's buildings, and volunteers are always needed.

The twin lights on Thacher Island can be viewed from spots along the Cape Ann shore, and they can be seen more closely from sightseeing cruises in the area. The Thacher Island Association usually holds a sunset fund-raising cruise in midsummer.

Members of the Thacher Island Association can visit the island on Saturday mornings from 9:00 to 11:00 a.m. from July through the end of August (weather permitting) aboard the Thacher Island launch. It's a 30-minute ride to the island. You must make reservations in advance by calling (978) 546-7697. Seats are limited because the Thacher Island launch accommodates only 15 passengers, and there's only one trip each Saturday.

You can also visit using your own boat or kayak, but there's no dock on the island, just the ramp used for the association's launch. Only small rowboats and kayaks are allowed to land on the ramp. Two guest moorings are available about 50 yards offshore. If you'd like to use one of these moorings, you must call the caretaker in advance at (617) 599-2590. Bring a dinghy to land on the ramp.

Those wishing to camp in the small campground on the island may obtain a permit by calling (617) 599-2590. A six-room apartment is available in the assistant keeper's dwelling; call (617) 599-2590 for information and reservations.

For more information or to join the Thacher Island Association, write to Thacher Island Association, P.O. Box 73, Rockport, MA 01966, or visit www.thacherisland.org.

CHAPTER 56

Straitsmouth Island Light in August 2006. *Photo by the author.*

Straitsmouth Island Light

1835, 1851, 1896

When the English explorer Capt. John Smith visited the area around Cape Ann in 1614, he found an abundance of timber and a "silver stream" of cod and other fish. He dubbed the area Cape Tragabigzanda, after a young princess who had shown him kindness while he was a captive of the Turks. It was later renamed in honor of Anne, queen of Denmark.

Smith's coat of arms depicted three Turks' heads on a shield, in commemoration of three consecutive jousting victories during a siege in Transylvania. As he traveled along Cape Ann's eastern shore, Smith encountered three prominent islands that he named the Turks' Heads. These islands are now known as Thacher, Milk, and Straitsmouth.

The area's vital granite business began in the 1820s, joining the fishing industry to put Rockport, which was then part of Gloucester, on the map. In fact, before it was incorporated as a separate town in 1840, many knew Rockport as Granitetown and its habitants were referred to as quarry people. Rockport granite built the locks of the Panama Canal, the Custom House tower in Boston, and countless other structures.

Rockport grew up around an indentation in the northeastern part of the cape known as Sandy Bay. A stone pier was built in the 1820s at Pigeon Cove, at the northwestern end of the bay, and it became an important location for the shipping of granite. It was determined that Straitsmouth Island, some 1,600 feet offshore near Gap Head at the bay's southeastern end, would be an ideal place for a lighthouse to guide vessels toward the harbor at Pigeon Cove, and to help vessels pass through the channel between Thacher Island to the south and the rocks known as the Salvages, northeast of Straitsmouth.

Congress appropriated $5,000 for the lighthouse on June 30, 1834, and the entire island of about 30 acres was purchased from Aaron and Solomon Poole for $600. A 19-foot brick lighthouse tower, showing a fixed white light 45 feet above mean high water, was built, along with a brick dwelling.

The first keeper was Benjamin Andrews, chosen because he was not likely to "serve as a juror, or to perform military duty." Andrews served until his death at the age of 58 in August 1840.

John Davis became keeper on July 1, 1841, at a yearly salary of $350. Davis was in charge when the engineer I. W. P. Lewis visited in 1842. In his report of 1843, Lewis described the tower as "laid up in bad lime mortar," its woodwork rotten, and the whole structure very leaky. The dwelling was also poorly built, but Davis had "repaired the house so as to make it tight and comfortable."

There were six lamps in use when Lewis visited, each equipped with a 13½-inch reflector. Four of the lamps were "out of plumb," and one of them faced the door to the lantern and had thus "burned for six years without the possibility of being seen."

In addition to its poor construction, Lewis pointed out that the lighthouse, on the island's central eastern shore, was built in the wrong place.

> The uses of this light, as originally designed, (apart from its local services as a harbor beacon,) was to enable vessels to run through the narrow channel between Thacher's Island and the Salvages; which purpose was completely frustrated by the contractor setting the tower about 500 feet west of the only position where it could serve as a mark to clear Alden's ledge and the flat grounds to the eastward.
>
> The present light is a positive injury to navigation, as it misleads strangers, who frequently get ashore on the low eastern part of the island, or strike on Alden's ledge, upon which there is no buoy or other mark. The tower is not worth repainting, and should be taken down, and a firm and substantial structure erected on the eastern point of the island. One lamp only is required for this locality, instead of six now used.

In a report for Lewis, Keeper Davis described how the dwelling was out of repair and leaky when he moved in, but had since been repaired and made "quite tight." A brick cistern in the cellar was so poorly built and leaky that it was useless, so Davis pulled it apart and paved the cellar floor with the bricks. Davis agreed with Lewis that the light was established far from its intended position. He believed that the contractor had done this simply because "it was more convenient for him to work there than on the other point."

In an April 1843 letter, Davis wrote that the light should have been 87 yards from where it was built. This would have placed it farther from the dwelling and thus would have represented an inconvenience to him, he wrote, "but that circumstance ought not to be thought of for a moment, when the property and lives of our seafaring brethren are in jeopardy."

Another inspection in 1843 by the local superintendent called the lighthouse—only eight years old—a "miserable old brick tower." The report called Davis "an excellent, attentive man, and careful of everything." The superintendent added that access to the station was difficult in high seas, and he recommended the addition of boat ways.

Several vessels were lost in storms in the 1830s and 1840s in the vicinity of Straitsmouth Island. Local navigation was improved somewhat by the addition of a buoy near Avery's Rock, north of the island, in 1845. A much-needed lifesaving station was established opposite the island on the mainland in 1874.

An 1850 inspection, when Henry J. Low of Rockport was keeper, reported that the tower and house were still leaky, but it included the good news that the tower was soon to be rebuilt. A 24-foot octagonal stone tower, at the northeast point of the island—where it had been intended in the first place—replaced the original lighthouse during the following year. In 1857 a sixth-order Fresnel lens was installed.

Many improvements were made to the keeper's dwelling in the 1867–69 period, including the addition of a new brick cistern in the cellar. But the repairs couldn't stave off the inevitable, and a new six-room wood-frame house was finally built in 1878.

For many years, a raised wooden footbridge connected the tower and dwelling. The footbridge was rebuilt in 1894. Two years later, the present 37-foot cylindrical brick lighthouse was built on the same foundation as the 1851 tower. For some time during the construction project, the light was exhibited from a wooden skeleton tower. Further improvements to the station were made in the early 1900s, including the addition of a derrick for the landing of supplies.

In 1932 the characteristic was changed from white to green. The light was converted to automatic operation by the early 1930s, and a license was granted for a time for a local man to live in the keeper's

The second (1851) lighthouse on Straitsmouth Island, with its original "birdcage-style" lantern. *U.S. Coast Guard photo.*

house. The island—except for the lighthouse itself—was declared surplus property and was sold in 1941 for $3,050 to Glenn Wilson of New York City. After World War II, a restaurant briefly operated on the island.

William Francis Gibbs, a naval architect who directed the production of

An early-1900s postcard view of Straitsmouth Island. *From the collection of the author.*

cargo-carrying Liberty ships during World War II, was the owner of the island for a time. His stepson, Adrian Larkin, fell in love with the property. In 1960 Larkin was given permission to live there as long as he didn't disturb the seagull population or change the character of the keeper's dwelling.

Larkin was dismayed at the condition of the house. Every window was broken and "the seagulls were having babies in the bedrooms," he told the *New York Times*. He began spending every weekend working on the property. "Between working and swimming and a few martinis and taking it easy," Larkin said, "the whole weekend is taken up." Friends visiting on the weekends were assigned work, and Larkin's sheepdog, Wayward, had a great time bounding around on the island's boulders.

Larkin eventually replaced the floors and a chimney and installed an electrical generator, a shower, and a flush toilet. Years later, Larkin recalled the island as "a very happy and active place to live."

After William Gibbs died in 1967, the property was donated by his brother, Frederic H. Gibbs, to the Massachusetts Audubon Society (MAS).

A modern electric foghorn was installed on the lighthouse tower in 1974. The lighthouse continued as an active aid to navigation, but the abandoned house rapidly deteriorated. In the early 1980s, a local resident, Charles Costello, did some renovation of the dwelling only to have his work immediately ruined by vandals. He once replaced some windows and saw them broken within days.

There was another short-lived restoration effort in 1983, initiated with the blessings of MAS. Four young men planned to live in the house. The old footbridge was long gone, so they first had to cut a swath through the island's luxuriant poison ivy before they could begin working on the house.

There were no windows left in the 1878 house, and it was filled with seagull droppings. The men were a bit startled when they first encountered the island's wildlife. One of them told the *Gloucester Daily Times*, "The first time my brother came out, he yelled, 'Hey, look at the seal on the rock!' Not until I saw the tail did I know it was a rat." The 1980s restoration effort eventually waned, and the house continued to deteriorate.

The lighthouse tower was refurbished by the crew of the Coast Guard cutter *Bittersweet* and personnel from Coast Guard Station Gloucester in 1982. The "Perfect Storm" of October 1991, which did great damage in the Cape Ann area, destroyed the old entryway to the tower. During the following year the Coast Guard built a new, smaller entryway, shored up the foundation, and completed some repointing of the tower's brickwork.

The Lighthouse Preservation Society, based in Newburyport, Massachusetts, at the time, tried to initiate the restoration of the keeper's house in 1998. MAS saw the need to maintain the island as a bird sanctuary as their primary mission, although officials have stated that they would be open to creative solutions concerning the care of the house. The Lighthouse Preservation Society suggested moving the house off the island to the city of Newburyport, but that notion met with opposition from officials in Rockport.

A restored light station would represent a significant improvement of the local seascape for thousands of boaters, tourists, and residents of Cape Ann. In the summer of 2001, there was talk in Rockport of a new restoration effort, but the more recent word is that there are no longer any such plans. The keeper's house has become an eyesore, and there is little hope that it will be saved from collapse.

The automated solar-powered light and fog signal remain active aids to navigation. A storage shed on the island has collapsed in recent years, although a brick oil house—its roof gradually being lost to the elements—still stands.

The lighthouse can be seen from the breakwater at the end of Bearskin Neck in Rockport. The Thacher Island Association runs occasional lighthouse cruises that pass close by; check www.thacherisland.org for more information.

For the few people who visit Straitsmouth Island by boat, landing is very difficult, as the landing ramp was removed years ago. Walking around on the poison ivy–covered island can be hazardous.

Straitsmouth Island is managed as part of the Ipswich River Wildlife Sanctuary. For more information, write to the Ipswich River Wildlife Sanctuary, 87 Perkins Row, Topsfield, MA 01983, call (978) 887-9264, or visit www.massaudubon.org/Nature_Connection/Sanctuaries/Ipswich_River/.

CHAPTER 57

Annisquam Light in August 2006. *Photo by the author.*

Annisquam Light

(Annisquam Harbor Light, Squam Light, Wigwam Point Light)
1801, 1851, 1897

The name "Annisquam" appears to be a combination of the word
squam—the local Indians' word for harbor—and "Ann," for Cape Ann.
The Annisquam River, technically an estuary that's open to the ocean
at both ends, separates most of Cape Ann—and most of the city of
Gloucester—from the mainland. The northern end of the river opens
into Ipswich Bay, and the southern end connects to Gloucester Harbor
via the Blynman Canal.

The cozy Annisquam village grew up on the east side of the river's
northern end beginning in 1631. The village grew into a fishing and
shipbuilding center that rivaled Gloucester Harbor in its early days.

The Blynman Canal, also known as "The Cut," had first connected
the southern end of the Annisquam River to Gloucester Harbor in
1623, but it was filled in and impassable for a century after 1723. Even
so, the Annisquam River was considered an important harbor of refuge
for vessels traveling along the coast.

Congress appropriated $2,000 in April 1800 for a lighthouse at
Wigwam Point, the northwesterly point of Annisquam village, where it
would "best serve the purpose of discovering the entrance of Anesquam
[a common early spelling] Harbor." The name Wigwam Point stems
from the long use of the point as a summer gathering place for local
Indians. Gustavus Griffin of Gloucester sold six and a half acres of land
for the station to the government for $140.

The first lighthouse was a 32-foot wooden tower, showing a fixed
white light 40 feet above the water. A two-room wood-frame keeper's
house was built near the tower. George Day, a Gloucester native who
was born in 1769, became the first keeper at a yearly salary of $200.
Day dug a well on the grounds himself.

A correspondent for the *Boston Post* visited the lighthouse in its
early years and provided the following glimpse of the keeper's family life.

> *A large milk pan, an iron pot, and a dozen wooden spoons, made*
> *up the greater portion of their housekeeping articles; and their live-*
> *stock consisted of a cow. It was their custom, while boiling their*
> *hominy for supper, to milk the cow into the pan, and after placing*
> *it in the middle of the floor and turning in the hominy to gather*

*around with their wooden spoons, and all help themselves from the
same dish. On one of these occasions old parson F., their minister,
happened to be paying them a parochial visit; and one of the boys
being a little crowded, he thought he could better his position by
changing it to the opposite side of the dish. In attempting to do this,
by stepping across, he accidentally put his dirty foot square onto the
milk and hominy, and before he could take it out again the rest had
revenged themselves for the interruption by rapping him smartly on
his bare leg with their wooden spoons, and without taking any further notice of the affair, went on eating as before.*

Keeper Day was still in charge when the civil engineer I. W. P.
Lewis examined the station in 1842. By this time, the tower was in
such bad shape that it was propped up with several wooden spars. The
keeper, whose pay had advanced to $350 yearly, provided the following
statement for Lewis's 1843 report to Congress:

*I was appointed keeper of this light in the year of its erection,
A.D. 1800, and am now seventy-two years of age. The tower is a frame
building, standing upon a point of rocks, and is merely a harbor light,
showing the entrance to Annis Squam harbor. The frame of the tower
is rotted in all parts, and has been shored up with spars for about
twenty years. In heavy gales the tower is so shaken as to be very
unsafe, and I hardly know what has kept it standing. Two years ago
the walk or bridge leading from the house to the tower was swept away
by a heavy sea only a few minutes after I crossed it. In winter the ice
collects on the stairs so as to render passage up and down very dangerous. I expect every storm that comes the tower will be destroyed.*

Day's statement went on to describe the deplorable condition
of the dwelling, which was "leaky and rotten, and quite as bad as the
lighthouse." He had repaired the roof himself several times. About 10
years earlier, rats had undermined the chimney. Day summed up the
situation: "I consider the whole establishment to be in a very dilapidated and ruinous state."

Lewis concurred. He called the lighthouse "a local harbor beacon
of exceeding usefulness to the fishermen," and said that it required
"rebuilding entirely." The lighting apparatus was "rude and ill-contrived,"
according to Lewis, and he recommended that the existing six lamps
could be reduced to one "of a proper form."

As it turned out, the 1801 lighthouse outlasted George Day's stay
as keeper by a few months. William Dade became the light's new
keeper in 1850, and a new 40-foot octagonal wooden lighthouse tower

was built during the following year. The original keeper's house was repaired and remained in use. It still stands today, enlarged and altered over the years.

A fifth-order Fresnel lens, rotated by a clockwork mechanism, replaced the old lamps and reflector about 1857. A 109-foot covered walkway between the house and tower was added in 1867. The covered walkway remained in place until some time after 1900, but a simple uncovered footbridge eventually replaced it.

Dennison Hooper was keeper from 1872 to 1894. His son, Edward, was born at the lighthouse in 1879. In a 1964 letter to the historian Edward Rowe Snow, Edward Hooper recalled some shipwrecks from his childhood days.

On September 26, 1888, according to Edward Hooper, two schooners went aground on Coffin's Beach, across the mouth of the river from the lighthouse. One was the two-masted *I. W. Hine*. The crew of the *Hine* got ashore without assistance, and the schooner was refloated.

The other wreck that day was the *Abbie B. Cramer,* a three-masted coal schooner from Baltimore that was heading for Portsmouth, New Hampshire. The *Cramer* went ashore at the west end of Coffin's Beach. All hands had to hang on to the vessel's rigging all day as they waited for help. The crew of the Davis Neck Lifesaving Station arrived and tried to land a line for a breeches buoy, but they couldn't hit their target with several tries.

Annisquam Light Station, circa early 1890s. *From the collection of the author.*

The Massachusetts Humane Society had kept a lifeboat at the lighthouse since the days of Keeper George Day. A group of volunteers took the lifeboat across the river to help the crew of the *Cramer.* They had to land the boat on the west side of the river and then carry it two miles to the beach near the wreck. From there they launched it into the surf and succeeded in rescuing the entire crew of the *Cramer.* The schooner was a complete loss, and Hooper claimed that years later he could see wood from the schooner protruding from the sand at low tide.

In a 1966 letter to the Coast Guard, Edward Hooper recalled the supply boat's yearly visits. Kerosene was delivered in five-gallon cans covered with wood, and a barrel of lime would be supplied to make whitewash for the tower. Keeper Hooper kept several cows in a barn at the station and sold milk in Annisquam village to help support his family. Edward recalled that he sometimes had to bring back the cows when they wandered away from the station at low tide. His father also kept an extensive garden and grapevines. In his later years at the station, he rented adjacent vacant property for a larger garden and a place to keep his flock of chickens.

Dennison Hooper connected George Day's old well to the house and installed a pump in the kitchen. A small second well provided water for the cows.

There was much more open space around the light station in the nineteenth century than there is now, and Edward Hooper recalled that there was plenty of room for baseball games, played with baseballs made of "wound yarn covered with buttonhole stitching." The pastureland near the lighthouse—owned by George Norwood—was subdivided into house lots around 1900, and the settlement was named Norwood Heights.

The present 41-foot cylindrical brick lighthouse tower was built in 1897, on the same foundation as the previous two towers. Four years later, the keeper's house was renovated, a 3,000-foot wire fence was added along the boundary of the station, and a stone wall was built along the beach.

John Davis was keeper from about 1900 to 1936, and he and his wife, Ida (Birch), saw many changes in their years at Annisquam. Telephone service and the city water supply reached the station in 1907. In 1922 the old fifth-order lens was replaced by a more powerful fourth-order lens, operated by electricity.

A foghorn was installed in 1931, but the following year it was decided that the signal would operate only from October 15 through May 15, so that local summer residents could have peaceful nights. In 1949 it went into operation in the summer, but only during the day.

Al Sherman of Delaware recalls life at Annisquam Light in the early 1950s, when his father was the Coast Guard keeper. Although the light—changed some years before from fixed to flashing—was powered with electricity, the mechanism that rotated the lens still needed to be wound by hand. "I can recollect memories of scaling the rocks beneath the light and most importantly going up the light every night with my dad to wind the turning mechanism," Sherman said in 1997.

The lighthouse was automated in 1974. The last keeper was removed, but the Coast Guard retained the buildings and 1.3 acres at the station to serve as housing for an officer and family. After the devastating blizzard of February 1978, the wooden walkway between the house and tower was rebuilt.

A controversy soon erupted when the Coast Guard deactivated the fog signal. Local boaters and fishermen complained, and one collected thousands of signatures on a petition to save the fog signal. Some said the Coast Guard was silencing the signal to appease tourists. "To hell with the tourists," said one fisherman, "They don't go fishing. We need that horn when we're coming in, especially when our radar breaks down." In 1975 a switch to activate the fog signal was installed at the local police station. The fog signal is now automated, activated by a sensor.

Some repointing of the lighthouse was done in 1985. Inspections in the 1990s found that iron beams in the tower, installed to support a landing below the lantern level, had badly rusted, which caused the upper part of the tower to lift more than three inches. The beams needed to be replaced, along with about five to six feet of brickwork all the way around the tower.

Marsha Levy, a Coast Guard architect from Civil Engineering Unit Providence, completed the design work for the rehabilitation, and the Campbell Construction Group of Beverly, Massachusetts, carried out the work. Marty Nally and his crew removed and replaced about 3,000 bricks in the tower during the restoration, which was completed in August 2000. As part of the restoration project, glass block windows—of recent vintage—in the tower were replaced with new ones, and the dwelling's roof was replaced, using durable, wind-resistant shingles.

A Coast Guard family lives at the station. There is limited parking, but visitors should respect the privacy of the residents. Some tour boats from Gloucester pass Annisquam Light, and it can also be seen distantly from Wingaersheek Beach across the Annisquam River. The Thacher Island Association of Rockport offers occasional cruises that pass by; see www.thacherisland.org for more information.

CHAPTER 58

Early-1900s postcard of the rear range light at Ipswich.
From the collection of the author.

Ipswich Range Lights

1838, 1881–1939

Ipswich, on the north coast of Massachusetts, was once part of a larger area known to the local Indians as Agawam. In 1614 Capt. John Smith noted the potential for a "good and safe harbour" on the Ipswich River. The first English settlers, led by John Winthrop Jr., arrived in 1633, and fishing and shipbuilding soon prospered. Today Ipswich is said to have more seventeenth-century homes than any town in America.

Because of increasing maritime traffic in the early 1800s, reliable aids to navigation in the vicinity became a necessity. The federal government paid John Baker and Tristram Brown $10 for four acres of land and rights to "pass and repass" in 1837 for the purpose of establishing a light station on Castle Neck, east of the mouth of the Ipswich River.

After a congressional appropriation of $7,000 on March 3, 1837, two lighthouses were built, along with a brick one-and-a-half-story dwelling. The 29-foot brick towers—542 feet apart from each other on a nearly east-west axis—both originally held 10 lamps and reflectors each and exhibited fixed white lights. There were complaints that they could not be distinguished from the pair of fixed lights a few miles to the north on Plum Island, so the western light was soon given a revolving mechanism. When they were first built, the two lights served as a range for mariners coming through the main channel toward the mouth of the river.

The first keeper was Thomas Smith Greenwood, a native of Boston. Greenwood had gone to sea as a young man and eventually became the captain of clipper ships. He and his wife, Paulina Adams (Thurlow), had eight children. Greenwood also owned a large tract of land to the west of the light station, originally given to him by his wife's family. That land is now operated by the Trustees of Reservations as the Greenwood Farm Reservation.

On December 23, 1839, the coast was hit by the second of what became known as the triple hurricanes of 1839. The dramatic events that unfolded as the storm battered Ipswich are detailed in Edward Rowe Snow's book *Famous Lighthouses of New England.*

A Maine schooner, the *Deposit,* ran aground close to the light station. At dawn, a neighbor, Joseph Marshall, alerted Greenwood, who

Thomas Smith Greenwood was the first keeper of the Ipswich Range Lights. *Courtesy of Jim Danforth.*

ran to the scene to find that the remaining people on the vessel—including the captain's wife—were clinging to the rigging. Two crewmen had already died. The situation appeared dire, but the terrified screams of the captain's wife prompted Greenwood to make a desperate rescue attempt.

The keeper instructed Marshall to hold one end of a 200-foot line. Tying the other end around himself, Greenwood swam through the powerful, icy waves and reached the schooner. Marshall tied the other end of the line to a lifeboat, which he then boarded and launched into the breakers. Greenwood pulled the lifeboat, with Marshall in it, to the schooner.

Greenwood first tried to save Captain Cotterill, who was barely alive. As the captain was being lowered into the lifeboat, a great wave hit and the man was lost, along with the lifeboat. The captain's wife, witnessing her husband's drowning, became hysterical. Greenwood and Marshall convinced the woman to jump from the rigging into their arms. Two other survivors managed to reach shore by clinging to wreckage; Greenwood, Marshall, and the captain's wife were carried safely to shore by a great wave.

Captain Cotterill and three crewmen who died in the wreck were buried in Ipswich a few days later; 16 sea captains served as pallbearers. Greenwood and Marshall were awarded gold lifesaving medals by the Massachusetts Humane Society.

In his landmark 1843 report, I. W. P. Lewis was critical of the sloppy construction of the towers, which were planted in the sand with no foundations. Despite the newness of the station, the towers and dwelling were leaky, and the woodwork was rotten. The eastern (fixed) light had seven lamps with 13-inch reflectors, and the western (revolving) light had seven lamps with slightly larger reflectors. The apparatus in both lights, according to Lewis, was "of the rudest kind." The weight used for the revolving light was an old nail cask filled with stones, and the revolutions stopped frequently because of the "awkward arrangement of its machinery, and the dusts that sifts through the lantern above."

Lewis also noted that since the channel had shifted, the range lights no longer provided proper guidance into the Ipswich River. "A stranger attempting to enter the Ipswich river by aid of these lights," he wrote, "would run ashore in the south spit of Plum Island, which has increased in extent very much within a few years."

Joseph Dennis became keeper in 1841 at a salary of $400 yearly. In a statement for Lewis, he pointed out many shortcomings at the station. The towers were leaky, and the stairs became encrusted with ice in the winter. Dennis mentioned that he had hired a man to make an embankment around the dwelling "to prevent the sand from blowing away, and also to keep the vegetables from freezing in the cellar."

Greenwood returned for two more stints (1847–49 and 1853–61), as the keepers came and went depending on the political winds. Ebenezer Pulisfer (1843–47) and John Philbrook (1849–53) served between Greenwood's stays. Pulsifer was in charge in 1850 when an inspection reported that the towers were still leaky around their soapstone decks. The revolving mechanism in the western tower had apparently been replaced by this time, as it was reported that the "clock runs well."

Because the channel continually shifted, the towers had to be moved several times. At some point before 1867, the front light was replaced by a shanty-like affair known as the "bug light." In 1867 the front light had to be moved 550 feet. A great deal of repairs to the dwelling were carried out in the 1867–69 period, and the 989-foot

The original (1838) rear range lighthouse. *U.S. Coast Guard photo.*

plank walkway from the rear light to the dwelling was rebuilt.

In 1869 the Lighthouse Board announced that the front light had been "remodeled" and moved again, this time 120 feet. It was moved 97 feet to the south in 1885. The front light was briefly discontinued on August 2, 1898, but it was reestablished in a new structure six months later after vehement complaints from the local herring fishermen. It was moved at least one more time, in 1905.

By 1878 the rear tower was badly cracked, and the dwelling was severely deteriorated. To pay for the rebuilding of the house and rear tower, and to purchase additional property needed for the front range light, an appropriation of $10,000 was asked for, and Congress complied on March 3, 1879.

A new one-and-a-half-story dwelling was completed in 1880, and the new rear range tower was erected the following year. It was a 45-foot conical cast-iron tower similar to several built in New England during the 1870s and 1880s.

Succeeding Greenwood in 1861 was Benjamin Ellsworth, a native of nearby Rowley who turned to lightkeeping after years as a local pilot and fisherman. Ellsworth, whose initial salary was $400 yearly, moved to Ipswich with his wife, Lora, and seven children. He would stay until he was nearly 90 years old, a beloved local fixture and faithful public servant. He was also an "earnest Son of Temperance," according to one article; he didn't drink alcohol or smoke tobacco after the age of 15.

Ellsworth was responsible for several rescues of shipwreck victims during his long stay. In October 1863, he went to the aid of the passengers of an English schooner that had run aground. He later said he

The 1881 Ipswich rear range lighthouse and the front light, known as the bug light, circa late 1800s. *From the collection of the author.*

Keeper Benjamin Ellsworth and unidentified children at the light station, circa 1900. *Courtesy of Edith Sturtevant.*

could "scarcely help from laughing" when he reached the wreck, because the passengers thought he was there to rob them. One of the passengers, a lawyer, had to convince the others to go with Ellsworth, and they all survived.

Ellsworth was twice awarded bronze lifesaving medals. The first was for his rescue of two men from the rigging of a fishing vessel that had struck a sand bar near the station during a wintry squall in March 1873. Before Ellsworth came to their aid at 7:00 that morning, the men had clung to the frozen rigging of the boat for 15 hours.

During their long hours of agony, the men sent a canine companion swimming toward shore in the hope it would attract attention, but the dog was killed by ice floes before it reached the beach. Ellsworth later said that the men kept the circulation going in their faces by passing a plug of chewing tobacco back and forth.

About 5:00 a.m., Ellsworth's daughter Susan spotted what she thought were two smokestacks on a lighthouse tender. Ellsworth was able to discern that the dark shapes were not smokestacks, but men. He frantically rounded up two neighbors, and the three men launched a surfboat. They swiftly rowed to the nearly frozen men and brought them back to the warmth of the keeper's house.

The second medal-winning rescue occurred far from Ellsworth's home. He was visiting the Willows section of Salem, Massachusetts, when he spotted a boat that had capsized in rough seas. Two men were clinging desperately to the craft. Ellsworth rowed in a small boat against high wind and waves and managed to pull the two men from the water, just as one of them was about to slip under.

On another occasion, four women schoolteachers who were staying nearby tried to help Ellsworth launch a surfboat to go the aid of a local vessel. The surfboat—and the women—became mired in the sand. "You can't understand how hard we worked," said Ellsworth, "with those poor wretches howling for mercy." Luckily, the crew from a lifesaving station at Annisquam came to the victims' aid and all eight on the wrecked vessel were saved.

Ellsworth was widowed three times and was father to 12 children. During much of his 41-year stay at the light station in Ipswich, his daughter Susan served as his housekeeper and unofficial assistant keeper. An 1898 newspaper article described the station:

> About the house are several beautiful shell pictures, the result of Miss Susan's skill and artistic taste, and the house also contains the government circulating library. This is replenished every year by the lighthouse tender Verbena, when she brings the supply of oil, chimneys, wicks, and coal for the station. A plank walk, 400 feet long, leads from the keeper's dwelling to the lighthouse, and from there to the "bug light" near the beach, is another plank walk, 1,000 feet in length.
>
> Like his own home, everything about the lighthouse shows the nicest of care and is the very acme of neatness. . . . Mr. Ellsworth is still hale, hearty, and ruddy with the health-color that comes from the brisk sea-breezes that have whistled about him for nearly 40 years of life at the beach. He is one of the prize packages of Ipswich.

A 1902 article praised Ellsworth, but it also emphasized the work of his daughter Susan:

> It is Miss Susan Ellsworth who has tended the light. As a vestal virgin of old Rome fed the sacred fire on the altar, that it should never die out, or as a nun watches over the altar lamp and keeps it ever shining brightly, so this New England daughter of a lighthouse keeper has tended, with almost reverential feeling, this great light. . . .
>
> "It is my life," declared Miss Ellsworth recently, and as she said it, softly and with shining eye, a flush crept across her face, such as is seen on the face of a maiden when her lover's name is spoken.

Keeper Benjamin Ellsworth can be seen feeding his chickens near the rear range lighthouse in this view, circa late 1800s. *Courtesy of Edith Sturtevant.*

When Benjamin Ellsworth died of kidney disease in his ninetieth year in February 1902, it was said that he didn't appear to be more than 60 years old. His funeral at the Methodist church in Ipswich was well attended. A male quartet performed, and a newspaper reported, "Miss Harriett F. Gove rendered an old-time favorite, 'I Will Sing You a Song,' in a very impressive manner." Susan Ellsworth lived to be more than a hundred years old, surviving her 11 brothers and sisters.

Undated photo of the keeper's house and rear range light at Ipswich. *Courtesy of Barbara Kezer.*

The changes in the contours of the beach have been dramatic. According to Charles Wendell Townsend's 1913 book, *Sand Dunes and Salt Marshes*, the corner of the lighthouse property was originally about 82 feet from the high-water mark. In 1911 the same spot was 1,090 feet from the water. Townsend wrote that when Keeper Ellsworth first took charge, he could stand at the top of the main light, which was close to the water's edge at the time, and converse with men in boats offshore.

The front range light was discontinued for good in 1932, and the rear tower—which showed a fixed red light in its later years—was automated. By 1938 the sand was so high around the tower that maintenance personnel had to enter through a window high up on the tower. It was decided that a simple steel skeleton tower would be easier to maintain, and there would be no worry if sand built up around its base.

When government officials announced plans to remove the former rear range tower in 1938, many letters were sent in protest. Susan Ellsworth, then 90 years old, was one of the loudest voices of opposition. The local complaints couldn't stop the wheels of government, and the lighthouse was soon gone.

In 1939 the iron lighthouse was floated by barge to Edgartown on Martha's Vineyard to replace an earlier structure that had been badly damaged in the hurricane of September 1938, and the lighthouse in Ipswich was replaced by a utilitarian skeleton tower.

The keeper's house was used for a time as a meeting place by the Girl Scouts, Boy Scouts, and church groups. Then, for a while, it was rented by the week or by the weekend to summer vacationers. After a period of extensive vandalism, it was engulfed by fire in the early morning hours of a Saturday in October 1973. Town officials had the remains of the house removed a short time later.

Other than the decidedly unpicturesque modern steel light tower, there is no longer any reminder of this old light station in Ipswich. Crane Beach, the site of the former light station, is one of the North Shore's most beautiful beaches, but is not worth visiting as a lighthouse destination.

CHAPTER 59

Plum Island Light in October 2004. *Photo by the author.*

Plum Island Light

(Newburyport Harbor Light, Plumb Island Light)
1788, 1809, 1898

Plum Island, a nine-mile-long barrier island off the northern coast of Massachusetts, is divided among four communities: Newbury, Newburyport, Ipswich, and Rowley. The Plum Island River (actually a tidal estuary) separates the island from the mainland; a bridge first reached it when a small hotel was built on the island in 1806. During its nineteenth-century heyday as a resort, steamships and a trolley line serviced Plum Island.

Newburyport was an important port by the late 1700s. The approach to the harbor was dangerous, with a sand bar and shifting channels at the mouth of the Merrimack River, near the northern end of Plum Island. To aid shipping entering the river, local mariners at first built fires on the beach and erected poles holding torches. Two day beacons were erected in 1783, and for a time the Marine Society of Newburyport employed men to hoist lanterns on the beacons at night.

These methods proved inadequate, and in November 1787 the General Court of Massachusetts authorized the building of "two small wooden lighthouses on the north end of Plumb Island," provided the construction did not exceed "the sum of £300 lawful money." The lights would be an early example—possibly the first in the United States—of range lights, allowing mariners to keep one light lined up behind the other as they proceeded in the correct channel.

Financed by the merchants of Newburyport, the wooden light-houses were finished in the following year at a cost of a little more than £266. Each of the towers exhibited a fixed white light 37 feet above the sea. A notice in April 1788 announced:

> When any vessel shall fall into this Bay, or shall be forced in by distress of weather, and shall make these lights, she may run safely in, over Newbury Bar, observing the proper time of tide, and taking care to keep the two lights in one, until she gets within twice her length of the shore; then, directing her course by the beach, where is bold water, she may proceed, until abreast of the Western Lighthouse, where is good and safe anchorage in three fathoms of water.
>
> The Lighthouses now bear due East and West of each other, and are constructed as to be movable; and care will be taken, in case the

Bar shifts, to place them in such a situation as that the foregoing directions will always be a good guide to strangers.

The towers had to be moved often as the channel shifted; they were repositioned at least twice in 1795.

Aids to navigation came under federal jurisdiction in 1789, and the General Assembly of Massachusetts officially granted the light station to the United States in 1790. It isn't clear who maintained the lights in their earliest days, but President George Washington approved the appointment of Abner Lowell of Newburyport as keeper in March 1790.

Lowell, who may have served as keeper before his federal appointment, was known to all as "Uncle" because he was so kind-hearted, according to Fanny Louise Walton's book *Historic Nuggets of Newburyport*. He served for about 20 years and was succeeded by his son, Lewis Lowell.

In 1795 Tench Coxe, commissioner of revenue and supervisor of federal lighthouse operations at the time, suggested that Lowell's pay be raised from £66 to $266 (about £80) yearly, as the soil was unfit for a garden and the station was relatively isolated.

A signal tower was also in use at the station, enabling the light-keeper to signal with flags that a pilot was needed or a vessel was in trouble. A cannon was placed at the station to help the keeper summon aid in an emergency. Keepers at Plum Island frequently were involved in the rescue of shipwreck victims.

In May 1808, a violent tornado did much damage in Newburyport and knocked both lighthouses to the ground. Congress appropriated $10,000 in February 1809 and the towers were soon rebuilt.

In December 1823, 56-year-old Keeper Lewis Lowell lit a charcoal fire under the lantern in one of the lighthouses one cold night to keep the whale oil in the lamps from congealing. Lowell was overcome and died at his post of asphyxiation. The next keeper was his son, Joseph Lowell, who left in 1837, ending an almost half-century dynasty of Lowell family keepers.

Congress appropriated $4,000 for the "rebuilding" of the light-houses in July 1838, but it isn't clear if the towers were rebuilt or simply altered or repaired. Since only $950.44 of the appropriation was actually spent, it seems doubtful that they were completely rebuilt.

Three destructive storms swept the area in December 1839, destroying more than 300 vessels and taking at least 150 lives. During the first, on the 15th, many vessels were wrecked in the harbors of Gloucester, Newburyport, and Salem. At Plum Island, Keeper Phineas George reported that the island's hotel was surrounded by water during the storm, and a great deal of the eastern side of the island had washed away.

Also in 1839, the brig *Richmond Packet,* carrying a cargo of flour and corn into Newburyport, was driven by a gale onto the rocks. The captain of the ship managed to leap to a ledge and secure a line holding the ship. His wife attempted to cross to the rocks on the line, but the rope snapped. The crew tried to lower her down on a spar, but the heavy seas washed her away. The crew was saved and the captain's wife was the only casualty.

I. W. P. Lewis visited Plum Island during his survey of 1842. He described the two towers as "dilapidated, leaky, and out of position, as to the bar channel." Lewis noted that the keeper's dwelling, with three rooms on the first floor and two small rooms upstairs, was out of repair and "leaky on all sides."

Lewis stressed the value of the lights, writing that the "importance of ranging lights here to give the true direction of the channel can only be estimated by those acquainted with the hazardous nature of the navigation, which the many fatal shipwrecks on Plum Island sufficiently testify."

The wrought-iron lanterns on each tower were equipped with eight lamps and 12-inch reflectors when Lewis visited. He found the practice of moving the towers as the channel shifted to be unwieldy, and he proposed an innovative alternative to Stephen Pleasanton, the man in charge of lighthouses at the Treasury. Lewis's plan, he suggested,

Postcard view of Plum Island Light, circa 1890s. *From the collection of the author.*

would be much more practical and less expensive than the "old system of marshalling two crazy old towers about and over the sand hills."

Lewis proposed to erect two iron rails, 108 feet long, parallel to each other and about 100 feet apart, at heights of about 20 and 30 feet, respectively, from the ground. Each rail would support a lantern holding three lamps with 14-inch reflectors, and the lanterns would be moved along the rails as shifts in the channel dictated. Lewis quoted a sum of $1,315.91 for the construction of this ingenious system.

Pleasanton apparently wasn't impressed. Instead of the implementation of Lewis's plan, the two towers were fitted with new cast-iron lanterns, repaired, and moved into new positions more advantageous to navigation.

In 1855 a strange-looking small tower that became known as the "bug light" was added to the station. On August 8, 1856, one of the lighthouses was destroyed by fire during a thunderstorm. It was decided not to rebuild the tower. Both the remaining lighthouse and the bug light were moved periodically, including a move of one-third mile to the northeast in 1869.

The Lighthouse Board's annual report for 1871 announced that a fourth-order Fresnel lens had replaced a fifth-order lens in the lighthouse. In 1874 the lighthouse was moved close to the spot where the present lighthouse stands.

The shifting sands left the remaining tower and the bug light too far inland; they were moved several times between 1870 and 1882. In 1898, a new 45-foot conical shingled wooden tower was built next to the old one. The lens was transferred to the new lighthouse, and the old tower was removed. The present tower was first lighted on September 20, 1898.

George Kezer, seen here with his wife, was keeper at Plum Island 1924–33. *Courtesy of Barbara Kezer.*

Kerosene, used since 1877 in Plum Island lights, was replaced by electricity in 1927. For some years, keepers had the added duty of maintaining range lights across the mouth of the river at Salisbury Beach, as well as the range lights on the Newburyport waterfront. Harry Dobbins was keeper at the time of a 1940 article that stated that local Coast Guard personnel looked after the lights when the keeper was away.

Keeper Harry Dobbins and family, circa 1940. *Courtesy of the Friends of Plum Island Light.*

In 1951 the light was automated, and in 1981 it was changed to flashing green. It remains an active aid to navigation. The keeper's house is used as housing for an official of the Parker River National Wildlife Refuge.

The Coast Guard did a great deal of work on the lighthouse in 1993. Among other improvements, it replaced all the lantern glass, repainted the tower, dug a drain around the lighthouse, and created a new oak door and exterior storm door. The work was a team effort utilizing active duty, Coast Guard reserve, and Coast Guard Auxiliary personnel.

The lighthouse is now cared for by the Friends of Plum Island Light, a nonprofit organization founded in the 1990s. Among the organization's volunteers are Barbara Kezer and Arthur Woods, both descendants of Plum Island Light keepers.

The Coast Guard paid for the reshingling of the tower and the placement of new roofing tar on the catwalk in 1997. The Friends have taken over the maintenance of the lighthouse, and they have recently had the tower painted inside and out. They hope eventually to restore the 1898 keeper's house to the turn-of-the-twentieth-century period.

On May 10, 2003, ownership of the lighthouse was turned over to the City of Newburyport. The Friends of Plum Island Light continue to care for it under a lease agreement with the city.

Plum Island Light is easily reachable by car, and the lighthouse is sometimes open to the public on summer weekends. The Friends of Plum Island Light are selling commemorative bricks that are incorporated into the landscape design as a walkway in front of the lighthouse. Bricks are available for $50.00 each. For more information, write to the Friends of Plum Island Light, Inc., P.O. Box 381, Newburyport, MA 01950, or visit www.newburyportharborlighthouseplumis.org.

The Newburyport rear range lighthouse (top) and the front range lighthouse (bottom) in October 2004. *Photos by the author.*

Newburyport Harbor Range Lights

1873

There were privately maintained range lights in Newburyport's harbor as far back as 1790. In 1873 the Lighthouse Board reported:

> *Two range lights to guide up the River Merrimack to the city of Newburyport have been established . . . and were lighted June 1, 1873. The front light is on an iron tower, conical in form, 14 feet six inches high, located on Bayley's new wharf, and the focal plane is 25 feet above the sea. The rear light is about 350 feet . . . from the front light, on a brick tower, pyramidal in form, 32 feet high, and the focal plane is 47 feet above the sea.*

The lights were tended by local caretakers and later by the keepers stationed at Plum Island, a few miles away. The first keeper (until 1886) was George Stickney, at an initial salary of $250 yearly.

The front range light was altered early in its history, when a shingled, hexagonal wooden section was added to the top of the cast-iron tower. The rear tower was raised to its present height of 53 feet in 1901.

The range lights were discontinued in 1961, and the rear tower was sold into private ownership. The front range light was later moved a short distance onto the grounds of a Coast Guard station. In 1990 the front range light was given a more traditional appearance with the restoration of its original iron lantern.

David Hall, a developer and the owner of the rear range light, has been responsible for some refurbishing of the tower. The Lighthouse Preservation Society now offers gourmet dinners at the top of the lighthouse, May through October. Diners choose from the menus of some of Newburyport's finest restaurants.

☀ **The rear tower is at 61 Water Street, and the front tower is on the nearby grounds of Coast Guard Station Merrimack River. For information on the dinners at the top of the rear range light, write to the Lighthouse Preservation Society, 4 Middle Street, Newburyport, MA 01950, or call (800) 727-BEAM (2326).**

CHAPTER 61

The LV 112 underway. *U.S. Coast Guard photo.*

The Buzzards Bay "Texas tower" replaced a
lightship in 1961. *U.S. Coast Guard photo.*

Miscellaneous Lights and Lightships

Miscellaneous Lights

Pamet Light, 1849–1856

This lighthouse, on Cape Cod Bay near the mouth of the Pamet River in Truro, was in operation for a mere seven years. Built with a congressional appropriation of $5,000, it was a typical "Cape Cod–style" lighthouse of its day, a brick dwelling with an octagonal tower and iron lantern on its roof. A fixed red light was shown from 31 feet above mean high water.

According to payroll records at the National Archives, the light's three keepers were James Davis (1849–52), Reuben Burdett (1852–53), and John Kenney (1853–56). The light was discontinued on November 20, 1856, and the property was sold to a private owner. The final fate of the building isn't clear, and there are no known photographs in existence.

Nantucket Cliff Range Beacons, 1838, 1889

A light known as the Nantucket Beacon went into service in 1831; the light served as a rear range light used in tandem with Brant Point Lighthouse to aid mariners entering the harbor. As the channel shifted, it was decided a new pair of range lights was needed, and the Nantucket Cliff Range Beacons went into service in November 1838. Soon after the two small wooden square pyramidal towers (300 feet apart and about a half mile from Brant Point Light) were erected, they gained the nickname "Bug Lights." Their first keeper was Peleg Easton, at $300 yearly.

In his 1843 report to Congress, I. W. P. Lewis noted that the keeper's dwelling was often flooded in spring tides, and the lights were "not much better than a farthing candle." An 1850 inspection report called Keeper Easton a "fine old man" and announced that one of the towers had been moved "to suit the channel."

The original structures were replaced by round, wooden, shingled towers in 1889. The lights were eventually made obsolete as the channel shifted, and they were discontinued in 1912. The towers were purchased in 1921 by Frank B. Gilbreth and incorporated into his family's

cottage, known as "The Shoe," near Bathing Beach Road. Gilbreth's son
Frank Gilbreth Jr. later described the moving of the rear range tower:

> *An unforgettable sight for your chronicler, then a deliriously excited
> freckle-faced tyke of ten, was that of a group of Nantucket men with a
> horse and a ship's capstan, moving the larger lighthouse to its current
> location, close aboard and just abaft our present cottage. . . . The
> tower, jacked up and placed on rounded logs, was pulled at the rate
> of about thirty feet an hour. This was a ticklish job, fraught with
> considerable danger to all hands and the horse, and was performed
> bravely and successfully.*

Frank Gilbreth Jr. went on to author more than 12 books, including
the popular *Cheaper by the Dozen* (coauthored with his sister Ernestine
Carey), based on the true story of the family's life.

Salisbury Beach Range Lights, 1891–circa 1950

In 1891 a range light station was established at Salisbury Beach, at the
mouth of the Merrimack River, across from Plum Island Lighthouse.
The original structures were simply lanterns on poles, 12 feet high; the
rear light had a focal plane height of 32 feet, and the front light had a
focal plane height of 22 feet. By 1922 two pyramidal skeletal towers
were in place. Taller skeleton towers were in use by the early 1940s,
with focal plane heights of 56 and 36 feet.

At first, a keeper lived in a small wood-frame house near the range
lights. From 1891 to 1910, the keeper was William H. Pierce. Pierce and
his family were the first year-round residents of Salisbury Beach.

For some years, the keeper of the light station at Plum Island had
the additional duty of tending the lights at Salisbury Beach, so he
frequently had to cross the river. The range lights were deactivated
around 1950.

Lightships

Nantucket Lightship (Nantucket New South Shoal Lightship, Nantucket South Shoal Lightship, Nantucket Shoals Lightship), 1854–1983

A lightship was first placed about 19 miles from Nantucket, near Davis
South Shoal, in 1854. The spot warned mariners of the treacherous
Nantucket South Shoals, and it also marked the eastern end of the
Ambrose Channel into New York Harbor.

Over the years, the station was relocated a number of times, up
to 50 miles from Nantucket, in some of the most isolated and exposed
positions of any American lightship. Gustav Kobbe, in an 1891 article,

quoted an old whaling captain who told him the loneliest thing he had ever seen at sea was a polar bear adrift on a piece of ice in the Arctic Ocean; the second loneliest thing was the Nantucket South Shoals Lightship.

In his 1917 book, *Lighthouses and Lightships of the United States,* U.S. Lighthouse Commissioner George R. Putnam wrote: "Life on a lightship is somewhat dreary, but on such a station as this, it is not without excitement. During every fog the crew on the Nantucket ship knows that many vessels are heading directly for them, and in a storm, anchored as they are in the open sea, they may be far from comfortable."

The first wooden-hulled vessel here, the LV 11, was blown ashore during its initial year at the station and was stranded near Montauk Point, Long Island, New York. It was relocated to Brenton Reef, Rhode Island, in 1856.

The LV 1, a 103-foot wooden vessel built at Kittery, Maine, served at the station from 1856 to 1892. It broke anchor in August 1866 and was towed to Edgartown by a fishing schooner. In March 1872, a storm set the vessel drifting all the way to Tarpaulin Cove in the Elizabeth Islands, where it was recovered and towed to New Bedford. In all, the LV 1 went adrift 12 times during its years at the station.

A British steamship, the *Castle City,* was wrecked a few miles south of the lightship on Christmas Eve 1887. The crew made it to the lightship in their lifeboats, and they remained there about a week before a tender arrived and removed them; the provisions on the lightship had almost run out.

The iron-hulled LV 54 was next at the station, which was relocated 10 miles southwest of its former position. It was succeeded in 1896 by the steel-framed, iron-plated LV 58, built at Toledo, Ohio. It was the first American lightship to have a complete upper deck above the main deck.

The 123-foot steel- and wood-hulled LV 66 was at the station from 1896 to 1907. On October 11, 1896, a storm sent it drifting for about 6 miles before the tender *Azalea* was able to get it under tow. Just a few days later, it was relocated more than 17 miles southwest of its former position, and the station was officially renamed Nantucket Shoals. It broke loose several more times, including February 3, 1897, when it drifted 65 miles to Falmouth in a gale.

During a bad storm on December 10, 1905, a relief vessel at the station developed a leak in its fire room. By the time the tender *Azalea* arrived, the pumps had failed. The tender crew attempted to tow the lightship to New Bedford, but the lightship crew was forced to abandon their vessel shortly before it sank about 18 miles northwest of its station.

The next vessel stationed here was the LV 85, a 136-foot steam-powered, steel-hulled ship built in Camden, New Jersey. In October 1917, the lightship provided refuge for more than a hundred seamen whose merchant vessels had been sunk by German U-boats just a few miles to the south. The LV 85 was succeeded by the LV 106, a 132-foot steel-hulled vessel built in Bath, Maine. The LV 106 remained at the station until 1931, when it was replaced by the 135-foot LV 117, built at Charleston, South Carolina. The LV 106 was sold to Suriname in 1968 and served in that South American nation until 1981; it is now an abandoned hulk on the Suriname River.

The LV 117 was sideswiped by the ocean liner *Washington* in January 1934. The collision did serious damage, but the crew escaped injury. The incident proved minor compared with the tragedy of May 15, 1934.

In thick fog in the midmorning, with visibility only about 500 feet, the White Star liner *Olympic*—sister ship to the *Titanic*—smashed directly into the LV 117 while cruising at 16 knots. Within minutes, the lightship sank to the bottom. Four of the crewmen died instantly, and three others died later of their injuries. George Braithwaite, in command of the vessel, and three crewmen survived.

In 2004 a diving crew called the Boston Sea Rovers recovered the 1,200-pound fog bell and other artifacts from the wreck of the LV 117, with the intention of displaying the items in museums. The federal government, charging that the divers didn't have the rights to the artifacts, filed suit. The items were ultimately handed over to the government.

Because the *Olympic* was British, as reparation England paid for the construction of a new lightship, the LV 112. After interim service by the LV 106, the LV 112 was placed at the station in 1936. The 148-foot steel-hulled, steam-powered vessel, constructed by Pusey and Jones at Wilmington, Delaware, for about $300,000, was the largest American lightship ever built. It remained at the Nantucket Shoals until 1942, when it was withdrawn and replaced by a lighted buoy for the remainder of World War II.

The LV 112 returned to the station after the war. Except for a two-year period (1958–60) when it served as a relief vessel, it remained at the Nantucket Shoals until 1975. It then became a floating museum at Nantucket until 1984. After spending some years as an educational vessel in Portland, Maine, it was on display at Captain's Cove Seaport in Bridgeport, Connecticut, from 1997 to 2002. It was then acquired by the National Lighthouse Museum on Staten Island, New York. The development of the museum on Staten Island has stalled, and in late 2006 the lightship faced eviction from its temporary home at Oyster Bay,

Long Island, New York. The board of directors of the National Lighthouse Museum, in an attempt to save the vessel, offered it for sale in December 2006 for one dollar to any nonprofit group willing to care for it. The WLV 612, built in 1950 at Curtis Bay, Maryland, was at the station beginning in 1975. In 1985, after its decommissioning, the WLV 612 was sold to the Boston Educational Marine Exchange. It was subsequently acquired by the Metropolitan District Commission (MDC) in Boston. The vessel suffered severe damage when its pipes were allowed to freeze. The MDC sold it in 2000 via auction on eBay to Bill and Kristen Golden, who have turned it into a charter vessel with luxurious accommodations. See www.nantucketlightship.com for details. At this writing, the lightship is for sale at an asking price of $7.6 million.

From 1979 to 1983, the WLV 612, designated *Nantucket I,* alternated 21-day stints at the station with the WLV 613, also known as *Nantucket II.* The WLV 613, built in 1950, was the last vessel at the station. After its decommissioning in December 1983 as the last active lightship in the United States, it became a floating museum at Boston's Charlestown Navy Yard. It was eventually sold to a private owner, a businessman named Jack Baker, and ported in Wareham, Massachusetts. It has a single lantern on a tripod tower, which replaced its two original lights in 1953.

Pollock Rip Lightship, 1849–1969

This station was about four and a half miles east of Monomoy Point, at the east end of the shallow area known as Pollock Rip. Thousands of vessels passing along the coast relied on the lightship for more than a century. The first vessel placed here in 1849 was the 98-foot oak-hulled LV 2, originally launched as the *General Taylor.* The 1850 edition of *Blunt's American Coast Pilot* called the LV 2 a "miserable light" that was "often out of place."

The LV 2 was plagued by ice and stormy weather, and it went adrift at least four times in its 26-year stay at Pollock Rip. The LV 40 stayed at the station less than two years and was followed by the wooden-hulled, schooner-rigged LV 42. The LV 42 was struck by other vessels several times and occasionally went adrift in rough weather. The ship was off its station so frequently that it was nicknamed the "happy wanderer."

The 120-foot schooner-rigged LV 47 spent more than 30 years (1892–1923) at the Pollock Rip station. Collisions continued with sickening regularity; on December 5, 1899, a steamer ran into the lightship, breaking the lamp chimneys and knocking the crewmen to the deck.

In 1923 the station was relocated to the northeast end of a newly dredged channel. A buoy marked the station during World War II. The last vessel here was the 133-foot steel-hulled LV 114 (WAL 536), which was at the station from 1958 to 1969. Finishing out its career at the Portland, Maine, station, it was decommissioned in 1971 after 41 years of service. The LV 114, built at the Albina Iron Works in Portland, Oregon, had been the first lightship to make the voyage from the West Coast to the East Coast via the Panama Canal.

The LV 114 was acquired by the city of New Bedford in 1975, and the name "New Bedford" was emblazoned in white on its bright-red hull. After some restoration work and several years as an attraction on the city's waterfront, the vessel was ultimately neglected. In May 2006, it developed a leak and rolled to one side at its berth. The city paid more than $200,000 to a company to right the ship, but thieves soon stripped it of many of its fittings.

Despite objections from preservationists, New Bedford city officials announced that the lightship would be auctioned in the fall of 2006. A public auction and an attempt to sell the vessel on eBay were negated. A New Bedford firm then agreed in June 2007 to buy the lightship for scrap at a cost of $10,000, after its historic artifacts had been removed. As this book goes to press, it appears the vessel, one of the last of its kind, will soon be history.

Pollock Rip Slue Lightship (Pollock Rip Shoals Lightship), 1902–1923

The Pollock Rip Shoals lightship was established in 1902, about four miles north of the Pollock Rip lightship. The name of the station was officially changed to Pollock Rip Slue in 1913.

Only one vessel served at this station, the LV 73 (WAL 503). Built in 1901 at Baltimore, it was a two-masted, 124-foot, steel-hulled, steam-powered vessel. The lightship was plagued by ice and broke adrift in storms on more than one occasion. A February gale in 1921, its winds exceeding 75 miles per hour, washed over the ship and did extensive damage. The LV 73 was relocated in 1924 to the Vineyard Sound station.

Cross Rip Lightship (Tuckernuck Shoal Lightship), 1828–1963

This station, off the northeast end of Tuckernuck Shoal in Nantucket Sound, was established in 1828. The first small 76-foot vessel, designated simply as "H," was soon repositioned to Cross Rip Shoal, in mid–Nantucket Sound. It remained there until a gale tore it loose from anchor and drove it ashore at Cape Poge on Chappaquiddick Island.

The second vessel, the G, was very similar to the H. Three days after Christmas in 1866, the ship was set adrift in a storm. It was sighted in distress by the keeper of Nantucket's Great Point Light, and there was a widespread belief that it must have been lost with all hands.

Word reached Nantucket in early February that the lightship crew had been picked up by a passing vessel shortly before it sank. The crewmen were taken all the way to New Orleans, and they returned to Nantucket about two weeks later. Several more lightships served here during the station's long history. In early 1918, the 80-foot LV 6 was surrounded by ice during a bitterly cold stretch. The captain requested permission for his crew to abandon ship, but he was ordered to remain at the station. On February 5, the lightship was torn from its mooring as the ice broke apart. It was last seen drifting to sea 23 miles from its station; the ship and its six-man crew were never seen again.

A 1960 article in *Yankee* magazine by Lawrence F. Willard described the daily routine of the crewmen of the Cross Rip Lightship. "On off hours," wrote Willard, "they read, watch television, play cards, fish, and watch the evening movie—there is a different one each night. Quarters are cramped, with one room serving as both recreation and dining room and the sleeping area consisting of tiny two-man staterooms with double bunks."

The last vessel on the station, the LV 102, was decommissioned in 1963. It was converted into a fishing vessel out of Ketchikan, Alaska.

Great Round Shoal Lightship, 1890–1932

The Great Round Shoal station was about 5.8 miles east of Great Point Lighthouse, at the northern tip of Nantucket. It was an important aid, used by many Cape Cod fishermen as well as coastal shipping traffic. The initial vessel at the station, the 81-foot LV 9, served only a little more than a year; it was followed by a succession of five other vessels in the station's forty-two-year history. An improved system of buoys replaced the lightship in 1932.

One of the most notable incidents here was the April 1893 wreck of the Norwegian bark *Mentor,* while the LV 42 was at the station. The crew from the vessel was able to reach the lightship in a lifeboat. The *Mentor* remained afloat, and 14 Nantucket islanders rowed 25 miles to recover the vessel. They were awarded $1,000 each for their trouble by the underwriters of the bark.

As part of Boston's celebration of the Fourth of July in 1940, the LV 42, which had been sold after its decommissioning, was set on fire. The remains were used as scrap.

Handkerchief Shoal Lightship, 1858–1951

This station was established in 1858 at the eastern end of Nantucket Sound, about 5 miles north of Nantucket's Great Point. The LV 4, originally built for the Bishop and Clerks Station, served here until 1916.

The schooner-rigged vessel, only 64 feet long, was replaced by an older and even smaller vessel, the LV 3, in 1916.

The 121-foot LV 41 served here from 1924 to 1930, followed by the 101-foot LV 98 (WAL 521). The LV 98 was struck by a freighter in a thick fog early one morning in July 1951, and one of the crewmen was injured. The LV 98 served until it was replaced by a lighted buoy later in 1951.

Stonehorse Shoal Lightship (Shovelful Shoal Lightship), 1852–1963

This station, about a half mile off the southern tip of Monomoy Island, was originally called Shovelful Shoal, after the tiny bit of shoal that showed above water. The shoal was part of a much larger formation said to have the shape of a horse's head at low tide. The station was officially renamed Stonehorse Shoal in 1916.

The tiny single-masted, schooner-rigged LV 3, only about 70 feet long, served at the station until 1916. The lightship was rammed by other vessels many times in its career, including more than a dozen times between 1884 and 1906. After retiring from lightship duty in 1924, it became a floating clubhouse in Boston for a time.

The station was replaced by buoys in 1963. The last vessel to serve here, the 102-foot LV 101 (WAL 524) eventually went to Virginia, where it was painted with the name "Portsmouth" on its side. Designated a National Historic Landmark in 1989, it is operated as a museum by the Portsmouth Naval Shipyard Museum. See www.portsnavalmuseums.com or call (757) 393-8741 for more information.

Succonnessett Shoal Lightship, 1855–1912

This station was off Cotuit on Cape Cod, in the north channel of Nantucket Sound. A light vessel in the vicinity was first suggested in 1838, but concerns with ice delayed the establishment of the station until $12,000 was appropriated by Congress in 1852.

Only two vessels served here, the LV 13 (1855–62) and the LV 6 (1862–1912). After serving faithfully at the Succonnessett Shoal for a half century, the LV 6 was lost with all hands at the Cross Rip station in 1918. The Succonnessett Shoal Lightship was replaced by a buoy in 1912.

Hedge Fence Shoal Lightship, 1908–1933

This lightship was located off Edgartown on Martha's Vineyard, marking a dangerous shoal in Vineyard Sound. It was established, at least in part, in response to a plea from the Boston Chamber of Commerce in 1903: "The depth of water in the approach to Hedge Fence Shoal is such that little or no indication is given of its proximity until a vessel is practically on the shoal."

Five vessels served here in the station's 25-year history, beginning with the 135-foot steel-hulled LV 90, built at Quincy, Massachusetts.

Late at night on November 11, 1925, the 120-foot LV 49, which had been at the station only a few months, was rammed by the Scandinavian streamer *M. C. Holm* and sank within 15 minutes. The crewmen were all able to row safely ashore. The LV 49 was raised and repaired, and it went on to serve until 1941 at various stations. The final vessel at Hedge Fence Shoal was the LV 41, formerly at Handkerchief Shoal. It was the last wooden-hulled lightship in the Lighthouse Service.

Hen and Chickens Lightship, 1866–1954

Named because it consists of one large rock (the hen) and a number of smaller ones (the chickens), Hen and Chickens Shoal is about 3.7 miles from Cuttyhunk Island, at the entrance to Buzzards Bay. The first vessel stationed here in 1866, the 81-foot wooden-hulled LV 5, was replaced after a brief period by the 98-foot LV 8.

The LV 8 was actually the former U.S. Navy brig *Arctic;* it had been altered for use as a lightship in 1859. In its first incarnation, the vessel had taken part in the rescue of a party of explorers near the North Pole. The LV 8's first station assignment was Frying Pan Shoal, North Carolina, where it was seized and subsequently sunk by Confederate forces. It was raised, repaired, and assigned to Hen and Chickens Shoal in 1867.

The 98-foot schooner-rigged LV 2 was at the station from 1877 to 1907. The vessel was knocked from its station more than once by ice and storms, but it never had a serious mishap. Tragedy touched the station in 1897, however, when two crewmen died at sea on route to the lightship from New Bedford.

The last lightship here, the 136-foot steel-hulled LV 86, was removed in 1954 when the station was replaced, along with the Vineyard Sound station, by the new Buzzards Bay station.

Vineyard Sound Lightship (Sow and Pigs Lightship), 1847–1954

Sow and Pigs Reef was long a scourge to mariners at the western end of Vineyard Sound, about 2.3 miles southwest of Cuttyhunk Island. The 78-foot schooner-rigged lightship designated "Z," also known as the *President,* was first stationed here in 1847. The little vessel was frequently swept off its station in rough weather. It was succeeded in 1861 by the 98-foot LV 7, fresh from six years at the Minot's Ledge station.

The LV 41 spent more than 40 years (1876–1910 and 1915–24) at the station. It broke adrift several times, including March 4, 1891, when it parted chain in a gale; it eventually was able to anchor off East Chop Light on Martha's Vineyard.

The 124-foot LV 73 was stationed here in 1924 after more than two decades at the Pollock Rip and Pollock Rip Slue stations. It had survived punishing storms in 1921 and 1924, but the steel-hulled lightship met its match in the hurricane of September 14, 1944. The vessel went down with all hands, and all 12 crewmen on board were lost. (See chapter 10 for more on this disaster.)

Divers discovered the wreck of the LV 73 in 1963, and the ship's bronze fog bell was recovered. It was later incorporated into the U.S. Lightship Memorial on New Bedford's waterfront. When the memorial was dedicated in September 1999, Harold Flagg, the last living crewman from the LV 73 (he was on shore leave at the time of the hurricane), read the names of the men lost as the bell was tolled for each one. Seamond Ponsart Roberts, who had watched from Cuttyhunk Lighthouse with her father, Keeper Octave Ponsart, as the lightship's lights disappeared in the sea on the night of the hurricane, traveled from Louisiana to attend the memorial dedication.

New Bedford's U.S. Lightship Memorial also memorializes the men lost on the Cross Rip Lightship (LV 6) in 1918 and the Nantucket Shoals Lightship (LV 117) in 1934.

Buzzards Bay Lightship and Tower, 1954, 1961, 1997

A lightship was first stationed at the entrance to Buzzards Bay, about four miles southwest of Cuttyhunk Island, in 1954. Until 1959, the LV 86—built in 1907 at Camden, New Jersey—served at the station. It was succeeded by the LV 110, then by the Buzzards Bay Light Tower (Buzzards Bay Entrance Light) in 1961.

The Buzzards Bay Light Tower, commissioned in November 1961, was the first so-called Texas-tower lighthouse in the U.S. The towers are named for their resemblance to Gulf Coast oil-drilling platforms. The tower consists of four concrete-filled steel pilings, topped by a 75-square-foot deck and helicopter platform, living quarters, and a light tower with rotating DCB 224 aerobeacons. The structure was staffed by resident Coast Guard personnel until its 1980 automation.

By the early 1990s, the tower's legs had become unstable and the boat-landing facilities had been washed away. Faced with restoration costs in the hundreds of thousands of dollars, the Coast Guard decided instead to replace the tower with a smaller, three-legged structure. The current tower, painted red and exhibiting a flashing white light every 2.5 seconds, was completed in 1997.

Boston Lightship, 1894–1975

In 1892 the Lighthouse Board suggested that a lightship should be moored six miles southeast of Boston Light. "The well-known difficulty in determining the location of the Boston Light in thick weather," read the recommendation, "and the doubtful utility of the bell at Minot's Ledge are strong reasons why this aid to navigation should be established."

The first 100-foot iron-hulled vessel at the station, the LV 54, was built in 1892 at West Bay City, Michigan. It had two lanterns on its masts, each with eight oil lamps and accompanying reflectors. Before it was stationed in Boston Bay in October 1894, the vessel had served briefly at the Nantucket South Shoal Station.

The LV 54 served until 1940 at the Boston station, then returned for three more years (1943–46). It narrowly averted disaster on September 29, 1915, when it was struck by the steamer *Quantico*, which opened a 10-foot hole two feet above the waterline. The lightship was towed to the buoy depot at Lovell's Island and quickly repaired.

One of the most memorable incidents of the vessel's career occurred on December 8, 1935, when it was rammed by the British steamer *Seven Seas Spray*. The collision left a gash at the waterline, but the quick-thinking crewmen plugged the hole with bags of coal. The vessel stayed afloat long enough to be towed to a drydock for repairs.

James Dean, a Boston stock exchange executive, took it upon himself to make life for the lightship men a little less lonely. For some years before his death in 1942, Dean delivered the Sunday editions of Boston newspapers to the lightship. Upon his death, Dean left $10,000 to the Permanent Charity Fund of Boston so that the deliveries could continue.

Four more vessels were stationed here before the station was discontinued in 1975, including the 115-foot LV 118 (1962–72). Built in 1938, the LV 118 was the last lightship designed and constructed by the Lighthouse Service. The final vessel here was the WLV 189, a 128-foot steel-hulled ship built at Bay City, Michigan.

The WLV 189, which had spent most of its career at the Diamond Shoals station off North Carolina, was decommissioned in 1975. It was sold for use as a floating museum in Atlantic City, but while under tow it was struck by a tanker and severely damaged. It languished until 1994, when it was deliberately sunk as part of New Jersey's artificial reef program.

SELECTED BIBLIOGRAPHY

For more extensive bibliographies for each lighthouse, see www.lighthouse.cc

Adamson, Hans Christian. *Keepers of the Lights.* New York: Greenberg, 1955.

Allen, Everett S. *A Wind to Shake the World.* Boston: Little, Brown, 1976.

Baker, William A. *A History of the Boston Marine Society 1742–1967.* Boston: Boston Marine Society, 1968.

A Baker's Island Chronicle 1964–1988. Salem, MA: Baker's Island Association, 1989.

Ball, David. *To the Point: The Story of Scituate Light and Cedar Point.* Published by the author, 1994.

Banks, Dr. Charles Edward. *Annals of Tisbury.* Circa 1908; published online by the Historical Records of Tisbury at www.history.vineyard.net.

Barnstable Patriot, various articles 1855-2005.

Bates, Raymond, Jr. *Shipwrecks North of Boston,* vol. 1, *Salem Bay.* Beverly, MA: Commonwealth Editions, 2000.

Bayley, William H., and Oliver O. Jones. *History of the Marine Society of Newburyport, Massachusetts.* Newburyport, MA.: Daily News Press, 1906.

Becker, Gloria. "Gurnet (or Plymouth) Light and Its Children." Undated typescript, Plymouth Public Library.

Bentley, William. *The Diary of William Bentley, D.D., Pastor of the East Church, Salem, Massachusetts.* Gloucester, MA: P. Smith, 1962.

Berger, Josef. *Cape Cod Pilot.* 1937. Reprint, Boston: Northeastern University Press, 1985.

Blasdale, Mary Jean. *Artists of New Bedford: A Biographical Dictionary.* New Bedford, MA: Old Dartmouth Historical Society, 1990.

Bliss, William Root. *Quaint Nantucket.* Boston: Houghton Mifflin, 1896.

Blunt, Edmund, and George W. Blunt. *Blunt's American Coast Pilot.* New York: Edmund and George W. Blunt, 1850.

Boston Globe, various articles 1875-2006

Boston Herald, various articles 1921-96.

Boston Post, various articles 1933-50.

Boston Transcript, various articles 1880-1916.

Bosworth, Janet F., ed. *Cuttyhunk and the Elizabeth Islands from 1602.* Cuttyhunk, MA: Cuttyhunk Historical Society, 1993.

Brewington, M. V. "The Backon on Backer's." *Essex Institute Historical Collection,* vol. 101. Salem, MA: Essex Institute, 1965.

Butler, Karen T. *Nantucket Lights.* Nantucket, MA: Mill Hill Press, 1996.

Candage, G. F. "Boston Light and the Brewsters." *New England Magazine,* October 1895.

Cape Cod Chronicle, various articles 1987-93.

Cape Cod Times, various articles 1979-2005.

Claflin, James W. *Historic Nantucket Lighthouses: Brant Point.* Worcester, MA: Kenrick A. Claflin and Son, 2003.

——— . *Historic Nantucket Lighthouses: Sankaty Head.* Worcester, MA: Kenrick A. Claflin and Son, 2003.

Clark, Admont G. *Lighthouses of Cape Cod, Martha's Vineyard and Nantucket—Their History and Lore.* East Orleans, MA: Parnassus Imprints, 1992.

Clifford, Candace. "The First Minot's Ledge Lighthouse." *Keeper's Log,* Spring 2002.
Clifford, Mary Louise, and J. Candace Clifford. *Women Who Kept the Lights: An Illustrated History of Female Lighthouse Keepers.* Williamsburg, VA: Cypress Communications, 1993.
Coast Guard Bulletin. 1939-43.
Columbian Courier, various articles 1799-1803.
Copeland, Melvin T., and Elliott C. Rogers. *The Saga of Cape Ann.* Freeport, ME: Bond Wheelwright, 1960.
Currier, John J. *The History of Newburyport, Massachusetts, 1764–1905.* 1906. Reprint, Somersworth, NH: New Hampshire Publishing Company, 1977.
Cusack, Betty Bugbee. "Bishop and Clerks Lighthouse." *Lighthouse Digest,* May 1995.
——— . *Collector's Luck: A Thousand Years at Lewis Bay, Cape Cod.* Stoneham, MA: G. R. Barnstead Printing Company, 1967.

Davidson, Donald W. *America's Landfall: The Lighthouses of Cape Cod, Nantucket and Martha's Vineyard.* West Dennis, MA: Peninsula Press, 1993.
D'Entremont, Jeremy. "Bill Grieder's Lighthouse Boyhood." *Cape Cod Today,* May 30, 2002.
——— . "Eastern Point Light." *Lighthouse Digest,* May 1999.
——— . "From Sparkplug to Matchstick: Boston's Deer Island Light." *Lighthouse Digest,* November 1999.
——— . "Graves Light: Granite Guardian of Boston's Outer Harbor." *Lighthouse Digest,* February 2001.
——— . "Josephine Norwood: First Lady of Boston Light." *Lighthouse Digest,* September 2003.
——— . "The Lighthouse Inn: A Shining Beacon for Travelers." *Lighthouse Digest,* September 2001.
——— . "The Lost Light of Egg Rock." *Lighthouse Digest,* February 1999.
——— . "Memories of Coast Guard Days at the Gurnet." *Lighthouse Digest,* March 2003.
——— . "Sally Snowman's Lighthouse 'Soul Work.'" *Lighthouse Digest,* May 2002.
De Wire, Elinor. *Guardians of the Lights: The Men and Women of the U.S. Lighthouse Service.* Sarasota, FL: Pineapple Press, 1995.
——— . "Keeping Boston Light." *Mariners Weather Log,* Summer 1991.
——— . "A Point of Light." *Navy Times,* March 9, 1992.
Deyo, Simon. *History of Barnstable County.* New York: H. W. Blake, 1890.
Digges, Jeremiah. *A Modern Pilgrim's Guide to Cape Cod.* Provincetown, MA: Modern Pilgrim Press, 1947.
Dobbins, Ruby Kelly, *The Additional Keeper.* Published by the author, 2003.
Drake, Samuel Adams. *Nooks and Corners of the New England Coast.* New York: Harper and Brothers, 1875.

Eckels, Donald, and Robert Fraser. "Minot's Ledge." *Keeper's Log,* Fall 1995.
Ellis, Margaret Francis. "Life in a Lighthouse." Originally published May 1963 in *Quest.* Reprinted in *Ebb and Flow of Life on Sandy Neck,* privately printed, 1998.
Emerson, Amelia Forbes. *Early History of Naushon Island.* Boston: Thomas Todd, 1935.
Emerson, Willie. *First Light: Reminiscences of Storm Child and Growing Up on a Lighthouse.* East Boothbay, ME: Post Scripts, 1986.
Fall River Herald News, various articles 1967-2006.
Falmouth Enterprise, various articles 1968-88.

Folger, Eva C. G. *The Glacier's Gift*. New Haven, CT: Tuttle, Morehouse, and Taylor, 1911.

Fraser, Robert. "I. W. P. Lewis: Father of America's Lighthouse System." *Keeper's Log,* Winter 1989.

Fraser, Robert, and J. Brian West. "The Three Sisters of Nauset." *Keeper's Log,* Summer 1990.

Fred's Place, www.fredsplace.org.

Garland, Joseph. *Boston's Gold Coast: The North Shore 1890–1929*. Boston: Little, Brown, 1981.

———. *Eastern Point*. Beverly, MA: Commonwealth Editions, 1999.

———. *The Gloucester Guide*. Rockport, MA: Protean Press, 1990.

Gibbs, Alice M., with Irene Flanagan. "Bourne's Lighthouse at Sandwich Harbor Entrance." *Falmouth Enterprise*, May 11, 1984.

Gleason, Sarah C. *Kindly Lights: A History of the Lighthouses of Southern New England*. Boston: Beacon Press, 1991.

Glennon, Beverly Morrison. *Dartmouth: The Early History of a Massachusetts Coastal Town*. New Bedford, MA: Garrison Wall Publishers, 2001.

Gloucester Daily Times, various articles 1974-2001.

Grubb, Russell. *Thacher Island . . . An Adventure with Keeper Russell Grubb*. Published by the author, 1988.

Hardy, Josiah. Diary, 1870–95. Typescript, Chatham Historical Society.

Harris, C. E. *Hyannis Sea Captains*. Yarmouth Port, MA: Register Press, 1939.

Haskell, Louise T. *The Story of Cuttyhunk*. New Bedford, MA: American Press, 1953.

Hawes, Charles Boardman. *Gloucester by Land and Sea*. Boston: Little, Brown, 1923.

Hewitt, Arthur. "Signals of the Sea." *The Outlook,* November 1904.

Holland, Francis Ross, Jr. *America's Lighthouses: An Illustrated History*. 1972. Reprint, New York: Dover, 1988.

Howland, John A. "Family Tragedy at Cape Poge Light." *Dukes County Intelligencer,* February 1989.

Hoyt, Henry Sears. "Want to Buy a Lighthouse?" *Yankee,* November 1939.

Jennings, Harold B. *A Lighthouse Family*. Orleans, MA: Lower Cape Publishing, 1989.

Jennings, Herman A. *Provincetown; or, Odds and Ends from the Tip End*. 1890. Reprint, Provincetown, MA: Peaked Hill Press, 1975.

Johnson, Arnold Burges. *The Modern Light-House Service*. Washington, DC: GPO, 1890.

Killen, Jeanette Haskins. Interview by Nantucket Historical Association, August 5, 2001.

Kittredge, Henry C. *Cape Cod: Its People and Their History*. 1930. Reprint, Hyannis, MA: Parnassus Imprints, 1987.

Kobbe, Gustav. "Life in a Lighthouse." *Century,* January 1894.

Kruza, J. A. *Lighthouse Handbook for Massachusetts and New Hampshire*. Franklin, MA: Kruza Kaleidoscopix, 1988.

Lawrence, Charles A. "Egg Rock." 1933. Typescript, Lynn Historical Society.

Lawson, Ellen N. "Sandy Neck Lighthouse History." Typescript, May 2001. Copy on file at Sturgis Library, Cape Cod Community College.

Lewis, A. N. *The Picture of Nahant*. Lynn, MA: T. Herbert and Co., 1855.

Lighthouse clippings files Records Group 26, National Archives, Washington, DC.
Lighthouse Digest, various articles 1993-2007.
Lighthouse Directory, www.unc.edu/~rowlett/lighthouse/.
Lighthouse Explorer Database, www.lhdepot.com/database/searchdatabase.cfm.
Lighthouse Friends, www.lighthousefriends.com.
Lighthouse letters, 1792–1809. Publication number M63 (microfilm), National Archives, Washington, DC.
Lighthouse Service Bulletin. 1931-35.
Lighthouse site files. Records Group 26, National Archives, Washington, DC.

Macy, William F. *The Story of Old Nantucket.* Boston: Houghton Mifflin, 1915.
Marcus, Jon. *Lighthouses of New England.* Stillwater, MN: Voyageur Press, 2001.
Massachusetts Historical Commission, Boston. Lighthouse information forms for National Register of Historic Places nominations.
Massachusetts Magazine. February 1789.
Mikal, Alan. *Exploring Boston Harbor.* North Quincy, MA: Christopher Publishing House, 1973.
Mills, Robert. *The American Pharos, or Light-House Guide.* Washington, DC: Thompson and Homans, 1832.
Morison, Samuel Eliot. *The Maritime History of Massachusetts.* 1921. Reprint, Boston: Northeastern University Press, 1979.
Morris, Charles W. E. "The Gurnet." *Pilgrim Society Notes,* July 1982.
Motta, Arthur P., Jr. "A History of Palmers Island and Its Lighthouse." In 150th Anniversary Relighting Program, August 30, 1999. New Bedford, MA: City of New Bedford, 1999.

Nantucket Inquirer. and *Nantucket Inquirer and Mirror,* various articles 1850-2005.
National Historic Landmark Nomination, Cape Ann Light Station (Thacher Island Twin Lights). Prepared by Paul St. Germain, Thacher Island Association, December 1998.
New Bedford Mercury, various articles 1818-1837.
New Bedford Standard and *New Bedford Standard Times,* various articles 1923-2006.
New England Lighthouses: A Virtual Guide, www.lighthouse.cc.
New England Magazine. "The Building of Minot's Ledge Lighthouse." October 1896.
New York Times, various articles 1857-1985.
"Night Beacon," www.nightbeacon.com.
Noble, Dennis L. *Lighthouses & Keepers.* Annapolis: Naval Institute Press, 1997.

Orr, Molly Tornberg. Interview transcript, August 29, 1990. OH 90-28, Sound Archives, G. W. Blunt White Library, Mystic Seaport Museum.

Parsons, Eleanor C. *Thachers: Island of the Twin Lights.* Canaan, NH: Phoenix, 1985.
Paterson, Stanley C., and Carl G. Seaburg. *Nahant on the Rocks.* Nahant, MA: Nahant Historical Society, 1991.
Perley, Sidney. *History of Salem.* Salem, MA: Sidney Perley, 1924.
Pratt, Enoch. *History of Eastham, Wellfleet, and Orleans, Massachusetts, 1644–1844.* Yarmouth, MA: W. S. Fisher and Co., 1844.
Provincetown Banner, various articles 1995-2002.
Putnam, George R. "Beacons of the Sea." *National Geographic,* January 1913.
———. *Lighthouses and Lightships of the United States.* Boston: Houghton Mifflin, 1933.

Quincy Patriot Ledger, various articles 1958-2004.

Quinn, William P. *Shipwrecks around Cape Cod.* Farmington, ME: Knowlton and McLeary, 1973.

Railton, Arthur. "Cape Poge Light: Remote and Lonely—First Part of the History of Our Least Known Lighthouse." *Dukes County Intelligencer,* November 1983.

——— . "Cape Poge Light: Remote and Lonely—Part Two." *Dukes County Intelligencer,* February 1984.

——— . "Cape Poge Light: Remote and Lonely—Concluding Part of the History." *Dukes County Intelligencer,* May 1984.

——— . "Gay Head Light Gets the Wondrous Fresnel." *Dukes County Intelligencer,* May 1982.

——— . "Gay Head Light: The Island's First." *Dukes County Intelligencer,* February 1982.

Rich, Earle. *Cape Cod Echoes.* Orleans, MA: Salt Meadow Publishers, 1973.

Ricketson, Daniel. *The History of New Bedford.* New Bedford, MA: Published by the author, 1858.

——— . *New Bedford of the Past.* Boston: Houghton Mifflin, 1903.

Rickmers, Ruth E. *Wellfleet Remembered, Past to Present in Pictures,* vol. 1. Wellfleet, MA: Blue Butterfly Publications, 1981.

——— . *Wellfleet Remembered, Past to Present in Pictures,* vol. 2. Wellfleet, MA: Blue Butterfly Publications, 1982.

Roberts, Seamond Ponsart. "Lighthouse Memories." Cuttyhunk, MA: Cuttyhunk Historical Society, 2001.

——— . Mail, e-mail, and phone correspondence with the author, 1999–2006.

Romaine, Lawrence B. "Yankee Pluck at Bird Island Light." *Old-Time New England,* Winter 1963.

Ryder, Marion Crowell. *Cape Cod Remembrances.* Taunton, MA: William S. Sullwold Publishing, 1972.

Salem Evening News, various articles 1919-2006.

Salem Gazette, various articles 1798-1835.

Salter, Harry. "Bug Light." Bookards, a Salter Publication, 1995.

Searle, Richard Whiting. *Marblehead Great Neck.* Salem, MA: Newcomb and Gauss, 1937.

Small, I. M. *Highland Light, North Truro, Massachusetts: This Little Booklet Tells You All about It.* Truro, MA: Town of Truro, 1927.

Small, Isaac M. *Shipwrecks on Cape Cod.* 1928. Reprint, Chatham, MA: Chatham Press, 1970.

Smith, Fitz-Henry. *Storms and Shipwrecks in Boston Bay.* Boston: Privately printed, 1918.

——— . *The Story of Boston Light.* Boston: Privately printed, 1911.

Smith, Mary Lou. *The Book of Falmouth.* Falmouth, MA: Falmouth Historical Commission, 1986.

Snow, Edward Rowe. "America's Most Dangerous Lighthouse." *Boston Herald,* April 18, 1971.

——— . *Famous Lighthouses of America.* New York: Dodd, Mead, 1955.

——— . *Famous Lighthouses of New England.* 1945. Updated edition (as *The Lighthouses of New England*), Beverly, MA: Commonwealth Editions, 2002.

——— . *The Islands of Boston Harbor.* 1935. Updated edition, Beverly, MA: Commonwealth Editions, 2002.

————. "Keepers of Boston Light." *Quincy Patriot Ledger,* April 22, 1967.

————. "Keepers Busy at Eastern Point." *Boston Herald Traveler,* April 12, 1971.

————. "The Maritime Benjamin Franklin." *Brockton Enterprise,* August 9, 1955.

————. *Minot's Light: 120 Years of Service to Mariners.* Quincy, MA: Quincy Cooperative Bank, 1981.

————. "A Needless Tragedy." *Yankee,* January 1958.

————. "New Facts Trace Busy Career of Man Who Built Minot's Light." *Quincy Patriot Ledger,* October 2, 1958.

————. "Nobska Point Lighthouse." *Quincy Patriot Ledger,* February 2, 1965.

————. *A Pilgrim Returns to Cape Cod.* 1946. Updated edition, Beverly, MA: Commonwealth Editions, 2003.

————. *The Romance of Boston Bay.* Boston: Yankee Publishing Company, 1946.

————. *Storms and Shipwrecks of New England.* 1946. Updated edition, Beverly, MA: Commonwealth Editions, 2003.

————. *The Story of Minot's Light.* Boston: Yankee Publishing Company, 1940.

Snowman, Sally, and James G. Thomson. *Boston Light: A Historical Perspective.* Plymouth, MA: Snowman Learning Center, 1999.

Starbuck, Alexander. *The History of Nantucket.* Boston: C. E. Goodspeed, 1924.

Stevenson, D. Alan. *The World's Lighthouses from Ancient Times to 1820.* 1959. Reprint, Mineola, NY: Dover, 2002.

Surveyor. "The Sea-swept Lighthouse of Minot's Ledge." February 1981.

Swan, Marshall W. S., annotator. *Thacher's Woe and Avery's Fall.* Rockport, MA: Sandy Bay Historical Society and Museum, 1985.

————. *Town on Sandy Bay.* Canaan, NH: Phoenix, 1980.

Sweetser, M. F. *King's Handbook of Boston Harbor.* Boston: Houghton Mifflin, 1882.

Talbot, Frederick A. *Lighthouses and Lightships.* Philadelphia: J. B. Lippincott, 1913.

Theriault, Albert A., and Elizabeth A. Theriault. *Ned's Point Lighthouse, Mattapoisett, Massachusetts: A Chronicle and Related Information.* Mattapoisett, MA: Ned's Point Publishing, 2002.

Thompson, Frederic L. *The Lightships of Cape Cod.* Portland, ME: Congress Square Press, 1983.

Thoreau, Henry David. *Cape Cod.* 1864. Reprint, Orleans, MA: Parnassus Imprints, 1984.

Tower Notes. Newsletter of the American Lighthouse Foundation, 1998–2006.

Townsend, Charles Wendell. *Sand Dunes and Salt Marshes.* Boston: D. Estes and Company, 1913.

Transactions of the American Society of Civil Engineers. "Minot's Ledge Lighthouse." 1870.

Trayser, Donald. *Barnstable: Three Centuries of a Cape Cod Town.* Hyannis, MA: F. B. and F. P. Goss, 1939.

U.S. Bureau of Light-Houses. *Two-Hundredth Anniversary of Boston Light.* Washington, DC: Government Printing Office, 1916.

U.S. Congress. Condition of the Light-houses on the Eastern Coast. Rep. no. 282, 27th Cong., 3rd sess., 1843.

————. Report of the General Superintendent of the Light-house Establishment. Ex. Doc. no. 11, 31st Cong., 2nd sess., 1850.

————. Report on Light-house Establishment from I. W. P. Lewis. H. Doc. 183, 27th Cong., 3rd sess., 1843.

U.S. Coast Guard District One Aids to Navigation Office, Boston. Aids to navigation files.

U.S. Coast Guard Historian's Office, Washington, DC. Lighthouse files.

U.S. Coast Guard Historian's Office, www.uscg.mil/hq/g-cp/history/collect.html.

U.S. Coast Guard Lightship Sailors, www.uscglightshipsailors.org.

van Roden, Mary Daubenspeck. *Nauset Light: A Personal History.* Lyme, NH: Blackrabbit Press, 1995.

Vineyard Gazette, various articles 1940-90.

Vineyard Voices: Words, Faces and Voices of Island People. Edgartown, MA: Vineyard Oral History Center of the Martha's Vineyard Historical Society, 1998.

Walton, Fanny Louise. *Historic Nuggets of Newburyport.* Newburyport, MA: Newburyport Press, 1958.

Washington Post, various articles 1904-91.

Watson, Elizabeth. "The Modern Settlement of Cuttyhunk." *Old Dartmouth Historical Sketches,* no. 1, 1903.

Weare, Nancy V. *Plum Island: The Way It Was.* Newbury, MA: Newburyport Press. 1993.

West, J. Brian. *Life on the Edge: The Lighthouses of Nauset.* Published by the author, 1989.

Wheeler, Wayne. "America's First Lighthouse: Boston Light." *Keeper's Log,* Fall 1984.

Willard, Lawrence F. "Last Days of the Lightships." *Yankee,* December 1960.

Willoughby, Malcolm F. *Lighthouses of New England.* Boston: T O. Metcalf, 1929.

Wilson, Fred A *Some Annals of Nahant.* 1928. Reprint, Nahant, MA: Nahant Historical Society, 1977.

Wise, DeWitt D. *Now, Then, Baker's Island.* Salem, MA: Baker's Island Association, 1964.

Worthylake, George. "Only Yesterday: Mayo Beach." *Keeper's Log,* Summer 1994.

Writers' Program (Mass.). *Boston Looks Seaward: The Story of the Port, 1630–1940. Compiled by Workers of the Writers' Program of the Work Projects Administration in the State of Massachusetts.* 1941. Reprint, Boston: Northeastern University Press, 1985.

Yarmouth Register, various articles 1850-1998.

INDEX

Abbie B. Cramer (schooner), 417–418
Aberdeen Hall Hotel, 137
Acushnet River, 21
Adams, John Quincy, 28
The Additional Keeper (Dobbins),
210–211, 250
A.J. Miller (schooner), 332
Alexander, Barton S., 273–274
Alger, Cyrus, 161, 266
Alice (powerboat), 297
Allen, Eben W., 108
Allen, Ethan, 130
Allen, James, 108
Allen, Joseph Chase, 84
Allen, W.S., 117
Allison, James T., 173
American Lighthouse Foundation, 206,
211, 217, 263
America (warship), 402
Anderson, Russell and Mazie, 327
Anderson, William L., 118, 233
Andrews, Benjamin, 409
Annisquam Light, 414–419
Antoine, Joseph, 271–272
Aquinnah, 71
Aquinnah Light. *see* Gay Head Light
A.R. Tucker (bark), 16
Art Moderne style, 41
Atchison, William, 53, 75
Attaquin, Max, 75
Atwood, William and Sarah, 221, 237
Azalea (tender), 117–118, 439

Babcock, Maurice A., 38, 321–323, 324,
335
Bailey, George, 226–227, 390
Bailey, James S., 353–354
Baker, Amos C., Jr., 13, 15–17
Baker, Amy, 17, 19
Baker, Charles A., 15, 18–19
Baker, Franklin, 144
Baker, Jack, 441
Baker, John, 421
Baker, W.W., 139
Baker's Island Association, 379–380
Baker's Island Light, 370–381
Ball, David, 257, 263
Ball, Robert, 314
Barker, Benjamin, 255

Barlow, Samuel, 45
Barnard, John Gross, 273
Barnstable, 143, 229
Baron, Joseph Barboza "The Animal,"
404
Barrett, Moses, 319–320
Barrus, J.E., 101
Barry, Joseph, 357
Barton, Otis, 181–182
Bass River Light, 148–153
Bates, Abigail, 256–257
Bates, James Y., 259
Bates, Rebecca, 256–257
Bates, Simeon and Rachel, 256
Bates, Thomas, 320
Bates, William, 261
Baxter, Henry, 229, 230
Baxter, James, 229
Baxter, Lucy Hinckley, 231
Baxter, Thomas P. D., 230–231
Bearse, David, 165
Bearse, George Smith, 165–166
Bearse, James, 144
Beck, Charles, 286
Bennett, John W., 268–273
Bentley, William, 371
Benton, Chris, 392
Berger, Josef, 213
Berry, Judah, 117–118
Bettencourt, Arthur and Rita, 76
Beverly, 367
Bicknell, Alvin, 242
Bicknell, Dolly, 242–243, 252–253
Billingsgate Light, 219, 222–227
Bird Island Light, 31, 32–39
Bird Island Preservation Society, 38–39
Bishop and Clerks Light, 138–141
Bittersweet (cutter), 206, 413
Blake, Solomon, 372
Blanchard, Howard, 241
Blizzard of 1978
    Monomoy Point Light, 167
Bohm, Fred, 239–240, 298
Bonney, Pelham, 161
Boonisar, Richard, 246
Borden Flats Light, 1–3
Bostel, John, 392–393
Boston Harbor Association, 328
Boston Light, 256, 259, 310–329

Boston Light: A Historical Perspective (Snowman and Thomson), 329
Boston Lightship, 447
Bowdoin, James, 59
Bowers, Larry, 336–337
Boyd, Everett F., 296
Bradley, Charles J., 38–39
Branco, Thomas and Charlotte, 205–206
Brant Point Light, 104–111
Bray, Alexander and Maria, 400, 406
Brennock, Michael Neptune, 275
Brewster Islands, 311, 312
Broad Sound Channel Range Lights, 290–293
Brown, Benjamin, 130
Brown, Ephraim, 351
Brown, Ira P., 339
Brown, Tristram, 421
Bruce, Jonathan, 317
Bryant, David, 178–179
"The Bug" (Hyannis), 143
Bug Light (Duxbury Pier Light). *see* Duxbury Pier Light
Bug Light (Narrows Light). *see* Narrows Light
Bug Light (Salter), 240
Bunker, Alexander D., 127–128
Bunker, Obed, 114
Bunker Hill (schooner), 384
Bunker Hill (steamer), 66
Burdett, Reuben, 437
Burdick, Albert, 277
Burgess, Eunice, 247
Burgess, Joseph, 247
Burgess, Nathaniel, 246
Burgess, William W., Jr., 237
Burnham, George, 387
Burt, Bill, 183
Butler, John, 299
Butler Flats Light, 13, 14–19
Buzzards Bay, 5, 41, 45
Buzzards Bay Lightship and Tower, 446
By Monomoy Light (Cairn), 167

Cagney, James, 83
Cairn, North T., 167
Cameron, George I., 66
Cameron, Ned, 405
Campbell Construction Group, 111, 199, 243, 289, 407
Camp Wightman, 287
Cape Cod Canal, 46, 249
Cape Cod Echoes (Rich), 221

Cape Cod Light. *see* Highland Light
Cape Cod Museum of Natural History, 167
Cape Cod National Seashore, 206, 207
A Cape Cod Native Returns: You Can Go Home Again (Sparrow), 178
Cape Cod Pilot (Berger), 213
Cape Cod Remembrances (Ryder), 150
Cape Cod (Thoreau), 179, 192–193, 209, 214, 225, 267
Cape Neddick Light, 65
Cape Poge Light, 46, 93, 96–103, 123
Capron, Harry, 221
Carney, Walter, 141
Carpender, Edward W., 5, 11, 30, 35, 52, 59–60, 64, 79–80, 92, 98, 106–107, 114–115, 135, 160, 169–170, 179, 189–190, 201, 213, 219, 223–224, 229–230, 247, 257–258, 286, 317
Carroll, George and Dottie, 404, 405
Carson, Frank S., 61
Carter, John B., 288
Castle City (steamship), 439
Cavanaugh, John, 348
Cedar Point Association, 262–263
Center for Coastal Studies, 206
Chace, Malcolm G., 137
Chamblin, Delaney, and Scott, 354
Chapman, George, 372
Chapman, John, 110
Chapman, Luther, 141
Chappaquiddick Island, 46, 93, 97
Chase, James, 150
Chase, Theodore L., 118
Chase, Thomas L., 217
Chatham, 155, 169
Chatham Light, 168–175
Cheaper by the Dozen (Gilbreth and Carey), 438
Chesapeake (frigate), 317
Children's Memorial (Edgartown Light), 94–95
Christian, Bud, 250–251
Christian, Paul, 250–251
Christiana (schooner), 99–100
City of Columbus (steamer), 74
City of Salisbury (freighter), 336, 337
Clark, Admont G., 156
Clark, Charles A., 36
Clark, John, 34–35
Clark's Point Light, 10–13
Clear, Warren J., 233
Cleveland, Grover, 17, 41

Cleveland Ledge Light, 40–43, 49
Coast Guard Auxiliary Flotilla 11-1, 175
Coast Guard Auxiliary Flotilla 11-02, 69
Cobb, Elizah, 223
Coffin, Daniel, 114
Coffin, David, 106–108
Coffin, Jonathan, 114
Coggeshall, George Folger, 115–117
Cohasset, 265
Cohasset Rocks, 265
Coleman, Amanda, 182
Coleman, Eugene L., 181–182
*Collector's Luck: A Thousand Years at
Lewis Bay, Cape Cod* (Cusack), 140–141
Collins, Michael, 223
Conrad, Hawkins, 183, 184–185
Conry, Joseph A., 301
USS *Constitution* (frigate), 372
Cook, John, 402
Cook, John Newell, 275
Cook, Mrs., 140
Cook, Samuel, 202
Cook, Tobias, 318
Cory, Charles Barney, 136–137
Coskata-Coatue Wildlife Refuge, 123
Coskata Lifesaving Station, 117
Covo, Joseph, 3
Cowie, George, 22
Coxe, Tench, 188, 430
Craig, Frank W., 110
Crea, Vivien S., 369
Creed, Levi L., 276–277
Creed, Winfield L., 292
Crocker, Crosby L., 75
Crocker, Sylvanus, 92
Crosby, Joshua, 180
Cross Rip Lightship, 101, 116, 442–443
Crowell, Warren, 149, 150
Cummings family, 181
Curran, Michael J., 296
Cusack, Betty Bugbee, 140–141
Cushing, Zeba, 258
Cushman, J. Frank, 261
Cuttyhunk Light, 50–57, 248, 302

Dade, William, 416–417
Daggett, Peter, 64
Daggett, Silas, 87
Daggett, William, 403
Dan, or the Gale of Seventy-Three
(Eisener), 302
D and K Building Movers, 252
Darling, Ezekiel, 351–352

Dartmouth, 5
Daubenspeck, Mary, 183, 185
Davidson, Richard, 206
Davis, Frank Allen, 61, 241, 249
Davis, Frank Arthur, 249–250
Davis, George, 241, 384
Davis, James, 404, 437
Davis, Jeff, 175
Davis, John, 410, 418
Davis, Olive, 249
Davis, William, 65
Day, George, 415–416
Dean, James, 447
Dearborn, Henry, 255, 317, 397
Dearborn, Henry A.S., 33, 189, 201,
255–256, 285, 373
Deer Island Light, 122, 239, 240, 294–299
Delano, John, 34
DeMille, Archie, 3
Dennis, 149
Dennis, Joseph, 423
Deposit (schooner), 421–422
Derby, Charles, 213–214
Derby Wharf Light, 358–361
Desharnais, Armand and Betty, 405
Devens, Richard, 316
Dever, Dennis, 327–328
Dewey, Mary Drayton, 355–356
Dexter (cutter), 74
Diligence (brig), 220
Dill, Herman, 225–226
Dixon, Richard, 111
Doane, Solomon, 161
Dobbins, Harry, 432
Dobbins, James Hickley and Ruby Kelley,
210–211, 250
Dodds, Paul, 326
Doherty, Patrick, 326
Dolby, George, 81, 101
Douglass, Hugh, 319
Downton, George and Ruth, 263
Drake, Samuel Adams, 128–129
Drayton, Henry T., 354–356
Drayton, Lawrence, 354
Dripps, Craig, 77, 94
Duane, James Chatham, 203
Dubois, Joseph, 101
Duff, Peter, 19
Dumpling Rock Light, 4–9
Dunbar, George, 165
Dunbar, Jesse, 255
Dunham, Charles, 342–344
Dunham, Isaac, 267–268, 270

Dunham, Isaac A., 268
Dunham, Jack, 214
Dunham, John Thomas, 214–215
Duvall, Harry, 327
Duxbury Pier Light, 231, 236–243, 277

Earcularious (schooner), 61
East Chop Light, 86–89
Eastern Point Light, 386–393
Eastham, 177
Eastman, Russell B., 31, 151, 356
Easton, Peleg, 437
Edgartown, 91
Edgartown Harbor Light, 65, 79, 90–95, 100
Edge, John, 313
Egg Rock Light, 338–349
Eisener, Alfred G., 53, 248, 302–303
Eldredge, Enoch, 155
Eldredge, Wallace and Louise, 46–47
Elizabeth Foley (schooner), 118
Elizabeth Islands, 51, 59
Ella M. Storer (schooner), 384
Ellis, Francis and Margaret, 233–234
Ellis, George and Nancy, 45
Ellis, George E., 257
Ellis, William B. and Dorcas, 369
Ellsworth, Benjamin, 424–427
Ellsworth, Susan, 426–427
Elsie M. Smith (vessel), 164–165
Elwine Frederick (bark), 115
Emerson, Willie, 323
Enterprise (schooner), 229
Etrusco (freighter), 261–262
Eva (scow), 31
Eventide (catboat), 137
Everett, Edward, 275
Exile (brig), 339

Fall River, 1
Falmouth, 63
Famous Lighthouses of New England (Snow), 23, 28, 260, 286, 318, 421–422
Fanny Pike (ship), 320
Farrah (dog), 326
Farley, John, 296
Figarado, Manuel, 282
First Light (Emerson), 323
Fisher, George H., 100–101
Fisher, Peggy, 175
Fiske, Augustus, 38
Fitzpatrick, George H., 282–283, 336
Flagg, Harold, 446

Flanagan, Frank and Irene, 49
Flanders, Samuel, 74
Flo F. Mader (schooner), 390
Flying Fish (whaleboat), 27
Flying Santa, 23, 28, 57, 67, 84–85, 120, 206, 304
Folger, George Franklin, 129
Folger, George W., 155
Folger, Peter, 129
Fontenot, Henry, 7–9
Fontenot, May, 8–9
Fort Andrew, 246
Fort Pickering Light, 362–365
Fort Pickering Light Association, 365
Fort Strong, 288–289
Fort Taber, 12–13
Foster, Ada, 345, 346, 348
Fraize, Clem, 153
Franklin, Benjamin, 129, 313, 323
Fratus, Joseph, 277
Freeman, Gershorn C., 308
Friend, Charles, 389
Friends of Flying Santa, 85
Friends of Plum Island Light, 433
Friends of Plymouth Light, 252–253
Friends of the Boston Harbor Islands, 328
Frothingham, Ted, 141
Fuller, A.W., 146
Fuller, Sam, 94

Gallatin, Albert, 71–72
Gallatin (steamer), 237
Gallop, Fred P., 85
Gardiner, Samuel, 269
Gardner, Henry R., 116
Gardner, Oliver C., 115
Garland, Joseph, 383
Gartland, Emma, 12
Gay Head Light, 70–77, 88
Gay Head (steamer), 109
General Arnold (brigantine), 246
George, John, 311–312
George, Phineas, 430–431
Georgie, Herman, 1
Ghosts
    Bird Island Light, 34, 39
    Boston Light, 326–327
    Long Island Head Light, 285
    Minot's Ledge Light, 279
    "Sea Witch of Billingsgate," 227
Gibbs, Frederic H., 412
Gibbs, William Francis, 411–412, 412
Gifford, Albert, 46

Gifford, Carry H., 46
Gilbreth, Frank B., 437–438
Gilbreth, Frank B., Jr., 438
Gill, Abijah, 224
Gill, Charles, 255
Gill, James B., 160
Gill, Nathan, 180
Gill, Nathaniel, 255
Glass, Ronald E., 43
G Lightship, 442
Gloucester, 383, 387, 415
Goodwin, John, 353
Gorham, Edward, 320
Gosnold, Bartholomew, 51, 63, 71, 125
Government Island (Cohasset), 275
Granby, Alan, 146–147
Graves, Ebenezer, 351
Graves Ledge light station, 131
Graves Light, 330–337
Great Brewster Island, 307
Great Island, 135
Great Island Club, 137
Great Point Light, 112–123, 157, 166
Great Round Shoal Lightship, 160, 443
Greely, Philip, 268–269, 270–271
Green, Edward Howland Robinson, 6
Green, Joseph W., 351
Greenwood, Thomas Smith, 421–422
Grieder, Bill, 75–76, 118–120, 239
Grieder, Frank, 75–76, 118–120, 239
Griffin, Gustavus, 415
Grocier, John, 189, 193
Grubb, Russell, 405
Gunderson, Mills, 156
Gunderson, Stanley, 156–157
Gurnet Light. see Plymouth Light
Gustavus, George T., 38, 54, 66, 174

Hadley, Elliot C., 38, 333–335, 378, 401
Hadley, Elliot C., Jr., 335
Hale, Albert Giddings, 400
Hale, William, 398
Hall, David, 435
Hall, Larnet, Jr., 30
Hallett, Almoran, 144
Hallett, Daniel Bunker, 143
Hallett, Daniel Snow, 143, 144
Hallett, Osborne, 67, 69
Hall family, 183
Hamblin, Calvin, 129–130
Hamilton, Enoch, 191
Hamilton, Frederick M. and Bonnie, 68
Hammond, Charles H., 173

Hammond, Joseph, Jr., 255
Hammond, Leonard, 28
Hancock, John, 396
Hancox, Frederick J., 69
Handkerchief Shoal Lightship, 160, 443–444
Harding, Joseph, 155
Harding, Walter C., 155–156
Harding, Warren G., 47
Harding's Beach Light. see Stage Harbor Light
Hardy, Grace, 172
Hardy, Josiah, II, 172–173
Harmon, George, 38
Harrington, Rick, 94
Harris, John, 364
Harris, Walt, 240
Hart, John Leland, 293, 321, 322
Haskell, Sydney, 400
Haskins, A. G. "Ted," 216
Haskins, Archford ("Ted") Vernon, 120–121, 132
Haskins, Beverly, 120–121
Haskins, Gregg, 283
Hatch, Henry Y., 178
Hayden, John, 59–61
Hayes, John, 313–314
Hedge Fence Shoal Lightship, 444–445
Hen and Chickens Lightship, 55, 445
Herman Melville (whaleboat), 27
Hewitt, Arthur, 248–249
Higgins, Russell, 268
Higgins, Willis, 248–249
Highland Light, 169, 180–181, 186–199
Hill, Carl Deland, 391
Hinckley, Charles, 6, 7, 140–141
Hinckley, James W., 204
Hinckley, Kee, 234
Hindley, Charlotte, 67
Hindley, Joseph, 67, 69, 77
The History of New Bedford (Ricketson), 11
H Lightship, 442
Hobbs, George, 376
Hodgson, Thomas, 19
Holbrook, Jesse, 191
Holbrook, Joseph, 220
Holmes Hole Light. see West Chop Light
Homer, James Lloyd, 286
Homer, Winslow, 384
Hooper, Charles, 342
Hooper, Dennison, 417–418
Hooper, Edward, 417–418
Hooper, Nathaniel R., 307

Hopkins, Constant, 189
Hopkins, Michael, 189
Horte, Albert M., 354
Horton, Henry, 180
Hospital Point Light, 366–369
Hovey, Chandler, 357
Howard, Alfred A., 118, 155–156
Howard, George Addison, 47–48
Howard, William James, 47–49
Howe, Collins, 170–171
Howe, James M., 43
Howes, Eunice Crowell, 231
Howes, Jacob S., 231
Howes, Marcus E., 117
Howland, Cornelius, 12, 51–52
Hoyt, Henry Sears, 157
Hurricane of 1938
    Bird Island Light, 38
    Borden Flats Light, 3
    Butler Flats Light, 18
    Dumpling Rock Light, 7–9
    Edgartown Harbor Light, 93
    Palmer's Island Light, 24–25
    Prudence Island Light (R.I.), 174
Hurricane of 1944, 240
    Bass River Light, 152
    Cleveland Ledge Light, 42
    Cuttyhunk Island Light, 56
Hurricane of 1954 (Carol)
    Bass River Light, 152
    West Chop Light, 83
Hurricane of 1991 (Bob)
    Bass River Light, 152
    Chatham Light, 175
Hurricane of 1996 (Edouard), 184
Huse, Malcolm N., 309, 348
Huston, Samuel, 396
Hyannis Harbor, 135
Hyannis Harbor Light, 142–147
Hydro-Dredge, 122
Hyland, Carol, 280
Hyland, Janice, 146–147

Ida Lewis (cat), 326
"I Love You Light," 280
International Chimney Corporation, 39,
    184, 198, 206
Ipswich, 421
Ipswich Range Lights, 420–427
Irene and Mary (tugboat), 141
Isherwood, Benjamin F., 127
The Islands of Boston Harbor (Snow), 289
I.W. Hine (schooner), 417

J. Goodison Company, 185
Jacobs, Cindy, 95
Jamieson, George A., 231–233
Jansson, Ron, 235
Jason, Herb, 263
Jasper, John, 192
Jefferson, Thomas, 72
Jenkins, Thornton A., 108
Jennings, Charles, 165, 303–305, 320–321,
    322
Jennings, Harold, 165, 183, 303–305,
    320–321
Jennings, Herman A., 213
J.F. Fitzgerald Company, 41
Johanson, Robert L., 123
Johnson, Arnold Burges, 312
Johnson, Charles, 196
Jones, Asa L., 163
Jones, Maro B., 163–164
Jones, Payson A., 69
Jorgeson, James, 233
Joseph, William A., 196
Joseph Fish (schooner), 287
Josephus (bark), 191–192
Joy, Benjamin Whitford, 46–47
Joy, Everett, 110–111

Kalisz, Frederick M., Jr., 27
Kearny (freighter), 67
Kennedy, Edward M., 122, 123, 241, 385
Kenney, John, 437
Kerigan, John, 314
Kezer, Barbara, 433
Kezer, George, 305, 401, 432
Kezer, Harlan, 401
Kezer, Thatcher Warren, 401
Killen, Jeanette Haskins, 121, 123
King, Cabet, 127
King, Caleb, 73
King, Harold D., 25
King, Merrill B., 298
Kirby, Edward P., 241
Kirkwood, James, 396
K & K Painting, 166, 385
Knox, Thomas, 316
Kobbe, Gustav, 278–279, 438–439
Krogram, Francis, 225

La Hogue (warship), 256–257
Laidlaw, Kathleen, 262, 263
Landseer, Edwin Henry, 341
Lang, Fred, 234
Larkin, Adrian, 412

Larnard, Joe, 326
Larsen, Eugene N., 131–132
Lavigne, Joseph and Mary Ellen, 324
Lawrence, Charles A., 344–345, 349
Lawrence, Edward D., 45
Lawrence, Jonathan, 285–286
Leighton, Waldo, 67, 146
Levy, Marsha, 419
Lewis, Alonzo, 339
Lewis, I.W.P. (1843 report), 6, 21, 35, 52, 64,
    72–73, 80, 92, 98–99, 107, 115, 125–126,
    136, 160–161, 179, 190–191, 202, 220,
    224, 230, 258–259, 265–266, 318, 331,
    352, 375, 383–384, 388, 397–398, 410,
    416, 422–423, 431–432, 437
Lewis, Stephen, 180
Lewis, Winslow, 72, 81, 99, 170, 178, 189,
    190, 191, 202, 223, 256, 258, 285, 317,
    318, 389, 397, 398
Lewis Bay, 135
"Lighthouse Army of Two," 256–257
A Lighthouse Family (Jennings), 165,
    303–304
Lighthouse Inn. see Bass River Light
"The Lighthouse" (Longfellow), 276
Lighthouse Pennant, 132
Lighthouse Preservation Society, 413
Lighthouses and Lightships of the United
    States (Putnam), 439
Lighthouses of Cape Cod, Martha's
    Vineyard and Nantucket (Clark), 156
"The Lighthouse Tragedy" (Franklin), 313,
    323
Lincoln, Benjamin, 187, 371–372
Lincoln, Frederick W., 275
Lincoln, Keith, 167
Lincoln, Levi, 286
Lincoln, Marshall, 257
Lincoln, Theodore, 188
Lindberg, John and Helen, 293
Liscom, Samuel, 308
Little Brewster Island, 318
Lodge, Henry Cabot, 261, 430
Loftus, Matthew, 2
Long, William, 318
Longfellow, Henry Wadsworth, 276
Long Island Head Light, 284–289
Long Point Light, 212–217
Lopaus, Roscoe, 278
LORAN, 174
Lord, Richard, 403–404
Loring, Harrison, 307
Lothrop, Alonzo, 144–145

Lothrop, "Pilot John," 144
Lovell's Island Range Lights, 292, 301–305
Lovering, William C., 301
Low, Henry J., 411
Lowe, Edward, 75
Lowe, Thomas, 209–210
Lowell, Abner, 430
Lowell, Joseph, 430
Lowell, Lewis, 430
Lowther, William H., 203–204
Lubec Channel Light (Maine), 65
Luce, Abijah and Mary, 79
Lumbert, Zaccheus, 59
"Lumpkin's Light," 227
Luther, Royal, 332
LV 1 Lightship, 439
LV 2 Lightship, 441, 445
LV 3 Lightship, 444
LV 4 Lightship, 139, 443
LV 5 Lightship, 445
LV 6 Lightship, 443, 444, 446
LV 7 Lightship, 445
LV 8 Lightship, 445
LV 9 Lightship, 443
LV 11 Lightship, 439
LV 13 Lightship, 444
LV 41 Lightship, 444, 445–446
LV 42 Lightship, 441, 443
LV 47 Lightship, 441
LV 49 Lightship, 445
LV 54 Lightship, 439, 447
LV 58 Lightship, 439
LV 66 Lightship, 439
LV 73 Lightship, 442, 445–446
LV 85 Lightship, 440
LV 86 Lightship, 445, 446
LV 90 Lightship, 445
LV 98 Lightship, 444
LV 101 Lightship, 444
LV 102 Lightship, 443
LV 106 Lightship, 440
LV 110 Lightship, 446
LV 112 Lightship, 440
LV 114 Lightship, 442
LV 117 Lightship, 440, 446
LV 118 Lightship, 447
Lyle, A. G. "Sandy," 196–197
Lynch, John, 360
Lyndon, Florence, 296
Lyon, George L., 278, 344–348

Macy, Francis R., 391
Mahan, F. A., 279

Maloney, Martin, 26
Marblehead, 351
Marblehead Light, 350–357
Marcus L. Urann (vessel), 122
Maria Bray (tender), 406
Marion, 38–39
Maritana (ship), 319–320
Marsden, Harry S., 357
Marshall, Joseph, 421–422
Martha's Vineyard, 71, 79, 87, 91
Martha's Vineyard Historical Society, 77,
    89, 94–95
Marticio, Pedro, 299, 337
Martin, Ambrose, 374–375
Martin, Elbridge Gerry, 374–375
Martin, Frank F., 277
Martin, Jane C., 352–353
Martin, Joseph G., 374–375
Mary E. O'Hara (fishing schooner), 336
Mattapoisett, 28
Maxim, John, 45
Mayflower, 223
Mayflower (tender), 335, 348
Mayhew, John, 73
Mayhew, Matthew, 97–98
Mayhew, Thomas, 91
Mayo's Beach Light, 218–221
McBean, Duncan, 79, 97
McCabe, Joseph, 297
McClain, Scott W. and Gaynetta, 392
McDuffie, John, 347
Mendonca, Manuel, 19
Messenger (whaler), 16
Meyer, Joseph, 2
Mikelonis, William "Mike," 326
Milo (dog), 340–341
Minot's Ledge Light, 259, 264–283
Minot's Ledge Lightship, 273
Minot's Ledge light station, 131, 231, 259,
    264–283
Minot's Light Storm, 271–272
The Modern Light-House Service
    (Johnson), 312
Mone, Michael, 391
Monomoy National Wildlife Refuge, 166
Monomoy Point Light, 123, 158–167,
    287
Monte Tabor (bark), 204–205
Moore, William S., 33–34, 223
Morong, Clifton S. and Shirley, 205
Morse, Nathan A., 377
Morton, Ken, 234–235
Mott, Elmo C., 297, 379

Muirhead, Don, 242
Murray, Hugh, 18, 19
Murray, Peter, 36–
My Dad Fixed the Lighthouse (Nally), 381
Myrick, George, 126

Nadeau, Pierre, 280–281
Nahant, 339
Nally, Marty, 153, 380–381
Nantucket, 104, 106, 109, 113, 125
Nantucket Beacon, 107
Nantucket Cliff Range Beacons, 437–438
Nantucket Lightship, 438–441
Nantucket Shoals Lightship, 132
Nantucket South Shoals Lightship, 128
Napoleon, Tomas, 95
Narrows Light, 298, 306–309
Nauset, 177
Nauset Light. *see* Three Sisters of Nauset
Nauset Light: A Personal History
    (Daubenspeck), 183
Nauset Light Preservation Society,
    183–185
Naushon Island, 58–61
Ned's Point Light, 28–31, 49, 151
New Bedford, 13, 15, 18
New Bedford Harbor, 5, 11, 21, 23
New Bedford's Story for New Bedford's
    Children (Gartland), 12
Newburyport, 429, 435
Newburyport Harbor Light. *see* Plum
    Island Light
Newburyport Harbor Range Lights,
    434–435
New Empire (bark), 274
New England Almanac (Clough), 311
Nickerson, Andrew S., 348
Nickerson, Angeline, 171
Nickerson, Edward D., 46
Nickerson, Florence, 65–66
Nickerson, Herman, 67
Nickerson, Joseph, 229
Nickerson, Joshua, 171
Nickerson, Oliver A., 65–66
Nickerson, Simon, 171
Niger (frigate), 246
Nix's Mate Island, 316
Nobili, Pam, 183
Nobska Point Light, 62–69, 146
Nooks and Corners of the New England
    Coast (Drake), 128–129
Northern Construction Service, 252
North Truro Light, 169

Norton, Aaron, 99
Norton, John Presbury, 98
Norton, Lott, 98–99
Norton, Nicholas, 121–122
Norton, Richard, 61
Norwood, Albert, 323
Norwood, Georgia, 324, 325
Norwood, Ralph C. and Josephine,
    323–325
Now, Then, Baker's Island (Wise), 378
Noyes, Harry K., 152

Ogden, C.A., 108
Olympic (liner), 440
Once Upon a River (Frothingham), 141
O'Neil, Jean, 262
Ordway, Chris, 197
O'Rourke, Rick, 391
Orr, Molly Tornberg, 281
Osborne, Ebenezer, 258–259
Osgood, William M., 360
O'Toole, John B., III, 18–19, 26
O-who (dog), 347

Palmer's Island Light, 20–27
Pamet Light, 437
Parker, James, 2
Parsons, James Collins, 400
Paul, John H., 2–3
Paulding (cutter), 210
Payne, Arthur L., 379–380
Peak, John A., 135–136, 139
Peak, John A., Jr., 145
Peak, Martha, 136
Peak, Samuel Adams, 135, 139, 151
Pease, Horatio N., 74–75
Pease, Jeremiah, 91–92
Pease, Joseph T., 73
Peirce and Kilburn Shipyard, 23
Pemaquid Point Light (Me.), 267
Penobscot Bay (C.G. cutter), 132
Pequot (tug), 41
Percival, John "Mad Jack," 177
"Perfect Storm" of 1991, 175, 183
Perkins, Joseph, 372–373
Petit Manan Light (Me.), 201
Petty, Alice Terpeny, 54
Phelps, Elizabeth Stuart, 390
Philbrook, John, 423
The Picture of Nahant (Lewis), 339
Pieffer, Marcus, 101
Pierce, Charles M., 21
Pierce, William H., 438

A Pilgrim Returns to Cape Cod (Snow),
    173, 204, 230, 234
Pingree, Henry L., 233, 320
Pingree, Philip, 297
Pingree, Wesley A. and Josephine,
    296–297
Pinkham, Paul, 113–114
Pleasanton, Stephen, 98, 179, 247
Plum Island Light, 421, 428–433
Plymouth Bay, 237
Plymouth Light, 53, 243, 244–253, 277, 302
Pocasset, 45
Point Gammon Light, 134–137, 139, 143,
    201
Pollock Rip Lightship, 160, 441–442
Pollock Rip Slue Lightship, 442
Polly (whaling ship), 213
Pomeroy, Benjamin, 266
Ponsart, Bette, 7–9, 54–57, 82–85
Ponsart, Emma, 7–9, 54–57, 82–85
Ponsart, Octave, 6–9, 18, 54–57, 76, 82–85,
    89, 94, 101–102, 120
Ponsart, Seamond, *see* Seamond Ponsart
    Roberts
Ponte, Franklin, 26
Ponte, Joseph, 26
Poole, Aaron and Solomon, 409
Portland Gale (1898), 101, 131, 180, 195,
    215–216, 296–297, 308
Portland (steamer), 180
Pratt, Bela, 33
Pratt, Enoch, 223
Project Gurnet and Bug Lights, 241–243,
    253
Prouty, John E. O., 260
Provincetown, 201
*Provincetown; or, Odds and Ends from the
    Tip End* (Jennings), 213
Prudence Island Light (R.I.), 174
Prunty, Patrick, 197
Pulisfer, Ebenezer, 423
Purdy, Alice, 88–89
Purdy, George Walter, 88–89
Purdy, Mary Jane, 88–89
Putnam, George, 156, 439

Quantico (steamer), 447

R. B. Forbes (towboat), 273
Race Point Light, 135, 146, 200–207
Rathbeg, Frances Murray, 36–3
Ray, Frederick, 65
Readdy, Al, 251

Reamy, Milton H., 248, 277
Reamy, Octavius H., 280, 335, 336
Redfield, William C., 297, 309, 379
Reece, Priscilla, 324–325
Reed, Gerald M., 110, 111
Reed, Lon D., 391
Reich, Lou, 337
Remsen, Joseph, 130–131
Republican (schooner), 114
Restoration and preservation efforts
  Annisquam Light, 419
  Baker's Island Light, 379–381
  Bird Island Light, 38–39
  Boston Light, 328–329
  Butler Flats Light, 19
  Cleveland Ledge Light, 43
  Derby Wharf Light, 360–361
  Duxbury Pier Light, 241–243
  Fort Pickering Light, 365
  Gay Head Light, 77
  Graves Light, 337
  Highland Light, 198–199
  Nauset Light, 183–185
  Palmer's Island Light, 26–27
  Plum Island Light, 433
  Plymouth Light, 252–253
  Race Point Light, 206–207
  Sandy Neck Light, 234–235
  Scituate Light, 262–263
  Ten Pound Island Light, 385
  Thacher Island Light, 405–407
  Wing's Neck Light, 49
  Wood End Light, 211
Ricci, Bill and Debbi, 252
Rich, Earle, 221, 226
Rich, Matthias, 201
Rich, Stephen D., 195
Richardson, George W., 149
Richardson, Henry N., 342
Richardson, Maurice, 227
Richardson, Thomas, 260
Richmond Packet (brig), 431
Ricketson, Daniel, 11
Riker, Charles, 403
Rob and Harry (ship), 53–54
Roberts, Seamond Ponsart, 6–9, 54–57,
  82–85, 101–102, 120, 446
Robicheau, Joseph and Leanne, 251
Robinson, Angie, 37
Robinson, John, 379
Robinson, Zimri Tobias "Toby," 31, 37
Rockport, 395, 409
Rogers, Edwin C. "Sparky," 356–357

Rogers, Llewellyn, 336
Rogers, Walter Scott, 376
Romance (vessel), 336
Rosado and Sons, 122
Rose, Leland S., 18
Rouillard, Mrs. Kenneth, 232–233
Rowe, Kelly and Nancy, 398
Russell, Gordon, 198
Ryder, Harry, 231
Ryder, Marion Crowell, 150

S-4 (submarine), 210
Saint John (brig), 267
Salem, 359, 363, 371
Salisbury Beach Range Lights, 438
Salter, Harry, 240
Salty (dog), 326
Salty II (dog), 326
Sand Dunes and Salt Marshes
  (Townsend), 427
Sandy Neck Light, 228–235
Sandy Neck Lighthouse Restoration
  Committee, 234–235
Sankaty Head Light, 46, 88, 124–133
Saunders, Robert, 313
Savage, James Sullivan, 266
Saved (painting), 341
Save Our Sankaty, 133
Save Our Shores, 337
Save the Light Committee (Truro), 198
Sawyer, Truman, 3
Sayre, Keeper, 51–52
Sayward, Joseph, 397
Scharff, John M., 67
Schley, Winfield Scott, 301
Scituate, 255
Scituate Historical Society, 262
Scituate Light, 254–263, 265
'Sconset Trust, 133
Sears, William, 248
Seavey, George, 403
"Sea Witch of Billingsgate," 227
Seven Seas Spray (steamer), 447
Sevigny, Susan, 251
Shadwell (dog), 326
Shannon (warship), 317
Shark (schooner), 340
Shephard, Douglas, 210
Sheridan, Carrie May, 150
Sherman, Al, 419
Sherman, Marcus, 137
Sherman, William, 21
Shipwrecks on Cape Cod (Small), 191

Shirley Gut, 295
Siasconset, 125
Sibley, Frank, 296
Silvia, David, 241
Simmons, Marshall V., 36
Simmons, William A., 36
Sippican Harbor, 33
Skiff, Ebenezer, 71–72
Skiff, Ellis, 72–73
Skolfield, John, 383
Skylark (whaleboat), 27
Small, Albert, 318
Small, Arthur, 22–25, 309, 369
Small, Isaac, 187–189
Small, Isaac Morton, 194–195
Small, Judson, 298, 309
Small, Mabel, 22, 24–25
Small, Morton, 191–192
Small, P.B., 287
Small, Tom, 298, 309
Small, Zebedee, 319
Smith, Daniel, 99
Smith, Ephraim, 156
Smith, F. Hopkinson, 15
Smith, Fitz-Henry, Jr., 311, 322
Smith, James P., 164–165
Smith, John, 409
Smith, Joshua, 99
Smith, Levi, 5–6
Smith, S. Austin, 53
Smith, Samuel Soper, 215–216
Snow, Edward Rowe, 23, 28, 57, 67, 84–85, 114, 120, 173, 204, 230, 234, 242–243, 260, 286, 289, 305, 308, 318
Snow, Joshua, 318
Snowman, Sally, 328–329
Somerset (warship), 187
Souza, Anthony, 282
Spanish-American War, 117
Sparrow, Donald B., 178
Spectacle Island Range Lights, 290–293
Spencer, Tolman, 238–239
Squam Light. *see* Annisquam Light
Stackpole, Matthew, 94
Stackpole, Renny, 131
Stafford (bark), 16
Stage Harbor Light, 154–157
Stetson, Dexter, 340
Stickney, George, 435
Stone, Bob and Mary, 152–153
Stone, Everett and Gladys, 152
Stone, Greg and Patricia, 152–153
Stonehorse Shoal Lightship, 160, 444

Storms and Shipwrecks of New England (Snow), 114
Story, Amos, 383
The Story of Boston Light (Smith), 311
The Story of Minot's Light (Snow), 268
Stowell, James, 31
Straitsmouth Island Light, 408–413
Studds, Gerry, 241
Succonnessett Shoal Lightship, 444
Swain, Charles F., 117
Swain, George, 114
Swain, Samuel G., 128
Swain, W.H., 108
Swampscott, 339
Swift, William H., 266, 271, 272–273

Taft, William Howard, 367–368
Tailer, William, 312
Talbot, Edward P., 19
Tallman, Charles F., 100
Tanzy Bitters (schooner), 61
Tarpaulin Cove Light, 58–61, 79, 249
Tarr, Addison Franklin, 401–402
Tarr, Edwin, 288–289, 402
Taunton River, 1
Taylor, George B., 340
Taylor, John, 119
Tebo, Charles, 68
Ten Pound Island Light, 382–385
Terpeny, Eugene, 53–54, 377
Thacher, Anthony and Elizabeth, 395
Thacher Island Twin Lights, 131, 248, 302, 394–407
Thaxter, Leavitt, 73
Thomas, Charles, 91
Thomas, Henry L., 93
Thomas, John, 246–247
Thomas, John and Hannah, 245–246
Thompson, Mary, 313
Thompson, Winfield Scott, Jr., 280
Thomson, Jay, 328–329
Thoreau, Henry David, 179, 192–193, 209, 214, 225, 267
Three Sisters of Nauset, 173, 176–185
Tierney, John F., 405
Tierney, Rosemary S., 19
Tisbury, 79, 87
Tornberg, Per Frederick, 281–282
Totten, Joseph G., 273
Tower, David, 317–318
Tower, James, 276
Townsend, Charles Wendell, 427
Treasure, buried, 308

Trenn, Edward, 85
Tripp, H. Edmund, 34
Trull, Peter, 167
Truro, 187
Truro Historical Society, 198
Tuell, Charles D., 22
Turner, Charlie, 221
Turner, James, 307–308
Turner, Jamie and Jessie, 261
Turner, John, 371

Union (ship), 373
United Lifting System, 198–199
U.S. Lightship Memorial, 446

Vanderhoop, Charles, 75, 77, 131
Vina, John, 45
Vineyard Environmental Research
    Institute (VERI), 94
Vineyard Haven, 79, 87
Vineyard Sound, 71
Vineyard Sound Lightship, 55, 56–57,
    445–446
Von Braun, Werner, 6
Vose, Joseph, 315

Wadleigh, George, 342
Walker, Jim, 206, 211
Walsh, Otis, 282
Walsh, Otis E., 118
Walter, Gertrude, 297
Ward, Herbert, 390
Ward, Nathaniel, 374
Washington, George, 315
Washington (liner), 440
Water Witch (schooner), 201
Webber, Bernie, 196
Webster, Russell and Elizabeth B., 68–69
Wellfleet, 219, 223
West, Charles, 81
West, James Shaw, 79–81
West Chop Light, 57, 78–85, 101
West Dennis Light. see Bass River Light
West Yarmouth, 135
Whaling City Rowing Club, 27
Whaling industry, 91, 104, 106, 113
Wheeler, Austin, 397
Wheeler, Charles, 397–398
White, Geoffrey, 94
White Heath (cutter), 299
Whitten, Albert, 401
Widger, Abraham, 342
Widger, Thomas, 341–342

Wigger, John, 404
Wigwam Point Light. see Annisquam
    Light
Wilbur, Harry A., 69
Wilder, Joshua, 276
William H. Atwood (schooner), 209
Williams, Charles J., 376
Williams, Edward T., 85
Williams, Gary and Donna, 67
Wilson, Glenn, 411
Wilson, Joseph, 271–272
Wincapaw, Bill, 120, 304
Wing's Neck Light, 44–49
Winter Island Light. see Fort Pickering
    Light
Wise, DeWitt D., 378
Wixon, Zelotes, 150–151
WLV 189 Lightship, 447
WLV 612 Lightship, 441
WLV 613 Lightship, 441
Wonson, Carroll, 392
Wonson, Samuel, 387
Wood End Light, 208–211
Woodman, George F., 174
Woods, Arthur, 433
Woods Hole, 63
Woods Hole Oceanographic Institute, 63
Worth, Edward, 100
Worth, Jethro, 100
Worthylake, George and Ann, 312–313,
    327

Yates, James, 348
York, Javan D., 204

Z Lightship, 445